edited by
ALBRECHT ROTHACHER

corporate globalization
business cultures in
ASIA and EUROPE

ASIA-EUROPE RESEARCH SERIES

© 2005 Marshall Cavendish International
(Singapore) Private Limited

Published 2005 by Marshall Cavendish Academic
An imprint of Marshall Cavendish International
(Singapore) Private Limited
A member of Times Publishing Limited

Times Centre, 1 New Industrial Road,
Singapore 536196
Tel:(65) 6213 9288
Fax: (65) 6284 9772
E-mail: mca@sg.marshallcavendish.com
Website:
http://www.marshallcavendish.com/academic

All rights reserved. No part of this publication may be reproduced, stored in a retrieval system, or transmitted, in any form or by any means, electronic, mechanical, photocopying, recording or otherwise, without the prior permission of the publishers.

ISBN: 981-210-373-2

A CIP catalogue record for this book is available from the National Library Board (Singapore).

Printed by Times Graphics Pte Ltd, Singapore
on non-acidic paper

London • New York • Beijing • Shanghai
• Bangkok • Kuala Lumpur • Singapore

International Board of Advisors

Dr. Abdul Rashid Moten, Professor
International Islamic University, Malaysia

Dr. Amitav Acharya, Professor
Institute of Defence & Strategic Studies
Nanyang Technological University, Singapore

Dr. Anne Pakir, Associate Professor
National University of Singapore, Singapore

Arun Mahizhnan, Deputy Director,
The Institute of Policy Studies, Singapore

Dr. Ban Kah Choon, Professor
Mahidol University, Thailand

Dr. Chua Beng Huat, Professor
(Current Chair of Board of Advisors)
National University of Singapore, Singapore

Dr. Eddie C. Y. Kuo, Professor
Nanyang Technological University, Singapore

Dr. Gerald Tan, Associate Professor
Flinders University, Australia

Dr. Hong Hai, Professor
Nanyang Business School
Nanyang Technological University, Singapore

Dr. Jason Tan, Associate Professor
National Institute of Education
Nanyang Technological University, Singapore

Dr. Jon Quah, Professor
National University of Singapore, Singapore

Dr. Josephine Smart, Professor
University of Calgary, Canada

Dr. Lee Lai To, Associate Professor
National University of Singapore, Singapore

Dr. Leo Suryadinata, Professor
Institute of Southeast Asian Studies, Singapore

Dr. Lim Hua Sing, Professor
Waseda University, Japan

Dr. M. Sornarajah, Professor
National University of Singapore, Singapore

Dr. Ramadhar Singh, Professor
National University of Singapore, Singapore

Dr. Roxanna Waterson, Associate Professor
National University of Singapore, Singapore

Dr. S. Vasoo, Associate Professorial Fellow
National University of Singapore, Singapore

Dr. Tan Tai Yong, Associate Professor
National University of Singapore, Singapore

Ten Chin Liew, Professor
National University of Singapore, Singapore

Dr. Tong Chee Kiong, Associate Professor
National University of Singapore, Singapore

Dr. Victor Savage, Associate Professor
National University of Singapore, Singapore

Dr. Wang Gungwu, Professor
National University of Singapore, Singapore

Dr. Wang Ning, Professor
Tsinghua University, Beijing, China

Yu Xintian, Professor
Shanghai Institute for International Studies
Shanghai, China

Marshall Cavendish Academic

ASIA-EUROPE RESEARCH SERIES

This series is based on peer-reviewed research from Asia-Europe Foundation, a think-tank based in Singapore. The series will publish comparative research and policy papers in a variety of disciplines which include regionalism, regional security, economics, business, management, geography and the environment.

Other titles in the series (including forthcoming titles)
- Paths to Regionalisation: Comparing Experiences in East Asia and Europe
- New Security Challenges for Asia and Europe
- Democracy in Asia, Europe and the World: Toward a Universal Definition

Contents

Preface   ix

Chapter 1   1
A Coming Clash of Business Cultures? Coping with Globalization: Corporate Experiences from Europe and Asia
Albrecht Rothacher

Chapter 2   21
SingTel: Connecting Asia and Beyond
Jason Alexander Villanueva

Chapter 3   41
High-Tech Toshiba in Drift
Albrecht Rothacher

Chapter 4   48
Siemens: Engineering Locomotives, Cell-phones, and Corporate Culture Change
Albrecht Rothacher

Chapter 5   60
Matsushita: Happiness in Appliances
Albrecht Rothacher

Chapter 6   69
Hyundai's Flight of Icarus
Paresh Mistry and *Albrecht Rothacher*

Chapter 7   84
The Elusive Mr Li: Hutchinson Whampoa and the 3G Phones
Albrecht Rothacher

Chapter 8   90
On the Wings of British Airways
Lim Chee Hong

Chapter 9   117
Honda Dares to be Different
Herbert Pang Shen Hong

Chapter 10   129
Forza Ferrari: The F1 Legend and its Corporate Story
Justin Tai Wei Chuen

Chapter 11   151
As Solid as Steel: ThyssenKrupp, the Rise and Fall of Two Steel Dynasties
Albrecht Rothacher

Chapter 12   160
Nestlé: A Reliable Cash Cow Feeding the World
Albrecht Rothacher

Chapter 13   168
Alltech: Irish Know-How in the New World
Frank Bradley

Chapter 14   188
Haribo: The King of Jelly Bears
Albrecht Rothacher

Chapter 15   195
Chupa Chups: The Lollipop Company
Albrecht Rothacher

Chapter 16   200
Born by Committee: Baileys
Frank Bradley

Chapter 17   222
Tsingtao Brewery: China's Newest Multinational
Justin Tai Wei Chuen

Chapter 18   **243**
Harrods: Making it Big
Chua Yi Fen

Chapter 19   **254**
Nomura: A Tale of Greed and Money?
Albrecht Rothacher

Chapter 20   **264**
Saatchi & Saatchi: Make, Break, Lost and Found
Terry Tan

Chapter 21   **289**
The Chinese *Nouveau Riches* as Movie Moguls: The Stories of Run Run Shaw and Loke Wan Tho
Stephanie Chung Po-yin

Chapter 22   **302**
Hello Kitty: A Silly Cat Earns a Lot of Money
Albrecht Rothacher

Chapter 23   **306**
Corporate Sponsorships in Asia and Europe
Wei Shen

Contributors   **321**

Index   **323**

Preface

The investigation of differences in business cultures and branding strategies between major Asian and European companies is an exciting field of inquiry. Are not all supposed to become uniform in an age of seemingly irresistible globalization, which after all is driven by business interests? Indeed, the research undertaken by young graduates in the context of the course "Comparative Business Cultures," held in 2004 at the Economics Department of the National University of Singapore, showed that far from any uniformity, strong national differences and remarkably vital and distinct corporate identities persist among major European and Asian companies in terms of management style, ownership preferences, personnel policies, marketing and branding strategies. The resulting case histories also make a good, well-researched and informative read in their own right, which clearly warrants an affordable book aimed at a wider readership. This book in fact builds on and expands on an earlier recent publication of mine, entitled *Corporate Cultures and Global Brands* (Singapore, 2004) with an entirely different set of corporate histories.

For this volume, we are very grateful for the pertinent contributions received from Professor Frank Bradley of the Michael Smurfit Graduate School of Business at University College Dublin, and from Professor Stephanie Po-yin Chung of Hong Kong Baptist University. The support of the Asia Europe Foundation (ASEF), led by Ambassador Dr. Delfin Colome, is gratefully acknowledged, as is the efficient secretarial support by Zareen Tia Siew Keng and Jenny Tang at ASEF in Singapore. I am also thankful to Gael Lee from Bonyfish for her hard, dedicated editorial work, and to Anthony Thomas, Managing Editor at Marshall Cavendish Academic, for his unfailing support of this pioneering new venture.

I would like to dedicate this book to my son Jan-Ulrich, who at the tender age of 15, secretly read most of the German business monographs which I used, late in his bed and later confronted me with his discoveries. This proves that it is never too early to start with well-written business studies!

Dr Albrecht Rothacher

CHAPTER 1

A Coming Clash of Business Cultures? Coping with Globalization: Corporate Experiences from Europe and Asia

ALBRECHT ROTHACHER

Corporate culture has been famously defined as "the way we do things around here."[1] In other words, it reflects patterns of shared values and beliefs created over time in the work life of a company. It also sets the norms for acceptable behaviour in organizations, starting from attitudes to risk, innovation and quality control to leadership behaviour, customer orientation and interaction between colleagues. When I joined Deutsche Bank for my first real job back in 1982, one of the first things I was told was: "In other banks, people may shout at each other. But at Deutsche we are polite." On occasion, this politeness could turn slightly acidic.

Corporate culture has nothing to do with the company's mission statement. The latter is an artificial product dreamt up by PR consultants and superimposed by senior management as a typically unwieldy slogan of no operational consequence. Rather, corporate culture is the complex result of interacting variables, like the company's real philosophy and its practised values, its organizational procedures (formality vs. informality), structures (degree of hierarchisation), management behavior (authoritarian, participative or laissez faire), the heritage of corporate history from the legends of the founding fathers to anecdotes of more recent heroic exploits, and finally personnel policy of recruitment, promotions and dismissals: who gets in, who leads and who gets fired?

It is obviously a big difference whether the upper ranks in an industrial company are dominated by engineers or by marketing people. Equally, a company, which prefers to hire female liberal arts graduates, will have a different corporate style than one that prefers rugby players as its staffers. Cultures within large corporations are not uniform. The trucking department has different norms and ways of interaction than the accounting people, who in turn are a different breed than the guys in public relations. Management norms surely belong to a corporate subculture distinct from the shop floor. Regional branches have their own ways of going about corporate business. Yet within these broad bands of variation, ideal types of organizations can be distinguished depending on business types and management styles.

Charles Handy defined four such types of organizational cultures:[2]

1. *Power Cultures*: There is one cultural source of power, which often rests within an authoritarian and/or charismatic founder-owner. Typical are family firms, who prefer to hire and to promote loyal retainers. Middle management has little initiative as decisions are made by the "old man" at the top. These decisions are quick, forceful and decisive, but often strong on intuition and short on full information and analysis. If correct, they propel the company to rapid growth, but when wrong, as high-risk decisions they could spell disaster and threaten corporate survival. Power cultures are typical for the early entrepreneurial stage of a company, when it moves out of its proverbial garage. It is also typical for the overseas Chinese tycoon-run conglomerate. The main problems for such companies are: will they survive generational succession and corporate consolidation?

2. *Role Cultures*: Job descriptions, formal roles and procedures count rather than personalities. Decisions are predictable and routinised. Technical expertise is valued. The organization has become bureaucratized, inflexible, slow and reactive. Role cultures are typical in large mature management-run capital-intensive companies. The risk is that they become self-referential, immunised to changing market realities and go the way of the dinosaur. Typical are statutory companies, big capital-intensive operations like utilities or airplane makers, or Japanese *keiretsu* companies with management due to corporate cross-shareholdings, answerable only to itself.

3. *Task Cultures*: Dominant are small work groups which consist of individuals with high control over their work. Qualification, creativity and networking skills count rather than rank. Task cultures are typical for high-tech start-up companies, ad agencies, marketing departments, and M&A units of US brokerage firms.
4. *Person Cultures*: Such organizations are based on individuals' professional talents: like lawyers in law firms, journalists in newspapers, researchers in a lab, musicians in an orchestra. Personal professional values count. Organizational loyalty is weak.

A well-developed corporate culture in a reasonably managed organization should reflect the specific needs of the institution and of most of its members as well. It also mirrors the social, regional and national business environment. A robust corporate culture, which as a living organism has gradually evolved over time, is hence a precious asset: in socialising the newcomers and in sustaining its older members, it saves precious management time, safeguards long-term performance and acts as an institutional memory. Such organizations then are almost an autopilot. Management does not have to intervene, enforce rules, motivate and direct people—it can limit itself to occasional corrections and focus on the pursuit of strategic objectives.

The laws of human nature and of social interaction have made corporate cultures conservative. They evolve gradually and change course only imperceptively—contrary to the unproven assertions of overpaid and underperforming change managers. Yet corporate cultures increasingly face more real threats by external shocks, caused by downsizings, outsourcing and mergers. In a secular tendency, the social fabric of many large corporations is being destroyed by overemphasising the short-term interests of maximised shareholder values.[3] Fund managers are now in charge of most corporate capital allocated by stock exchanges. As they are under strong pressure to outperform their competitors' "benchmarks," they are naturally obsessed with short-term stock price movements, which allows them to churn over their assets profitably—the quicker the better. News about planned large-scale redundancies, closures and divestments, which have an immediate bottom line effect, are the most welcome as are M&A activities, the rumour of which alone will drive up the share prices to unimaginable heights. In order to let senior management join in the game, their pay is tied to stock performance through sizable stock options. No longer are they interested in empire building, or in costly ventures like the development of new products, new markets or new distribution channels. The quarterly bottom line is the objective. Aggressively vocal PR road shows to impressionable financial markets are the means. As most work places have become insecure, employees react in a defensive "me first" mode. Since corporate trust and loyalty have been betrayed so often, the rational response of survivors is to maximize personal benefits in "mental divorces" foremost. Lower morale, absenteeism, outward conformity, low quality input, distrust of colleagues and management are the result.[4]

Once destroyed by large-scale job cuts—made worse when "outsourced" workers continue at lower pay and status in their old jobs—or by mergers, rebuilding a shattered corporate culture is notoriously difficult. Corporate subcultures need to be nurtured and tenure be offered to re-establish trust.

To make mergers succeed, it takes more than just organized merry get-togethers, flowery speeches and PR gimmicks by senior management. If jobs cuts are necessary, they should be instant and then be done with. People from companies taken over need to be given the justified feeling to be welcome, not to suffer a permanent career stigma with efforts undertaken—best through a large measure of autonomy—to preserve the major desirable elements of their corporate culture.

While national mergers and acquisitions are difficult enough, international mergers are notorious for their frequency and costliness of failure. Yet the lure of shortcuts to global playerdom, management hubris and delusion ("We will succeed where all others have failed") and the manifest incentives of the short-term stock market make the repetition of the ever-same mistakes irresistible. Some companies survive the ordeal, and after cutting losses and licking their wounds for one decade, start again with a generation of managers successfully immunized to learning experiences and corporate memory. Others like Swissair, Seibu-Season and Vivendi did not survive and hence will not repeat.

Corporations recruit people who already went through their primary (familial) and secondary (schooling/military/university) socialization. Hence their way of speaking, thinking, working and interacting clearly reflects the national culture in which they grew up. It may be a truism that society at large is reflected in corporate cultures, but this surely also applies to the national characteristics of the corporate environment. In large countries also regional variations are famously pronounced. In the

US, the quintessential symbol of the melting pot of interregional mobility and of ultra capitalist profit maximization, for instance, the business styles of brash New York, the patrician North East, the folksy South, the aggressive yet formal Texans, the staid Mid West and the relaxed self-confident Californian remain clearly distinct. All the more so this applies to different national styles of doing business. When a US senator back in 1945 remarked that once the world had become like Kansas City, peace would be assured, not only was he wrong but he was also asking for the impossible (if anything then the world should take care these days not to look like and turn into a big Lagos instead).

Although being *the* key obstacle against effective globalization, curiously not much research has been conducted into national differences of corporate cultures. In the 1970s, Geert Hofstede, an intrepid Dutchman, had done a world survey of the major highbrow multinational of the day, IBM—and found striking differences within one and the same company's national subsidiaries.[5] He categorized them valiantly, and although distinctly dated and no longer always plausible, his research results tend to be quoted and recycled endlessly—basically because nobody else has ever bothered to undertake this Herculean effort again. Hofstede quite rightly started out with the concept of different "layers of culture." There is a national level, but there are also "sub-levels" of a regional, ethnic, religious and linguistic sort whenever nations are sufficiently large or heterogeneous enough. Variations of gender, generation, social class and company specific ("tertiary") socialisation also played their role.

In the light of his survey results, Hofstede then sorted the world's national business cultures along five different parameters:

1. *Power Distance*: the degree of authoritarianism vs. egalitarianism. He measured the emotional distance between bosses and their subordinates with questions like whether the latter were able to express disagreement or to admit mistakes, whether leadership styles were more autocratic, paternalistic or consultative. Latin America, the Arab Word, Southeast Asia and India scored highest. At the bottom were unsurprisingly Scandinavia and perhaps more surprising, the British Isles, with the US with their insistence on management prerogatives, in spite of all appearances of informality, in the middle. As the results in part also depended on the behavior of the subordinates, there was also an element of social class. The

less educated and the lower their skill level, the more authoritarian the workforce usually was. Reflecting a pattern instilled already during their primary and secondary socialization, they expected and accepted the social distance practised by senior management, including their privileges and status symbols.

2. *Consensus Orientation*: the degree of individualism vs. collectivism is measured. To what extent do group interests (like of the extended family or of clan/tribal elders) prevail over individual interests? To what extent is meritocratic individualism accepted? Predictably the US and most Europeans scored highest on the individualism scale, while Latin Americans and Asians scored lowest. These results also may have reflected the differences between more modern welfare societies and those of a more traditional sort that rely on protection and solidarity of the family. With economic development since, a shift toward more individualism should be expected.

3. *Style and Gender*: estimating "masculinity" (pre-industrial and industrial toughness, assertiveness and materialism) vs. "feminity" (post-industrial modesty, tender care and quality of life objectives). While these categories are interesting, the results did not make much sense. The Scandinavians scored high as feminine soft eggs, but so did Turks, Yugoslavs, Africans and Koreans.

4. *Uncertainty Avoidance*: Insistence on predictability was highest in Japan, in Germany (remember that in the 1970s German trains still ran on time!), and curiously in Southern Europe. In contrast, tolerance of ambiguity was relatively high in Scandinavia, the UK, then the land of improvised muddling through, and places like Jamaica, and even implausibly Singapore!

5. *The Concept of Time:* measured as "short-termism" vs. "long-termism." The latter was highest in Confucian cultures like China and Japan, while Nigeria and Pakistan scored the lowest, living as they do very much in the present tense.

Richard Lewis took a more deductive approach. He synthesized his perceptive gems of wisdom—some of which were anecdotal, but no less true—after conducting hundreds of intercultural management seminars in dozens of countries. He starts out by stating forcefully that deep-rooted national attitudes and beliefs resist the transformation of values in multinational enterprises.[6] This applies to corporate objectives—US companies will go after profits, Japanese companies after market share—and to the behavior of individuals. McDonald's will not get its Russian sales staff to smile at customers. German Wal-Mart employees will not sing the company hymn, and Matsushita has given up on foreign hirelings reciting the founding father's corporate morning prayer. The result of such intercultural encounters is a mutual culture shock, which after digesting the initial experience may either result in a possibly enriching practice of mutual tolerance and gradual adaptation, or slide into mutual antagonism and a mental divorce ("us" vs. "them"). It should be understood that natural characteristics in corporate behaviour should not be seen as simple stereotypes. National cultures are not static. For better or for worse, they evolve. Surely also individual behavior cannot be inferred simply from one's nationality.

There is also plenty of regional variation, like between Catalans and Andalusians in Spain, Friulians and Sicilians in Italy, Bavarians and Hamburgers in Germany, but also within countries located along the Germano-Romanic divide in Western Europe like in Switzerland with her German, French and Italian speaking parts, and in Belgium between the Flemish and the Walloons (and a few Germans).

Richard Lewis developed interesting distinctions in the main modus operandi of these cultures. The Germanic way in his view is "linear active": as a planned linear activity ideally one thing is done at a time until it is finished. In contrast, Romanic, Arabic and Indian cultures are "multi-active": multiple activities are undertaken at the same time, often as spontaneous actions. Multi-active cultures in his view are interaction oriented, while companies in linear active societies are data oriented.

Lewis also observed "reactive" ways among Finns, Estonians and East Asians. Before becoming active, they observe, listen, try to understand and guard their reactions. In his view, they are both data and interaction oriented.

These three cultures then affect companies' and their employees' key concepts of space and time, leadership, corporate strategies, negotiating behaviour, including listening habits and body language.

A Finn will usually be an excellent listener with his body language and facial expression revealing very little about his likes and dislikes. The opposite will be true with a multi-active Greek. His attention span will be short and he will quickly volunteer his own pronounced conclusions. This is not a European speciality. In East Asia for instance, the same could be said about the more "reactive" Japanese and Chinese on the one hand, and the relatively more "multi-active" Filipinos and

Koreans on the other. Business cultures are surely more complex than popular stereotypes of "East" vs. "West," or "European Ways" against "Asian Values," will have it.

It is true that basic concepts of human intercourse are shared between the great civilizations of Asia and Europe (and in the Americas as essentially derived European cultures). These are concepts like truth, honor, duty, courtesy, love and family. Yet there are different notions. While for the Dutch and Australians, the truth is a blunt notion to be adhered to straightaway, for the British it may be used "economically" (selective), for the Italians it is negotiable, but for Asians and Latin Americans, there is a serious risk of destroying harmony and losing face, which needs to be avoided.

Contracts in Germany, the US and in Singapore are strictly binding. All eventualities are foreseen and covered. In Japan, Korea and in Latin America they represent a temporary amicable intention for ceremonial functions. They describe ideal arrangements, which may however, need to be changed once circumstances change. Legislative practice also affects attitudes toward the law. In Switzerland, there are only a few laws, but they are well-known and hence well observed. In Italy, in contrast, there are many laws, many of which are obscure and unclear. Hence one is invited to pick and choose. In more authoritarian countries like China, it is not rule of the law, but rule by law. It is the authorities, which pick and choose the law, which they then apply for a special treatment.

Communication patterns vary similarly. Take silence for example. Romanic cultures and the action-paced US show least tolerance. After a few seconds, they feel the urge just to say something to fill the airwaves. In Japan and Finland, silence is rather a means to show respect. You reflect carefully what your opposite has just said, which merits a well-considered answer that takes time. A Spaniard will misread this silent reflection as a signal that the audience is over, since everything seems to have been said. Similarly, tolerance for noise is strongly different, with Italy and Sweden at the two opposites on the European scale.

Language also can pose difficulties. Even native English speakers use their national language differently. Americans love tough idiomatic language laced with expletives, wisecracking verbal threats with a tendency to exaggerate. British English is more articulate with a wider vocabulary range and a more correct grammar. Like its Canadian variant, it is more relaxed, low key and used for understatements as well as for studied ambivalence and vagueness in order to avoid confrontations at meetings, which Brits (in difference to their US cousins) abhor. As the Brits insist on doing business with grace and humor, and their style inevitably appears as polite, casual and helpful, the occasional subsequent ruthlessness then appears as devious to their unsuspecting victims. Irish English will be more poetic, philosophical or humorous. Language for the Irish is a means to convey vision, warmth and to tell a good story, sometimes with the truth embellished ("blarney"). Australian and New Zealand English display their distinct ancestral origins. Aussies speak the blunt and colourful slang of lower classes of the London East, which also reflects the outback and the nineteenth century jail experience. The slower-paced Kiwis rather speak in the bygone ways of the South English countryside.

Among Romanic languages, the Mediterraneans speak in famously flowery, emotional and circumlocutous terms. The French rather submit their discourse to the structure of Cartesian logic, and can be quite cuttingly direct in speeches. If their logic is correct, then they must be right, and anybody disagreeing must be wrong and put in a corner (and if he insists, by logical implication, he must either be an idiot or acting in bad faith—both not very enviable positions).

German and Dutch are very precise in their terminology. Their language is a serious instrument to convey facts and to check detail. The opposite is probably true in Japan. Language is used to convey empathy and feelings. What is left unspoken counts as well. Public speeches are full of platitudes and leave Japan's partners inevitably wondering about the real intentions and meanings.

Humor is used with equal differences: in the US when you open a meeting; in the UK to relax the mood during a meeting; in Germany once a difficult meeting has been concluded; and in Japan only during the drinking session afterwards.

Meetings with Germans and Americans start promptly and follow a preset agenda without much ado. In Japan, meetings begin on time as well, but a long time is spent on introductory rituals and explaining the obvious. In Italy and Spain, they start with long exchanges of gossip, soccer news and politics—while people continue to arrive. In the fast-paced US, in order to prolong the day, the working breakfast has been invented, which for more civilized people like the Spaniards, is an inexcusable act of barbarity.

The Americans want their meetings as expeditious as possible, with a handshake and a deal with a written agreement at the end. Details can be worked out later. Their full range of available instruments from friendly informality to brutal bullying is employed to this purpose. The Brits dislike this confrontational approach (which actually also poses no problems to the French and to most East Europeans), but rather want polite diplomatic discussions, with disagreements often papered over with vague wording. The Germans want to work down a lengthy prepared agenda, ask a lot of detailed difficult questions from the start, with hopefully no uncertainties left in the end, when they are ready for a decision. The Japanese ask the same questions like the Germans. But they ask them 10 times, and at the end of the meeting they are surely not ready for any decision. Ultimately, a deal with them is not determined by technical detail, but whether mutual trust is established or not.

Similarly, the Spaniards will not study details, but will use the meeting to study you. If they think you are a honorable person, the deal is on; if not, forget it. During negotiations, their own obsession with honor and "face" makes it difficult for them to climb down. Negotiations with the French are notoriously difficult, since they hate compromises which smell of a deal and don't fit their preconceived logic. But a lengthy boozy lunch can help. The strategic moment with the senior manager in charge is toward the end between the peach and the cheese (*entre la poire et le fromage*).

Business information required in US and other Germanic organizations are hard data, market studies and other reliable printed or electronic information. In a Romanic or Chinese business context, it is network information which counts: oral news on business opportunities and risks coming from relations or trusted informants.

The concept of time is probably the strongest differential between the world's business cultures. It is very much a function of linear vs. multi-activity. Germany, for instance, is punctual and deadline-oriented. Mediterranean countries, the inventors of *mañana*, are more flexible. Insistence on punctuality is seen as disruptive to ongoing activities (and useless since one's counterpart is unlikely to be punctual either).

In the US clearly, "time is money," a scarce, precious commodity, which if used unproductively leads to irreplaceable income losses. The US insistence on hard driven urgency is supported by the Puritan ethic and the first mover advantage of the frontier myth: the *Homestead Act* and the Gold Rush rewarded speed and roughness of those who filed and asserted their claims first. Decisiveness, assertiveness, risk taking, mobility and hard work are clearly prized. One American friend once told me: "If I had as many vacations as you Europeans, I would take a second job" (I did not tell him that I had a second job and still had plenty of leave). This attitude is a secular heritage of the Protestant work ethic in an achievement-oriented society: the more you work and the more efficiently you use your time, the higher your wealth and—especially in the US—the higher your social standing. Interestingly, the Confucian work ethic is similar, once East Asians are released from governmental constraints.

In countries with strong class divisions and inherited wealth, like Latin America or the Philippines, this time-driven work ethic does not make sense, nor does it in the fatalist world of the Middle East, or the traditional sectors of Indian and Thai society, which in line with centuries of monsoon experience see time as cyclical, the repetition of the ever same seasons and life cycles, with the monsoon destroying regularly what has been built up. Clearly in these cultures, the cultivation of human interaction or contacts with the divine are a more worthwhile use for time than the sweat-covered lust for more money than one needs.

Cultural concepts of leadership have a direct bearing on corporate structures. Germanic tribes typically elected their leaders. If a Viking raid did not work out, the next time they would try it under a different boss, with their erstwhile chief back in the ranks. For a thousand years (800–1800 A.D.), German and Swedish kings were elected. Romanic cultures in contrast inherited the autocracy of the Roman emperors. Catholicism built up the Vatican's hierarchy to deal with God. North European Protestantism however, encourages each believer to read the Bible for himself and to make his own personal contacts. In the East European Orthodoxy authoritarianism was even more pronounced, with the head of church and state as one and the same remained absolute rulers ("czars"). In China, the emperor ruled with similar absolute power via a mandate from the heavens, a role into which now in China, Vietnam, Laos and North Korea, a party dictatorship with unchecked powers has succeeded.

In corporations of a Germanic tradition (most pure in Scandinavia and in the Netherlands), hierarchies are flat, consensus-oriented, open to information flows, and derive their legitimacy from peer acceptance, managerial competence and business success (Note that in the UK since William the Conqueror, Germanic leadership has been replaced by Romanic nobility with lasting effects!). Within German companies, there is less social distance than among the Latins. Senior management—in difference to France—has typically risen from within the ranks, sometimes even proudly from the shop floor on the strength of hard work and technical expertise. Middle management and the foremen on the shop floor ("Industriemeister") have larger powers of discretion. As motivated technical experts, they typically insist on solid engineering and strict manufacturing requirements. The focus on technical expertise leads to a certain measure of over-engineering and to being more product than market led. Departmental rivalries are also fairly strong. As supervisory boards are stuffed with stakeholders—mostly friendly bankers, suppliers and trade unionists (thanks to a co-determination law favouring industrial democracy in the 1970s), German companies can take a long-term view (which in Europe means 5–10 years, in the US: 2–3 years). The focus on technical expertise, financial solidity and careful planning, overall makes for a more managerial than entrepreneurial business culture in Germany.

Sweden has driven the Germanic management model even further. Hierarchies are flat. Business and status symbols are frowned upon (similar as perhaps only in Australia—settled by a Germanic underclass). Yet decision-making is cumbersome—in endless meetings an internal consensus (almost like in Japan) needs to be reached and conflicts avoided at all cost. Then committed employees deliver well-designed quality products on time. Interlocking non-executive directorships of the leading Swedish companies equally allow a healthy long-term orientation.

Business leaders in Romanic countries frequently enjoy their position thanks to academic qualifications (in France notably) or family connections. Management is autocratic. Power distance and status differentials are big. Information is shared only on a need-to-know basis.

French companies cultivate elaborate hierarchies and rituals. Top managers are obsessed with status and act in a studied aristocratic aloofness as *le patron*. While in other countries educational credentials are just an entry ticket into a decent company, in France it is less job performance, but graduation from their highly competitive *Grandes Ecoles*, which determine the incumbency of most senior ranks. In well-connected privileged old boys networks, these high-flyers ("grand corps") move around in musical chairs between executive positions of the private sector and ministerial and senior administrative postings in the public sector. French bosses think big, prefer abstract and conceptual thinking—they actually often prominently participate in philosophical and political public debates—and hate mediocrity and technical detail. Whilst their bosses are omnipotent, running centralized, often idiosyncratic top-down operations, their subordinates with their truncated career prospects react with the national sport of circumventing rules and by carving out their own little territories. With this village mentality below and alienation from the top, intra-corporate cooperation is often difficult.

In East Asia, the Confucian heritage ("Asian Values") makes for a paternalist leadership style. Ideally bottom-up feelings of loyalty and dependence are matched by top-down obligations of benevolence and support in emergencies. In Korean and overseas Chinese companies, leadership is mostly exercised by the controlling families. In Japan in the larger companies it is done by managers promoted by seniority-based bureaucratic merits. In the non-Confucian parts of East Asia, like Indonesia, Malaysia, Thailand and the Philippines, the native non-Chinese businesses are equally mostly family-owned and their leadership normally inherited, sometimes with a feudal background, or if in public companies owed to the favouritism by governments.

For the overseas Chinese enterprise, the classical rags-to-riches story of self-made entrepreneurs is typical. As émigrés of Southeast China's war-torn coast, they worked their way up through hard work, frugality, keen business acumen and strong family connections in Hong Kong, Taiwan, Singapore and the rest of Southeast Asia. These tightly-run family owned conglomerates strongly profess Confucian values like discipline, trust, hard work, learning and paternalist benevolence[7]—which to others probably seems like autocratic rule. For analysts like Backman,[8] the problems of these overseas Chinese conglomerates with their haphazard collections of disparate businesses (consisting typically of a lot of real estate, a bank, a stockbroking firm, a trading company, an odd selection of manufacturing companies, and inevitably a major hotel) lies in the loose, intransparent and informal arrangements, with only clansmen hired and family members put in positions of trust. Marketing and production decisions are not based on market research, but on intuition and connections. Like in similarly structured Indian and Korean conglomerates, succession struggles often destroy the life work of the autocratic polygamous founder. Their settlement is not helped by purposefully intransparent corporate structures, and inexistent accounting.

Also in China itself, the non-availability to legal recourse forces businessmen to rely on structures of trust. In China, these are less family members and clansmen, but the need to purchase political protection, the root cause for endemic corruption.

Korea's *chaebol* after the Korean War were quite consciously modelled with government support along the lines of Japan's pre-war *zaibatsu*. As diversified, aggressively growing, export driven and highly leveraged family conglomerates, their internal structures are autocratic founder-owner power cultures, which still in many cases have to survive the first generational succession.

In post-war Japan, however, the family owned *zaibatsu* had been expropriated by the US and were replaced by management-run groupings (*keiretsu*). Through interlocking shareholdings, these are entirely management self-controlled. After the hard and diligent post-war reconstruction and catching up development work of the first generation, the *keiretsu*, aided by political protection and free capital, by the 1980s degenerated into a bureaucratized corporate clubland, with wasteful capital-eating practices, which not even the decade of stagnation after the asset deflation of 1992 managed to end.

In US companies, the preference for informality camouflages the high degree of hierarchisation, of differences in income and social status, and strong pressures to conform with corporate norms. The need to achieve ever-tougher profit objectives and to comply with endless detailed numerical reporting requirements for HQ bureaucracies is stronger than probably anywhere. Within these parameters, promotions are almost exclusively by highly competitive merits.

National corporate cultures, ways of business communication, negotiations and work ethics are obviously strongly distinct. They have shown a remarkable resistance against the pressures and promises of globalization—which after all is said to be business driven.

An awareness of these deep-rooted differences is all the more important for managers, as businesses—in difference to international organizations, like the UN, which have learned to live with a fair amount of organizational inefficiencies, frictions, waste and dead wood—have to make money in order to survive. Hence at one point, the niceties of cross-cultural mutual understanding seminars will be over, and the straightforward regard of no-nonsense bottom line performance will be on, with careers, jobs and entire production sites at stake.

Hence during global expansion—notably when foreign acquisitions are involved—a real knowledge of distinct national corporate cultures and their nuances is a must. Leaving the subject to a bunch of specialist consultants and putting some tired managers through a few awareness-raising seminars is asking for serious trouble, which ultimately, if the stakes are high enough could put corporate survival at risk. If badly handled, in any event the costs are likely to surpass the price of the initial foreign acquisition.

How did our companies, which achieved global reach, cope with these challenges? Almost inevitably born by a mythical founder-owner some 30 to 180 years ago, at one point they had to cope with generational succession and ultimately the transition to professional managerial rule (or they will still need to do so). They also had to survive external shocks like WWI, the post-war depression, the world economic crisis of 1929, WWII, Allied Occupation (for German and Japanese companies) and communist expropriations, and to have had the capacity to restart, reconstruct and re-launch. Products, branding and marketing had to be adjusted to cope with the needs and demands of the world markets. Being born and bred into a district national corporate culture, companies had to cope with the consequences of internal growth—the recruitment of foreigners with decent career prospects—or of growth by foreign acquisitions and mergers, in which case the consequences are more imminent and dramatic.

Corporate progress and growth is never linear and assured. After 100 years, at best, only one out of a hundred start-ups will have survived. Who remembers for instance, the Hornbostel Silk Weaving Plant of Leobersdorf (Lower Austria) and the Hansen Turbine Works of Gotha (Germany). I do, because my ancestors some 150 years ago had set them up. They faded away three generations ago having been sold due to inheritance problems or the unwillingness of sons to take over. Subsequently, the hyperinflation of post-WWI ate up the proceeds of the sales. The new owners lacked the means to modernize and to expand. What is left? A few gilded patents, street names of the founders, museum exhibits in Gotha and in Vienna, and two footnotes in Thyringia's and Austria's industrial history. It is hence important to remember that century-old corporate histories represent the rare exception of success rather than the rule of failure and oblivion. This makes the survivors' case histories all the more instructive.

We picked 21 such histories—12 from Europe and 9 from Asia—to see whether there were specific European or Asian ways (or perhaps common ways) to cope with survival, growth and cultural adjustment in the globalised economy. They represent a wide variety of sectors: telecoms, electronics and electrical appliances, motor cars, construction, steel, air transport, foodstuffs, confectionary, finances, advertising and branding.

The first generational succession is still ahead for Hutchison Whampoa, Sanrio, Haribo and Alltech. It just succeeded with Chupa Chups to the second generation and failed in the autocratically-run Hyundai. With companies like Matsushita, Honda and Ferrari, transition from an owner-founder power culture to a managerial role culture had been achieved one or two decades ago. With Saatchi & Saatchi, this was done by throwing out the erstwhile owners. Siemens, Nomura, Thyssen and Krupp did the transition only after successive generations of family-controlled management. Thyssen and Krupp had run out of suitable heirs. The Nomuras were expropriated by the US occupants. Nestlé has been run by professional managers for more than one century and is probably the most straightforward success story. There are, however, also government-founded companies like SingTel, Toshiba, British Airways and Tsingtao Beer. Their problem was rather the absence of an entrepreneurial culture and an overdose of bureaucracy during much of their existence. Finally, there is Baileys, a rare breed: the entrepreneurial creation by a managerial structure. Created by artificial insemination, so to speak, not by the real lifeblood of a maverick entrepreneur in his garage, but successful nonetheless.

The prospects for the inherently more unstable family-run companies are decidedly mixed. Haribo and Chupa Chups as medium-sized global operators service niches in the confectionary market. Provided entrepreneurial talents are born, motivated and trained, familial management poses no problems. For a brand icon producer like Sanrio, this is more of a problem. Essentially it is a one-man one-product show. If one of the two goes without adequate succession (which is likely), the show will be over. The same may also apply to Hutchison Whampoa, the most successful and diversified of all overseas Chinese conglomerates. Once Li Ka-shing's successor loses the old man's Midas touch on high-risk ventures, the holding could disintegrate quickly.

Successive family owners have managed Harrods successfully. They maintained corporate values on product quality, customer service and staff loyalty. But running the world's best department store with no plans to expand is perhaps the least difficult management brief of all the 21 case histories.

The most difficult succession story was surely Hyundai, built up in no time by the autocratic, charismatic as well as despotic Chung. His empire did not survive him for long. It is still unclear which components will continue under which management.

The issue of generational succession and/or transfer to managerial control is the most crucial stage in the midlife of a successful company. Failure is often blamed on degenerate sons, squabbling siblings or incompetent widows. But equally frequent the owner-founder may have planted the roots for disaster unwittingly himself. Being obsessed with *his* company, he failed to bond with his children, did not delegate managerial tasks in time, remained aloof and critical of his offspring. Clearly, their youth experiences could not have been more different. The founders, often ill educated, grew up in relative poverty and felt driven to succeed. The next generation was born into affluence, with an authoritarian absentee (and of polygamous) father and vastly wider opportunities, a better education and wider worldview—but also with the pressure of high expectations, to which sooner or later one or the other generation refused to comply.

For centuries, hereditary nobility faced the same problem—with four decisive differences. They put more care and thought into their children's upbringing. They had more children, hence a larger pool of talents to choose from. As a rule, they also had more intelligent marital policies, and finally they were not measured publicly by bottomline performance.

Founder or successor generations were not always one-man shows. Interestingly, one frequently finds also complementary two-man teams—either close brothers (like August and Joseph Thyssen, the Saatchis, or Hans and Paul Riegel [Haribo]), a group of early orphaned siblings (like the Benettons), or two close friends from early professional days (like Takeo Fujisawa and Soichiro Honda, or Masaru Ibuka and Akio Morita [Sony]).[9] In these cases, both play strictly complementary roles. Almost inevitably one is the technical innovator, the man dealing with production management, and the other, the marketing genius acting as the externally visible face of the company. This division of managerial labor can work well throughout long, high-tensed working lives. Once, however, the division of tasks is muddled, a split is almost inevitable.

Most Japanese case studies offer more predictable scenarios due to their advanced managerial bureaucratization. Like most Japanese high-tech companies (post-Morita Sony comes to mind as well), Toshiba displays a bureaucracy with a sense of drift in the pursuit of fuzzy slogans. Honda and Matsushita after the death of their founders have also been taken over by managerial bureaucrats. Yet their founders' foresight bequeathed both with more solid old economy business and less *keiretsu* clubland distractions. Hence, they are in a much better shape.

Nomura, after burning a lot of cash and its reputation in Japan's bubbly asset inflation, is now back at square one, where it was in the 1920s and 1960s: namely as Japan's first domestic securities house. A place where it should remain, as corporate history knows of no third chances. Saatchi & Saatchi was an even more aggressive up-start, with a mad binge of undigested acquisition. This proved: the faster the pace, the higher the risk, and the quicker the game is over. Having been retooled under new management, its life expectancy has increased. Ferrari, a purely technology-driven power culture, turned out to be a marketing and branding gold mine as well. Now an autonomous part of the shaky Fiat empire, it should continue to do well as long as its autonomy remains.

On a larger scale, ThyssenKrupp does well having digested its major intra-national merger with no job losses and injecting modern technology into a mature old economy product range. Their turbulent family and political histories, including Allied tribulations, are a distant past.

Companies of public origin like SingTel or British Airways continue in their advanced efforts to inject entrepreneurialism into their bureaucratic culture of origin. This is surely more difficult than the opposite challenge: to prevent the cosy bureaucratisation of erstwhile power cultures.

For most of our globally operating multinationals, globalization did not affect their national corporate culture fundamentally. Essentially they set up well-staffed international sales/production departments, hired well-paid foreign nationals and established a pool of experienced expat staff for overseas assignments. One or two executive board members were in charge of international operations and had to travel a lot. That was it. Such globally operating companies kept and still keep their national identities; in our cases: Japanese, Chinese, Korean, Singaporean, Spanish, Italian, German, British and Irish.

Amongst them, Alltech as a global feed-enzyme maker appears to be a fairly unique case. Its Irish-US management blend is very science-driven. Supplying agro-industrial clients with commodities and strong marketing know-how, a national cultural focus appears to have been transplanted successfully by a transatlantic corporate orientation.

Two cases stand out for having gone further than the rest to cope with real or perceived requirements of globalization: Siemens and Nestlé. Siemens retooled itself entirely from a solid German quality electrical engineering company into a marketing and bottom line-driven corporation, mimmicking Jack Welch's GE. The jury is still out on whether this corporate cultural revolution, whose initial wake up call—like all wake up calls—was healthy, really works, and more importantly, whether an imported US model of corporate governance can work in Europe—except as imitating mispronounced US jargon and mannerisms, which appears like wearing cowboy boots in a beer hall.

What really works well is the Nestlé system, which did as admirably well as does Swiss federalism. A lean, mean but well-informed headquarters limiting itself to the barest essentials like strategy, finance, brand policy, quality assurance and executive personnel and leaves product and country managers the largest measure of entrepreneurial autonomy possible. A good food manager is humbled by the persistence of the healthy diversity of national tastes. Only pet food knows no borders (although some people eat it, they clearly care for price, not for taste). Hence our prize for best practice on internationalization goes to Vevey, Switzerland.[10]

Our volume of pertinent case histories from Europe and Asia clearly shows that globalization will not necessarily throw us into an "orcas" run by conformist bottomline number crunchers. The American way of running companies is surely not the only option. Up to a certain size—very large (like 200,000 employees)—and a sizable home market and domestic production base, national corporate cultures, displaying a country's unique managerial strengths, creativity and work ethic, can be maintained with no harm done. For successful branding in addition a positive intact national image is a major asset: from Ikea's elk to the Singapore Girl.

Once a company—like Siemens and Nestlé—has decided on global manufacturing, then the option for decentralization and highly autonomous national and regional operations appears as the more suitable one. This approach will allow multinational corporations to harness the wealth of distinct national corporate cultures without incurring the wrath of intra-corporate clashes of civilizations, which not even the most profitable of companies would be able to survive. Europe and Asia offer plenty of profitable and well-run alternatives to the US way of doing business. Reflecting their culture of origin, none of them has any claim to exclusivity, but in combination they surely beat the US model.

ENDNOTES

1. John Middleton. *Culture*. Oxford: Capstone, 2002, p. 2.
2. Charles Handy. *Understanding Organizations*. 4th edition. Harmondsworth: Penquin, 1999, p. 180.
3. Terence Deal, and Allan Kennedy. *The New Corporate Cultures*. London: Texere, 2000, p. 2.
4. Corinne Maier. *Boujour Paresse*. Paris: Editions Michalon, 2004.
5. Geert Hofstede. *Cultures and Organizations: Software of the Mind*. New York: McGraw-Hill, 1991, p. 23.
6. Richard D. Lewis. *When Cultures Collide: Managing Successfully across Cultures*. London: Brealey, 2002, p. 25.
7. Chan Kwok Bun, and Claire Chiang See Ngoh. *Stepping out: The Making of Chinese Entrepreneurs*. New York: Prentice Hall, 1994, p. 267.
8. Michael Backman. *Asian Eclipse*. Singapore: John Wiley & Sons, 2001, p. 51.
9. For the Benetton and Sony stories, see Albrecht Rothacher (ed.), *Corporate Cultures and Global Brands*. Singapore: World Scientific, 2004.
10. Note, however, that Nestlé has recently embarked on a controversial attempt to centralize management functions; see "Special Report Nestlé", *The Economist*, August 7, 2004.

CHAPTER 2

SingTel: Connecting Asia and Beyond

JASON ALEXANDER VILLANUEVA

PROLOGUE

After Singapore's independence in 1965, massive efforts were undertaken by the Singapore government to improve the country's infrastructure as a means to attract foreign MNCs. It was clear that this strategy, characterized as the industrial take-off phase, would form the basis for economic growth in Singapore's drive toward a cosmopolitan hub. Through rapid capital formation, Singapore emerged with a highly developed telecommunications system. The adoption of new foreign technologies by government-linked firms and statutory boards was evident, and especially so in telecommunications. As the sector evolved, a corporate giant in the making, SingTel, was born. Since its inception, SingTel has continuously and aggressively adopted cutting edge technologies, resulting in Singapore possessing one of the most advanced telecommunications infrastructure deployment and services in the Asia-Pacific region. As the title suggests, we shall be taking an in-depth look at Singapore's most successful company from its background and evolution to its leadership and corporate culture. In addition, SingTel's business strategies involving the expansion of its core business to overseas markets amidst an increasingly competitive domestic market will be analysed.

COMPANY PROFILE[1]

SingTel is Asia's 6th largest and Southeast Asia's largest telecommunications company with operations and investments in more than 20 countries and territories around the world.

Together with its regional partners, SingTel is Asia's largest multi-market mobile operator, serving more than 40 million customers in six markets—Australia, India, Indonesia, the Philippines, Singapore and Thailand.

It is to date the largest company listed on the Singapore Exchange with a market capitalisation of about S$40 billion.

The SingTel Group (including SingTel Optus) has subsidiaries whose businesses include mobile phone, paging, Internet, IT consultancy services, investments, repair of submarine cables and sale of telecommunications equipment.

The SingTel Group has more than 20,000 employees in total, headed by its President and Chief Executive Officer, Lee Hsien Yang.

SingTel operates two main hubs in Singapore and Australia. SingTel also has interests in several communications companies outside Singapore. This primarily includes a presence in developed and rapidly growing markets in Asia through strategic investments in Hong Kong, India, Indonesia, the Philippines, Taiwan and Thailand. In addition, SingTel has global offices based in 15 countries and territories worldwide. These points of presence, together with its global infrastructure, are seen as "enhancing the Group's competitiveness by providing it with expanded reach and enabling it to offer high quality, seamless services to its customers across borders".[2]

The SingTel Group provides a wide range of communications services in Singapore and Australia, including:[3]

- national telephone services
- mobile communications services, including cellular, paging and satellite services
- public data and private network services, including leased line, switched data, broadband, IP and Internet access services
- international telephone services, including international direct dialling, calling cards, facsimile services and international corporate voice and wholesale voice services

In Singapore, SingTel operates slightly under two million direct exchange lines, which works out to approximately one line for every two persons in Singapore. SingTel is also the leading mobile operator in Singapore with a 40 per cent market share, and leads the broadband

Internet market with a 62 per cent market share. In Australia, Optus serves more than six million customers. It has driven the competition as the challenger brand to Telstra and contributed to technological innovations and breakthroughs.

SingTel has been recognized Best Asian Telecom Operator by industry publication, *Telecom Asia*, for six consecutive years since 1998, giving a clear indication of its success in the region.

COMPANY HISTORY

SingTel has had more than 120 years of operating experience in Singapore and has played an integral part in the development of the city as a major communications hub in the region. SingTel traces its roots back to 1879 when Singapore became one of the first cities in the East to acquire telephone services, three years after Alexander Graham Bell patented his invention. At that time, a Mr Bennet Pell started a private telephone exchange which had 50 lines. As a British colony, telephone services in Singapore were managed by British interests until the mid-1950s. In 1955, the Singapore Telephone Board (STB) was incorporated as a statutory board with exclusive rights to operate telephone services within Singapore. A merger of STB and Telecommunications Authority of Singapore (TAS) took place in 1974. Up until that time, STB was responsible for local services, while TAS provided international services. 1982 saw the merger of the Postal Department with Telecommunications.

In 1988, a subsidiary, Singapore Telecom International, was formed and this marked the beginning of SingTel's expansion into overseas markets. The corporatisation of SingTel in 1992 was followed by its Initial Public Offering a year later. It remains Singapore's largest ever IPO.

The Singapore telecoms market was fully liberalized in April 2000. Despite the competitive environment, SingTel continues to maintain its leadership position in the Singapore market.

CORPORATE OWNERSHIP

SingTel is majority owned by Temasek Holdings.[4] Temasek has an aggregate (direct and deemed) interest of 65 per cent in SingTel's issued share capital. The Capital Group of Companies holds 5.92 per cent while the rest of the shares are in public hands.

Liberalization of the company

SingTel was for the most part of the early days a government-owned monopoly for telecommunications services provision. Even as SingTel went public in 1993, the government's stake in the company through Temasek stood at approximately 80 per cent of issued capital. In an effort to deregulate the telecommunications industry, that figure has been and continues to be pared down periodically. The latest divestment by Temasek occurred in January 2004 whereby a deal worth around US$1.25 billion, comprising shares and convertible bonds, was on offer– making it the biggest share sale in Singapore in recent years.[5]

The share sale is in line with the government's undertaking to cut its stake in SingTel under Singapore's free-trade agreement (FTA) with the US. A significant reduction in Temasek's stake is viewed as positive in the long term as it increases the free float and liquidity of the stock, not to mention the indirect benefits of its corporate image as a publicly listed firm.

LEADERSHIP AND COMPANY CULTURE: BUSINESS, THE SINGTEL WAY

Every successful company has its own set of shared beliefs, practices and leadership style which distinguishes itself from its competitors. In this section, we shall look into the corporate culture that has made SingTel the most profitable company in the country.

Leadership at SingTel

SingTel's senior management comprises of the Chairman, CEO and board of directors. However, like many other MNCs, there is an apparent power culture observed at SingTel, with decisions regarding major investments made by a key figure often spotlighted in the press. We shall focus on this individual who is synonymous with the company.

The man at the helm is SingTel's President and Chief Executive Officer Lee Hsien Yang. Born in 1957, he is the youngest of three siblings. He is the son of Singapore's Minister Mentor Lee Kuan Yew, and the brother of Prime Minister Lee Hsien Loong. Coming from a family with strong Asian values, Lee Hsien Yang was enrolled in Catholic High School, a premier Singapore school known for its academia, discipline and bilingual culture. Lee's tertiary education was primarily undertaken in the West. He obtained a first class honors degree in engineering from Cambridge and subsequently a Masters in management from Stanford. Lee joined SingTel as its executive vice-president for local services in 1994. He became the President and CEO a year later. Prior to this, Lee served in a number of command positions in the Singapore Armed Forces.

Being a former brigadier-general in the military coupled with his ambitions for SingTel, many would have drawn conclusions of the company being run in a highly hierarchical and regimented way. This has been a misperception perhaps, as it is known that he endears himself to his staff on a first-name basis. This casual approach was undertaken to shake up the bureaucratic mindset of the staff, and such corporate culture even warranted publication in the local newspaper.[6] Anyone who has seen him around the office may be inclined to agree after drawing a certain degree of inference regarding his personality and informal style.

Having a foreign education has in all likelihood shaped the way Lee Hsien Yang runs the company. While having Asian values, Lee's approach to corporate management is clearly inclined toward the American way. Highly conscious of the company's bottomline, he has sought to carry out the company's mission of maximizing shareholder wealth. Indubitably, Lee has become a household name in the corporate world for his aggressive risk taking style in forging SingTel as a global player in the telecommunications industry. His strategic planning and bold investments as the CEO of the company may be attributed to his days as a military leader. These have garnered much attention, on occasion drawing criticism from some analysts and market watchers. This notwithstanding, in an industry with rapidly changing technologies, power culture of this nature may be deemed appropriate.[7] In fact, his management of the company has led him to the title of the Best Telecom Executive for 2001 and 2002 by magazine *Telecom Asia*.

In a later part, we shall take a closer look at some of the high profile corporate deals orchestrated by Lee, including the acquisition of Australian telco Optus, and their implications for the company. One thing is unmistakable though. Lee Hsien Yang has no intention of shifting gears and his commitment to the company has been reinforced by his personal accumulation of the company's stock.

SingTel: A model IS organisation

It is often said that knowledge is power. In order for a company to stay ahead of the competition, it is necessary for it to maintain a free flow and exchange of information. The hierarchical system of the old school companies fails in this respect, and such a style could be said to be somewhat archaic and irrelevant in the telecom industry today. SingTel has been quick to recognize this, and has endeavored to respond to changes in the industry by taking an Information System (IS) approach to its staff development program.[8]

In an IS organisation, task culture is the order of the day. There is not much room in middle management for the role culture that is seen in certain older companies, where a pre-determined fixed role is usually appointed for every manager, providing a sense of job security to the more senior staff.

The training of staff at SingTel thus needs to be intensive and effective. Enter the Chief Information Officer (CIO), whose responsibility lies in ensuring that the company staff are well equipped to handle the demands of its customers while readily absorbing the latest cutting edge technologies.

From the technical IT skills point of view, SingTel has been able to recruit people from the market. It is somewhat more difficult from a telecom business skills perspective due to the fact that SingTel has for many years been the only telecom player in Singapore and has trained most of the people in the industry with telco business experience. The company as such has been training employees internally from the beginning: firstly, to learn the business, and secondly, to upgrade their technology skills. The latter appears to be of greater importance now with the presence of domestic competitors Mobile One and StarHub.

The company invests 4 per cent of payroll in skills.[9] Much of the training is done through the SingTel Academy under the human resources department at SingTel, which is responsible for instilling employees with corporate norms and culture, but does not handle the technical areas. For that, SingTel posts people overseas to work in subsidiaries, attend business schools or relevant courses. These are critical for the development and retention of necessary skills within the company, as all IT staff desire to keep abreast of the various technologies in the industry. IT training at SingTel was bolstered on the back of the company's acquisition of NCS in 1997. The aim was to realise its vision of providing seamless, end-to-end telecommunications and IT services to its customers in Singapore and the region. NCS's ability to support SingTel's needs in Singapore and Australia have facilitated this objective.

Worker role-playing and interaction with colleagues are also part and parcel of SingTel's training program as they are seen as essential for instruction and team-building skills needed in dealing with the other business units they will provide IT support to. Having people skills is especially important as SingTel expands into foreign markets where understanding those businesses and cultures will be imperative to the company's long-term success.

What does all this training translate to? A task-cultured team of middle management employees equipped to meet daily challenges. Nonetheless, depth of expertise is essential for employees working directly with high cost and advanced technologies and this still requires a role culture.[10] As such, procurement of workers with relevant skills to fill highly specialized positions is important. Since SingTel only monitors trends that the present marketplace dictates, requirements must be satisfied quickly. This is 3–6 months typically, or a year at most in the case of big projects. The IS group, of which the CIO heads, aims to meet such necessities. SingTel's team of IS soccer players are on hand "to tackle" fluid situations (The soccer player is defined as one who responds to challenges within the flow of the game). Where tight schedules mandate, the take-charge attitude of the marine is sought to accomplish tasks (The marine offers leadership, taking the lead role to solve crises or capitalize on opportunities).[11] It therefore comes as no surprise that most of the specialists sought by the IS group are contract-based employees. Evidently, most of the job openings at SingTel are basically of this nature at present.[12]

In a nutshell, the culture at SingTel may be characterized as one of power culture at the top decision-making level. Task culture and role culture are somewhat integrated for middle management employees and those directly under them. What seems apparent and logical is that task culture takes centre stage for IS middle management while role culture gains importance as the job becomes more specialized, whether technical or otherwise.

SingTel received the People's Developer Award from the Singapore Productivity and Standards Board (PSB) in March 1999 for its efforts in skills training,[13] giving testimony to SingTel's overall development plan's success.

Corporate image

Despite a Western style approach to business and management, SingTel presents itself as a company with a strong Asian orientation with regard to its public image.

The values espoused by the company are a reflection of the Confucian principles that are prevalent amongst countries in the East.[14] This is probably due to the nature in which the company has evolved from its days as a government entity. As such, the majority of the television advertisements presented by SingTel Mobile indicate a strong bias toward Asian family values, centered around communication between family members. This is in contrast to its competitors having corporate images that endear themselves as being more trendy and appealing to the younger generation.

While competitor StarHub has sponsored events such as the 2004 MTV Asia Awards, SingTel is more inclined to the sponsorship of community and national projects. Its charitable endeavours include the "Touching Lives Fund" which has successfully raised millions of dollars for the less fortunate. This was extended to healthcare workers and patients during the SARS epidemic in 2003. In addition, SingTel was the Telecom Service Provider for National Day Parade 2003 where it sponsored the provision of services and support for the e-balloting ticket distribution system.

The advent of competition in telecommunications industry has thus produced a dichotomy in the types of sponsorship.

SingTel has, albeit not very successfully, tried to add pizazz to its image by engaging in a joint venture with Sir Richard Branson's Virgin Mobile in 2001. The objective of creating a flashy and trendy mobile phone service provider in Singapore was short-lived however due to harsh economic conditions and a saturated market. Domestic operations that were part of the venture were scrapped in 2002 and SingTel has since appeared content on focusing on its strengths. This has benefited SingTel in a way since the promulgation of its Asian values through increased advertising expenditure has assisted in providing the company top branding in terms of local enterprises.[15]

SingTel still strikes many people as a government controlled company with its leadership tied to the country's politics. This view will continue, considering CEO Lee's pedigree and the fact that it will be quite a while before Temasek divests its stake in SingTel completely. On the positive side, there is the belief that such factors provide the basis for a fundamentally sound company, where corruption and fraud are virtually non-existent. The downside to this as will be seen later is that these same factors may be a stumbling block for the company as it seeks to increase its presence overseas.

An example of the company's links with the government that was not viewed favorably by some customers involved SingTel's subsidiary Internet service provider SingNet in 1999.[16] Apparently, the Internal Security Department secretly scanned 200,000 computers at SingNet's request to trace a virus that allowed hackers to steal computer passwords and credit card numbers. This came to light after a student who installed anti-hacking software filed a police report. Not only did the company appear to have close ties with the Ministry of Home Affairs; it clearly intruded into the privacy of its customers, for which it had to issue a public apology.

SingTel has noticeably been trying to distance itself from the government and establish itself as a distinct corporate entity. In a case which drew nation-wide interest in 2002, SingTel emerged victorious in its dispute against the Infocomm Development Authority (IDA), Singapore's telecommunications regulator. In 2001, the IDA claimed it had over compensated SingTel by S$388 million in 1997 for bringing forward the end of its exclusive license to operate by seven years. The disputed amount was due to a mistaken tax provision in IDA's compensation of S$1.5 billion. In the clash of the titans, SingTel came out on top, and in the process signalling the corporate strength of the company. Different conclusions may however be drawn from this outcome.

A number of other legal tussles involving its competitors over telecommunications infrastructure has also been brought before the IDA. While it should be noted that many of these only impact SingTel's earnings revenue marginally, it does illustrate the company's commitment to its mission of creating value for shareholders. To put it in a somewhat more arcane fashion, it fights for every penny it believes it deserves.

In essence, the corporate culture of SingTel is one that may be fairly characterized by its company vision and mission statements:

> SingTel's vision is to be the communications company that breaks barriers and builds bonds.

SingTel's mission:

- To provide customers with innovative solutions to meet their communications needs
- To develop staff with challenging careers in a nurturing environment that foster excellence
- To create value for the shareholders

CHANGING TRENDS IN THE TELECOMMUNICATIONS INDUSTRY

Sharing the pie: competition in the domestic markets

SingTel's position as the dominant player in fixed line, mobile line and Internet services stems from its days as a government monopoly when it benefited greatly from the government's involvement in developing the country's telecommunications infrastructure. The government's recognition of the strategic and economic importance of the telecommunications industry provided SingTel virtually total protection from market forces until 1997.[17] Government ownership at that time was justified on the grounds that the telecommunications sector was a natural monopoly, in that there existed high fixed costs but falling marginal costs of running the services. In order to prevent welfare inefficiencies usually associated with monopolies, the pricing of many SingTel services were regulated to be close to or at the most competitive world rates. World-class standards of service were also required.

Singapore, being a small country, has little option but to follow worldwide trends. One of these trends was the European-led movement towards privatization, deregulation and increased competition in the telecommunications sector in the early 1980s. This spread to Southeast Asia and was motivated by the belief that telecommunications infrastructure is a national asset which could be exploited to gain a competitive advantage. Privatization was also seen as improving the efficiency of monopoly telcos. The shift in mindset had huge implications for monopolies like SingTel, which had to react quickly to the rapid change in the industry from one of the most protected to one of the most internationalized in the 1990s.

With the full liberalization of the telecommunications industry in 2000, SingTel faced direct competition on multiple fronts. Starting from 1997, SingTel had begun to face competition from rival MobileOne in the mobile line market. Aggressive price competition between the two firms ensued and within two years, M1 was able to grab a 32 per cent share of the mobile phone services market from SingTel.[18] The entrance of StarHub into the fixed line market in 2000 together with its provision of Internet and mobile phone services further intensified competition in these key markets. Certain telecommunications infrastructure such as underground cabling with which SingTel had full access to would now have to be shared with competitors. Advertising expenditure at SingTel also rose significantly during this period, growing from S$27.4 million in 1996 to an estimated S$100 million in 1999.[19] With competitors eating into the pie of the domestic markets, SingTel needed a sound business strategy to counter the erosion in home revenue.

CONNECTING THE WORLD: ENHANCING THE COMPANY'S GLOBAL OUTREACH

Sensing that the small domestic telecommunications market would become saturated eventually, SingTel embarked on a growth path in the late 1980s that hinged on expanding into foreign markets. The expansion was also motivated by SingTel's success in the domestic market coupled with its large cash reserves.

With the benefit of hindsight, one can clearly see that as a government-owned company prior to privatization, SingTel was able to plan ahead its business strategy to meet the challenges stemming from future liberalization of the telecommunications market.

SingTel adopted a three-pronged approach to internationalization.[20] These were namely international marketing through joint marketing programs with other telcos, alliances with foreign telecom authorities and the setting up of a consultancy firm involved in planning, operations maintenance and seeking investment opportunities.

There were three main types of investments made by SingTel. First, joint investments were carried out for the purpose of providing global services. Second, SingTel invested in infrastructure such as participation in a consortium involved in laying and owning submarine cables (C2C). The third main focus was investing in sound foreign telecommunications companies with the objective of acquiring overseas profits from these firms.

Venturing into Europe

The first forays into foreign territory included small investments in the US, Sri Lanka, Mauritius and Vietnam in the late 1980s and early 1990s. In 1990, SingTel made its first major venture in Thailand, acquiring a 40 per cent stake in the data and paging services of Shinawatra Group.

Prior to Lee Hsien Yang's appointment as CEO of SingTel, the company was led by Chairman and CEO Sung Sio Ma. Under him, SingTel consolidated its position by acquiring, partnering and building strategic relationships in Asia, Europe and America. Sung was responsible for creating the world's first nationwide digital telecommunications system and the first submarine fibre-optic cable between Singapore and Europe. He also built the first paging network in China and the second largest cellular network in the Philippines. The focus of SingTel at the time was primarily toward Europe however, and by early 1995, SingTel had three quarters of its foreign assets in European ventures.

SingTel had two main reasons for moving into Europe. Firstly, it believed that the potential returns in Europe would exceed that from Asia significantly, considering the much larger telecommunications market of the former. Secondly, the 1998 liberalization deadline set by the European Union made the region an attractive place to establish a foothold ahead of the competition. SingTel thus became the only Asian telco to have substantial investments in Europe in the mid-1990s. The European investments were however not profitable by 1995. Keeping a long-term view of the market, SingTel chose to ignore the short-term losses.

Shifting focus

By mid-1995, SingTel had set a target of 20 per cent of total revenue from foreign sources by 1998 and 50 per cent by 2004.[21] It has been a common practice for the company to review its investments and concentrate on areas in which it has competitive advantages. Coming to the realization that the new high-growth areas would be in emerging markets, SingTel began to set its sights on Asia. This view was reinforced by the idea that the growing momentum of deregulation in telecommunications industry in Asia would provide many opportunities for the company. The company meanwhile sold its stakes in some smaller ventures to concentrate on new and larger investments.

The orientation toward Asia also signified the company's objectives under its new leadership in 1995. Since his appointment, CEO Lee Hsien Yang has striven to turn the company into a nimble multinational giant. As such, Lee has been instrumental in the investments made by the company ever since. While acknowledging that the European investments provided invaluable lessons, Lee felt that SingTel's image as an Asian company would put it at an advantage against Western firms in Asia.[22] Nonetheless, this new direction did not inhibit the company from making new strategic investments in Europe.

SingTel surprised the market in December 1995 with an announcement that it intended to purchase 13.5 per cent of Belgacom for S$945 million. It concluded its largest European venture to date in 1996. SingTel was part of a consortium which purchased 49.9 per cent of the state monopoly from the Belgian government. This would prove to be a prudent investment for SingTel, contributing $111 million to the company's profits in 1997. In addition, this more than offset the other loss making ventures, allowing SingTel to make its first foreign profit of S$47.6 million that year.[23]

Emerging markets: Asia beckons

As part of its reorientation, SingTel engaged in a joint venture in 1997 with the Singapore government's investment arm to make investments in telecommunications and complementary businesses. This was in line with SingTel's strategy of having foreign investments playing a significant part in its long-term growth.

SingTel's plans for regional expansion suffered a temporary setback in 1997 as Southeast and East Asia was struck by a severe financial crisis. There was speculation that the Asian miracle was over and that the region would no longer be able to reproduce the stellar growth seen in the 1980s and early 1990s. This led to the question as to whether SingTel had erred on its European strategy by missing out on Asian opportunities. One can always argue that the fall in company valuations caused by the Asian crisis made a number of companies in sectors and countries with strong growth potential ideal investments for SingTel. It therefore came as no surprise when SingTel acquired sizable stakes in Advanced Info Service Co. in Thailand and Globe Telecom in the Philippines.

In the last few years, SingTel has continued its strategy of achieving revenue and profit growth from the region. In 2001, SingTel concluded its largest overseas investment ever, with the S$13 billion acquisition of Optus—the second largest telecommunications provider in Australia. SingTel's aim was to exploit the extensive investments in regional infrastructure comprising submarine cables and satellites made by Optus.

SingTel also invested in Telkomsel in Indonesia and the Bharti Group in India, and increased its stake in Globe Telecom in the Philippines. These companies were seen as attractive investment opportunities due to their leading positions in their respective markets where mobile phone penetration is set to increase markedly. At the same time, SingTel completed the C2C and i2i regional cable networks, providing new low-cost bandwidth with multiple connections from Japan to India. These investments, according to the company, have led to a more efficient capital structure without compromising its financial strength and flexibility.

THE CHALLENGES FACED WITH REGIONAL EXPANSION

Expansion effects on the company's stock price

While the regional expansion bodes well for SingTel's image as an Asian telecommunications powerhouse, the main concern of investors is undeniably its stock price. Apart from the competition in the domestic market, SingTel's share price has been dampened by the market's concern over its rapid expansion. Some of the major investment decisions made by CEO Lee Hsien Yang have been questioned.

Many observers felt that SingTel had overpaid for Optus at 50 times price earnings, in a deal which caught much attention in the region. SingTel financed the deal partly by issuing 1.4 billion new shares of stock, representing 8 per cent equity dilution.[24] The shares went on a downward trend after the announcement of the deal, declining 29 per cent and wiping out over S$9 billion of the company's market capitalization. At that point of time, the company's shares were trading at 47 per cent of their price at its 1993 initial public offering, drawing the ire of many investors. Furthermore, SingTel had amassed a net debt of S$10.1 billion in 2002 compared with a cash balance surplus of S$6.6 billion in early 2001. This led to the subsequent downgrading of SingTel's long-term credit rating from "stable" to "negative" by both Standard & Poor's and Moody's. In a separate deal in 2001, when SingTel bought 22 per cent of Indonesia's PT Telekomunikasi Selular (Telkomsel) for S$600 million, it valued the entire company at S$2.7 billion, a much higher value than independent estimates.[25] Had SingTel been too optimistic with its investments?

SingTel's focus on potential high growth areas has also implied higher risks involved in ventures. The investments in Indonesia and Philippines have been politically risky ones, with political uncertainty rife in those countries. In addition, the accounting practices of the companies have been seen as less than transparent. The currencies have also been unstable over periods of time, providing a high degree of exchange rate risk as far as overseas revenue is concerned. This uncertainty over the earnings potential of SingTel's many investments has impacted its share price adversely. Such factors have played a part in affecting investor confidence in the company.

Yet another issue: intercultural and cross border communication

An area that is often neglected when a company expands beyond its shores is one of cultural and national differences. Be it an investment stake, a merger or acquisition, ignoring the roles of intercultural and cross border communications can result in undesirable outcomes. These range from lower productivity and earnings in subsidiaries to the more serious consequence of being shut out of important markets.

In spite of its many secured investment bids in Asia, SingTel has had its fair share of high profile corporate misses. These were mainly due to differences in national objectives caused by the high level of involvement in SingTel by the Singapore government. For example, SingTel had unsuccessfully tried to purchase Hong Kong's Cable and Wireless HKT in 2000. The latter was acquired by PCCW, a company controlled by Hong Kong tycoon Li Ka Shing's son, Richard Li, after it submitted an outrageous bid of US$36 billion. It was believed by bankers and diplomats that SingTel's failure in securing HKT was due to Beijing not wanting the Singapore government controlling Hong Kong's largest telephone utility.[26]

Singapore's reputation for having an overbearing mother-knows-best attitude may have hurt SingTel's chances to attract certain regional partners. A classic case is SingTel's unsuccessful attempt in 2000 at acquiring a minority stake in Malaysia's Time Engineering, a telecoms and fibre-optics company. Although the company was in financial trouble, SingTel viewed its extensive link of optical cables to Thailand as a strategic and hence attractive factor. The deal fell through at the eleventh hour, with a widely held belief that Malaysia's Prime Minister at the time, Mahathir Mohamad, had blocked the deal and instructed the Malaysian government's investment arm to rescue Time. Apparently, he did not like anybody linked to the Singapore government wielding influence in industries he saw as strategic.[27]

This incident had deeper political undercurrents than just the fact that a foreign government-controlled company having influence over a strategic industry. There are intercultural differences at play historically between Singapore and Malaysia. This goes back to the emotionally intense days of the merger and separation of the two countries in the 1960s involving Lee Kuan Yew and to a certain extent, Mahathir.[28] Basically, the difference could be considered one of work ethics between the Chinese and the Malay communities. In the latter culture, the work ethic is not as strong as the former.[29] Hence, the resultant disparity in economic development between the groups. Over the years, Mahathir has often been critical of Singapore, perhaps due to its perceived hubris associated with its success. SingTel's CEO, needless to say, fits that description perfectly. As one article put it bluntly, Lee Hsien Yang "is a living embodiment of the Singapore its neighbours love to hate."[30]

A fine example of the importance of intercultural communications occurred when SingTel acquired Optus. In Australia, there was an attempt to prevent the deal from succeeding. Apparently, there were some Australians who did not agree much with the Singapore government's, and in particular Lee Kuan Yew's, style of leadership. This may stem partly from the Australian culture where there is significant cynicism toward people in power or with too much wealth.[31] Thus, there existed a segment of the population that was unhappy about SingTel's acquisition of an Australian company. The difference in corporate cultures of Optus and SingTel were also seen as a challenge. SingTel was still viewed as having the vestiges of a civil service mindset, while Optus with its young workforce, had a freewheeling culture. How would the less pressurized style of some 8,000 new Australian employees be incorporated into the performance-driven one of an aggressively expanding Singapore firm?

SingTel has eschewed an intercultural dilemma by keeping Optus' day-to-day operations autonomous, while combining divisions between the two companies to allow opportunities for synergies. In that way, transition would appear to be almost seamless without the need to overhaul Optus' system of management. However, in order to improve Optus' performance, SingTel had to cut costs and capital expenditure and also restructure loss-making divisions. In the process, SingTel inevitably laid off 1,000 employees at Optus. Nevertheless, Optus' CEO Chris Anderson praised SingTel's direction, leadership and strict financial discipline as it turned profitable in the year following the acquisition.[32]

LOOKING AHEAD

We have looked at SingTel's corporate culture and international business strategies along with the challenges faced in its expansion plans. Looking to the future, what are the implications of SingTel's current business strategy of focusing on Asia?

SingTel's objective of having 50 per cent foreign revenue by 2004 has been achieved successfully with its acquisition of Optus and other regional investments. Latest reports have this figure at 77 per cent on the back of strong earnings by Optus and associated companies in Thailand, Indonesia, Philippines and India.[33] The strong showing from Optus should placate SingTel shareholders somewhat, considering the negative reaction to the news that SingTel overpaid for it initially. Ironically, it is the smallness of Optus in relation to Telstra that has allowed it to gain market share in Australia.

With healthy earnings from its regional investments, SingTel is well positioned to service its long-term debt incurred in its expansion plans and also to look to new investments in other parts of Asia. This ability to grow is further enhanced with the company's liquidation of its major European investment stake in Belgacom in March 2004. This sale has resulted in the realisation of significant capital gains to the tune of over S$1 billion and is in line with the company's strategy of concentrating within the region.

In an effort to focus on its core telecommunications services business, SingTel sold 69 per cent of Singapore Post (SingPost) in an

Initial Public Offering in May 2003. SingTel also divested its stake in Yellow Pages, its directory business, in June 2003 to CVC Asia Pacific and J. P. Morgan Partners Asia for S$220 million in cash.

SingTel's corporate image as a privatized firm will gain credibility in time as connotations of it as a government company fade with Temasek's decreasing stake.

This will assist in its future quest to enter deregulated markets seeking free competition. Changes in the regional political landscape may also work in SingTel's favor. At present, there is speculation of SingTel looking toward Malaysia once again for investments with the retirement of Mahathir. The new premier, Abdullah Ahmad Badawi, is seen to be less confrontational in his dealings with Singapore and also less likely to veto commercially-driven deals involving major companies on both sides of the Causeway.[34]

While the inherent risks of SingTel's regional investments will continue to be a source of concern, the company has shown immense resilience amidst a global slowdown in the telecommunications industry. SingTel has reaped profits throughout its history as a corporate entity and its associated firms have been profitable at an aggregate level since 1997, allowing for continuous dividend payouts to shareholders. This gives the impression that the company has been highly adaptable and able to stay ahead in an ever-changing industry. While the past performance of a firm is often said to be no guarantee of its future success, corporate results produced by the current leadership show highly encouraging signs for SingTel as it moves forward.

At this juncture, the company is already preparing for the next challenge; competing in the provision of services in the new 3G mobile technology. However, it is clear that the domestic mobile line market will be of reduced importance to SingTel as it increases its presence across Asia. The greater challenge would thus be for it to penetrate new markets ahead of its rivals. If SingTel is able to maintain its growth for the long haul amidst stiff competition in adopting new technologies, it may very well emerge as one of the companies that is "most likely to change the world."[35]

ENDNOTES
1   Company profile information from SingTel's official website, http://www.singtel.com/.

2   http://www.ncs.com.sg/. NCS is a wholly owned subsidiary of SingTel.
3   http://www.singtel.com/.
4   Temasek Holdings is the Singapore government's domestic investment arm. Ho Ching, wife of PM Lee Hsien Loong, is the company's executive director.
5   Wong Wei Kong, January 7, 2004, "Temasek to divest significant SingTel stake," *Business Times*.
6   Hansen, Jeremy, & Assif Shameen, February 16, 2001, vol. 27, no. 6, "SingTel Blues," *Asiaweek*.
7   Handy, Charles. B., 1976, *Understanding Organisations*, Penguin Books, pp. 189–90.
8   Miller, James, October 1999, "The IS organisation," *CIO Asia*.
9   Ibid.
10 Handy, op cit., p. 189.
11 Miller, op cit.
12 http://www.singtel.com/.
13 http://www.singtel.com/.
14 Lewis, Richard D., *When Cultures Collide, Managing Successfully Across Cultures*, Nicholas Brealy Publishing, 1997, pp. 81–2.
15 Most Valuable Singapore Brand with brand value of S$2.6 billion (Singapore Brand Awards 2003).
16 Kulwant Singh, Nitin Pangarkar, & Loizos Heracleous, "Singapore Telecom: Strategic challenges in a turbulent environment." In *Business Strategy in Asia: A Casebook*, second edition, p. 11.
17 Kulwant Singh, Nitin Pangarkar, & Loizos Heracleous, "SingTel in Europe." In *Business Strategy in Asia: A Casebook*, second edition, p. 122.
18 Singh, op cit., p. 9.
19 Ibid., p. 9.
20 Singh, op cit., p. 126.
21 Ibid., p. 130.
22 "Foreign ventures are slow to pay off," March 24, 1997, *Asian Wall Street Journal*.
23 SingTel annual report (various years).
24 Shari, Michael, December 3, 2001, "SingTel is soaring beyond Singapore," *Business Week*.
25 Ibid.
26 "Singapore should set its companies free," March 13, 2000, *Business Week*.
27 "Sing, tell, cry," May 20, 2000, vol. 355, issue 8,171, *The Economist*.
28 For a political perspective regarding this issue, see Lee Kuan Yew's memoirs.
29 Lewis, op cit., p. 295.
30 Hansen, Jeremy & Assif Shameen, February 16, 2001, vol. 27, no. 6, "SingTel blues," *Asiaweek*.

31 Lewis, op cit., pp. 182–4.
32 "Hsien Yang makes good on Optus," February 8, 2003, *Straits Times*.
33 http://www.singtel.com/.
34 Toh, Eddie, September 24, 2003, "SingTel may get 3rd chance to enter M'sian market," *Business Times* (Malaysia).
35 Chong, William, February 27, 2002, "SingTel, Flextronics in Top 100," *Straits Times*.

REFERENCES

William Chong. "SingTel, Flextronics in Top 100," *Straits Times*. February 27, 2002.

Toni Clarke. "SingTel expands as competitors flood domestic market," *Finance Asia*, April 7, 2000. http://www.financeasia.com/

Charles B. Handy. *Understanding Organisations*. Penguin Books, 1976.

Jeremy Hansen & Shameen Assif. "SingTel Blues," *Asiaweek*, vol. 27, no. 6. February 16, 2001.

Loizos Heracleous & Kulwant Singh. "SingTel: Venturing into the region." In *Business Strategy in Asia: A Casebook*, second edition, 2003. Edited by Kulwant Singh, Nitin Pangarkar & Loizos Heracleous, Thomson. Earlier version under review at *Asian Case Research Journal*.

Loizos Heracleous & Kulwant Singh. "Singapore Telecom: Strategic challenges in a turbulent environment." In *Business Strategy in Asia: A Casebook*, second edition, 2003 & 2001. Edited by Kulwant Singh, Nitin Pangarkar & Loizos Heracleous, Thomson. Also published in *Asian Case Research Journal*, 2000, vol. 4, 49–77; and in T Wheelen & J Hunger, *Strategic Management and Business Policy*, Prentice Hall, 2002.

Richard D. Lewis. *When Cultures Collide: Managing Successfully across Cultures*. Nicholas Brealy Publishing, 1997.

James Miller. "The I.S organisation," *CIO Asia*. October 1999.

National Computer Systems website, http://www.ncs.com.sg/

Michael Shari. "SingTel is soaring beyond Singapore," *Businessweek*. December 3, 2001.

Kulwant Singh. "SingTel in Europe." In *Business Strategy in Asia: A Casebook*. 2003 & 2001. Second edition, Edited by Kulwant Singh, Nitin Pangarkar & Loizos Heracleous, Thomson. Also published in Proceedings of the *Asian Case Research Journal Conference*, Singapore.

Singapore Telecommunications website, http://www.singtel.com/.

Eddie Toh. "SingTel may get 3rd chance to enter M'sian market," *Business Times* (Malaysia). September 24, 2003.

Wong Wei Kong. "Temasek to divest significant SingTel stake," *Business Times*. January 1, 2004.

CHAPTER 3

High-Tech Toshiba in Drift

ALBRECHT ROTHACHER

Toshiba, Japan's electrical giant turned electronics conglomerate, lost its way following the Japan crash of 1992 and the IT crash of 2000/1 amidst mounting debts and losses. The company's current publications and Press Releases feature various products, development and research projects, which all seem to center around digital TVs and a portable wireless personal digital assistant (PDA) working as a telephone, camera, pocket computer and Internet access all in one. At the same time, there are the ongoing activities of the 20-odd Toshiba semi-autonomous "in-house companies," which produce "old economy" products like white household appliances, locomotives, power generators, electrical pumps, light bulbs and X-ray machines, as well as new economy IT stuff. There is a lot of IT jargon among Toshiba's senior management. But at the same time there seems a belated rediscovery of the beauties of low-margin, neglected old economy products compared to the loss-making IT production into which Toshiba ploughed most of its R&D and capital investments. It now accounts for the bulk of its mountain of debts. Yet, Toshiba's senior management has not quite given up on the elusive "next generation" IT breakthrough, which miraculously would allow Toshiba to become profitable again within the overcrowded IT competition.

Toshiba was founded with Meiji government support 130 years ago in 1875 and run by Hisashige Tanaka, who as "Japan's Edison" had invented water pumps and weapons' systems. Originally set up as a plant for telegraph equipment, it soon branched out into other electrical appliances and became a major facilitator of the electrification of Japan. After a merger in 1939 it became the Tokyo Shibaura Electric Works as part of the Mitsui *zaibatsu*. During the war some 100 factories, including those in China and Korea, were in operation. When in post-war Japan, 100,000 of these workers remained unpaid for months, they became a strategic target for the JCP (Japan Communist Party) and the unions, which the communists controlled. When unending militant labour strife threatened the survival of Toshiba, Mitsui Bank drafted Taizo Ishizaka, the tough wartime president of Dai-ichi Life Insurance as Toshiba's new president in 1949. He quickly managed to crack the labor troubles, threw out incompetent managers at the same time, restructured the company, set up proper accounting, and negotiated a technical support agreement and a 25 per cent capital participation with General Electric (GE), thereby resuming their traditional pre-war ties. In 1957, when Toshiba's course was firmly embedded in Japan's post-war recovery, Ishizaka moved on to become Chairman of Keidanren, Japan's powerful business federation, the equivalent to the country's "economic prime minister" for the decade to come.

Subsequently, in the course of the Tokyo Olympics boom of 1964, Toshiba overinvested, with debt levels threatening corporate survival. Again, a tough outsider was drafted by the Mitsui *keiretsu*. This time it was Toshio Doko, erstwhile of the Ishikawajima-harima shipyards, who in 1965 engineered a turn-around by empowering factory managers with new competencies and by pruning seniority-based promotions and the bureaucratization in headquarters. By 1973 it was his turn to move on and to assume the chairmanship of Keidanren for Toshiba and the Mitsui *keiretsu*.

Toshiba's full-hearted move into the electronics sector started under Shoichi Saba (1980–7). Under his reign, the first DRAM (1985) and portable PCs were developed, typically in joint ventures with Siemens and Motorola. Saba's career was ended by the revelation of the sale of submarine sound-deafening equipment to the Soviet Navy by a Toshiba subsidiary, Toshiba Kikai, which had falsified export papers to circumvent Cocom export controls.

The prospect of a Japanese electronics competitor fraudulently aiding the Soviets to threaten the security of the US and their allies was too much to go unnoticed on Capitol Hill. US lawmakers used their dismay at the duplicity of the Toshiba plutocrats to set up a photo opportunity to smash a series of Toshiba ghetto-blasters against a White House background. After a public apology, Saba resigned in atonement.

Toshiba was part of the crowded field of Japanese electrical appliance makers: Hitachi, Matsushita, Mitsubishi Electric, Fujitsu, NEC, Oki Electric, which after the war were joined by Sony, Sharp and Canon. To this sector MITI up to the 1980s applied its industrial policy of "controlled competition," facilitating competition over price and quality in the domestic market while using import protection and government procurement to support the domestic makers. For Toshiba, the tie-up with GE permitted a steady stream of technological concepts and innovative products. Amongst a wide range of electrical goods, like the electrical rice cooker, which was famously invented by Toshiba in 1955 and changed the lives of all East Asian housewives, or electric fans, refrigerators, vacuum cleaners, washing machines, X-ray tubes, locomotives or turbines, Toshiba became a market leader for decades.

During the boom and bubble decade of the 1980s, Toshiba—like the rest of the Japanese electrical industry—ploughed its profits and cheaply raised capital into semiconductor and IT developments. While investments and subsequent post-bubble debts were huge, they failed to deliver. Curiously, it was the size of the capital invested into semiconductor manufacturing, where Toshiba hoped in vain to become a world market leader, which retarded innovation of the memory chips and allowed the Koreans and Taiwanese to catch up. The Japanese maker had avoided to retool and to redesign their expensive brand new plants and operations in time. Since 2001, the production of DRAMs accumulated huge losses. Yet still in mid-2000, just prior to the IT crash, ¥170 billion were again invested by Toshiba into chip production. For IT equipment, competition and innovation simply worked too quickly to generate profits. Consumers learned to expect a cheaper and improved generation of PCs every six to eight months.

Toshiba had some successes in developing Japanese language word processors, automatic letter sorting machines, point-of-sales (POS) systems (which integrate the cash register, accounting and stock keeping systems), liquid crystal displays and DVDs, where it largely went ahead of Sony to set the world standards in 1995. Yet Toshiba flopped with its desktop computers, and as a latecomer, ranked only 10th with mobile phones. Sales of its expensive digital TVs never took off. PCs, semiconductors and liquid crystal displays are hit by persistently low demand. Yet like an addict to its fuzzy science fiction visions, the company seems unable to cut the losses and let go. There seems always the promise of a next generation product, like the wireless server ("3G Phone"), combining digital TV, cell-phone, computer, Internet and camera functions, just around the corner, thus discouraging Toshiba from stopping current loss making production and R&D in all related fields in order to be able to produce the entire system in-house in the future.

The notion that the wireless server will face similar competition and innovation cycles—with first products from Motorola, Nokia and Siemens already entering the market—and hence similar profitability levels like their IT predecessors did not seem to materialize.

Toshiba's R&D efforts are legendary. One thousand scientists are engaged in fundamental research. Each in-house company has its own development center under a chief technology executive. Each plant has an engineering department on-site for continuous product innovation and improvement. Toshiba has somewhat cut back its research staff, but is reluctant to give up any of its broad research drives for fear of missing out unforeseeable breakthroughs on any of the many fronts on which it is engaged. As even a major player like Toshiba cannot afford the huge costs of being engaged in all electronics R&D fields, since years it has expanded on its GE experience and engaged in a lengthy lists of strategic alliances for joint developments and purchases and for shared costs and risks.

Such alliances exist with Electrolux for home appliances (including a joint factory in Thailand), with Sony on LSI and work for the Playstation, with Matsushita for liquid crystal displays and cell-phones, with Microsoft on e-books, with Samsung on clothes dryers, with United Technologies on fuel cells, with Fujitsu on DRAM processing technology, and with Time Warner on multimedia content. Occasionally the alliances end in divorce, like with Philips on DVD development (1993) and with IBM on display technologies (2001), due to incompatible strategies and commercial interests—only to be followed by remarriages with new partners.

Toshiba's management is convinced that its polygamous corporate lifestyle is only made possible by continuing to stay attractive by maintaining a world lead in the respective technology field. The alliances allow it to take part in full product development and to avoid becoming a parts supplier whose "commodities" would inevitably suffer a relentless pressure on prices and margins.

Glamorously overinvested and high-tech loss-making ventures aside, Toshiba remains a leading producer of mid-technology electrical machinery and appliances. Like most "old economy" products, they have typically low-margin profitability, as increasingly dominant retail discounters in Japan squeeze prices and the Korean and Taiwanese competition enters world markets and even the Japanese home market, where replacement cycles in an ageing population have become longer.

As two-thirds of Toshiba's total sales are domestic, also its wide range, a 20,000 product long list of machines and appliances with strong electrical motors, like power pumps, blowers, compressors, injector machines and industrial air conditioners continue to depend mainly on the stagnant Japanese market.

Toshiba's "social infrastructure systems"—meaning electrical buses, locomotives, radar installations, and water supply and treatment plants—equally depend mostly on civil engineering projects in Japan. They are hence affected by the cutbacks of its overextended public budget. When Toshiba was awarded the contract to set up a high-speed Shinkansen-type railroad between Kaohsiung and Taipei in Taiwan, this did not just include lowly profitable equipment for construction and rolling stock, but also signal systems, ticketing machines and the management of stations, thus assuring a steady stream of revenue.

All color TV production in 2001 has already been shifted to China, the world's most rapidly growing TV market. There they are made by Dalian Toshiba TV Co., which just manages to break even.

For Toshiba's barely profitable thermal and nuclear power plants, in which it holds a share of one-third in Japan, all hopes rest on a resurrection of nuclear energy generation in the US. Since the 1979 Three Mile Island accident, none of the US ageing plants were substantially modernized, let alone replaced—thus creating a potentially huge and profitable demand—which however, as usual with Toshiba's forward planning, still awaits realization.

Toshiba is also prominent in diagnostic medicine, like in X-ray systems, computed tomography, ultrasound, magnetic resonance imaging and nuclear medicine. For Toshiba's management, their medical department serves mainly to contribute a "positive image" to the company (Cutts, p. 222).

With profits of around $1 billion, Toshiba as a company of $54 billion turnover had never been particularly profitable. Since 1999, however, net losses occurred and kept mounting to $1.5 billion (2002). Management reaction has been the usual Japanese mixture of fashionable "sloganeering," half-hearted measures to cut costs and to establish a semblance of focus, as well as outsourcing of manufacturing to China.

Some peripheral productions, like car headlights, automated teller machines (ATMs) and home air conditioners were sold off or hived off to subsidiaries. The money-bleeding DRAM production was sold to Micron Electronics (US).

The already mentioned structure of 20 semi-autonomous in-house companies clustered around related product groups was created, with their own CEOs and profit/loss accounts. Given Toshiba's "minefield" of messy accounting with multiple sales channels and trade between subsidiaries, this was no small feat.

Outside consultants were brought in and for the first time, listened to. Toshiba's unwieldy Board of Directors was reduced in size from 34 to 13. The most senior chieftains, however, retained their posts. Still, Toshiba claims that the automatic approvals of investment and project plans have become a thing of the past.

Expecting a series of high-tech gadgets to turn around the losses as miracle weapons for the next fiscal year, an ultra-optimist objective of 14 per cent return on equity was introduced—only to be painted in red, and postponed to the subsequent year.

Belatedly, President Tadashi Okamura discovered in 2001 that Toshiba had focused too much on the overcrowded IT sector in the past two decades (Cutts, p. 235). Rather value added in neglected promising non-IT areas like heavy electrical machinery, water and power grids and home appliances needed strengthening. Toshiba is now supposed to listen to the "voice of consumers" and to change from an engineering company to a marketing culture. Given its poor brand image—7th in rankings for its electrical and electronic products in Japan—this change is overdue.

As losses mounted, Toshiba was forced to announce a 10 per cent retrenchment of its 188,000 strong global workforce. Some 20,000 left on early retirement or were redeployed to subsidiaries, as production left high-cost Japan for China.

Yet even measures of crisis management typically took one year to allow a consensus to emerge for their watered down implementation. The hard choices facing Japan's cosy corporate clubland are still clouded in fuzzy "sloganeering," camouflaging the persistent urges of empire building. Like the military of 1944/5, corporate Japan appears unable to retreat tactically, thus putting the survival of all at risk.

Although this strategy is protective of current employment levels, Robert Cutts' interviews with a handful of employees reveal an atmosphere of profound pessimism, professional dissatisfaction and a very un-Japanese readiness to change the employer. For a research-intensive company, which on all of its management levels relies exclusively on

Japanese males and needs to retain and to recruit the best and the brightest, this is an inauspicious omen.

REFERENCES
Robert L. Cutts. *Toshiba*. London: Penguin, 2003.
Taiga Uranaka. "Toshiba forecasts heavier losses," *The Japan Times*. September 17, 2003.
"Toshiba Corporation," *The Oriental Economist*. May 1981, p. 34.

CHAPTER 4

Siemens: Engineering Locomotives, Cellphones, and Corporate Culture Change

ALBRECHT ROTHACHER

Siemens, the German electronics and electrical appliance giant, offers an interesting case study on how a conservative business conglomerate with a strong and proud engineering culture transformed itself into a revenue-oriented multinational corporation driven by US reporting standards. The process was drawn out and painful, and the results were often mixed. Yet corporate survivors claim that the transformation was unavoidable if Siemens was to survive the deregulation of markets in Europe, ever-shorter high-tech product cycles, and globalized markets for goods and capital.

Siemens was founded more than 150 years ago. It was started in 1847 by a young artillery officer, Werner von Siemens, and a mechanic, Johann Halske. Von Siemens had improved on an existing telegraph model and sought to capitalize on his invention. Once Morse constructed his apparatus, von Siemens again managed to improve it. Siemens & Halske also soon arrived to produce the first sea cables for telegraph wires. Sustained by public procurement, the company went on to develop dynamo generators, signalling systems for railways, alcometers for the Russian fisc, and since 1877, the first telephones in Germany. In 1870, Siemens built the first Indo-European telegraph line from London to Calcutta. It actually worked over 8,000 km of distance. When in 1863 a first attempt at laying a sea cable between Oran and Cartagena failed, Halske left the company in disgust.

For a long time then, Siemens became the family property of the Siemens clan, foremost led by the inventor and patriarch Werner von

Siemens (until his death in 1892), seconded by his brothers in senior management positions. This obviously limited their access to capital and prevented them from expanding as quickly as their competitors in the booming market for electricity and electrical appliances. Additional capital was only available through expensive credit—supplied by a friendly Deutsche Bank. In the German Empire then, Siemens was outflanked by AEG, which was a more daring and better financed competitor, created by banker Emil Rathenau.

Initially they attempted to agree on a complementary strategy—with AEG building capital-intensive power stations, and Siemens supplying the equipment and wiring. The agreement, however soon stood in the way of AEG's more aggressive drive for expansion. Through investments in power generation and transmission networks, electrical appliance makers then had to create their own demand.

In 1873, Siemens took over the Schuckert electricity company in Nuremberg. Until the 1960s, all high voltage operations were located within Siemens Schuckert. The low voltage business was run by Siemens & Halske.

Keen competition aside, Siemens and AEG were also ready to cooperate. Upon request of the pre-war military, they set up a jointly owned "Telefunken," which supplied military communications equipment to the Imperial Army and Navy. A joint venture "Osram" was created in 1919 to produce electrical bulbs.

After WWI, all patents and overseas possessions were lost. With its more solid finances, Siemens, however survived the world economic crisis better than its competitor AEG. In the 1930s, it became Europe's largest electrical appliance maker. In 1930, Siemens employed 137,000 people. Armament orders for electrical equipment for submarines, airplanes, detonators and signals boosted employment to 244,000 by 1944. Its ranks depleted by the draft, most workers were women but also POWs, foreign civilian labor, including forced labor. With the increasing frequency of Allied bomb attacks, Siemens production sites were dispersed to 660 different locations. In anticipation of Germany's defeat and foreign occupation, by 1944, sites were discreetly shifted to the West and to Austria, with the corporate HQ moving partly from Berlin to Munich.

Nonetheless, as a result of WWII, 80 per cent of corporate assets were lost. All foreign possessions and patents were again expropriated, and so were all remaining assets in Communist-occupied territories, including in East and Central Germany. The facilities that had escaped the bombing were now stripped and shipped off as reparations. In Austria, Siemens was nationalized to protect it from the grasp of the Allied Occupation. Some senior managers like Hermann von Siemens were interned or committed suicide during "de-nazification." Thousands of Siemens workers and engineers had died during the war or were held captive as POWs for years.

Initial US plans to break up Siemens like IG Farben, Deutsche Bank or their Japanese competitors came to naught with the advent of the Cold War when the reconstruction of West Germany took precedence. When in 1952 foreign representations and capital participation were permitted again, Siemens was quick to re-establish itself in the rest of West Europe, in Latin America and in Japan.

Siemens' competitor AEG had greater post-war difficulties. Although the sales of its washing machines and refrigerators went well, its war losses had been higher and its urge to catch up by undertaking aggressive half-digested corporate acquisitions stronger. While Siemens was highly profitable with a turnover of DM6.5 billion (1966), AEG had a turnover of one-third less. The company was soon into debt and hit by costly technical problems with its nuclear power stations. By 1968, it had to sell its share in the joint ventures Osram and Kraftwerksunion, a power station builder/operator, fully to Siemens. In 1982, finally AEG had to ask for protection from its creditors. Two years later, it was absorbed by Daimler Benz, which under the chairmanship of Edzard Reuter, attempted a then fashionable, but ultimately ill-fated strategy of diversification. Once this strategy was terminated in 1996, 100 years of AEG ended as well.

With German unity in 1990, Siemens remained the only major player in the German electronics market. It took over dozens of run down state-owned factories and retrained some 20,000 workers, but also benefited handsomely from massive public procurement orders to modernize communication networks and railway systems in East Germany.

In these days of pre-deregulation, 80 per cent of Siemens' clients by volume were public or semi-public: postal services, railways, hospitals, energy distributors, city governments, etc. Purchasing decisions took a lengthy period, required political lobbying, and were oriented more toward longevity and technical quality rather than price. Sales prices were usually cost prices plus a "reasonable" mark up. Product cycles were slow, competition minimal. Everything was predictable, solid, profitable, and jobs seemed safe for life. Siemens was aware that it had fallen behind US and Japanese competitors in its rates of innovation and product development, but the process of catching up and of corporate restructuring and culture change was to take more than a decade. The initial steps today appear as insufficient half measures, like the slimming of the management board, and the set up of a more compartmentalized structure (splitting seven central business sectors into 18) in 1989.

The entire company—from personnel management to product development, design and finances—stood for conservative solidity and—unlike the failed more commercial AEG—was run by successful engineers. A very strong and change-resistant "Siemens culture" with sacred business principles going back to the founder had developed. It strongly disliked anything smacking of US shareholder orientation or Japanese high-speed product cycles.

A steady cash flow, high liquidity and plentiful hidden reserves (generated by decades of instant depreciations)—in the early 1990s estimated at $9 billion compared to a total Siemens turnover of $38.5 billion—spread a misleading sense of complacency. Then Siemens revenues from financial investments easily surpassed its losses from operational business. Sometimes it was jokingly suggested Siemens should give up production and turn itself into a fund manager instead.

Yet Siemens increasingly realized that its commercial products arrived on the markets too late. Development and implementation were too slow. Products were over-engineered and poorly designed. The first cell-phones were perfect, but as heavy as bricks. To handle fixed line office telephones, customers were asked to attend two-day seminars to handle complicated functions no one ever needed. In Europe, the days of public monopolies ended irrevocably with the advent of the EU's unified internal market in December 1992.

Although a publicly listed company since 1897, the Siemens clan relinquished the CEO office only in 1981. And it was only in 1991 that Peter von Siemens, great great grandson of the founder, left the management board. He still has an office in headquarters in Munich. One family member remains represented on the supervisory board. Although their preferential voting rights have been abolished, they still control some 7 per cent of the shares. Together with a sizable block of employee-held shares, they rather opt to safeguard the traditional corporate culture and a diversified electrical engineering production structure. In the German system of social partnership and trade union co-determination, the employees' elected representatives fill half of the supervisory board. The price for the union's acceptance of restructuring are lengthy concerted efforts and promises to keep expensive German production sites as long as possible.

First attempts at culture change began in 1990, with a range of fairly uncoordinated attempts to cut costs and to improve productivity. When Heinrich von Pierer, a lawyer and nuclear engineer, became CEO in 1992, many old-guard managers were retired. Then a more systematic program aiming at "time optimized processes" (TOP) was introduced to speed up the cycles of innovation, product development and market introduction. Overall productivity was to be improved by 30 per cent. Cross-subsidization of products was to end, as were highly exacting quality standards, which irrespective of costs and user needs were based on engineering perfection alone. This was a time when market prices for electronic goods, like for fixed line telephone sets, were slashed by more than 50 per cent in no time.

An army of highly paid consultants descended upon Siemens. They tore down departmental walls and cut the production sequence into a series of steps for each of which one team and its leader were made responsible. Managers' individual responsiveness and leadership behaviour were scrutinized by regular employee surveys. Like in China's Cultural Revolution, two-thirds of Siemens 30,000 management functions were subsequently declared redundant.

By 1996, each of the new units had to present their own profit/loss accounts. Management pay now contained a sizable variable component, which was tied to reaching profitability, but also to performance and marketing objectives.

Jack Welch's GE and ABB (a 1988 merger of the Swiss BBC and the Swedish Asea) and their earlier brutal restructurings loomed ominously large in the background. Yet Siemens' approach was less radical, insisting on keeping the full product range of electrical appliances and electronics in production. This generated the public reproach of half-heartedness—especially when the business results of 1997/8 disappointed.

Restructuring during 1993/7 had cost some $8 billion. 40,000 jobs had been eliminated in Germany alone. Costs were cut by $10 billion. Overall productivity gains of 8.5 per cent were realized. Yet during the same period, most product prices had fallen by around 50 per cent. A strong Deutschmark and increasing wage costs in Germany hurt Siemens' price competitiveness. Corporate indebtedness climbed to new heights.

Hence, von Pierer decided to re-launch a renewed restructuring exercise, this time more focused on profitability—as recommended by the McKinsey people. All managers and their units henceforth had to maximize "economic value added", that is quarterly returns on corporate and borrowed capital used. Benchmarking toward the best competitors became *de rigueur*. Successful units were supposed to engage in "best practice sharing." Managers would be regularly reviewed in front of their peers in terms of quality, innovations and asset management. Underperformers were warned off and lost their variable performance bonus.

The most dramatic initial turnarounds were achieved in transport and in medical equipment, for Siemens both fairly traditional sectors—with its first electrical tram produced in 1879.

Transport electronics used to be one of the most stable branches, with the need to cultivate monopoly clients like the German, Austrian and Swiss railways with reliable quality products. With the liberalization of the sector, the retooled clients opted for "turnkey" projects, locomotives and rolling stock delivered by one manufacturer according to pre-set specifications. In anticipation, Siemens had purchased a series of rolling stock suppliers, like Duewag, Krupp and Mantra, without really integrating them fully. Only once the reforms began to bite, two rolling stock factories were merged, one closed down, with the remaining one now producing 50 per cent more than the two previously taken together. 1,000 jobs were shed. The production time of one complete train was reduced to less than 25 days. In 2001, Siemens managed to acquire the largest UK railway order ever awarded with a volume of $2.5 billion.

Siemens medical technology had suffered from the hubris of technical perfectionism. The ambition was to be the "Roll Royce" in hospital equipment. Cost pressures in the health sector, however, made these Rolls Royces unsellable. Prices of competing ultrasound and computer tomographs fell quickly. In a massive reinvesting and flexi-time effort, the production site in Erlangen was modernized. Production was streamlined, dental technology, for instance, was sold (so patients will no longer stare at the Siemens logo of their dentists' lamps while they are being tortured). After purchasing Shared Medical Systems and Acuson, Siemens advanced towards world leadership in medical IT services.

Equally, after encountering heavy losses up to 2000/1, the merger of Mannesmann's vehicle components division with Siemens electrical car parts achieved its turnaround by 2002/3.[1]

As a result of these restructuring efforts, of US accounting standards and a new slick tech image, Siemens was able to ride high during the IT bubble of 1999–2001, having moved from placid appliance maker to shiny high-tech value—until the bubble burst.

The main addresses of the recurrent restructuring work were not the small shareholders of old—in Germany they had gotten used to miserable dividends since long—but the US fund managers, new fearsome creatures in the German corporate power equation, who turned traditional relations (management, supported by friendly bankers, cooperating nicely with in-house trade unionists) of Rhineland Capitalism upside down. By 2001, the share of foreign investors in Siemens stocks had grown to 45 per cent. Already in 1997, the share of banks, insurances, pension and other funds had equally grown to 45 per cent. Hence, performance driven fund managers were calling the shots, ready to sacrifice their stocks anytime for a lucrative takeover battle. After purchasing Westinghouse (bought in 1997 for US$1.5 billion), and the industrial part of the Swiss Elektrowart in 1996, Siemens' debts had grown considerably. As an unwieldy conglomerate it had become a possible candidate for a similar takeover, to which Mannesmann, a venerable steel pipe producer turned cell-phone operator, in 1999 had just fallen victim to a British upstart called Vodaphone.

Hence, feeding New York and London analysts with aggressive stories of strategic acquisitions, divestments, large-scale dismissals, and quarterly improved price earnings ratios became a mainstay of new corporate and CEO communication.

But the working capital was also improved by relatively simple measures like using and divesting Siemens' extensive real estate more effectively, by reducing excessive inventories, by speeding up invoicing and by avoiding a build-up of hidden reserves. Financial services were no longer automatically procured from Deutsche Bank, but increasingly also from Merrill Lynch and Goldman Sachs.

Following the IT crash of 2001, Siemens' communication divisions—until 2000 shiny and investment-pampered new economy flagships—suffered, while the old economy transport, medicine and power generation sectors rescued the company. Unfashionable business diversity had won over the high-tech pig cycle.

Siemens' corporate takeovers—much in favour with hurried and simple-minded analysts advising their fund managers—also showed predictably mixed results. Since 1992, more than 1,000 companies had been bought for the total price of $17 billion plus. Mannesmann Atecs (sold by Vodaphone) alone cost $9.5 billion.

Since 1997, the strategic principle had become simple: in a given sector, Siemens—aided by acquisitions—was either No. 1, No. 2 or at best No. 3 on the world market, or the production would be divested or cease entirely.

Although dearly loved by analysts, fund managers and their securities houses (who gross in most of their profits during such transactions), most M&A famously turn out to be flops, notably so international mergers where on top of incompatible corporate cultures, different national work ethics and management styles clash under the intense pressure of deadlines and profit targets. Global estimates consider 50–85 per cent of all such mergers as failed, while Siemens internal studies view 20 per cent of its acquisitions as miscarried, destroying more value in the process than the initial purchasing price.

The acquisition of Nixdorf Computers offers a tell-tale case in point. Nixdorf until the death of its founder, Heinz Nixdorf, in 1986 had been Germany's leading computer maker, specializing in integrated hardware/software packages for medium-sized companies. As a "power culture" built upon the model of its founder, its sales and development policies were quick, risk taking and aggressive. Siemens was rather strong in large-sized computers, which it supplied to the public sector and to big industry. Although both thought little of PCs, their complementarity appeared like a perfect match in 1988. Then Siemens bought a controlling stake in Nixdorf for $300 million. Soon it was discovered that Nixdorf had cheated on its accounts. During their first three years, the merged computer operations produced some $800 million of cumulative losses. It took Siemens a long time to cut staffing from the combined size of 50,000 and to close the Nixdorf factory in Berlin, a decision deeply resented by the proud independence-minded Nixdorf people.

There were also frequent divestments. The largest was the spin-off of Siemens semiconductor manufacturing as Infineon in 1998. Then 60,000 people and a quarter of its total turnover left the company. As a high growth area, the sector is strongly volatile with extremely high investment and development costs ($1 billion for one chip generation), ultra-quick product cycles and forceful up and downswings of demand. For 1994–6, semiconductors contributed nicely to the Siemens bottomline. But in 1998, there were $600 million of losses, and a brand new factory in North Tyneside in the North of England, inaugurated by the Queen only 15 months earlier, had to be closed.

Since 1984, Siemens had invested $12 billion for the development and $300 billion for the production of semiconductors (as well as $120 million of German public subsidies) in order to catch up with Japan. Yet 14 years later, after staying in the race and catching up, it was happy to let go this destabilising business. When Infineon shares were placed on the stock exchange, the new company was profitable. It was run by a brash young executive, Ulrich Schumacher. Benefiting from the IT boom, the IPO of 2000 was vastly oversubscribed, allowing Siemens to gross in $6.1 billion for 29 per cent of the shares. 13.5 per cent of the shares were moved to the Siemens pension funds. By 2001, the volatile Infineon was no longer part of Siemens' consolidated balance sheets. With the IT crash of 2001 and the persistent erosion of chip prices, Infineon's losses soon mounted to $1 billion. Recently hired employees were quickly fired, and those who had failed to buy its shares thanked their lucky stars. In 2004 also, Schumacher, after a short boardroom struggle, resigned in the face of continuing losses.

Although Siemens had always been strong in the white goods sector, its mainstay had been public and corporate procurement. After earnestly and expensively going through corporate culture change for years, it needed to communicate its brave new corporate world to the rest of mankind with a rebranded corporate image. No longer refrigerators, power generators or dentists' lamps, the hip market for cell-phones was to be the flagship battle for rebranding and repositioning. Yet in 2001, "Siemens" as a brand name remained far behind Sony, Nokia, let alone General Electric, BMW or Coke, amongst the world's top 100. Particularly galling for a conglomerate remodelled along US ideals, it was the US public, which, as usual, took the least notice.

In 1998, the "Be inspired" campaign was born. Lifestyle feelings were to be in the foreground of corporate communications and advertisements—not the technical specifications of which the engineers were proud. Designers and marketing people were now to be at the beginning of product development—not at the end of the engineering process as in the past. Siemens went into Formula 1 and soccer sponsorships—an effective tool for publicity notably in Italy, France and the UK. Yet also the high profile cell-phone market was not free from boom and bust. After the euphoria of 2000, suddenly the markets with penetration rates of up to 70 per cent seemed saturated. Except for Nokia, all competitors wrote red figures. Siemens bought out Bosch, which had dropped out of the race. Siemens in turn had abandoned entertainment electronics (radios, CD-players, video recorders, TV sets) already in 1996. Uninspired, it never managed to be successful in the PC business either.

R&D with 7 per cent of turnover remains stronger than most competitors, including IBM and most Japanese electronics firms. On occasion, German public policies intervened, not just in subsidizing heavily new East German production sites—like a very small Silicon Valley near Dresden, but also in promoting nonsense like the Maglev, a low flying train designed to solve the world's transportation problems. Unfortunately, in spite of massive subsidies, it proved unsellable except for an empty airport shuttle in Shanghai. More seriously, the development of more conventional high speed trains like the TGV or Shinkansen was critically neglected by Siemens and Germany as a result.

Within less than 10 years, for Siemens its share of overall sales in Germany have fallen from 47 per cent (1992) to 22 per cent (2001). Sales to the rest of Europe have remained almost constant at 30 per cent. But the rest of turnover is now achieved in the Americas (30 per cent) and Asia (13 per cent)—with a tendency to grow.

Siemens' global shift was aided by an aggressive acquisition policy in the US: Westinghouse ($1.5 billion), Acuson ($700 billion), Shared Medical Systems ($2.1 billion) and Efficient Networks ($1.5 billion). As a result, 80,000 people in the US now work for Siemens, although the company remains less known than its subsidiaries. Was it worth it? Surely not. Most of the overblown US dot-coms, who were Siemens' new customers dropped dead in 2001. US losses in that year amounted to $600 million alone. Like for DaimlerChrysler, Deutsche Bank, Bertelsmann, Sony and Matsushita, it seems an exhilarating experience for German and Japanese CEOs to lose money by the billions in God's own country, an experience that gets more exciting only by its repetition.

With Efficient Networks, losses continued to mount with a certain efficiency well into 2003. But the Westinghouse acquisition—announced fictitiously as a "merger of equals" with Kraftwerksunion (KWU)— developed more successfully. It was helped by a certain boom for gas turbines, aided by widespread US power shortages up to 1998. With extensive exchanges of workers and engineers, accompanied by social activities like friendly soccer games between Westinghouse and KWU plants, like in Hamilton, Ontario; Charlotte, N.C.; Berlin, Erfurt and Mülheim technical and managerial expertise on turbine production was exchanged as well.[2]

The lure of China promises similar excitements. Some 50 joint ventures, many of them deeply in the red, produce practically the entire Siemens product range for the rapidly expanding domestic market. 25,000 Chinese are employed by Siemens producing a turnover of $4 billion (2001). German government support was always forthcoming for the state economy controlled part of the Chinese market. The empty Maglev of Shanghai alone cost the German taxpayer $200 million.

What is left of Siemens' German identity—except for getting public subsidies and political support? Out of 570 Siemens plants, 170 are left in Germany. The number of German employees has fallen from 253,000 (1991), 61 per cent of the total, to 198,000 (2001)—41 per cent, while employees from the rest of the world have grown from 160,000 to 286,000 in the same decade. Put simply, the jobs disappearing in high-cost Germany were relocated to low-cost China (and the US).

US management routines have taken over, like campaigns to weed out the 10 per cent low performers amongst employees. Large numbers of dismissals are announced (but luckily not always implemented) to impress impressionable analysts and to jack up the share price. Then, are there any of the traditional German virtues left in Siemens—like hard work, discipline, honesty, persistence and reliability—which had made the company innovate, grow and recover from all misfortunes during its 150 years?

This is a good question, which will ultimately decide corporate survival—not the finicky reports of half-baked New York analysts—but a question about which the jury is still out.

For CEO Heinrich von Pierer, however, the situation is clear. Taking GE's $9.5 billion takeover of Amersham, the UK biosciences company, as a role model, he signalled Siemens' readiness for a further big acquisition involving a radical shift toward profitable segments like medical equipment, power, automation and controls, directed toward Japan or East Europe (where Siemens is still weak) or purchasing a chunk of Alstom, the troubled French power system group.[3] Anything goes, or so it seems.

ENDNOTES
1   *Financial Times*, August 19, 2003.
2   *Financial Times*, July 5, 2002.
3   *Financial Times*, March 1, 2004.

REFERENCES
Daniela Decurtins. *Siemens. Anatomie eines Unternehmens*. Wien: Ueberreuter, 2002.
"Das Geschaeft von Siemens stabilisiert sich langsam." *Frankfurter Allgemeine*, July 25, 2003.
Peter Marsh. "Siemens clocks up top results." *Financial Times*, August 19, 2003.
Peter Marsh. "Siemens generates goodwill in North America." *Financial Times*, July 5, 2002.
"Siemens positions itself for expansion." *Financial Times*, March 1, 2004.

CHAPTER 5

Matsushita: Happiness in Appliances

ALBRECHT ROTHACHER

If there is a classical "rags-to-riches" story in Japan, it is surely represented by the life of Konosuke Matsushita. Matsushita himself was an active self-publicist. His self-made "philosophies" fill entire library shelves, and Matsushita Electric, his company, is given to a certain measure of personality cult, which on occasion has a sectarian streak in it. Yet the "real" Konosuke Matsushita has always been enigmatic nonetheless. He was an interesting complex character, who at the time of his death in 1989 had built Matsushita Electric out of nothing into Japan's largest electronics company with 100,000 employees producing a turnover of US$42 billion per year.

Konosuke Matsushita was born in 1894 in rural Wakayama prefecture—today part of Osaka's metropolitan region. The circumstances of his birth seemed promising enough. He was the youngest son (amongst eight siblings) of an affluent rural landlord, who owned 150 hectares and lived off the rents of his tenant farmers. Tragedy struck when Konosuke's father began gambling on the nascent commodities market on rice futures, and in 1899 lost his family's entire fortune. Their land and spacious home had to be sold off, and bereft of status and means, the family had to move into a cramped three-room apartment in Wakayama City. Living conditions, food and clothing became fairly miserable. Their father opened a shop for *geta* (wooden sandals), which for want of business had to close two years later.

During 1900/1, tragedy turned disaster, when three of his siblings, all young adults aged 18–24, were killed by infectious diseases due to the non-availability of medical treatment. His father moved out to Osaka to become a lowly paid clerk in a school for the deaf and blind. After less then four years of schooling, Konosuke then aged 10 was made to work in the shop of a maker of *hibachi* (ceramic vessels holding charcoal for heating) as an apprentice.

Then an apprentice working long hours often did heavy, but also auxiliary works (like cleaning and running errands) in the shop and in the house of his master, in exchange for food, shelter and some pocket money. Later, Matsushita went to work in a bicycle shop where he worked, lived and learned for the next six years.

In 1906, fate struck again, two of his older sisters aged 18 and 21, and his father aged 52, died, all again after short illness. Aged 16 in 1910, he left the bicycle shop to work briefly in a cement company doing heavy physical labour, but then quickly moved on to Osaka Light, a new high growth company servicing the electrification of Osaka City. Working in a work gang installing electrical wirings, he was promoted from unskilled laborer to foreman after three months. When he was 19, he was already organizing very complex lighting installations, like those for a theatre, with dozens of workers reporting to him.

After the death of his mother, Konosuke, aged 20, married 19-year-old Mumeno Iue, a merchant's assistant, hailing from Awaji Island. Her eight years of schooling was twice as long as Konosuke's. Two years later, he was promoted to inspector. As this position entailed fairly low productive, supervisory work, Matsushita had the time to develop a lamp socket. When his superiors refused to appreciate his invention, he quit Osaka Light in order to produce his own products for the market in 1917, then aged 22—but with already 13 years of varied work experience! He started his company with ¥100 of savings (five monthly salaries he saved from Osaka Light) and five employees, two of whom were his wife and his 14-year-old brother-in-law Toshio Iue, in his two-room rented apartment. These inauspicious beginnings were compounded by the fact that none of the novices knew how to produce the new lamps sockets, the production and design of which soon hit serious flaws. With a weak product, poor finance and little demand, his employees shrank from five to three. The company was saved by a sudden large order for isolation materials, which Matsushita with his small team working without a break for some months, could execute in time. More orders followed, and in 1918, he could move into a larger two-storey workshop.

Apart from electrical isolators and lamp sockets, they also produced plugs. With his low-cost production, based on self-exploitation and no frills, Matsushita could undercut his competitors' prices by 30 per cent.

Finally, a fourth product became his best-selling item: a twin plug allowing two appliances to be connected to the then habitual single source. By the end of 1918, his company employed 20 people, including some apprentice boys. Some corporate principles already became established practices then: Matsushita produced lower-priced—and sometimes better quality—versions of products developed by his competitors. Low production costs were created by frugality, low overheads and long work hours. Employees were treated like family members. The product emphasis was on quick, flexible and innovative reaction to new market needs. Given his past experience, Konosuke Matsushita remained a down-to-earth businessman with a keen eye for detail and empirical consumer needs. Decisive factors for early success were less intellectual brilliance or charisma of the founder, but rather his commercial customer orientation and an enormous willpower to succeed driven by hope and fear of failure.

Matsushita cut costs by evading basic research and product development investments. Rather he copied and improved the products developed by the competition. Also he did not invest in cultivating political connections and ties with the economic ministries. As a small upstart company, he left this part to the established politically privileged *zaibatsu* companies.

In 1919 and 1921, his only two surviving sisters of his family of 10 died. Aged only 27, Konosuke had become the only survivor.

With his business expanding, he threw himself into the construction of a new small factory in 1922, which offered workstations to his 30 employees. A newly developed battery-driven bicycle lamp sold extremely well. Its market introduction had succeeded after leaving free samples with the retailers, then an innovative sales method. By 1924, 10,000 lamps were produced each month. Aged 30, Matsushita even ran for a seat in Osaka's municipal council and as a successful young local businessman, was promptly elected. As local politics turned out to be too time consuming, he did not present himself for re-election.

For a new square bicycle lamp and its batteries, Matsushita Electric in 1927 introduced the brand name "National," followed by a massive and attractively designed advertising campaign. A low-priced electrical iron followed. Much cheaper than the competition, it was made affordable to average income earners. The resulting mass demand permitted the economies of scale and cost savings thus justifying the price. By 1928, Matsushita Electric had outgrown its infancy with 800 employees.

A daughter, Saduko, was born in 1920 and a first son in 1926. When the latter was one, he died however after a sudden illness, much like Matsushita's brothers and sisters. This tragedy led to Matsushita's gradual alienation from his wife Mumeno, who was described as strong willed and combative and who had so energetically helped him set up his company. No other children were born, but with a concubine, Matsushita, who himself suffered from regular recurrences of an undiagnosed lung disease, later had four children.

Matsushita Electric had just completed a credit-financed new production site when in 1929 the world economic crisis spread to Japan. As demand for electrical appliances collapsed, his advisors urged Matsushita to retrench production and to fire employees. He reacted by reassigning redundant production workers to the sales force. After a few months, the inventories were sold and full production resumed. With better labor relations, lower costs, greater customer orientation, more imaginative marketing and aggressive pricing, Matsushita made a decisive difference and the company had its breakthrough in the pre-war years.

When Matsushita Electric in 1929/30 entered the market for radio sets by taking over small manufacturers, it encountered a series of persistent quality problems. A systematic redesign was then ordered by Matsushita and the quality problems were eliminated. By 1942, its "National" brand held 30 per cent of the Japanese market with a monthly production of 30,000 sets. Regularly reduced costs were translated into lower retail prices and helped to gain market share over the competition. In the late 1930s, through a series of takeovers, Matsushita Electric also became Japan's largest maker of batteries.

The production of the 200-strong product range was strongly departmentalised. Each department had to be its own profit centre and write black figures—and there was no management literature around to recommend this concept. The main divisions were:

1. radios
2. lamps and batteries
3. electrical installations and synthetic resins
4. electrical heaters, all with their own production and distribution centres

Their relative independence motivated the creativity and drive of division members. Within each division, there were semi-autonomous production teams of five to 15 co-workers, also responsible for their own profitability and product quality. If positive results were not forthcoming, Matsushita would call in the manager in-charge. He did not hesitate to raise his voice when straight explanations and deadlined improvements were not provided. This decentralization allowed the company to remain flexible and reactive and to train leadership personnel for a future without Matsushita, which given his fragile health, was possible anytime.

Following his private tragedies and his search for meaning in his business success, Matsushita was drawn to the Buddhist Tenrikyo sect, which he supported henceforth materially and whose influence is visible in his subsequent corporate visions and mission statements. In 1932, he announced to his 1,100 employees the purpose of his enterprises was not profits or market share, but the happiness of mankind in supplying it with ever cheaper quality consumer products. Matsushita insisted that all employees should subscribe publicly to this objective and profess to ideals of honesty, fairness, teamwork, permanent improvement, politeness, modesty, gratefulness and progress. These syrupy ideals were to be pronounced aloud collectively at the beginning of each working day. This touch of sectarianism has never left Matsushita's public pronouncements or his corporate publications ever since.

In 1932, an export department was set up. Soon the production was expanded with electrical lamps, ventilators, record players, loudspeakers, watches, microphones, hairdryers, etc. The number of employees grew from 1,100 (1932) to 9,300 (1941). Corporate training institutes for sales and production skills were created.

During WWII, Matsushita Electric was ordered to curtail its production for civilian uses, and to supply the military with electrical goods and bayonets. In the desperate last years of the war, Matsushita was asked to produce wooden ships and wooden airplanes, which could escape detection by enemy radar, although it had no experience in either field. Matsushita Shipbuilding was led by Toshio Iue, and against all odds began completing wooden ships by December 1943. Matsushita managed to produce also three wooden airplanes. But it is not reported whether these actually ever flew or saw any action.

With Japan's military expansion, production sites were also set up in the Philippines, Indonesia, Taiwan, Korea and in China. When the war ended, in spite of all disruptions, destruction and rationing, Matsushita had grown to 26,000 employees and into one of Asia's largest electrical companies.

In September 1945, the US Occupation ordered Matsushita to cease production. Production for civilian uses was allowed to resume after six weeks. In June 1946, Matsushita was listed as a *zaibatsu*, and Konosuke Matsushita banned from exercising any management office. Seventeen of his subsidiaries in Japan were declared independent enterprises. All foreign holdings were confiscated and Matsushita Electric was left with all debts (which hyperinflation quickly ate up).

The number of employees shrank to 8,000 in 1947. In January 1946, Matsushita Electric workers, like everywhere else in Japan, set up their own trade union. Typically most were Communist influenced, militantly leftist and hostile to management. Uninvited, Konosuke Matsushita showed up at the founding assembly. Equally uninvited, he made a short speech pledging good cooperation with the new union, a speech which to the dismay of some leftist organisers was strongly applauded by the workers. As a result, in difference to most large Japanese companies, labor relations remained harmonious in Matsushita Electric in the post-war era.

With MacArthur's post-war purges, Matsushita and his top managers had to leave the company. His two lieutenants, Toshio Iue, his brother-in-law, and Takeo Kameyama, a nephew, left the company permanently. Iue later founded Sanyo. Konosuke Matsushita meanwhile worked incessantly at his company's and his own rehabilitation. Supported by the trade union in May 1947, Matsushita was officially "depurged" by the occupiers and could resume his old function.

He still had to struggle with administrative barriers set up by US authorities. At the same time, deflationary policies in 1949 strangled demand, tax arrears mounted and credit lines were stretched to the limit. In order to cope with the financial crisis in 1950 for the first time, Matsushita had to resort to dismissals. Only then a turnaround was achieved and the company became profitable again.

In 1951, aged 56, Konosuke Matsushita made his first voyage abroad, a study trip to New York. There he extended his pilgrimage to the cradle of modern capitalism to almost three months.

Upon his return, he vowed publicly that Matsushita and Japan needed to catch up with the US in terms of lifestyles and technology. In order to gain access to Western technologies, a joint venture was set up with Philips, with Philips owning 30 per cent of the shares and supplying the technology. Matsushita would manage the enterprise with 70 per cent of the shares and pay a net technology provision of 1.5 per cent to

Philips. Based in Osaka, TV tubes, lighting tubes and other electrical parts were thus jointly produced since 1952.

In 1953, Matsushita Electric set up its own research laboratory in an Osaka suburb. True to corporate tradition, it did not undertake fundamental research nor any new product development, but rather investigated incremental improvements in existing appliances like TV sets, refrigerators, microwave ovens, rice cookers, washing machines, etc. In the 1950s, Matsushita then was well positioned with an expanding range of low-priced quality products for the protected domestic and later the more competitive overseas markets, where they were marketed under the "National" and "Panasonic" brands.

Like Honda and Sony, who were similar post-war "power culture" maverick upstarts, Matsushita's expansion was explosive since the 1950s. Yet compared to Sony with its pioneering developments, Matsushita was then more of a copier, skimping R&D costs and sticking to incremental improvements. Also, the corporate chieftains were strikingly different. Akio Morita was urbane, well educated, articulate, at ease with the mighty and glamorous. Konosuke Matsushita had only had minimal schooling, had grown up in poverty, was less charismatic, struck with personal tragedies and a weak constitution. As his companies became more and more successful, he immersed himself ever more into a self-made philosophy of humility and devotion to mankind. His staff was thus early impregnated against the spirit of arrogance and overbearing attitude, which permeated much of corporate Japan in the 1980s until the bubble economy burst in 1992.

Matsushita's expansion was also fuelled by acquisitions, like of Nakagawa Electric, a maker of refrigerators, and of Victor Company of Japan, which produced record players. In order to enhance intra-enterprise competition and innovation, Matsushita left the old management and their product range in place, even when it competed with Matsushita's own products.

Even at an advanced age, Matsushita was still good at surprises. In 1961, he announced to his startled employees a quadrupling of turnover within five years. In 1960, he declared Matsushita to be the first large Japanese enterprise to introduce the five-day working week by 1965 without pay cuts. Matsushita also made sure that his employees' pay was significantly better than his competitors. This was made possible by persistent and continuous efforts at productivity improvement. In 1977, Konosuke Matsushita, then aged 82, appointed Toshihiko Yamashita, the head of the air conditioners department, as the future CEO (1977–86), thus leapfrogging over 24 more senior managers. Yamashita had turned around the struggling department, showed strategic sense and was more outspoken and less deferential then many of the others. His son in-law, Masaharu Matsushita (1961–77) had exercised this function earlier. In 1973, Konosuke Matsushita formally retired from the supervisory board, and as honorable senior advisor was less and less involved in operational business, but continued to act ad hoc from behind the scenes.

His main interest now became the PHP (Peace and Happiness through Prosperity) Institute, which he had set up in 1946 presumably to prove his pacifist credentials to the Americans. After 1950, PHP had became dormant, except for publishing a moderately interesting monthly journal exhorting the virtues of peace and prosperity for Japan and the world.

With Matsushita retiring to his PHP, its activities quickly expanded into a plethora of publications, symposia and management seminars. By the time of his death in 1989, 300 people were employed. The simple homilies about peace, prosperity and the goodness of mankind were dispensed million-fold on glossy paper, but usually—intellectually undernourishing as they were—left as an afterthought the search for a hidden agenda, perhaps of a sectarian origin. His core beliefs focused on what he termed the *sunao* mind, by which he meant an untrapped personality with an open-hearted innocence and a willingness to be sincere. From this a "natural" way of management followed, which was commonsensical, temperate, consultative and socially responsible.

Konosuke Matsushita wrote—or did let write—some 46 books and brochures to his name. Partly this wealth of output may have been motivated by the urges of a self-educated man in a highly educational status and intellectual value-oriented Confucian society like Japan. But essentially, Matsushita was driven by the strength of his own convictions, which he followed up not only through PHP activities, but also by sizable donations—$290 million from his own pocket, and $100 million from the company's coffers—to charitable causes of his eclectic liking. Some of his published pet ideas seem slightly eccentric—like doubling Japan's arable land by dumping all her mountains into the sea, abolishing all taxes after creating a public endowment fund from budget savings, or closing half of Japan's universities. To transmit his ideas to posterity in 1979, he set up the Matsushita Institute of Government and Management (MIGM). It is to train and to support future young political leaders in

Japan, by allowing them to do unconventional hands-on public project work in Japan and abroad and by teaching them the Matsushita philosophy. Only 23 out of some 1,000 applicants are accepted. In the early 1990s, already 15 of MIGM's then 150 alumni had been elected members of the National Diet, most—but not all—as members of recently founded conservative opposition parties to the LDP's rule.

REFERENCES
John P. Kotter. *Matsushita*. New York: The Free Press. 1997.
Konosuke Matsushita. *My Management Philosophy*. Kyoto: PHP Institute. 1978.
Teijiro Sato. "Konosuke Matsushita. His Life & his Legacy," *Asia 21*, January 2000, pp. 38–43.

CHAPTER 6

Hyundai's Flight of Icarus

PARESH MISTRY AND ALBRECHT ROTHACHER

Analyzing the extraordinary rise of Hyundai from a poor farmer's far-fetched dream to its materialization as the biggest and most successful Korean conglomerate, it would seem that Chung Ju Yung, Hyundai's founder, had discovered the formula to entrepreneurial success. Chung rose from poverty to start a small construction firm, which he developed into an over $70 billion conglomerate with 50 subsidiaries operating all over the world. While each industry presented its own set of challenges, Hyundai overcame them using a common set of core strategies. These strategies consisted of high-risk investments, a culture of authoritarian leadership and a ruthless commitment to hard work, which was used to drive a low-cost, fast-delivery business model. Up until the peak of their success in the mid-1990s the Hyundai story was nothing short of a fairy tale.

However, as financial crisis struck Asia in the late 1990s instabilities in the seemingly rock-solid giant became apparent. Fifty years of continual debt-financed risk taking had left many of the Hyundai companies with a highly unstable and insecure debt-ridden financial foundation. Moreover, the close connections and collaboration between the sibling companies that originally helped each one prosper, were now dragging down the few remaining successful businesses. Finally, as Chung stepped down as chairman, and later passed away, intra-family rivalry broke out as family members competed to be heir of his almighty throne. It quickly became apparent that Hyundai's strategy was far from flawless. While it was very effective in the short-term, it did not build a company of lasting success.

Through analysis of Hyundai's growth in four of its major industries—construction, automotives, shipbuilding, and electronics—

it is clear that the difficulties that they experienced on their way to success, and ultimately their tremendous collapse, were caused by over-use or inappropriate use of their strategies. Hyundai found business techniques that undeniably worked but failed to recognize their limitations and weaknesses. Indeed, there is no convenient formula for success in international business. All strategies have strengths and weaknesses making them optimal in some scenarios and detrimental in others. As a company grows and evolves and its environment shifts, strategies need to be continually re-evaluated.

The principles at the heart of the Hyundai Group, as well as the culture and strategies that they drove, all originated from Chung's upbringing and early career. From his past, it is apparent that the continual implementation of these strategies was not a deliberate action, but a consequence of his character.

The story of Chung Ju Yung is a genuine rags-to-riches classic. He was proud of his humble rural origins, and they always showed in his conservative Confucian rustic values, his autocratic yet paternalist management style, his risk taking drive for growth and for new untired business interests and a frugal family-centered way of life.

Chung Ju Yung was born in 1915 in a poor rice growing family in a coastal village along the Korean East Coast, just 30 miles north of today's DMZ. As a teenager, he made several attempts to escape from poor harvests and wretched poverty by running away from home and going to work in construction or taking accounting lessons. Finally at age 18 after a stint in stevedoring he began work as a deliveryman for a Seoul rice store. After a few years, he was able to take over the store only to be expropriated by the Japanese in 1939. Without knowing much about cars, he soon started a car repair business, which after learning on the job by 1943 had some 20 employees. After the war, he decided to move his new Hyundai ("modern") company into construction, starting out as a quick, reliable and low-cost contractor for the US military, delivering quality construction in time according to US specifications under the adverse conditions of the Korean War (1950–3). Reconstruction of the devastated impoverished country (often with foreign aid) offered new opportunities, with Hyundai branching out into unfamiliar bridge and harbor construction.

Hyundai Engineering and Construction (HEC) was to become and remain his main holding company and management pool ("mother company") for all subsequent subsidiaries and spin-offs. By 1957, Hyundai had grown into one of Korea's top five construction companies. It had also moved into warehousing, road transport and cement production, which were obviously related to the core construction business. Chung however, did not participate in the Rhee regime's "sale" of confiscated Japanese property and pre-war businesses and kept a safe distance from his corrupt and economically inept regime. Still, by 1960, he had expanded to become Korea's largest construction company. With Korea's new leader General Park relations became much closer, as Chung shared the new ruler's passion for national economic development and advances into untried areas of infrastructure and industrial technology in Korea.

In consequence, based on its ability to deliver infrastructural projects on time, to reach self sufficiency and export targets, Hyundai benefited handsomely from its close association with Park's 16-year-long developmental dictatorship, as the government could allocate credit and interest rates of the nationalised banks as well as procurement orders and business licences at will to well performing companies.

Hyundai's first large foreign project was a 60-mile motorway construction through Thai jungles in 1964. Low-interest government grants permitted Hyundai to outbid all international competitors. Even though the project brought huge losses due to the Koreans' inexperience of Southeast Asia's climatic conditions and labour relations, it permitted the right learning experiences to do construction work later for the Americans during the Vietnam War, building military camps, bridges and dredging rivers there.

Hyundai's strategy of learning by doing and plunging into unknown waters by undertaking big projects in areas of no previous expertise was to become a regular feature of the company's rapid expansion. In 1967, it began building a 126-m dam in Korea at a rock bottom price with no prior experience in dam building. Once the Park government set its sights on duplicating Germany's *autobahn* system in mountainous Korea, Hyundai led the consortium to build the first North-South Kyungbu Express Way with dozens of tunnels and bridges in forbidding terrain at breathtaking speed. Both Park and Chung regularly were unannounced and feared guests at the construction sites operating day and night. In 1970, the job was done. Cars and shipbuilding were to follow.

When in 1967 Kia and Shinjin (later: Daewoo) started assembling Japanese-made car kits, Hyundai joined the drive in a joint venture with Ford. Within the record time of six months, Hyundai set up a fully operated assembly plant in Ulsan, a deep water port well suited for export manufacturing. With Korean government pressure to increase local content quickly, a fight for management control soon started. Not without reason Ford soon felt that "Hyundai, supported by the government, was simply milking them for technology and engineering expertise" (Steers 1999, p. 77). After the breakup, Hyundai teamed up with Mitsubishi, which was happy with a licensing fee and a 10 per cent stake in the company in return for supplying the technology to build an ultimately all Korean-made car.

Workers had to put in 14 hours a day, six days a week. Poorly trained with little quality control in place and continuously pressured to increase output, the cars produced were of low quality. Export sales even to Third World markets were poor. Hyundai Motor remained unprofitable until 1978. Nonetheless even without visible viable markets, a massive increase in production capacity was implemented: with a planned output of 300,000, it was 10 times the size of Korea's market at the time (1980). Yet by 1986, sales had grown to 400,000 cars per annum.

In 1985, Hyundai began to attack the US car market at its subcompact segment with its Excel priced at only $5,000, aiming at low-end buyers who would usually only purchase Yugos or second hand cars. Initially sales were extremely successful, allowing even a plant to be set up in Canada to supply the US market. Yet by 1987, Hyundai began replacing its US managers with inexperienced Korean expatriates. Labor troubles, poor marketing, inexisting after-sales services and quality problems mounted. The resale value of the Excel cars became very poor. By 1992, sales had collapsed and in 1994, the Canadian plant was closed. In the meantime, Hyundai improved its quality in production as well as in R&D performance. Since then its capacity of 1.3 million cars at Ulsan is in full use again. Its dealer network and brand image in the US has been reconstructed.

Chung built his *chaebol* less by strategic design than by ad hoc needs. When his construction company needed a lot of cement, he decided to produce it in-house by Hyundai Cement. For engineering works Hyundai Engineering was formed; for pipes Hyundai Pipes; for the distribution of cars Hyundai Motor Service. When orders for supertankers were cancelled, Chung created his own shipping line to operate them.

As in cars, Hyundai started building ships in 1973 with almost no technical expertise. In order to cut costs, the new Hyundai Heavy Industries (HHI) operated within minimal supervisory and engineering staff. What looked like a recipe for disaster enabled HHI to undercut competitors' bids significantly and thus secured a series of supertanker orders.

By the mid-1980s, HHI was an established major competitor. Any slack of its cyclical business would be evened out by ready government purchases. Technical expertise was supplied by underemployed British naval engineers. Like its construction sites, Hyundai ran its shipyards in military style and with military discipline—helped by its workers' long military service and by patriotic appeals. By the mid-1990s, HHI, now the world's largest shipbuilder produced 40 per cent of Korea's output of ships and with the Kipo Dockyard also ran the world's largest repair and conversion facility, worth a total of $6 billion won in annual sales.

Following the oil crisis of 1973 and pushed on by the government, which needed the foreign exchange, Hyundai with little expertise moved into constructing turnkey projects in the Mid East, building naval shipyards in Iran, a dry dock in Bahrain and a huge oil terminal in Saudi Arabia.

Chairman Chung's pressure to bid for these projects aggressively and to complete them at seemingly impossible schedules was too much for his younger brother, Chung In Yung. He quit Hyundai and subsequently set up his own Halla Group.

Working conditions for Korean construction workers can only be described as atrocious. In a culturally hostile environment, with a short visit back home only once a year, they worked 10 hours a day, seven days a week. When labor troubles ensued, with even the Saudi military being called in, working conditions improved somewhat. Yet the Koreans were proud to survive a tough working environment better than the Japanese did.

During the two decades of Park's authoritarian rule, Korea grew from a Third World country to join the ranks of other developed nations. His pro-business development policies were appreciated by *chaebol* leaders and by Chung in particular. Yet Park's assassination and the coup of Major-General Chun saw an increase in corruption and arbitrary government decisions often contrary to common business sense. Richard Steers describes well the type of "donations" exacted by the Chun regime and its anti-competitive meddling in corporate investments and strategies (op. cit., p. 120).

In the early 1980s, Chung Ju Yung found his conglomerate too dependent on heavy industries and construction. Hence he decided to move into electronics. He formed KDK Electronics as a joint venture with the time-honored objective to acquire all the missing technological know-how from the US, to manufacture the products in Korea and to sell them cheap in the US.

In his attempt to leapfrog earlier stages of technological development and to push for grand scales of operation, Chung quickly ran into difficulties as Hyundai's classical approach to muscle itself through problems did not work in electronics development, which needed more subtle creativity and patient R&D. Hyundai had started with the construction of a huge electronics plant in Inchon with production capacities, which soon stood idle for the lack of products and demand. Similarly US electronics engineers found Hyundai's authoritarian climate difficult to accept and quit as soon as they were hired. Once the forcible attempt to produce workstations failed, the Inchon facilities by 1985 were converted to manufacture DRAM chips with more success after Hyundai belatedly discovered the value of R&D. By 1990, with strong government support Korean manufacturers had become major players in the semiconductor race, which hitherto had been an exclusive preserve of the US and Japan, ultimately knocking out Japan "by copying their marketing and pricing strategies" (Steers, p. 132). Hyundai Electronics had entered the memory chip business with a series of technology alliances, the most important being with Fujitsu. Having reached 7th in rank in the world in terms of DRAM sales by 1997, it still attempts to catch up with market leader Samsung.

In difference to Japan, labor relations in contemporary Korea have always been troublesome. The sacrifice of catching up in terms of hard work, long hours and little rewards has clearly been borne by its working classes. Although Hyundai instituted the usual trappings of corporate identification like on-the-job training, company songs and team spirit enhancing social events, the persistence of harsh working conditions, including mandatory overtime, and authoritarian management attitudes took its toll.

The toothless management controlled work councils could not hold up the workers' pent up discontent once the unions' activities were fully freed in 1987. Hyundai's foremost industrial town of Ulsan ("Hyundai City"), in which more than 80,000 people out of a population of 600,000 work for Hyundai was particularly hard hit. In violent protests the newly established radical unions fought with the existing company unions and with an unresponsive and hostile management. As a result of the labor struggles of 1987 finally the new unions won recognition, with more paid vacation days and mandatory overtime and military crew cuts abolished for Hyundai staff. One year later, it was pay demands with hike requests of up to 48 per cent, which led to riotous strikes at various Hyundai plants. They flared up again in 1989. In 1991, workers at Hyundai Motors even began to smash their own newly produced cars. In Europe only Fiat workers are able to do that. Many workers clearly had shifted their allegiance from the company to the radical unions (p. 149). With an ailing economy, President Kim sent the military in to quell the troubles. With two weeks paid vacations, vastly improved pay and an annual working time reduced from 2,800 hours to 2,300 hours, by 1994 relative calm set in until the Asian crisis broke in 1997.

The symbolics and subsequent economics of the 1964 Tokyo Olympics, which stood for Japan's miracle growth, were surely not lost on their Korean neighbours. Chung hence gladly took the government's hint to play a leading role to bring the 1988 Olympics to Seoul. As usual, against all odds—including violent threats from North Korea—by whatever means it took (including a platoon of former Miss Koreas and KAL stewardesses) to persuade the IOC meeting in Baden-Baden in 1981, he managed to win against the rival bid of Nagoya. Later Hyundai was to benefit handsomely from the construction of sports stadiums and related infrastructure, including a new subway system and an Olympic Expressway. Hyundai has always been a politically alert conglomerate. In the Gorbachev era it exuded keen interest to exploit Siberia's underutilized riches, even though subsequently, in spite of earnest efforts, little business materialized for the specifically created Hyundai Resources Development Corporation.

Taking off in 1990, Hyundai's activities in China became soon more substantial. Joint ventures ranged from container manufacturing, to naphtha production and semiconductor plants. Most dramatic however was surely Hyundai's patriotically motivated ventures into North Korea, from where the Chungs originally hailed. As the first Korean businessman with his government's blessings, Chung visited the North and his long lost relatives in 1989. He promised to develop the North's famous "Diamond Mountains" as a tourist resort as well as to build ship repair and rolling stock plants. Yet, as usual in the notoriously difficult dealings with the Stalinist North, none of his goodwill schemes ever materialized as originally agreed.

Annoyed by what he perceived to be anti-business policies of President Roh, who forced companies to sell off their hoarded land holdings and to streamline their widely diversified *chaebol* operations, Chung set up his own United People's Party (UPP) and at age 76, ran for the Korean presidency on a conservative pro-business ticket. A veritable army of Hyundai activists and corporate funds were duly mobilized. The UPP won 31 seats out of 299 in the National Assembly, and Chung a respectable 16 per cent in the presidential race. His political ambitions however cost Hyundai dearly, as it predictably incurred the wrath of the much criticized Roh administration and of the incoming Kim Yong Sam presidency.

Credit lines by government banks were suddenly tightened, tax audits followed, and Chung was charged with violating campaign financing rules. For this, in 1993 he ultimately received a three-year suspended sentence, thus effectively ending Chung's short-lived foray into politics, which had challenged in vain the Confucian order of Mandarin rule over business in Korea.

Within Hyundai itself, Confucian values were explicitly encouraged. The group spirit and group achievement (versus Western individualism), company loyalty, harmony through autocratic paternalism and personal relations (versus Western contractual bureauraticism) were said to rule. In difference to high-growth Japan, there were however no job guarantees. Chung frequently fired people on the spot when he was displeased with their performance, notably when they politely pointed out that his impossible demands for delivery dates could not be met. Already during recruitment decisions, the focus was to hire highly motivated, skilled candidates with traits of unquestioning loyalty and perseverance to be enforced during subsequent military-like training and corporate indoctrination, thus shaping Hyundai salarymen into legendary "road warriors" as secret weapons in international competition. As a result, employees were expected to work 16 hours daily, seven days a week and even to go to jail for their company. There were even women who put up with this work regime for years.

In its heyday in 1997, Hyundai consisted of 50 major companies, ranging from oil refining to securities, employing 170,000 people and counting for 10 per cent of Korea's exports. At its apex was Chung Ju Yung, his brothers and sons and the workaholic managers, who rose through his Hyundai hard school of construction business. Apart from his vision, unique drive for success and autonomy, and his insistence on autocratic order, Chung also had redeeming traits like his personal frugality, his patriotism to make economic sacrifices for better relations with the North, and a longing for life in the countryside, which he fulfilled by famously damming a large chunk of sea, reclaiming the land and creating South Korea's by far largest commercial farm. As a character larger than life, Chung helped to create and equally represented modern Korea's unparalleled stormy development.

Although HEC was experiencing considerable success, not everyone in the company agreed with Chung's risk taking business style. His younger brother, In Yung, had resigned from the company in protest (Steers, 1999). While at the time bold actions delivered incredible results, the dangers In Yung feared would later become reality. When Asia was hit by a financial crisis in 1997 Hyundai Construction was deeply affected. Difficulties experienced by their clients resulted in contract cancellations and payment defaults. Since Hyundai had used borrowed money to finance its rapid growth it quickly found itself in financial turmoil (Choe, 2000). The double-edged sword Hyundai used to fight its way to the top nearly crippled it financially. In 2000, banks and creditors were refusing to rollover its $4.7 billion in loans, bonds, and commercial papers, driving HEC dangerously close to bankruptcy (BBC News, 2000). This revealed the imperfection of its high-risk strategy. While the strategy is undeniably effective in moderation, using it exhaustively results in unmanageable debt. Corporations must constantly re-evaluate internal and external environments in order to select appropriate strategies. Clearly, Hyundai should have begun working toward lower levels of debt and better cash flow many years ago.

Faced with the repercussions of their past decisions, HEC managed to avoid bankruptcy by swapping some of their debt for equity (Duncan, 2004). They have also shifted their focus from labor-intensive to technology-intensive projects, which have improved their cash flow, allowing them to clear more debt. Combined with their downsizing and outsourcing efforts, these new strategies have greatly improved HEC's prospects for regaining their position as a competitive player in the construction business (Nho, 2002).

Unlike their construction counterparts, Hyundai Motors recognized and corrected these problems before they grew out of control. Although they still offer competitive prices Hyundai has now improved their product development and make better quality and more stylish cars. In fact, they have won design awards and sport rallies all around the world.

As well, recognizing that their ties to other debt-ridden Hyundai businesses were compromising their success, they have broken these connections. For instance, HMC refused to purchase any of the convertible bonds HEC issued as part of their debt repayment effort (Lord, 2000). They know that they have a 2.4 per cent of the US market share, and are the No. 9 automaker in the world (Armstrong, 2003).

When the economy improved, Hyundai Heavy Industries, with skilled workers and the appropriate technology, was in a position to compete in the industry (Steers, 1999). Once again they succeeded by undercutting and outpacing the competition. Frugality was instilled in every manager and worker using billboards that displayed the costs of supplies and materials. Everybody in the company was encouraged to preserve and conserve as much as possible. Chung would say, "My money is to be preserved at all costs" (Steers, 1999). To this end, they would often break rules and standards, such as making their own tools and using old equipment. But all of these savings allowed them to consistently underbid competitors. Moreover, the drive and diligence of their work force permitted them to complete ships in half the time required by competitors. An American supplier observed that Hyundai welders would work 10 hours a day, of which they would spend eight hours actually welding. He contrasted this to American welders who work eight-hour days but spent less than two hours actually welding. This productivity allowed HHI to produce ships in half the time compared to their competitors, without driving up the price (Steers, 1999).

Further aiding the diligence of the workers was the military-like power culture characteristic to Hyundai. David Gregg, a British engineer associated with HHI, noted that workers would stand at attention every morning to get their work assignment, and once a week the director would address them over loudspeakers to psych them up (Steers, 1999). This culture not only increased individual productivity, but it also allowed them to hire fewer managers and more technical workers, further increasing speed and decreasing costs.

In addition, HHI leveraged on its ties with other Hyundai businesses to become competitive in their industry. From HEC engineers they learned how to plan and schedule, and from HMC engineers how to reduce throughput, as well as how to establish and balance an assembly line. Finally, they attracted talent from other companies through competitive salaries and career opportunities that the Hyundai business group offered (Steers, 1999).

HHI is currently still the world's largest ship builder, and they have expanded their business into robotics and diesel engines (Williams, 2004).

Recently they have suffered from close ties with other Hyundai companies. As difficulties struck many of the groups' businesses HHI helped some of its sister companies by repaying loans on their behalf. These loan repayments, as well as the legal disputes that have ensued, weakened investor and creditor confidence (Lord, 2000). Lack of confidence in the company's future makes it difficult and expensive to acquire capital to fund expansion. Recognizing that their connection to the Hyundai group had become one-sided, HHI followed HMC in breaking these ties. They too refused to purchase HEC's convertible bonds (Lord, 2000).

HHI is an excellent example of how effective Hyundai's business style is, and explains why they used it so exhaustively. Beyond doubt their management techniques had clear and tangible benefits.

Like HEC, HEI's history of debt-leveraged growth left them in financial difficulties beginning in 2000, when 73 per cent of their debt matured over a span of only 15 months (Ann, 2000). While they went to great lengths to repay these loans, their future is still uncertain. This is another illustration of the ramifications of Hyundai's over-use of debt-financed expansion. They over-exposed themselves to the risk of an economic downturn, which materialized in the late 1990s.

More than other Hyundai businesses, HEI illustrates the ramifications of inappropriate use of sound business methods. Their earlier prosperity in Korea proves their ability to succeed using these techniques, but their original failure in America and current liquidity problems identifies the consequence of exploiting them and using them in unsuitable environments.

Hyundai's ventures gained competitive advantage by offering low prices and fast delivery. The ability to achieve results was dependent on their culture of ruthless dedication to hard work. Their employees worked long and intense hours in order to achieve demanding Hyundai goals. Hyundai took advantage of the low cost of labour and profited extensively from this drive and work ethic. However, as the compensation failed to keep pace with economic growth their strategy crossed the line into labor force exploitation. In its earlier stages Hyundai offered its industrial workers vast improvements in salary and quality of life compared to that of farming, which was their only other career option. However, as Hyundai and the Korean economy began to prosper throughout the 1980s the salaries of blue-collar workers grew slowly while the economy flourished. The result was a series of nation-wide strikes that cost Hyundai and its sub-contractors approximately $1.2 billion (Steers, 1999). While this was a nationwide problem, since Hyundai dominated the heavy industries they were a significant contributor to the problem and, consequently, its heavy industrial companies were most deeply affected. Hyundai Motors, for instance, experienced a 200,000-worker strike that lasted 26 days, resulting in a $500 million loss of sales (Steers, 1999). In addition to the financial losses Hyundai's image was also degraded due to the violence that broke out during protests. During one meeting between Hyundai Motor managers and assembly line workers to discuss grievances, the workers began breaking windows on cars on the assembly line. Public opinion of Hyundai further slipped when a union leader was kidnapped at the order of Hyundai executives (Steers, 1999). These problems were a result of Hyundai pushing their strategy to an extreme. Capitalizing on Korea's cheap labor and strong work ethic was an effective strategy; however, the harder employees worked and the less they were rewarded the greater the chance of internal revolt. Hyundai pushed this strategy to the point of exploiting their work force, and as a result violent and costly strikes ensued.

In addition, these management practices also caused significant detriment to the conglomerate as a whole. In particular, Chung's authoritarian control left his brothers and sons power hungry, resulting in a power struggle once he had stepped down. While Chung was in control, everybody obeyed his commands; however, when Chung stepped down, his potential successors began feuding for his throne. The problem initially became apparent between 1999 and 2000 during a power struggle between Chung's sons. This continued until Chung stepped in and divided the company. He assigned Hyundai Motors, Kia Motors and other profitable smaller units to Chung Mong Ku, his eldest surviving son, the debt-ridden Hyundai group to Chung Mong Hun, his fifth son, and the the profitable shipbuilding of Hyundai Heavy Industries to Mong Joon, his sixth son (Lee, 2003). This family feud was particularly detrimental to Hyundai because it took place while the financial situation of the firm was in shambles. While several of the firms such as HEC were facing bankruptcy due to liquidity problems, the Chung family was preoccupied with this power struggle. In addition, at a time when creditors were already refusing to rollover debt, these disputes only weakened investor and creditor confidence.

After Chung's death, the problem resurfaced after Chung Mong Hun committed suicide when it was revealed that he had been paying bribes estimated at $500 million (*Financial Times*, August 6, 2003) to North Korea for approval of seven projects (Brooke, 2003). The payments took place just before the historic June 2000 summit between President Kim Dae Jung and North Korea's dictator Kim Song Il.

Directly after Mong-hun's death, foreign investors purchased 11.5 per cent of Hyundai Elevator, the holding corporation for the left-over of Hyundai, which left the shrunken group vulnerable to hostile takeover attempts. Shortly after, Chung Mong Hun's widow, Ms. Hyun Jeong Eun, took office as Chairwoman of Hyundai Elevator and Hyundai Business Group. Upset that the Hyundai group was being run by someone outside the core family, Chung's younger brother and Chairman of Kumgang Korea Chemical Co (KCC), Chung Sang Young, purchased 20.9 per cent of the holding. Although this was an attempt to take control of the business group, it was unsuccessful as securities regulators forced Chung Sang Young to sell his newly acquired equity, citing his failure to report the purchase of over 5 per cent of a firm's equity. This is a requirement under Korean securities regulations. This conflict angered investors in KCC since company funds were being used to purchase equity in Hyundai Elevator (KIOS, 2004). After the court decision of March 2004, Hyun Jeong Eun is now firmly in control of Hyundai Elevators and its affiliates, like HEC, Hyundai Securities and Hyundai Asan, which assembles all of Hyundai's (and most of South Korea's) loss making ventures with the North (*AFP*, March 31, 2004).

This problem is inherent to authoritarian control and common to many *chaebols*. Only a handful of companies, such as Samsung and LG, have successfully transitioned the company to the next generation (Lee, 2003). While having one all-powerful leader has its advantages, it allows for only one successor with complete power—a role that everybody desires. In Hyundai's case, this power struggle has contributed to serious difficulties in individual companies and has caused the conglomerate to be divided into smaller groups.

Hyundai's success is undeniable. The creation of this mammoth international conglomerate amidst a backward Korean economy was a marvel. Their ambitious vision, and resilient commitment made them a dangerous threat in any industry they set their eyes on. While the rest of the world believed that Korea's primitive economy left Hyundai without any hope in the international market, Hyundai turned this into an advantage by leveraging the cheap workforce to undercut their way to the top.

Moreover, the authoritarian control Chung held over every part of the company ensured that everyone in the firm ruthlessly worked toward the same goals. Finally, the family of companies collaborated together providing financial support, and technical expertise to one another.

However, using these tactics also resulted in significant losses throughout their growth. From their unprofitable construction projects, their early failures in the American automotive and electronics markets, and labour disputes, it is clear that these strategies were not universally and inexhaustibly effective. It became apparent that cutting too many corners would result in costly failures, and that authoritarian control, collaboration with family companies, and brash entrances into industries was not applicable to all parts of the world and to all industries. While they were able to correct their ways and recover from some errors, others took longer to surface and may be beyond repair. Their over-use of debt-leveraged growth has left much of the firm battling bankruptcy and the authoritarian control that held the conglomerate together dissolved as interfamily rivalry prevented the appointment of a successor. As a result, the Hyundai group has been divided into smaller groups, and collaboration has virtually ceased.

Hyundai's strategies were built on sound principles of hard work, commitment, confidence, and family harmony—principles that seemed capable of guiding them through any challenge. However, from their downfalls it is clear that no set of strategies is infallible. They all have imperfections which make them unsuitable in certain environments. It is difficult to identify at what stage Hyundai should have begun shifting their strategies for optimal gains, but it is clear that they should have been open to new strategies, and continually assessed themselves and their environment. The Hyundai story provides a lesson in the hazards of the *chaebol* structure and uncontrollable debt-leveraged growth. However, more generally it illustrates the need for companies to analyze challenges and environments objectively, and adapt accordingly. Clearly, there is no formula for lasting success. The business world is far too complex and dynamic to be governed by any rigid methodology.

REFERENCES

Mi-Young Ann. "Hyundai Electronics needs $3B to survive debt load." *Electronics News*. December 4, 2004. http://www.findarticles.com/cf_dls/m0EKF/49_46/69237154/p1/article.jhtml.

Larry Armstrong, Gail Edmondson and Ihlwan Moon. "Hyundai's hurdles: Will union unrest slow the auto maker's global growth drive?" *Business Week Online.* July 21, 2004. http://www.businessweek.com/magazine/content/03_29/b3842131_mz033.htm.

"Hyundai's new rescue plan." *BBC News.* November 20, 2000. http://news.bbc.co.uk/1/hi/business/1032225.stm.

James Brooke. "Hyundai suicide leaves question marks over future cooperation." *Taipei Times.* August 8, 2003. http://www.taipeitimes.com/News/edit/archives/2003/08/08/2003062804.

Sang-hun Choe. "Hyundai struggles to overcome debt." *Detnews.com*, November 25, 2000. http://www.detnews.com/2000/autos/0011/25/autos-153056.htm.

"Hyundai pays off debt, renamed Hynix." *CNN.com.* March 9, 2001. http://www.cnn.com/2001/BUSINESS/asia/03/09/korea.hyundaieldebt/.

Bobby Duncan. "Hyundai Engineering & Construction Co., Ltd." *Hoovers Online.* March 2004. http://www.hoovers.com/hyundai-engineering-and-construction/—ID__57023—/free-co-factsheet.xhtml.

DSL Prime. *DSL Prime Industry Directory: Hyundai Electronics.* http://dslprime.mblast.com/presentations/page614-63047.asp

Kim Jung Min. "Partly cloudy." *Far Eastern Economic Review.* August 28, 2003.

Korean Overseas Information Service (KIOS). *Regulators Order KCC to Sell Hyundai Shares.* February 11, 2004. http://www.kois.go.kr/kwnews/News.asp?Number=20040211008.

John Larkin. "Will Hyundai find a lifeline?" *Far Eastern Economic Review.* November 23, 2000.

Chang-sup Lee. "Greed overrules family ties." *The Korea Times.* December 11, 2003. http://times.hankooki.com/lpage/biz/200311/kt2003111217065510760.htm.

Nick Lord. "What's in a name?" *Finance Asia.* October 31, 2000. http://www.financeasia.com/articles/2F52917D-AE46-11D4-8C180008C72B383C.cfm.

Laxmi Nakarmi. "Are Hyundai's problems over?" *Asiaweek.com.* June 9, 2000. http://www.asiaweek.com/asiaweek/magazine/2000/0609/biz.buzz.html.

Laxmi Nakarmi. "Of fathers and sons." *Asiaweek*, June 16, 2000.

Joon-hun Nho. "Hyundai Construction seeking to regain past glory." *The Korea Times.* November 21, 2002. http://times.hankooki.com/lpage/tech/200211/kt2002112118290710880.htm.

Richard M. Steers. *Made in Korea.* New York: Routledge, 1999.

Andrew Ward. "The glory days of Hyundai sit firmly in the past." *Financial Times.* January 29, 2001.

Andrew Ward. "Nation racked by shock and sorrow for revered family." *Financial Times.* August 5, 2003.

Andrew Ward. "Chung family feud." *Financial Times.* November 18, 2003.

Randy Williams. "Hyundai Heavy Industries Co., Ltd." *Hoovers Online.* February 2004. http://www.hoovers.com/hyundai-heavy-industries-co.,-ltd./—ID__57072—/free-co-factsheet.xhtml.

CHAPTER 7

The Elusive Mr Li: Hutchison Whampoa and the 3G Phones

ALBRECHT ROTHACHER

The rise of one of East Asia's most enigmatic and richest business tycoons, Li Ka-shing of Hong Kong, is a fascinating subject matter. Worth $12.4 billion in 2004, according to Forbes, Li Ka-shing started his business career under very inauspicious circumstances. Born in 1928 in Chaozhou, a town in Northern Guangdong, which for a century was a source of many Chinese emigrants (mostly to Thailand), a son of an impoverished school teacher who failed to make his luck in Java in the 1920s, the family fled the war to move to Hong Kong in late 1940. One year later this apparent safety was shattered by the Japanese Occupation, and two years later in 1943 his father died of tuberculosis, unable to afford treatment and medicine.

Having barely finished middle school education (in itself quite an achievement in starving war-torn HK), Li started as a sales clerk first in a shop for watches and then in one for plastic goods, hawking plastic belts and watch bands. During the day he would sell his goods, during evenings supervise production and at night work toward his high school diploma.

Having risen to general manager of this small outfit at age 20, he set up his own plastic company in 1948 producing first plastic combs, soap boxes and cheap toys. His sweatshop employed barely a dozen workers, and was thus indistinguishable from 100,000 others in postwar HK. It struggled until 1957, when Li hit upon the then US middle class craze for plastic flowers to "embellish" their new suburban homes. By 1958, he could purchase his first property and build a multi-storey mixed production and residential facility. Lauded in 1964 as the "King of Plastic Flowers," whose quality flowers had been better than the local competition and cheaper than overseas products, he however sensed a forthcoming change in US tastes and moved decisively into real estate development. In difference to the traditional Chinese preference for real estate and land holdings (and the corresponding disinclination to sell), Li took a vigorously modern approach: the purchase, development and sale of land as a commodity in the quickest possible time. A continuous stream of refugees from China, rapid economic development and the general scarcity of space fuelled an enduring real estate boom in the colony.

Li focused on strategic locations, which he quickly developed for high-rise housing and office purposes and then resold speedily. He also used local crises (like the riots engineered in 1967 by Beijing, the uncertainties about the political future of HK which culminated in 1983) to buy out cheaply those competitors with less confidence and less nerves of steel who were ready to abandon their HK properties. Having gone public with his holding company Cheung Kong in 1972, he subsequently moved into warehousing, rental properties, hotels, shopping arcades and cement production. By 1978, the Hong Kong and Shanghai Banking Corporation offered Li a controlling stake in one of the colony's most prestigious *hong* (trading conglomerate), Hutchison Whampoa, with its wide export trading, warehousing, cargo/container handling, engineering, quarrying and retail interests. Apparently, the Bank was worried about Hutchison's debt levels and dissatisfied with its management and seemed to have felt that Li's good Chinese mainland connections would be more helpful than continued expatriate management (which was soon eased out by Li).

Already in 1979 Li started his first joint ventures on the mainland, then involving Chinese partners only, like for cement production, residential developments or an aircraft maintenance depot; later also introducing Western partners like Procter and Gamble or the Singapore Government to the Chinese market, with schemes ranging from shampoo and hygiene products manufacturing to highways in Sichuan, power plants, steel plants in Guanxi and ports on Hainan.

Li is known to have undertaken joint ventures with Red Chinese "princelings" which left them with virtually no risks (Chan, p. 109) or donated to their causes (Chan, p. 195). Already in 1982 he met with the Beijing leadership and as early as in 1979 was appointed to the board of its CITIS agency to attract FDI.

Yet after the June 1989 Tiananmen crackdown, during the next two years Li strengthened his investments in Canada where he already owned 10 per cent of the Canadian Imperial Bank of Commerce, controlled the deficitarian oil and gas developer Husky Oil and was involved in a controversial, if highly profitable land development for the Vancouver Expo. In London he took over the Canary Wharf development from the cash bleeding Reichmann brothers, and similarly other promising real estate and resource developments in North America from their suffering owners.

Li's ventures in media activities, like shares in Pearson or a sizable stake in Star satellite TV (which covered most of East Asia up to the Mid East), however did not lead to much then, except in very profitable ultimate sales to Rupert Murdoch. By 1996, Li Ka-shing's net worth stood at $6 billion. He then controlled most of Southern China's seaports and with sizable interests in railways, airports, power stations and highways, was the most visible supplier of foreign capital to modernize China's coastal infrastructure.

Eight years later, after entering the telecom market forcefully his net worth more than doubled to $12.4 billion. Li Ka-shing had always been a classical asset trader: buying cheaply ("bottom fishing"), like Warren Buffet, undervalued assets in which no one seemed interested, but then—disregarding all niceties about "strategic holdings"—being ready to sell anything (in difference to Buffet) provided the price and the profit margin were right. He was aided in this strategy by high liquidity and the tendency to purchase—relatively speaking—small- to medium-sized business operations.

Li's involvement with the third generation phone (3G) was to change all this. In time-honored fashion, the initial funds to purchase 3G licenses in 10 countries came from the sale of Orange, the mobile phone operator set up in 1994, to the ill-fated Mannesmann at the height of the telecom bubble in 1999 at a hefty profit of $15 billion (*Financial Times*, December 4, 2003). Overindebted and undermanaged, Mannesmann was soon swallowed by Vodaphone. Li used the proceeds to buy 3G licenses in countries like the UK, Italy, Sweden, Australia, Austria, HongKong and Israel. In the UK and Italy alone for market development and the licenses some $11 billion were spent (*Financial Times*, March 1, 2003). Originally, the UK 3G risk was shared with the Dutch KPN and the Japanese NTT DoCoMo, who purchased shares in the operation Three UK. As software problems mounted, service was poor, and the handsets delivered by NEC and Motorola turned out clumsy, often defective and were delivered late and in insufficient qualities (*Financial Times*, November 18, 2003), subscriber numbers remained far below target. Handsets, which were supposed to be priced at $4,380, were sold at $90 in the UK (and at $435 for corporate customers in HK), with video calls being billed at the price of voice calls (*International Herald Tribune*, February 11, 2004). As losses mounted, KPN Telekom pulled out, with NTT DoCoMo considering the same (*Financial Times*, May 12, 2004).

Li now found himself in a strange new situation: being a strategic investor locked into a loss-making high-risk new market and product development situation. His 3G operations in total had required $22 billion so far. Since 2002 annual losses amounted to $2.0 to $2.3 billion. His 3G customer base had barely reached one million in the key markets of the UK, Italy and HK. In order to break even some 11 million are needed. This objective could at best be reached in late 2006 (*Financial Times*, November 18, 2003), if ever. Clearly out of favour with international investors and rating agencies, which like Standard & Poor's promptly downgraded Hutchison Whampoa and its sister company Cheung Kong, still local HK money continues to bet on Li's Midas touch and his track record of three decades (*The Economist*, February 17, 2002).

A series of—often highly profitable—sales followed, the proceeds of which were all used to stuff the holes which the 3G adventure had punched into the bottom line. Hutchison's stakes in Vodaphone and Deutsche Telekom were sold first, followed by its share in the China joint venture with Procter & Gamble (sold at $2 billion, with a profit of $1.8 billion) (*Financial Times*, May 12, 2004). Its HK fixed line network was shifted for $910 million onto another subsidiary Vanda, whose share prices subsequently halved. Two internet businesses, TOM online, a China-based Internet service company, and Priceline, an Internet-based discount travel service provider, were floated, as was a hotchpotch of joint venture and minority participations in mobile phone operations from Paraguay to Ghana and Macao, beautified as Hutchison Telecom International. As proceeds from sales and floatings alone were insufficient, also Hutchison's main revenue, accruing from its 32 ports, Hong Kong real estate, drugstores, supermarkets, and energy businesses in Australia and Canada, was equally mobilized to maintain a positive cash flow. Speculation has become intense as to when core businesses, like Husky Oil, would need to be sold (*Financial Times*, March 31, 2004).

Li Ka-shing's modus operandi is described as very much a one-man show: with quick analysis and quick decisions, embedded in a wealth of highly useful contacts, at the political level as one of Beijing's most trusted external advisors and a sizable contributor to the Tory Party at the same time.

When Li in 2002 bought the bankrupt US telecom giant Global Crossing with its global fibre-optic networks, he was publicly denounced as a security risk for US interests due to his close links with the Chinese Communist leadership and its military establishment (Rep. Dana Rohrabacher in: *NewsMax.com*, March 7, 2002). Equally at the core, he is part of an expatriate Chinese tycoon network with close ties to Robert Kuok (Malaysia), Raimond Chow (Taiwan) and the Lamsan family, which controls the Thai Farmers Bank .

According to the sources quoted by Anthony Chang, Li remains driven by a passion for business (making money not for himself but for reinvestment) and a persistent longing for status and respect (Chan, p. 90), while sticking to rustic principles of conservatism, trust, simplicity and self-restraint. Inevitably, Li's empire is foreseen for dynastic succession. While his oldest son, Victor (39 years old), an engineer and deputy chairman at Hutchinson, remains fairly nondescript in Chang's account, the second son Richard (37 years old), an economist, is described as an arrogant bully surrounded only by sycophants (Chan, p. 163). In the meantime, Richard Li is in the headlines with stories like no shows at court for speeding charges (*Straits Times*, March 5, 2004), for buying a $1 billion parcel of HK public land without tender (*Financial Times*, March 1, 2003), and for continued losses at PCCW, his own Hong Kong telecom business (*IHT*, March 24, 2003). His troubles started in 2000 when he took over HK's dominant phone company for $28 billion, a highly leveraged risk without his father's stable cash flow businesses. With succession prospects like that, the future of Li's empire appears as less than assured.

REFERENCES

Asia's Superman Swoops Again. The Economist. August 17, 2002.
Anthony B. Chan. *Li Ka-shing: HongKong's Elusive Billionaire*. Hong Kong: Oxford University Press, 1996.
Francesco Guerrera and Robert Budden. "How Li Ka-shing's gamble on 3G telephony is squeezing cash from Hutchison Whampoa." *Financial Times*, December 4, 2003.
Francesco Guerrera, and Justine Lau. "3G weakens 'Superman' Li's standing." *Financial Times*, March 31, 2004.

Rahul Jacob and Robert Budden. "Man in the news: Li Ka-shing." *Financial Times*, March 1, 2003.

Kate Linebaugh. "As elder Li prospers, son trails in distance." *International Herald Tribune*, March 24, 2003.

Charles R. Smith. "Global Crossing Buyout by Li Ka-shing Under Fire." *NewsMax.com*, March 7, 2002.

CHAPTER 8

On the Wings of British Airways

LIM CHEE HONG

INTRODUCTION

British Airways (BA) is one of the world's largest airlines and the largest in Europe. It is based in Heathrow Airport, London, one of the world's busiest international airports, and has a global flight network through partners such as American Airlines in the United States and Qantas in Australia. As the UK's sole global network carrier, it transports 36 billion passengers a year to approximately 268 destinations in 97 countries.[1]

History: linking the British Empire

BA's earliest predecessor was Aircraft Transport & Travel, founded in 1916. On August 25, 1919, this company inaugurated the world's first scheduled international air service with a converted de Havilland 4A day bomber leaving Hounslow (later Heathrow) Airport for London and also Le Bourget in Paris. Eight days later another company, Handley Page Transport, Ltd., started a cross-channel service between London's Cricklewood Field and both Paris and Brussels.

The same year Britain's advisory committee for civil aviation proposed plans for establishing a world airline network linking Britain with Canada, India, South Africa, Australia and New Zealand. Because airplanes were not yet available, the committee recommended that first priority be given to a route to India and be operated by a state-assisted private enterprise.

Progress was made quickly. Before the end of the year, the British government was operating a service to Karachi and had established a network of 43 Royal Air Force (RAF)[2] landing strips throughout Africa to the Cape of Good Hope. Meanwhile, strong competition from subsidized foreign airline companies forced many of the private British air carriers out of business. By March 1921, all British airline companies had suspended their operations. The government intervened with a pledge to keep the British companies flying, using its own form of subsidization.

In January 1923, British Parliament appointed a Civil Air Transport Subsidies Committee to form a single British international air carrier from existing companies. On March 31, 1924, Daimler Airway, British Marine Air Navigation, Instone Air Line, and Handley Page merged to become Imperial Air Transport.

In 1925, Imperial Airways operated a number of European routes, while a route across the Arabian desert linked Cairo to Basra in present day Iraq. The airline was faced with a number of problems on this route. The desert was featureless; radio stations were difficult to maintain. Basra was a major terminal on the route to India. However, on January 7, 1927, the Persian government forbade Britain the use of its airspace two years later, thus generating demand for longer range aircraft. Passengers flying to India from London, had to travel via Paris to Basel, where they boarded a train for Genoa. Next, a flying boat took them on to Alexandria, where they flew in stages to Karachi. The passage to India, previously three weeks by sea, had been reduced to one week by air.

Imperial Airways' service to Calcutta was established in July 1933, to Rangoon in September and to Singapore in December. In January 1934, Australia's Queensland and Northern Territories air service (Qantas) inaugurated a route linking Singapore with Brisbane. The passage from Europe to Australia could be completed in 12.5 days.[3]

A commercial service through Africa was opened in 1931 with flying boats linking Cairo with Kwanza on Lake Victoria. In April 1933 the route was extended to Cape Town, the trip from London taking 10.5 days. An east-west trans-African route from Khartoum in Sudan to Kano in northern Nigeria was established in February 1936. This route completed a world network that linked nearly all the countries of the British Empire.

The primary source of revenue on the network was not from transporting passengers but mail. Nevertheless, an increase in demand for more passengers seating and cargo space generated a need for larger airplanes. Britain's primary supplier of flying boats, the Short Company had developed a new model designated the C-class, with 24 seats and weighing 18 tons. Since it had an increased range and flew 145 miles per hour, it was able to simply "bypass politically difficult areas."[4] A year later, Imperial Airways made its first transatlantic crossing with a flying boat equipped with extra fuel tanks. It was Pan Am, however, that first scheduled a regular transatlantic service, employing more sophisticated and updated Boeing airplanes.

World War II and nationalization

Imperial Airways was formed with the intention of being Britain's "chosen instrument" for overseas air service. On its European services, however, Imperial was competing with the British continental airline and an aggressive newcomer called British Airways, which had been created in October 1935 by the merger of three smaller airlines. Three months later, the company acquired a fleet of Lockheed 10 Electras, which were the fastest airplanes available.[5] The competition from British Airways threatened the "chosen instrument" so much that in November 1937, a British parliamentary committee proposed the nationalization and merger of Imperial and British Airways. When the reorganization was completed on November 24, 1939, the British Overseas Airways Corporation (BOAC) was formed.

The creation of BOAC was overshadowed by the declaration of war on Germany the previous September. The secretary of state for air assumed control of all British air services, including BOAC. Within a year, Italy entered the war and France had fallen. Britain's air routes through Europe had been eliminated. British flying boats, however continued to ferry personnel and war cargo between London and West Africa with an intermediate stop in nominally neutral Portugal. The air link to Khartoum maintained Britain's connection to the "horse-shoe route", from Cape Town through east Africa, Arabia, India and Singapore to Australia. When Malaya and Singapore were later invaded by the Japanese, BOAC and Qantas opened a non-stop service between Ceylon and Perth in Western Australia. BOAC transported ball-bearings from neutral Sweden using a route which was dangerously exposed to the German Luftwaffe. BOAC also operated a service for returning flight crews to North America after they delivered American and Canadian built aircraft to the Royal Air Force.

When the war ended, BOAC had a fleet of 160 aircraft and an aerial network which covered 54,000 miles. The South American destinations of BOAC were assigned to a new state-owned airline, British South American Airways (BSAA), in March 1946. Similarly the European services were turned to British European Airways (BEA) on August 1, 1946. After the war, Britain established its overseas services to the nations of its Empire. Some of the nations which had recently gained independence from Britain received advice and often finance from BOAC.

In order to remain competitive with American airlines, BOAC purchased Lockheed Constellations, the most advanced commercial aircraft of the day. They were later joined by Boeing 377 Stratocruisers and Canadair Argonauts (modified DC-4s). BEA operated generally smaller airplanes and more frequent flights between the British Isles and Continental Europe. In 1948, it joined other Allied airline companies in the airlift to Berlin during the Soviet blockade.

Fleet strategies: from the Comet to the Concorde

Following a series of equipment failures at BSAA, the Civil Aviation ministry declared that the company should re-merge with BOAC. On July 30, 1949, BSAA was absorbed by BOAC. Even though the passenger load had steadily increased, BOAC accumulated a debt of £32 million in the five years from 1946 to 1951.[6] Much of this was due to "recapitalization" or purchasing new equipment; the British built Handley Page Hermes and De Havilland's DH Comet 1, the world's first jetliners, were delivered to BOAC.

In January 1954, one of BOAC's Comets exploded near Elba in the Mediterranean. Another Comet crashed near Naples only 16 days after an investigation of the first crash was concluded. As a result, the Comet's certificate of airworthiness was withdrawn and a full investigation was ordered. In the final report it was determined that the Comets' pressurized cabin was inadequately designed to withstand low air pressures at altitudes over 25,000 feet. When the airplane reached that altitude, it simply exploded. The cabin was strengthened and the jet introduced in 1958 as the DH Comet 4. The company was forced to purchase propeller-driven DC-7s to cover equipment shortages when the delivery of its Britannia turbo-props was delayed in 1956. When the Comet re-entered service, BOAC found itself with two undesirable fleets of aircraft which were later sold at a loss of £51 million.[7]

South American operations were suspended in 1954 when the Comet was taken out of service. Operation of the route with shorter range aircraft was too costly. At the insistence of Argentina and Brazil, which claimed that Britain had "lost interest" in South America, the routes were reopened in 1960. That same year, the first of 15 Boeing 707 jetliners was delivered to BOAC.

British European Airways used a wide variety of aircraft for its operations and remained a good customer for British aircraft manufacturers. In 1964 the company accepted delivery of the first de Havilland Trident 1, a three-engine airliner capable of speeds up to 600 miles per hour. A few years later, when the company expressed an interest in purchasing a mixed fleet of Boeing 727s and 737s, it was instructed by the British government to "buy British" instead. BEA complied, ordering BAC-111s and improved versions of the Trident.

BOAC's cargo traffic was growing at an annual rate of 27 per cent. Nevertheless, a sudden and unexplained drop in passenger traffic during 1961 left many of the world's airline companies with "excess capacity" or too many empty seats to fly profitably. At the end of the fiscal year, BOAC's accumulated deficit had grown to £64 million.[8] The losses, however, were underwritten by the British government, which did not allow its flag carrier to go bankrupt.

BOAC and Air France agreed to build a supersonic transport (SST) in 1962. In June, the company became associated with the Cunard Steamship Company. A new company, BOAC-Cunard Ltd. was placed in charge of the transatlantic air services in an attempt to capture a lager portion of the American travel markets.

The British government published a "White Paper" that recommended a drastic reorganization of BOAC. In response, the company's chairman Sir Matthew Slattery, and the managing director, Sir Basil Smallpiece, resigned. Britain's minister for aviation appointed Sir Giles Guthrie as the new chairman and chief executive officer. Under Sir Giles Guthrie, BOAC suspended its unprofitable services and rescheduled its equipment purchases and debt payments. After the financial situation had improved the company purchased new equipment and expanded its flight network. In April 1967, BOAC established its second around-the-world route and opened a new cargo terminal in Heathrow.

The company's sister airline, BEA, had been paying close attention to consumer marketing for holiday makers. In 1967, the company created a division called BEA Air Tours Ltd, offering complete travel packages to a number of vacation spots. In May 1969, BOAC opened a passage to

Japan via the North Pole. The route was shortened even further when the Soviet Union granted BOAC landing rights in Moscow and a Siberian airline to Tokyo.

On March 31, 1972, after six years of record profits, BOAC announced that it no longer owed any money to the government. Later, on July 17, following several recommendations on further reorganization of the state-owned airline companies, management of BEA and BOAC were co-ordinated under a new government agency called the British Airways Group. On April 1, 1974 the two companies were merged and renamed British Airways. A second reorganization of the internal management structure occurred in 1977.

The first British Airways' Concorde was introduced in 1976. Jointly manufactured by British Aerospace and the French firm Aerospatiale, the supersonic Concorde was capable of carrying 100 passengers at the speed of 1,350 miles per hour at an altitude of 55,000 feet. An eleventh hour flight from New York to London was cut nearly in half the time by the Concorde. British Airways employed additional Concorde planes on a limited number of international services.

THE ROAD TO PRIVATIZATION IN THE 1980s: FROM BLOODY AWFUL TO BLOODLY AWESOME

Existence of two cultures

The history of BA must be understood as the merger of two organizations: British European Airways (BEA) and British Overseas Airways (BOAC). These two organizations not only represented different kinds of economic and commercial interests, they represented two distinct sets of values and beliefs and in effect, two very different cultures.[9] On the face of it the two cultures could not have been further apart. BEA, reflecting the high frequency, short-haul, quick turnaround nature of its business, tended to display a street smart, can-do culture. BOAC, Britain's intercontinental airline at the time, viewed itself as the true flag carrier of Great Britain and could be characterized as having a cosmopolitan culture. Ultimately the strengths of the two cultures, brought together under the single banner of customer excellence, melded to grow into the BA of today. However for years after the formal merger the cultural differences stood out.

Fighter Command vs. Bomber Command
During the Second World War, there were two distinct services in the Royal Air Force: Bombers and Fighters. The fighter planes, like the famous Spitfire which distinguished itself in the Battle of Britain, were flown by a single pilot. These were highly manoeuvrable aircraft and required certain flair to fly. The fighter squadron tended to attract officer pilots from the upper class who were single and whose personalities and dress reflected the flair required to pilot the plane. The bomber squadron planes were flown by a crew: pilot, co-pilot, navigator and gunners. These were not manoeuvrable aircraft, but required a mechanic-like skill to fly and drop bombs accurately. The bomber pilots came from the ranks, working as ground crew before becoming co-pilots and pilots.

After the war, despite its long haul routes, BOAC attracted the officer pilots of both bomber and fighter commands while BEA attracted the enlisted men, non-commissioned officers (NCOs) of both commands. There was a timelessness in BOAC, whereas the focus of BEA was much more of an on-line, real-time orientation. BOAC still got the glory; indeed, it became world-renowned as more advertising money was spent to fill seats on the long haul routes. BEA, ever the unappreciated workhorse, was unknown to many. BEA was small and scrappy: "We'd rather get you there on time than worry about the uniform not pressed."[10] BOAC projected decorum and style, frequently at the expense of financial performance. This "cross ruff" of bomber-fighter officer-enlistees had a profound impact on shaping post-war BA culture.

The two cultures continue to exist within BA
While the merger was accomplished by 1982, the two cultures continued to exist within BA for years. For 1984–7, for example, terminal one at Heathrow continued to be dominated by people from BEA and continued to represent BEA culture; while terminal three (and later terminal four) continued whatever vestiges there were of the BOAC culture. Indeed, these turned out to be somewhat task-related, since terminal one originated all short haul flights out of Heathrow, including services to Europe and terminal three (later four) was the source of all long haul services around the world, a very different kind of task, with different kinds of passengers and totally different time perspectives.

In the end, one could begin to talk about a short haul culture and a long haul culture, values and beliefs congregated around the task rather than the completion and minimum time turnarounds. With this time perspective, an "operations" culture can be successful, whatever the background and education. Similarly, the service in terminal four is related to the kind of passenger who use long haul flights. The culture that emphasizes a higher quality of service and more concern for the overall health and psychological welfare of its passengers is appropriate to the long haul task.[11]

Since 1987, there have been numerous efforts to integrate the two cultures. People have been moved from one terminal to another so that there are more shared values. Within the terminal environment at Heathrow, there is now cross terminal management which sets overall standards for all staff no matter where they are. Managers have either worked their way up the ranks by performance or have been hired to meet specific technical and managerial needs.[12] In a certain sense, the BEA culture has won out. The ability to perform the job means a great deal more at BA today than one's background or schooling.

Problems of BA

At first, BA suffered from the problems of having to merge two organizations and to eliminate duplication. These problems were not helped by the way in which the two corporations were to continue as separate divisions with BA, each controlling its own marketing and operations. These problems were recognized in an April 1977 reorganization of the airline into four divisions covering commercial operations, flight operations, engineering and planning. Throughout the period, the BA Board's objective was to rationalize the operations of BA without resorting to layoffs, a policy that would have fitted well with political constraints (Labour government) even if it was not dictated by them. During the 1970s, BA had a reputation of overstaffing, low productivity and poor labor relations: strikes caused the loss of £11 million in operating profits in 1975 and £40 million in1978.[13]

The 1973–4 and 1979 oil shocks doubled the price of aviation fuel, while the slump of the British economy reduced the number of domestic and international passengers. Operating profits fell from £76 million in 1979 to £17 million in 1980 and as demand continued to fall, BA suffered an operating loss of £102 million in 1981 with an overall loss of £141 million.[14] Volume was falling, costs were rising and fares on the transatlantic routes, BA's most important market, were cut in response to deregulation of international air fares.

Lord King

In 1980, Prime Minister Margaret Thatcher appointed Lord John King as chairman of BA. The Conservative government had been elected to power under the leadership of Margaret Thatcher, with the commitment to sell into private ownership many of Britain's major nationalized industries, including BA. The new administration was determined to reduce the losses that almost all state enterprises showed each year and in many cases, to restore these enterprises to private ownership.

As Nigel Lawson, Chancellor at the Exchequer and the man with Cabinet responsibility for the privatisation program, said in 1982,

> The conservative party has never believed that the business of the government is the government of business.[15]

Lord King's first move was to adopt aggressive American-style marketing and management philosophies. As a result, he initiated a massive campaign to scale down the company and reduce costs. Employment had fallen from 57,741 in March 1979 to 52,310 in March 1981. It was down further to 43,000 a year later and reached a low of 36,794 in March 1984; a 36 per cent reduction.[16] King appointed Colin Marshall as chief executive in 1983, following a long search for someone capable of turning BA into a market-driven company and focusing attention on delivering a quality service to the customer. It is the partnership of these two men that is credited with the creation of the "new" BA. Other changes included a shake-up of the existing top and middle management structures in an attempt to clear out the old "engineering-driven" blood, which might resist change, training courses for staff at all levels to instil a customer-focused culture and increase motivation, the introduction of performance-related pay and a major marketing initiative with the emphasis on branding the airline's services.

Sir Colin Marshall

When Lord King recruited Sir Colin Marshall as the CEO of BA in 1983, the airline was already making profits. It was Sir Colin who with his experience of managing service industries crafted the winning strategy of quality-based service for BA. The reason for recruiting Sir Colin was that he knew a great deal about serving customers, without knowing much about the airline business. As Lord King commented:

> We were looking for someone who understood service. But there seemed to be an advantage in not knowing too much about the business. In my ignorance, I could do things I might not have done if I had been better informed.[17]

Sir Colin Marshall[18] was born on November 16, 1933 in north London. He left school at 17 to join the Orient Steam Navigation Company, now the P&O Line. He began as a management trainee purser, a position of responsibility for everything aboard the ship but navigation. He left the line in the mid-1950s, as the youngest ever deputy purser to join Hertz. At Hertz in Chicago he was posted to Toronto and at the age of 25 was given one day to relocate from Toronto to run Hertz Mexico. Just before his 30th birthday he was approached by Avis to head Avis Europe and subsequently become its CEO in 1976. After the conglomerate Norton Simon acquired Avis in 1979, Marshall's responsibilities expanded to include Hunt-Wesson foods, which instilled in him an appreciation for the power of brands. Sears, the British retailer and shoe manufacturer, lured him back to London in 1981 by offering him the deputy CEO's job. Then in 1983, John King came calling.

Sir Colin's approaches to BA

In retrospect, the arrival of Colin Marshall at BA was an auspicious event in the history of this organization. At the time there was considerable confusion about Sir Colin's role and a great deal of doubt as to what he would be able to accomplish. Prior to being selected to be the CEO of BA, Sir Colin ran Avis and was responsible for a number of customer service and technological initiatives in his career there. Thus, it was not just a British son returning home. Sir Colin was a person with an entirely new set of values, values concerned with the customer rather than with the transportation process. It is crucial to understand the importance of these changes.

Sir Colin's background gave him a perspective that was alien to BA at the time. His perspective was that you could compete through meeting or exceeding customer expectations. As a practical matter, Sir Colin became very aware early on that, given its combination of routes, BA could never be a low-cost producer. It could become much more cost effective and certainly break through the cost of doing business barrier, but it would never win on cost alone. His conviction that it could compete through customer service is the underpinning of the BA culture and undoubtedly, the underpinning of its success. This is further illustrated from his interview with The *Harvard Business Review* Nov/Dec 95:

> I mentioned that we strive to make our customers' travel experience seamless, personal, and caring. We continually ask customers in focus groups to tell us what such an experience should look and feel like, and we have distilled their responses into service principles that are enshrined in two of our corporate goals. The goals are: "To provide overall superior service and good value for money in every market segment in which we compete" and "to excel in anticipating and quickly responding to customer needs and competitor activity."

Focus on customers (PPF)
It is certainly true that a great deal of effort and energy went into shaping BA's culture. At the heart of this was the *Putting People First* (PPF) training program launched by Sir Colin Marshall, the company's new chief executive, in December 1983. Originally intended for staff who had direct contact with customers it was, in fact, attended by all 40,000 employees by 1986 and it aimed to revolutionize their attitude.[19] In a direct challenge to the hierarchical and militaristic culture which existed in BA at the time, staff was instructed not to attend in uniform and, once on the course, put into cross-functional and cross-grade groups. The course itself was consciously designed to modify behavior. Attendees were encouraged to take a more positive attitude to themselves, taught how to set personal goals and cope with stress and instructed in confidence building and "getting what they wanted out of life." Lapel badges inscribed with the motto "We're putting people first" provided a visible reminder of the course's message.[20]

The approach was self-consciously "indoctrinative." As Sir Colin said, "We ... have to 'design' our people and their service attitude just as we design an aircraft seat, an in-flight entertainment programme or an airport lounge *to meet the needs and preferences of our customers.*"[21]

Colin Marshall's own personal commitment is one of the most written-about features of the PPF program. He attended 95 per cent of all the PPF courses that ran, setting out his vision for BA and participating in question and answer sessions with staff.[22] This involvement extended beyond the PPF program. Each time he flew, the chief executive would introduce himself to front line staff and passengers and discuss their experience of BA. Once, when a queue formed at the launch of a new service, he helped to deliver breakfasts to customers.[23] In his presence all of the symbols of the "new culture" were expected to be in place—even down to the PPF lapel badges. Staff not wearing one of these had replacements pinned in place and Colin Marshall wore his own PPF badge for two years.[24]

But the most impressive aspect of BA's cultural change is not so much the sophistication of the PPF program itself, nor the commitment of executive time, but the extent to which other employment policies and practices were changed to fit the "new" culture and the continued emphasis on these practices and programs throughout the 1980s and 1990s. Three-quarters of the 100 Customer First teams, formed to propagate the message of PPF, survived into the 1990s.[25] Not only were team briefings and team working introduced but these were developed and refined with TQM (Total Quality Management), autonomous team working and multi-skilling introduced in many areas. Direct contact with all staff was considered so important that "down route" briefings were developed to ensure that mobile and isolated staff was not neglected and in March 1996 BA became the first company to make daily TV broadcasts to its staff.[26]

The way cabin crew were rostered was also changed. "Families" of staff were created to work the same shift patterns. These were intended to provide mutual support, make cabin crew feel happier about their work environments and, as a result, facilitate the production of emotional labor.[27] A new role of "Passenger Group Co-ordinator" was introduced and staff appointed based entirely on personal qualities. The importance of emotional processes was also reflected in the new appraisal and reward systems such that work was judged on the way in which it was performed as well as against harder targets.[28] Managerial bonuses could be as much as 20 per cent of salary and were calculated on a straight 50:50 split between exhibiting desired behaviors and achieving quantitative goals.[29] *Awards for Excellence* and an *Employee Brainwaves* program encouraged staff input. The Personnel Department was renamed "Human Resources" with many decisions devolved to line managers and, in the first few years of the program at least, a commitment was made to job security.[30]

Building a transparent organisation (MPF)
Closely following these developments, a *Managing People First* (MPF) program targeted managerial employees and aimed to bring their behaviors into line with a list developed by two consultancy firms.[31] As on PPF, the emphasis on this five-day course was on quasi-group therapy and experiential exercises. Outward Bound courses were also intended to support the re-shaping of personality and the small groups formed on these residential programs were expected to act as mutual support vehicles once back in the workplace.

Other courses were developed to maintain the momentum created by *Putting People First* and *Managing People First*. These included *Winning for Customers, A Day in the Life, To Be the Best, Leading in a Service Business* and *Leadership 2000* and, while each was different, they all shared a focus on shaping staff emotions.[32] The most, dramatic form of this was probably the "love bath" exercise in one of the early courses in which delegates took it in turns to sit in the centre of a circle while their colleagues complimented them.[33] Nearly 20 years after the launch of PPF, BA managers attending a training course are still being told about understanding themselves and taking responsibility: "understanding self is our starting point. ... That means that to make a change within the airline we need to start with you—what can *you* do differently?"[34]

The world's favourite cost cutter
Sir Colin Marshall's emphasis on putting people first and caring for one another had been preceded by a rule of fear. BA's first response to its problems had been a massive series of redundancies, the largest in British history at the time, with staff numbers reduced by 40 per cent between 1981 and 1983.[35] Senior staff was not exempt from this process, with 161 managers and senior executives being "removed" overnight on one memorable occasion in 1983 known as the "night of the long knives."[36]

Brave as the act was in the long term, no chief executive can make redundant such a large proportion of the top management without discomfort or regret. This event is particularly important because of the sweeping commitment to change that it represented. The values, beliefs and bureaucratic apparatus associated with the "transportation culture" were dealt a severe blow in a single action. Most of the mass termination included managers and executives who had come from the transportation/ technical culture. This is an important issue because the culture was very strong, based on values that the men had developed over many years of working together and trusting each other: it was clearly unable to cope with "the customer is boss." The total reversal of authority that was suggested by a customer point of view was anathema to quasi-military thinkers and the values they brought to the organization, while honest and sincere, they clearly would have represented an enormous obstacle for any further change efforts.

There must be some commitment break with the past, to reduce the significance of prior values. It should be recognized that this represents destruction but in my view, some degree of destruction is necessary before any real reconstruction can begin. At BA, the "night of the long knives" was a significant destructive event, clearing the way of debris and providing a fresh environment within which new kinds of managers and leaders could and would emerge very quickly.

Aftermath of the privatization of BA

In 1984, BA became a public limited company in preparation for privatization and was fully floated on the London Stock Exchange in February 1987. Since privatization, profits have continued to increase, often against the grain of the industry as a whole which suffered severely in the 1989–92 recession and BA continued to gain respect as an excellent company. This is in stark contrast to the days when it was said that BA stood for "Bloody Awful" and its service levels were an international joke.

By 1988, BA had reversed its fortunes by producing profits at record levels with pre-tax earnings exceeding £200 million for the first time.[37] The company was now more profitable than any of the large international carriers, including KLM, Cathay Pacific and United Airlines. Their success continued, with BA remaining highly profitable through 1990–5, when the worst recession the industry had ever known forced many operators out of the business, aggregate losses for the international airline industry reached almost US$16 billion in 1990–3, and it was not until 1994/5 that the industry as a whole managed to pull back into profits.[38] Meanwhile, BA was way ahead with pre-tax profits at £327 million (1994/1995), on a turnover of £7.23 billion, showing a near three-fold increase in profitability and a 45-per-cent increase in turnover during the five-year-period from 1990.[39] There was further improvement during 1995/6 with profit before tax up to a record £585 million and turnover reaching £7.8 billion.[40]

Profit margins rose from 2 per cent in 1982 to 6 per cent in 1984 and 1985 and 8 per cent in 1990 as market share was taken from other airlines.[41] The company was voted "Best Airline in Europe and Across the Atlantic" by a leading industry journal in 1991 and won numerous other awards.[42]

BA achieved a remarkable turnaround during the 1980s, from a loss-ridden state-owned organization to a highly competitive global company respected worldwide for its performance with profits and market-share continuing their upward trend into the 1990s. The sale of BA is widely regarded as one of the most successful of the UK privatization program.

Between 1991 and 1992, BA moved up 397 places from 908 to 511 on the Business Week Global 1,000 list, with a market value of US$3.85 billion. These changes have made it a fearsome competitor in the global skies, changing its image from "Bloody Awful" to "Bloody Awesome."[43]

Fundamentals of BA

More fundamentally, the company was well provided with slots in Britain's prestigious Heathrow airport and faced little competition on many of the routes that it served. European markets were still tightly regulated and market share often depended on negotiation skills rather than competitive success. In 1987 just before privatization, BA controlled some 60 per cent of the UK domestic market and only experienced competition on 9 per cent of routes into and out of the UK.[44] Post privatization its position was actually strengthened when it gained a 75 per cent share of domestic routes.[45] Such was BA's dominance during this period that it could almost charge what it liked. Moreover, BA built up a series of alliances and mergers to consolidate this position.[46]

POISED FOR INTERNATIONAL GROWTH: ACQUISITIONS AND ALLIANCES

British Caledonian (BCal) was formed in 1970 through the merger of Caledonian Airways and British United Airways. For many years, BCal was BA's only large domestic competitor, fighting vigorously under the direction of Sir Adam Thompson for more favorable operating rights from the British government. When Britain's Civil Aviation Authority recommended the reallocation of BA routes to BCal in 1984, Lord King threaten to resign. Instead BA was instructed to trade its profitable Middle East routes for some of BCal's less profitable Latin American destinations. The Middle Eastern routes became much less popular during 1986 as a result of regional tensions and falling oil prices. BCal which had been generating a fair profit started to lose money and was faced with bankruptcy.

In July 1987, BA acquired BCal for £237 million in shares.[47] The new airline had almost 200 aircrafts and by combining BA's 560,000 kilometre network, now formed one of the world's largest airline companies. Several smaller independent British airline companies unsuccessfully challenged the BA/BCal merger on the grounds that the new company would dominate both London's Heathrow and Gatwick airports, forcing them to relocate to the less accessible and underdeveloped field at Stansted.

With its dominance of the home market secure for the time being, BA aggressively expanded into Europe, North America and the Far East over the next several years aiming to become a global airline. Its foray into the then lucrative US market came in 1988 when it formed a marketing alliance with United Airlines designed to feed customers from one carrier to the other. This partnership set the pattern for BA's expansion. It would not be based on forming new airlines outside Britain or acquiring them, but rather through strategic alliances. Nevertheless, this partnership collapsed a little more than two years later. Then the two strongest US airlines had purchased the Heathrow rights from the floundering Pan Am and TWA, immediately increasing competition in BA's home market.

While the alliance with United was still operating, BA suffered losses in Europe in 1990 and 1991 because of the first Gulf War. Shortly after that, in July 1991, it entered into an alliance with Aeroflot in Russia to create a new airline called Air Russia. After several false starts over the next few years, the venture never got off ground. Additional proposed alliances failed for assorted other reasons. Officials from BA and KLM Royal Dutch Airlines held merger discussions in 1991 and 1992. But talks broke down over the valuation of the two firms. Later in 1992, BA attempted to purchase 44 per cent of USAir Inc. for US$750 million.[48]

American, United and Delta Airlines (the US "Big Three") vigorously lobbied against the deal and demanded enhanced access to the British market if the deal was to be approved by the US government. In December 1992 the USAir purchase was blocked.

That same month, the first in a string of alliances was struck when the airline paid £450 million for 25 per cent of Qantas, the Australian-based international airline.[49] BA next acquired a 49.9 per cent stake in the French independent carrier TAT European airlines and later launched a start-up in Germany called Deutsche BA with 49 per cent ownership.[50] Through these alliances, BA enhanced its position in Europe and the Far East. It then refocused its attention across the Atlantic where it restructured an offer for a piece of USAir into US$400 million purchase of 25 per cent of the company.[51] This alliance received the US government's approval. The US government also approved a code-sharing arrangement that enabled the partners to offer their customers a seamless operation where they use both airlines to reach their destinations.

The "Row" with Virgin's Sir Richard Branson

While the entire deal-making was going on abroad, BA faced an embarrassing and costly fight at home with Sir Richard Branson's Virgin Atlantic Airlines. Since starting operations in the early 1980s, Virgin had made some inroads against BA primarily by focusing on customer service, something "Bloody Awful" BA had neglected for years. Sir Richard filed a suit against BA in 1991 alleging that BA had smeared him and his airline, conducted "dirty tricks" such as spreading rumors about Virgin's insolvency, and that BA used its shared booking information with Virgin to persuade Virgin customers to transfer to BA, informing them (incorrectly) that Virgin flights were no longer available. In 1993, the suit was settled out of court with BA offering a public apology and paying £500,000 to Sir Richard and £110,000 to Virgin.[52] The case also led to the resignation of Lord King as the chairman of BA. Second in command Sir Colin Marshall took over as the chairman. Further litigation followed between the two rivals, most seriously a US$1 billion antitrust suit brought by Virgin in the US.[53] Various suits damaged BA's reputation and led to comments from *The Economist* (March 4, 1995): "BA now looks ... like an anxious, overbearing giant trying to squash a feisty little rival."

With its Virgin difficulties continuing, BA's overseas partners suffered huge losses: in 1993 Qantas lost US$271 million, while in 1994 TAT lost US$60 million and USAir lost US$350 million.[54] The situation at USAir was so grim that BA declared that they would hold back an additional US$450 million investment in the firm until the carrier re-established itself back in the black.[55] The alliances continued to deteriorate and in pursuit of more promising partnerships, BA eventually sold its stakes in USAir in 1997.

As it approached the long awaited 1997 deregulation of the European airline industry, BA was on solid ground. In the process of becoming one of the largest airlines in the world, it has also managed to remain one of the most profitable at that time. In mid-1996, BA announced plans for a broad alliance with American Airlines. Under this plan, the two carriers would coordinate schedule and pricing, code-share (sell seats) and more importantly, share profits and revenues. Together they submitted a joint application to the US Department of Transportation requesting approval of the proposed venture and granting antitrust immunity. The plan was vehemently attacked by competitors on the basis that it will permit the two airlines to monopolize cross Atlantic traffic between Heathrow and the US. Both airlines had, in fact, previously refused to relinquish takeoff and landing slots at Heathrow; combined they would control 85 per cent of the peak takeoff slots in the largest single aviation market in the world. Intermittent negotiations and attempts to secure antitrust immunity continued into 2001, with both airlines struggling to agree on terms more conducive to an "open skies" agreement between Britain and the US. Competitors United Airlines and Lufthansa had already secured antitrust immunity and prospered from the "open skies" between Germany and the US. Air France and Delta Airlines then threatened BA and American Airlines as well.

"One World" alliance

Separately, the "One World" alliance formed in 1998 by BA and a group of others eventually became one of the most successful. Officially launched in February 1999 by BA, American Airlines, Qantas and Canadian Airlines and Cathay Pacific, it provided an interchangeable network of frequent filers to claim rewards. The group eventually grew to eight members and 23 affiliates by 2001 and collectively served more than 200 million passengers in 133 countries with 566 destinations.

ON THE BRINK; PREPARING FOR INDUSTRY CONSOLIDATION AND A GLOBAL FUTURE

Starting in the mid-1990s, BA began investing in advanced information technologies to build a "virtual airline" to expedite ticketing, scheduling and customer service functions. It also began outsourcing "non-core" operations that had been previously overstaffed such as ground transport services, in-flight catering and heavy engine maintenance. This is to reduce costs and allow the company to refocus squarely on operating its air network. The outsourcing frustrated industrial relations and failed to significantly reduce employee numbers. Further, industry analysts speculated that the airline would be more vulnerable to an economic downturn because it would no longer have secondary resources of revenue to offset the accompanying downturn in air travel revenues. Not surprisingly, when the air travel market slowed in 1998, BA's net profits of US$330 million dropped precipitously to US$34 million.[56]

Bob Ayling

Bob Ayling's time as head of BA had been associated with a number of controversies such as the rebranding attempt, dropping the Union flag from the aircraft, and the attempt to match low-cost rivals. Between 1998 and 1999, profits fell by 61 per cent, and in 2000, BA announced losses of £244 million on its main business.[57] While gains from disposals succeeded in keeping the company out of the red this was its worst performance (and first loss) since privatization.[58] The new logo Bob Ayling had launched (at the expense of £60 million[59]) during the 1997 dispute was unpopular and had to be withdrawn. Subsequently, BA started to repaint its aircraft with Britain's national flag, only two years after the airline had announced the Union Jack would be phased out. BA then had the tail fins of its aircraft painted with a wide variety of ethnic designs from all over the world, which looked like junkyard graffiti. These failures so colored the public perception of the chief executive that even his attempts to refocus BA onto profitable routes and introduce a new seat for business class long-haul passengers were not entirely welcomed.

Subsequently, BA ditched the much-criticized "ethnic" tailfin logos on half of its fleet and replaced them with a red, white and blue Union Jack-based design. The airline said UK customers had not been won over by the abstract "world images" designs introduced two years ago.[60] The much criticized re-branding exercise featured designs from Delft pottery to Chinese calligraphy. They were commissioned from international and British artists in an effort to reflect the airline's "cosmopolitan" outlook. But the move in 1997 provoked immediate criticism. Baroness Thatcher famously draped her handkerchief over a model aircraft sporting one of the new tail designs at a Conservative party conference, calling it "awful."[61] Market research found that British customers, who make up 40 per cent of the airline's business, had not taken to the new designs.[62] On March 10, 2000, Bob Ayling resigned as chief executive.

Rod Eddington

Tapped for the role of chief executive in May 2000, Rod Eddington set out to reduce exposure in unprofitable and non-core areas, selling stakes in Air Liberte and even placing its own no-frills carrier, Go (launched only in 1998), on the market. Plans to build Gatwick into a second international hub were abandoned. Instead, unprofitable routes were suspended and key long-haul routes were relocated to Heathrow. Smaller aircraft, especially Boeing 777s, would replace the older, larger aircraft and play a major role in a new fleet strategy. With bigger business travel sections, each new aircraft could seat a greater number of premium business travellers and help cut excess capacity.

In an effort to create a more appealing environment for its premium business travellers, BA invested in costly product and service enhancements. These included passenger seats that expand into six-foot-flat beds for in-flight sleeping; new state-of-the-art in-flight entertainment; and modernized airport lounges with an upscale look and feel. A veteran of Cathay Pacific and Ansett, Eddington's approach improved both operations and morale. During his first year, the airline faced a number of adversities. Following a tragic Air France Concorde accident in Paris in 2000, BA's entire Concorde fleet was grounded. In addition, foot and mouth disease caused a serious decline in air travel and tourism in Britain, and rising oil prices doubled fuel prices.

Rod Eddington[63] was born on January 2, 1950 in Australia. He attended University of Western Australia, Perth. Being awarded the Rhodes scholarship, he completed a doctorate at the department of engineering and science in Oxford in 1974. Subsequently, he taught as a research lecturer at Pembroke College, Oxford from 1978–9. For this career, he joined the Swire group, the holding company for Cathay Pacific, in 1978. He worked his way through Cathay Pacific being based in Hong Kong, South Korea and Japan, eventually becoming managing director in 1992. Eddington left Swire in January 1997 to become executive chairman of Ansett, the Australian airline owned by Rupert Murdoch, based in Melbourne. In April 2000, he left after Murdoch had sold 50 per cent of Ansett's shares. He then joined BA as chief executive in April, soon after the dismissal of Bob Ayling. Currently, he still remains on the board of News Corporation.

Challenges facing BA

According to the House of Lords inquiry into airline competition, there are now more than 500 airline alliances involving around 200 airlines.[64] Many of these alliances involve code-sharing, where a particular airline books passengers onto another airline's plane that is operating on the same route. This allows airlines to maintain capacity on particular routes without the considerable fixed costs than operating a route on their own would bring. Since deregulation in the European airline market, in 1987, a wave of cooperative arrangements or alliances has occurred. These alliances have been designed to achieve fleet rationalization, expansion and rationalization of the structure of the flight path network, and purchasing and marketing economies of scale.[65] The largest of the major global alliances include the "Star Alliance" and "One World." The "Star Alliance" major partners include Lufthansa, Scandinavian Airline System (SAS), United Airlines, Air Canada, Thai Airways and Singapore Airlines. This is currently the most established of the alliances, beginning as it did with a 10-year agreement between Lufthansa and SAS, blessed by the European Union (EU), to set up "an operationally and commercially integrated transport system" in 1996.[66] "One World" comprises BA, American Airlines, Canadian Airlines, Cathay Pacific, Qantas, Finnair and Iberia. As the industry consolidates and passenger volumes decline, increasing importance is placed on the role of strategic alliances within the airline industry. Jean-Cyril Spinetta, the Air France chairman, believes that a shake-out in the European airline industry will eventually leave only BA, Air France and Lufthansa, as they currently lead the major strategic alliances with the European airline industry.[67] Recently BA and KLM have announced a "cooperation pact" which will see them selling tickets on each other's flights as well as their own. There was speculation that this could be the first stage in a full merger plan, although the two companies abandoned merger plans in September 2000.[68]

Emergence of Ryanair and Easyjet
As a result of the deregulation of the European airline industry, major national carriers like BA have seen a downturn in their economic outlook. Their experience has been similar to the US experience of deregulation in the late 1970s, in that the new competitive environment has allowed the entry of low-cost carriers. These include Go (set up, but since sold off, by BA), Easyjet and Ryanair (both newly formed independent operators). This mirrored the process of the development of low-cost airlines in the US, for example Southwest Airlines. In Britain, it seems that low-cost airlines are actually thriving while their larger, more established counterparts such as BA are struggling. For instance, passenger volumes on Ryanair have increased considerably since they were set up, while Easyjet currently has another 23 Boeing 737-700s on order for May 2001 to cope with a projected rise in demand for its no-frills airline service.[69] Meanwhile Ryanair has placed an industry advertisement for expression of interest to sell it 50 second-hand Boeing 737s with a preference for aeroplanes aged between seven and 14 years.[70]

Low-cost airliners seem to possess the competitive advantage of operating at significant lower costs than their larger national counterparts. They have achieved this partly by operating with lower wage costs, more flexible employment and quicker airport turnaround times. In addition, they have tended to cut costs of landing charges by flying to and from provincial, regional airports rather than major hubs such as Heathrow. Furthermore, they have reduced channel marketing costs by reducing their reliance on travel agents and other middlemen. The low-cost airline services tend to operate their own virtual customer service networks offering their customers quick book and search facilities through the Internet with minimum fuss and cost. Both Ryanair and Easyjet are growing rapidly, with a turnover of £487.7 million and £356.9 million and pre-tax profits of £123.4 million and £40.1 million respectively.[71]

September 11 and the war on terror
When the first plane flew into the World Trade Centre in New York at around 9 am local time on September 11, 2001, and a second plane crashed within the hour, the world and the aviation industry changed considerably. Airline passenger confidence took a considerable knocking. Passenger volumes dropped considerably as people, fearing further terrorist attacks, decided to stay at home. Governments around the world began to pass legislation to alter existing flight paths over cities and enforce extra security measures on airline companies as a consequence. In the wake of the attacks, Swissair (the Swiss national carrier) and Sabena (the Belgian national carrier) collapsed because of the considerable downturn in demand. Most other national carriers had operating losses for the 2001/02 financial year.[72] Passenger volumes declined within Europe by over 10 per cent, by 35 per cent from Europe to the US, and by 17 per cent from Europe to Asia, in September and October 2001. BA reported losses of around £750 million for the 2002 financial year.[73]

Conclusion: what's next for BA?

What's next? Or better: What's next after next? The ability to develop a vision for the business and convey all the airline resources in that direction will be the key to success in the future. The structure of the industry changes continually with new carriers entering the market and others revising their strategy. The pursuit of globalization seems to be the main concern of a handful of airlines trying to build up a network which could offer a global coverage, whilst most of the airlines look for niche markets to survive.

The implication for communications in globalization are enormous, starting from devising an international advertising campaign to the need of bonding staff scattered all over the world. A true marketing orientation, a focus on total customer care through excellent service and effective communications are the key elements for success. If BA wants to stay ahead and eventually realize its globalization strategy it will have to look carefully after its partner airlines to realize that perception of a seamless network.

ENDNOTES
1. Gretchen Antelman (2002).
2. Gretchen Antelman (2002).
3. Ibid.
4. Ibid.
5. Ibid.
6. Ibid.
7. Ibid.
8. Ibid.
9. George Litwin, John Bray, Kathleen Lusk Brooke (1996).
10. Ibid.
11. Ibid.
12. Ibid.
13. Ahmed Galal (1994).
14. Andrew Cox, Lisa Harris, and David Parker (1999).
15. Quoted in D. Heald and D. Steel (1982).
16. Andrew Cox, Lisa Harris, and David Parker (1999).
17. Madhukar Shukla (1997).
18. George Litwin, John Bray, Kathleen Lusk Brooke (1996).
19. I Grugulis and A Wilkinson (2001).
20. Ibid.
21. Barsoux J-L and Manzoni J-F (1997) p.14.
22. Georgiades, N. and Macdonell R. (1998).
23. Höpfl H. (1993).
24. Georgiades, N. and Macdonell R. (1998) p. 209.
25. I. Grugulis and A Wilkinson (2001).
26. Colling T. (1995).
27. J. L. Barsoux and J.F. Manzoni (1997).
28. N.Georgiades and R. Macdonell (1998); H. Höpfl (1993).
29. I. Grugulis and A. Wilkinson (2001).
30. Ibid.
31. N.Georgiades and R. Macdonell (1998) p. 174.
32. Ibid.
33. See H. Höpfl (1993) for an account of participants' reactions to this process.
34. I. Grugulis and A. Wilkinson (2001).
35. George Litwin, John Bray, Kathleen Lusk Brooke (1996).
36. J. L. Barsoux and J. F. Manzoni (1997).
37. Andrew Cox, Lisa Harris, and David Parker (1999).
38. Ibid.

39 Ibid
40 Ibid.
41 Ibid.
42 Ibid.
43 Matthew Bishop, John Kay, Colin Mayer (1994).
44 Monopolies and Mergers Commission (1987).
45 T. Colling (1995).
46 Ibid.
47 Gretchen Antelman (2002).
48 Ibid.
49 Ibid.
50 Ibid.
51 Ibid.
52 Ibid.
53 Ibid.
54 Ibid.
55 Ibid.
56 Gretchen Antelman (2002).
57 I. Grugulis and A. Wilkinson (2001).
58 Ibid.
59 *BBC World service* (1999a).
60 *BBC World service* (1999b).
61 Ibid.
62 Ibid
63 *The Guardian*, September 22, 2001.
64 House of Lords (1998).
65 J. Stragier (1999).
66 Ibid.
67 Airline Industry Information (2001).
68 Done and Odell (2002).
69 Done (2002).
70 Ibid.
71 Ross Brennan, Paul Baines, Paul Garneau (2003).
72 Ibid.
73 Ibid.

REFERENCES

Ahmed Galal. *Welfare Consequences of Selling Public Enterprises: An Empirical Analysis* Oxford, New York: Published for the World Bank [by] Oxford University Press, 1994.

Airline Industry Information. *Air France Chairman Sees Consolidation of European Airline Industry*, March 14, 2001.

Andrew Cox, Lisa Harris, and David Parker. *Privatisation and Supply Chain Management: On the Effective Alignment of Purchasing and Supply after Privatisation.* New York: Routledge, 1999.

Gretchen Antelman. *International Directory of Company Histories/Writers and Researchers.* Chicago: St. James Press, 2002.

J. L. Barsoux and J. F. Manzoni. *Becoming the World's Favourite Airline: British Airways 1980–1993.* Bedford: European Case Clearing House, 1997.

BBC World Service. Broadcast on January 28, 2004. *BA Slashes Another £300m in Costs.* http://news.bbc.co.uk/1/hi/business/3431815.stm, 2004.

BBC World service. Broadcast on June 6, 1999. *British Airways to Look More "British".* http://www.bbc.co.uk/worldservice/business/story_air120699.shtml, 1999a.

BBC World service. Broadcast on June 6, 1999. *BA to Fly the Flag Again.* http://news.bbc.co.uk/1/hi/business/362203.stm, 1999b.

Matthew Bishop, John Kay and Colin Mayer. *Privatization and Economic Performance.* Oxford, New York: Oxford University Press, 1994.

Ross Brennan, Paul Baines and Paul Garneau. *Contemporary Strategic Marketing.* Basingstoke, Hants: Palgrave Macmillan, 2003.

T. Colling. "Experiencing turbulence: competition, strategic choice and the management of human resources in British Airways," *Human Resource Management Journal*, 1995, vol. 5, no. 5, pp. 18–32.

K. Done and M. Odell. "BA and KLM ready for 'Cooperation Pact'," *Financial Times.* January 7, 2002.

K. Done. "No frills yet plenty of soaring ambitions," *Financial Times.* January 7, 2002.

H. Landis Gabel. *European Casebook on Industrial and Trade Policy.* New York: Prentice Hall, 1995.

N. Georgiades and R. Macdonell. *Leadership for Competitive Advantage.* London: John Wiley & Sons, 1998.

I. Grugulis and A. Wilkinson. *British Airways: Culture and Structure. Loughborough University Research Series paper 2001*, p. 4.

D. Heald and D. Steel. "Privatising public enterprise: an analysis of the government case," in *Political Quarterly*, July 1982, pp. 333–49.

H. Höpfl. "Culture and commitment: British Airways," in D. Gowler, K. Legge and C. Clegg, *Case Studies in Organizational Behaviour and Human Resource Management*, London: PCP, 1993.

House of Lords. "European Communities: thirty second report–airline competition," Select Committee on European Communities, November 1998, http://www.publications.parliment.uk/pa/id199798/idselect/ideucom/156/15602.htm.

George Litwin, John Bray and Kathleen Lusk Brooke. *Mobilising the Organization: Bringing Strategy to Life.* New York: Prentice Hall, 1996.

Madhukar Shukla. *Competing through Knowledge: Building a Learning Organisation.* Thousand Oaks, CA: Sage Publications Inc., 1997.

Monopolies and Mergers Commission. *British Airways plc and British Caledonian Group plc: A Report on the Proposed Merger*. 247 London: HMSO, 1987.

Steven E. Prokesch. "Competing on Customer Service: An Interview with British Airways' Sir Colin Marshall," *Harvard Business Review* Nov/Dec 1995, vol. 73 issue 6.

J. Stragier. "Current issues arising from airline alliances," 11th Annual Conference, *Recent Developments in European Air Transport Law and Policy*, Lisbon, November 5, 1999, http://europa.eu.int/comm/compeition/spppeches/text/sp1999678_en.html.

"We are flying into turbulence," *The Economist*. March 4, 1995, pp. 64–6.

The Guardian. Septmber 22, 2001.

CHAPTER 9

Honda Dares to be Different

HERBERT PANG SHEN HONG

INTRODUCTION

Honda Motor Company is today Japan's second biggest automobile maker after Toyota Motor. It has performed tremendously well recently, establishing a new ¥116.7 billion quarterly profit for the January–March period in 2004. Besides its astounding performance, Honda Motor has also incited much interest due to its unique management style and illustrious history. Though Honda Motor maintains the common characteristics of Japanese management, it is unique in many ways.

The story of the two founders of Honda Motor, Soichiro Honda and Takeo Fujisawa, actually casts light upon the unique principles of management adopted by the company as the company philosophy reflects in many aspects the characters of both Honda and Fujisawa. For a better understanding of the two dynamic personalities which led to a successful Honda Motor, a brief account of the formative years of the two men will be given. Then the management practices of Honda will be discussed.

SOICHIRO HONDA (1906–1992)

The eldest son of a poor blacksmith and bicycle repairman, Soichiro Honda was born in 1906. He was fascinated by machinery since he was young and his favourite pastime was to watch a gasoline-powered engine at a nearby rice-polishing mill. In 1922, after eight years of schooling, Soichiro became an apprentice at Art Shokai, an automobile repair shop in Tokyo. As an apprentice, Honda's job was to baby-sit his master's child. As the shop became busier, however, Honda was ordered to help out with auto repairs.

Then in 1923, an earthquake struck Tokyo, bringing Art Shokai to ruins. This catastrophic event brought Soichiro closer to his dreams. Honda and the senior apprentice stayed behind to learn auto repairs after Art Shokai ceased business operations. Encouraged by Yuzo Sakakibara, the owner of Art Shokai, who was a zealous racing fan, Soichiro built a racing car in his free time. Honda built a racer powered by an 8-litre, Curtis-Wright aircraft engine that had nearly 100 horsepower at 1,400 rpm. Apart from the engine, Honda built everything himself.

In 1928, Soichiro was granted permission to set up a branch of Art Shokai in Hamamatsu. He carried on his passion for racing, building more racing cars. As cars raced anti-clockwise in Japan then, Honda tilted a Ford engine to the left for better control and fixed a supercharger for more power. To overcome the heating problem of this car, he added an auxiliary radiator and made valve seats from a heat conducting metal.

Soichiro entered the 1936 All-Japan Speed Rally and set a speed record of 120 kph, a record which lasted 20 years. However, a collision with a car leaving the pit stop denied him of victory in that race and left him seriously injured. The next year, Honda set up Tokai Seiki Heavy Industry to manufacture piston rings which he thought would be a profitable business as piston rings were very costly then, and it seemed simple to make them by die-casting.

The task of producing piston rings proved to be more difficult than expected when the first piston rings produced had no elasticity and were useless. He approached the owners of neighboring foundries for help, but they would only teach the secrets of their trade to apprentices. Honda worked day and night but could not solve the impending problem. Until then he had been very sceptical about the value of education: "If a theory led you to an invention, all school teachers would become inventors". This time, he yielded to his lack of knowledge and called upon Professor Yoshinobu Fujii of Hamamatsu High School of Technology.

Soichiro was told that his piston rings did not contain enough silicone and he made the decision to go back to school. Nine months after his first attempt, Honda managed to make a satisfactory prototype.

The school principal Tei Adachi once summoned Honda to his office and told him that he would not be awarded a diploma, because he had not taken the examinations. "Diploma? That's worth less than a movie ticket. The ticket guarantees that you can get into the theatre. But the diploma doesn't guarantee that you can make a living," Honda is reported to have replied.

During the World War II, Soichiro's business did well due to the increased demand for machines and auxiliary parts. When most of Japan's able bodied young men were enlisted to fight the war, many production techniques could no longer be used as the factories were now staffed by women. Thus, Honda invented automatic machines which made it possible for women to take over the heavy production tasks. Honda also invented new tools to reduce the manufacturing time of aircraft propellers from a week to half an hour at the request of the military.

After the war, Honda sold Tokai Seiki to Toyota Motor for ¥450,000 and took a one year break. The passionate and enthusiastic Honda was the technical brain behind the rise of Honda Motor. He began early in life to learn technical skills and being adventurous, he tried many different solutions to various problems, making him quite a successful innovator in his field. This spirit was carried on in Honda Motor where employees are encouraged to try different methods of solving problems no matter how unconventional.

Though he had started with scepticism for education, he learned that there was value in education. But passion and drive always took precedence over education. This attitude can be seen from Honda's hiring of graduates from lesser known universities with a love for racing like him.

TAKEO FUJISAWA (1910–1989)

The other man who brought Honda to prominence, Takeo Fujisawa, was born in 1910 to Hideshiro Fujisawa, the owner of an advertising agency. As Japan was prosperous at that time due to the profits made from the World War I, Takeo led a comfortable life in his early elementary school years. However, the depression of the 1920s led to poverty and Takeo read novels by borrowing from his friends in his middle school days.

Though poor, Takeo's father was proud, like the *samurai*. He taught Takeo that he must have confidence in himself no matter how poor. He also taught Takeo the philosophy of equality which boosted his motivation as he did not get a university education.

Takeo graduated from middle school in 1928 and was forced to settle for writing addresses on envelopes and postcards for a living, earning

¥45 a month. In 1930, shortly after turning 20, he enlisted into military service as a cadet. This would enable him to serve one year to complete his obligation as a male citizen, instead of two years.

After he left the military, he continued his old trade of writing addresses. As such work had little status, Fujisawa was looked down upon and he was determined that he would respect the feelings of those under him if he could rise to a higher position.

In 1934, after a few years of searching, he found a job with Mitsuwa Shokai, a small scale commission trader dealing in steel. Takeo was happy as he had always wanted to be a merchant. But his father was displeased with his new job as his salary was only ¥15, a third of what he got previously. He felt that his choice was appropriate as this job did not look at his educational qualifications but at his efforts. Takeo performed well and became the best salesman in the company by the end of the second year, earning ¥150 a month.

In 1936, Takeo, then 27, was entrusted with the management of the company when the owner of Mitsuwa Shokai was called up for military service to fight the Sino-Japanese war. Takeo's leadership made Mitsuwa Shokai a profitable business, earning ¥200,000 in the final months of that year. The war made the government impose stricter controls over the economy, lowering commercial profits and Takeo decided to enter the manufacturing industry. He established the Japan Machine and Tool Research Institute in 1939 with ¥10,000 which he borrowed from his company.

Observing the hard life led by his workers, Takeo wrote to his boss, requesting permission to increase the wages in Mitsuwa Shokai. The owner instructed Takeo to freeze the wages until he returned from the war. Takeo was upset. He decided to run his own business and to leave Mitsuwa Shokai when the owner returned. As severance pay, Takeo received the ¥10,000 which he had used to start the Japan Machine and Tool Research Institute. Takeo was able to lead his new enterprise to produce high quality machine tools and to make good profits. To motivate his employees, he paid them handsomely, giving them good incentives to work hard.

As the tide of the World War II turned against Japan, American bombers starting destroying Tokyo in 1942. By 1945, the bombing raids on Tokyo became frequent, killing hundred thousands of people and devastating the city. In June, Takeo decided to move his company out of Tokyo to Fukushima to avoid the bombings.

Takeo Fujisawa was a practical business-minded individual who had a humane approach to management. He took care of the welfare of his employees and sought to grant them good levels of pay. The organization of Honda Motor was masterminded by the commercial expertise of Takeo.

UNION OF THE STRONG MEN

In October 1946, Soichiro Honda established the Honda Technical Research Institute to recycle engines which were left behind after the World War II. Coincidentally, Takeo Fujisawa had decided to move his business back to Tokyo since the war had ended. He remembered a friend mentioning a young inventor in Tokyo by the name Honda and decided to pay Honda a visit.

"I looked for a financier in Hamamatsu but all the potential investors wanted to recover their money quickly, and I didn't like that." Honda lamented about his difficulty finding a suitable financier for his company. After a lengthy discussion, Fujisawa decided to cooperate with Honda. "I don't have the money now, but I will find what you need to launch your technology." The end of the night marked the dawn of Honda Motor Company.

TRADITIONAL JAPANESE MANAGEMENT

There are many characteristics common to Japanese companies. Though Honda Motor is special in many aspects of its management, it still retains elements common to traditional Japanese management.

First, there is an emphasis on group identity in Japanese companies. The employees are nurtured to feel a collective responsibility for the success of the companies. This is made possible by the lifetime career offered to employees within the organization. Life-long employment and a collective identity are used to build loyalty and create the motivation to work. The underlying belief is that a worker who is protected by the company will feel safe to give his maximum effort in solving work problems. This is in contrast to the US where a culture of individualism exists and employment tends to be short-term.

Second, subordinates are given the trust they need to get on with their work. Employees are seen to have potential for development and the management trains to develop themselves. The training usually prepares employees for a large array of tasks so that they are flexible and are able to undertake multiple roles in the organization.

SPIRIT OF THE FOUNDERS

The resilience of both Honda and Fujisawa can be seen from the personal mottoes they set for themselves and Honda Motor:

- Be original
- Do not rely on the government
- Work for your own sake

All three are important parts of the spirit that dwelled in Honda Motor. But the first—to be original—brings the most pride for the company. Many Japanese firms in various industries took to imitating Western technology to manufacture their products. However, Soichiro Honda never resorted to copying and from the beginning, in his Art Shokai Hamamatsu, had started developing his own technology.

Honda believed that imitating and copying can help a company do well in the short-term but for a company to last, it has to put in its own research and development efforts to innovate new products. As an inventor himself, copying gave him no pride. Only new products which result from creativity could.

Since the day Honda Motor was established in 1948, the management of Honda had never sought government aid, unlike the general business population which usually turned to the government for support during tough times. Many companies even adopted the practice of hiring retired bureaucrats to establish a connection with the government, but Honda shunned such practices.

Thus, the second motto—do not rely on the government—embodies the true spirit of entrepreneurship, embracing free competition and self-reliance.

The third motto—work for your own sake—expresses the work-oriented culture that is present in the company. While traditional Japanese employees identify themselves with the company they work for, Honda focused on motivating the employees through the satisfaction they derive from work. In a modern capitalist economy, people are more motivated by their own interests rather than that of the company.

To guide employees in fulfilling their roles in the organization, company mottoes were developed. These five company mottoes actually summarizes Soichiro's and Takeo's view of an ideal employee:

1. Follow your dreams and keep a youthful outlook
2. Respect theory, new ideas and time
3. Love your work and make your workplace bright and positive
4. Ensure a smooth flow of work
5. Make research a dedicated and daily effort

DUALISM

In Western philosophy, dualism refers to pairs of ideas which are thought to be opposites: individual and group, cost and quality, efficient work and humane work. In the West, it is thought that the two elements in each pair are contradictory and cannot co-exist so management have to trade off the opposites for each other.

Recognizing the advantages of each element in a pair, Honda's management philosophy seeks to retain both sides of the pair, to get the "best of both worlds." Though it isn't easy, there are some examples of how dualism exists in Honda.

There is emphasis on both individuality and group identity in Honda. Individuality and group identity seem like irreconcilable opposites. Yet with certain guidelines, a fine balance can be achieved between the two. We must first note that being individualistic doesn't mean anti-social before we can understand how the two opposites co-exist. In Honda Motor, a group identity exists, just like in the other Japanese firms. Employees develop high levels of loyalty to the organization and co-operate with each other for the good of the company. It is within these limits that Honda allows individualism.

Freedom of expression is encouraged, to nurture a climate of freedom and creativity which allows employees to attempt solving work problems from various approaches. The freedom of expression is contained within the overall goals of the organization and thus, doesn't contradict the group identity.

This unique blend of individualism and group identity leads to an interesting research and development organization in Honda Motor. Honda R&D became a wholly independent subsidiary of Honda Motor so that Soichiro can concentrate on R&D, while Takeo took care of the organizational aspects of the business. In the early days, Soichiro would encourage the different researchers through his own interaction with them. After Honda Motor became a large organization, Kiyoshi Kawashima, the man who took over Soichiro Honda as the president, came up with a technique called "simultaneous competition among different approaches" to manage research work.

Researchers work as individuals or are divided into groups to develop their own solutions to problems. To make good project deadlines, the management signals the pace of research by telling researchers to work faster or slower. Individualism is maintained by the freedom given to researchers while group identity isn't compromised as the employees are constantly working on the same goal, to make Honda a better brand.

The other prominent example of how Honda uses the concept of dualism is in the organization of work to be both efficient and humane. The mass production assembly line system developed by Henry Ford is efficient, but the workers undergo much stress as the pace of work is dictated by the machine. This stress coupled with the monotony of the work would deny the employees a sense of satisfaction from work and leads them to poor performance which is reflected by an increase in defective products.

To make production more humane, the Ford production system is modified into a free-flow system. Instead of having the pace of work determined by the machine, the workers themselves determine the speed at which they work. After completing their tasks, workers would activate the conveyor belt to move the unit to the next station. The humane nature of the work gives the worker control over the work processes and thus, the worker derives more satisfaction and is motivated to do his best. The free-flow production line system shows the ability of Honda Motor to develop fresh and original ideas.

TOP MANAGEMENT ORGANIZATION

"I have burnt all the energy I had to give during these 10 years as president. I now need time off to recharge and refuel. In any case, a change of leadership is vital to keep the organization young and vigorous." Kiyoshi Kawashima said when he was the second president of Honda Motor at the age of 55.

Takeo Fujisawa also saw the need for the leadership of Honda Motor to remain young and vigorous. In 1973, he retired together with Soichiro Honda. After retirement, they did not retain control of the company and left the operations of the company to the new leaders. Such an attitude was passed down to the future leaders of the company, and Honda Motor has a record of young and energetic leaders.

In the early years of the company, the entire organization was very much directed by the forceful leadership of its founding leaders. When they were about to retire, they saw that Honda Motor had grown to become a big organization that needed a structure to ensure smooth operations. Thus, Fujisawa made sure that an organization scheme was set up before he retired.

All forms of communication are important to prevent the organization from becoming sluggish and bureaucratic. Vertical communication tends to be smoother than horizontal communication in an organization due to the usual competition between departments of a company. So Fujisawa came up with a Joint Boardroom (JBR) concept to encourage horizontal communication and group decision-making at the management level.

The JBR changes the nature of the organization from one of individual leadership to that of team leadership. The executives of the company have their desks in one large common room, rather than the conventional arrangement of each managerial executive having his own room. The JBR makes it easy for management executives from various departments to discuss projects and allows them to build a shared vision for the organization. Working relations between the various departments are good as constant interaction and co-operation on problems build team spirit. The seniority of the executives is reflected by the position of their desks in the JBR.

Though many other companies sought to improve communications within their organization, their attempts rarely go beyond leaving office doors open. Thus, the JBR concept again demonstrates Honda's creativity and boldness.

THE COMPLEMENTARITY PRINCIPLE

There is always a measure of risk in business as success is never guaranteed. Therefore an essential part of a company's management strategy involves the creation of a kind of safety net, which regulates the level of risk undertaken by the company. Honda's answer to this problem came in the complementarity policy. Risky ventures are balanced by more stable ones, and daring and sales-oriented executives are made to work alongside those who are more cautious and technologically-oriented.

The complementarity principle is the result of many experiences accumulated over the years. In 1966, sales to the US fell to a third of the level sold in the previous year. The Vietnam War had grown from a civil war within a Southeast Asian country into a major conflict. As the US committed itself deeper into the war, there were repercussions on the domestic and international economy. Stocks piled up, and as the company had concentrated on US and Southeast Asian sales, cash flow was tight and the company was facing a crisis.

Honda made model changes to the Super Cub motorcycle and reduced excess stock by reducing prices and throwing in accessories. Luckily, the growth of sales in Southeast Asia, ironically including war-torn Vietnam, were rising. The crisis gradually relieved and Honda Motor survived, learning a useful lesson. The rising Asian market had complemented the waning US market to enable the company to survive.

The complementarity principle is used to reduce the risk of running into a similar crisis. As Honda produced both motorcycles and cars, Honda can apply this principle across products. As the two products are quite different, they respond differently to economic changes. For example, in 1975 when the US went through a depression, motorcycle sales fell, while car sales rose. Thus, total sales in the US didn't fall but grew instead.

Honda used the complementarity in its product market in two other ways. Firstly, a balance is achieved between its domestic market and its overseas market. Secondly, Honda balances the various regional markets. Such a system can provide a substantial safety net if the company exports to a large number of markets. Today, Honda Motor exports to a hundred odd countries and has production facilities in over 30 countries, enabling it to use complementarity in its production and sales to cushion fluctuations.

Demystifying the Honda miracle?

There have been critics who remain cynical about such rags-to-riches success stories such as Honda. They believe that these stories are hyped up and are receiving attention beyond their educational value due to the eagerness of businessmen to recreate the success achieved by the industrial giants. These people doubt that business monographs reveal the essential ingredients to a successful business. Though there are lessons on management that may be acquired from the reading of the histories of great companies such as Honda, these critics have a point. There have been cases where business leaders fell after granting interviews and writing books on their successes. In these declines, businesses crumble quickly and are sometimes obliterated.

Honda's move into the limelight has been credited to the extreme growth which the company had over a short span of a few decades: from a small scooter manufacturer to a colossal multinationally-renowned car maker. This interest is strengthened by Honda's ability to withstand the test of time and partly also due to interest in the West on the secrets of Japanese industrial might.

The idealistic philosophical propositions about loving work and individualism have been seen as mere rhetorical statements. The company mottoes propagated seem too idealistic for practice. It would be difficult for all employees to hold onto the five mottoes due to the extreme variety of roles different workers fulfil.

All companies have a finite budget for research and development. Thus, a company has to limit the number of research projects undertaken and modern research requires large financial capital outlays, further reducing an organization's ability to embark upon several research projects. Management analysts question the extent to which individualism is encouraged by the commissioning of research projects to study different methods of solving the same problem.

Charges of imitation have been raised against Honda's management. The so-called "complementarity principle" is similar to the practice of diversifying risk by organizations in the West. It is as if Honda had re-discovered the wheel and renamed the technique into some fancy term.

Even the JBR concept was not spared from such attacks. Though Samuel Eilon pointed out that merchant banks in the UK and US used to have partners sitting together, I do not see how that can be likened to the JBR concept of locating all managerial executives together. The scale is too diverse for any form of comparison. Eilon, however, scored when he suggested that accounts of the JBR by books on Honda left many questions unanswered. Has the absence of privacy inhibited confidential discussions between individual directors and their subordinates? What arrangements were made for thinking and private contemplation?

CONCLUSION

Honda Motor has more than just its phenomenal success to boast. It has shown itself to be a nimble and effective company that is quick to adjust in key aspects such as product development and market strategies. Such organizational flexibility reflects a high degree of integration between the sales, engineering development and production departments, demonstrating the efficiency of horizontal communications channels within the company.

Blessed with a line of good leaders (perhaps successive capable leaders were the result of a culture of learning and training), Honda Motor had achieved great results with its bold decision-making. The learning culture of the company which sees the company evolving with the addition new management tricks enables it to effectively take risks.

Honda has shown itself to be a dynamic company with special management practices. Despite attempts to criticize Honda and depict it as "just another firm which happens to achieve," the Honda experience is just too different to be viewed in such a light. As long as the company continues to withstand the test of time and press on with its march upwards, it will remain an extraordinary case study for all students of international business practices.

REFERENCES

Tetsuo Sakiya. *Honda Motor: The Men, The Management, The Machines*. Kodansha International Ltd., 1982.

Setsuo Mito. *The Honda Book Of Management: A Leadership Philosophy for High Industrial Success*. The Anthlone Press, 1990.

A. Mair. *Honda's Global Local Corporation*. St. Martin's Press, 1994.

Eilon Samuel. *Management Strategies: A Critique of Theories and Practices*. Kluwer Academic Publishers, 2000.

M. Marquardt, and A. Reyolds. *The Global Learning Organization*. Irwin Professional Publishing, 1994.

H. Mintzberg, and J. B. Quinn. *Readings in the Strategy Process*, 3rd edition. Prentice Hall, 1998.

CHAPTER 10

Forza Ferrari: The F1 Legend and its Corporate History

JUSTIN TAI WEI CHUEN

INTRODUCTION

Not many brand names evoke great emotions identified in terms of national pride, but Ferrari is definitely in that class. Italians like to remark that only two things unite them: the soccer team and Ferrari (Andrews, 1993). Italy was, after all, born only in 1861, slightly less than 90 years before Enzo Ferrari found this small, but successful enterprise of making sports cars which dominates the racing track till this day. Officially established in 1947, Ferrari SpA. currently sells 4,000 high-performance cars every year, with each having a median price of US$140,000. Models such as the Modena, Spyder, Maranello, and most recently, the Scaglietti, are well-known and highly coveted by many, although to safeguard the exclusivity and high value of the brand, supply is very limited. Production is capped at 4,300 cars per annum and only the Ferrari factory, housing 2,706 employees, in the Italian village of Maranello produces Ferrari cars. Today, the company is owned and controlled by Fiat Auto, Italy's largest automobile maker, which has a 56 per cent stake in the company. Other shareholders include the Italian Bank Mediobanca (15 per cent), Germany's Commerzbank AG (10 per cent), the Lehman Brothers (7 per cent), and Piero Ferrari, son of Enzo Ferrari (10 per cent).[1] Ferrari has a presence in 43 countries worldwide. Its main market is the US, which takes up 25 per cent of its annual production. Germany, its second largest market, takes up 20 per cent, while the UK, Italy, Switzerland, Japan and France each demands around 10–17 per cent of its yearly quota (see Vukson, 2001, p. 151). The rest are sold in other parts of the world in Asia and Latin America. Up to 90 per cent of its production is exported from Italy.

FERRARI'S CORPORATE HISTORY

To understand the success of Ferrari SpA., it is imperative to look into the history of the company. This is analogous to the founder's life, since he was at the helm for 41 years. Enzo Ferrari, born in Modena on February 18, 1898, came into a world with the British Empire encompassing much of the globe. Motor cars and his country, Italy, were in their infancy. He had a quiet childhood and was already interested in motor races at a tender age, but WWI changed his life drastically. His father and elder brother died in the war and their steel business was sold. Thus, Enzo went to Turin to find a job. He was rejected by Fiat, but later took up jobs with small companies like CMN. Through frequenting the Bar de Nord on Turin's Porta Nuova, he made connections after knowing many people in the racing scene and finally landed a job in Alfa Romeo. Racers were no celebrity figures then. Nonetheless Enzo aspired to become one. From a mechanic, he was promoted to racing driver. This culminated in his appointment as an agent for the company in the Emilia Romagna region. He had a good racing record, finishing second in 1920 at Targo Florio and later winning the Acerbo Cup at Pescara, thus receiving the national order of "Commendatore" in 1928.[2] In 1929, Enzo retired from racing and established an autonomous arm of Alfa Romeo dealing with competitive racing, the Scuderia Ferrari in Modena. This is the much vaunted "Ferrari Idea" at work, whereby a team of amateur racers were organized together to compete in races. Co-founders of this team included Augusto and Alfredo Caniato, and Mario Tadini, all of whom were relatively well-off and provided Enzo with financial support. With this team, and by luring technical expertise such as Luigi Bazzi (a former Fiat technician) and Vittorio Jano (a highly respected engineer from Fiat), the Scuderia Ferrari was quite successful in the racing arena, with the most remarkable victory coming in the 1935 German Grand Prix by Nuvolari in an Alfa Romeo P3. Ferrari was hardly the favorite due to the presence of Mercedez Benz and Auto Union. This giant-slaying act brought the company into prominence for the first time.

However, in 1938, Alfa Romeo decided to re-enter motor racing using its own name, absorbing Scuderia Ferrari and shifting operations to its headquarters in Milan. This was seen as an affront by Enzo on his own "territory," and coupled with differences with Ugo Gobatte, one of the Alfa Romeo directors, and a great dislike for Wilfredo Ricart, a Spanish engineer (see Rogliatti et al., 1990), Enzo left Alfa Romeo in 1939. He and his team embarked on numerous small-scale projects, and in 1943, operations were shifted to Maranello, which would later be regarded as the capital of the world for high-performance automobiles.[3] Subsequently in 1946, the first real Ferrari car was built: the Tipo 125, founder member of the Ferrari cars we know today. It made its racing debut in Pescara in 1947. Participation in various races ensued with different models (e.g., the Tipo 166 at Monaco, and the "barchetta" 166 at Mille Miglia). 1950 was an important year with the beginning of the Formula One world championships (F1). Ferrari is the only racing car that has participated in every single season since its inception. The following year saw Ferrari's first victory over Alfa Romeo in F1 and its first Grand Prix win in Britain, with Froilan Gonzalez's 375 beating the Alfa Romeo 150 at Silverstone (Rogliatti et al., 1990, p. 20). Enzo exclaimed: "I have killed my own mother" (Lehbrink and Schlegelmilch, 1995), and in 1952, Ferrari won its first World Drivers' title with Alberto Ascari in the Type 500. This also marked the beginning of the partnership with Pininfarina bodywork, and in 1961, Ferrari won its first World Constructors' championship. Ferrari's racing history is very distinguished, with 159 Grand Prix victories out of 671 starts, 12 World Drivers' titles, 12 World Constructors' titles, and a total of 2,885.5 points accumulated.

In 1956, Enzo experienced personal tragedy with the death of his son Dino, but he continued his work on engines and motor cars relentlessly. After winning a couple of world titles, affirming Ferrari's supremacy on the race track and gaining international fame in its production models, the company changed its name to Societa Esercizio Fabbrische Automobili e Corse (SEFAC) in 1960. The factory was modernized and enlarged, and production increased with a new assembly line installed. In the meantime, accolades were still rolling in, although the 1960s were generally a tough time for Ferrari.[4] Frequent changes of technical regulations by the sporting authority CSI, and strong competition from the likes of Porsche, Jaguar and Maserati incurred great costs on Ferrari's production (Lehbrink and Schlegelmilch, 1995). This forced Enzo into negotiations with Ford in 1963, although eventually a compromise was not forthcoming. However, financial difficulties lingered on; therefore negotiations between Enzo Ferrari and Gianni Agnelli (patriarch of Fiat Auto) led to Fiat acquiring 50 per cent of Ferrari in 1969.[5] Enzo retained control over the competition department, and even after becoming its honorary chairman in 1977, he continued to captain Ferrari's motor racing. The 1970s saw Ferrari winning the World Drivers' titles in 1975, 1977 and 1979, along with the World Constructors' titles in 1975, 1976, 1977 and 1979. Output also exceeded 2,000 cars per annum in 1979. The 1980s saw Ferrari participating in various motor shows in cities like Turin, Geneva and so on. Despite winning more constructors' titles during this time, no drivers' titles were in sight although new models were built (e.g., the 512 BB and the GTO series). In 1987, in honour of Ferrari's 40th anniversary, the F40 was unveiled in a press conference attended by present and past Ferrari drivers at Imola.[6] However, in the following year, Enzo Ferrari died at the age of 90, and with this, SEFAC was renamed Ferrari SpA. in 1989.

AFTER ENZO: LUCA DI MONTEZEMOLO AT THE HELM

At that time, Ferrari was near bankruptcy (Larner, 1998), and Fiat had to inject new capital to keep it afloat. In 1991, at the personal request of Gianni Agnelli, Luca di Montezemolo, the present CEO of Ferrari, took charge. He overhauled the company, luring top talent to the racing team, boosting the quality of the cars and renewing the product range which stimulated the market (Edmondsen et al., 2002). New models were designed with an emphasis on fun when driving Ferrari cars.[7] Soon, Ferrari recovered, with sales increasing from US$600 million in 1997 to US$950 million in 2002, and profits increasing 2.5 times from US$22 million to US$55 million. Although the 1990s were relatively disappointing for Ferrari on the race track, its recent successes—winning the last five constructors' titles and Michael Schumacher winning the last four drivers' titles—cemented its position as the top racing car. In the luxury car department, noting Ferrari's impressive sales and performance, Fiat handed Maserati over to its management in a bid to rejuvenate this brand of cars. With its current success in Formula One and its status as a luxury car well-established, Ferrari is truly one of Europe's corporate success stories.

CORPORATE CULTURE

With this in mind, a look at Ferrari's corporate culture is useful for a deeper understanding of the inner workings in the company. Corporate culture is defined as the way things are done in a corporation, with shared practices and beliefs created over time. Here, Deal and Kennedy (2000) identified history, values and beliefs, ritual and ceremony along with management and practices, and stories as the main elements of culture.

FERRARI'S DEVELOPMENT

During the 1950s, Italy's industries grew with the backdrop of major regional differences. Italy is a relatively young nation. Strong cultural and linguistic differences exist to this day. These were reflected in Ferrari which has always been based in Maranello, near Enzo's hometown Modena. Despite never really leaving Maranello, which is the only place in the world that has produced Ferrari cars for the past 60 years, the company has reinvented itself to suit the tastes of consumers on its world market, thus operating in a manner which maintains its core while changing its peripheral practices (Deal and Kennedy, 2000). Enzo Ferrari very seldom left Maranello and worked incessantly on improving the quality and safety of his cars and engines (Lehbrink and Schlegelmilch, 1995), setting an example and precedent for future Ferrari workers. Regional differences can also be explained by Enzo's refusal to move with Alfa Romeo to Milan in 1939, and his adamancy in meeting people only in Maranello. He claimed that going elsewhere, he would "be just another person," thus when meeting people, he "gets them to come" to Maranello (Rogliatti et al., 1990, pp. 19–20). However, it can be said that Ferrari helped galvanize Italian unity, since its dominance of F1 has brought about a source of great national pride to many Italians. Ferrari is thus a symbol of national identity, but at the same time has its roots in the country's localized past.

In terms of values and beliefs, the most important to Italian companies are probably those that are associated with the family. This is true for Ferrari during its early years, but at present, there is a relatively stronger *clientelismo* relationship, an arrangement determined by particularistic relationships and personal contacts (Hickson, 1997, p. 124). For Enzo in his earlier days, Ferrari was his own company and he alone made the decisions, especially when it came to competition and motor cars. He "ruled in a personal manner" (Hickson and Pugh, 1995, p. 81) which was analogous to the captains of Italy's industries.[8] He might have envisaged keeping Ferrari as a family business, but unfolding events like the death of his son and financial constraints dissuaded him from this path of action, placing the continuity of Ferrari as his top priority.[9] When he sold 50 per cent of Ferrari to Fiat in 1969, it was with the condition that after his death, 40 per cent would revert to Fiat while the remaining 10 per cent stayed with the Ferrari family. Thus, although Italian business culture is very pro-family, the practicality of its founder allowed Ferrari to continue its operations under Fiat. Succession problems were not evident, since Di Montezemolo is not a member of the Ferrari clan. The family still owns 10 per cent of Ferrari's shares today, but has no direct control over management, leaving the CEO and his lieutenants free to decide on major issues and strategies, which is in contrast with the general business climate of having families own and run their enterprises. It is noted, however, that *clientelismo* is still evident in Ferrari, the best example being the CEO himself who started working for the company when he was 26. He left for a while and came back as he had connections within Ferrari and was under the patronage of Enzo himself in the 1970s (*BusinessWeek*, 2002). Thus when it comes to creativity and getting the best personnel, Ferrari did not have much problems in attracting top talent. At the same time it maintained loyalty amongst its workers to the company through *clientelismo* arrangements. Its reputation, however, is still important and effective despite being somewhat detached from the clan name (compared to, say, the Agnelli family and Fiat Auto). Ferrari is a relatively small enterprise compared to Italian counterparts like Fiat, Pirelli and IRI, thus enabling it to acquire a high degree of responsiveness to market conditions and adopt "flexible specialization" to find small adaptive niches. This is done through limited entrepreneurship, focusing on the efficiency of internal activities mainly in production, and with little interest in wider business environments and growth prospects (Hickson, 1997, p. 132). However, this is probably changing with Di Montezemolo's initiatives. Under Enzo, Ferrari concentrated on winning races and upgrading engines and car technology (e.g., V12, 246 Dino, and 360 Modena), with increases in production as secondary concern. This is still the main focus today, although venturing into greater merchandising and opening of theme parks may change this emphasis in the future. Nevertheless, F1 does retain utmost importance in Ferrari's priority list, and for the CEO on a personal level, the Formula One award for best car maker (Edmondsen et al., 2002).

Rituals and ceremonies are activities of culture, and Ferrari has some notable events which can be classified in this category. Anniversaries are celebrated with great pomp, for example, the 40th anniversary of Ferrari's founding in 1987 was a gala event, during which Ferrari drivers throughout its history joined the company in its celebrations. It was also the last event during which Enzo was still alive, and the special F40 was unveiled. The 50th anniversary in 1997 was also an important occasion, with the introduction of the F50. Only 349 F50s were produced. It is the only Ferrari consumer car which has Formula One engines. Another "ritual" was the annual Ferrari press conference, which was often seen as the top executive holding court and the press being "granted" a papal audience (Lehbrink and Schlegelmilch, 1995). Looking at management, Ferrari can be said to be a typical Italian firm. In Italian management, specificity is important since Italian managers have a highly politicised view of their organizations. There is preference for clarity and control of uncertainty. This was why Enzo split with Alfa Romeo in 1939 and refused the bid by Ford in 1963. He wanted control over the department deemed to be his turf and this he retained even after conceding half his company to Fiat. This reduces internal conflicts, although there is evidence of greater autocracy and paternalism in such organizations. Another aspect is control over key activities by the CEO or founding entrepreneur, and the delegation of peripheral functions to others within the family or business partners. Enzo controlled activities such as engine and motor car development, letting others like Fiat worry about commercial interests. Such practices are no longer as clearly evident with Luca, but it is certain that Ferrari is still very much autonomous from Fiat and that the CEO can decide on the future workings of the company. As for subordinates and workers of Ferrari, the general consensus is that Italian workers are heavily dependent on their superiors. Bosses are supposed to be paternalistic and have certain privileges, although in Ferrari, employees also enjoy many benefits. In fact, Ferrari is one of the top 10 workplaces in the EU (DG Employment and Social Affairs, 2003); with Internet courses from home provided and other benefits include wellness and sports-medical programs. The extension of such benefits to relatives of employees help to consolidate the *clientelismo* relationship, thus fulfilling obligations and responsibilities within the company as well as those pertaining to family members, inclusive of those in a quasi-familial personal network (Hickson, 1997, p. 135). Promotion and recruitment of personnel are not restrictive at Ferrari, since there is little family control over the company, although with *clientelismo* active, it is expected that relatives of people directly associated with Ferrari would be first in line. However, the relative flexibility of the company in this regard enables it to recruit expertise which is needed, whether or not this is within or out of personal networks. Also, when it comes to aesthetics, Italians are known for having a flair for design and visual appeal and in this sense, Ferrari is very much Italian. In fact, Enzo's favourite expression well describes the stylistic beauty of Ferrari cars:

> ... the epitome of mechanical beauty acquired by men who want to turn their dreams into reality and inject their life with a long period of youthful passion.

This is inherent in Italian society due to concerns over dress and plastic/visual arts. Thus there is no clear defining line between fashion, art, architecture and design, allowing an amalgam of all these practices and qualities to be concentrated in Ferrari cars. This is the result of flexible specialization exhibited by small enterprises like Ferrari. Including the South European quality of cultural aspects, it gives Ferrari cars a unique outlook which epitomises the reputation and artistry of them being "Made in Italy." This has "ceremonial" functions for Ferrari. Since the 1951 collaboration with Pininfarina has been an integral part in Ferrari's development.

Ferrari has its own unique stories, which contribute to its corporate culture. Basically, the main story is that of the Ferrari logo and how it came about. It was said that on the May 25, 1923, Enzo was at the Savio track near Ravenna, outpacing more powerful opposition and winning convincingly. He was sought by the parents of Francisco Baracca, the legendary WWI Italian fighter ace who shot down 34 enemy planes before being shot down in the hills of Montello just before the war ended. The Countess Paulina Baracca presented Enzo with Francisco's prancing horse emblem on the spur of the moment as an acknowledgement for his courage and audacity behind the wheel, saying that this emblem would bring luck to his cars. Whether or not this was true, the logo—a prancing horse symbol with a yellow background representing the city of Modena and having Italian state colours on top of it—is now carried on every road and racing Ferrari car today. Other stories related to Enzo Ferrari include the story of his racing car being stuck in a procession of cars following the then Italian President Vittorio Orlando in 1919, and one in which Enzo was caught in a snow storm and was attacked by wolves. These probably gave Enzo a larger-than-life persona to his workers and to subsequent generations of Ferrari fans and employees. However improbable such stories are, they brought spice to Ferrari's culture at the workplace and probably contributed to some measure of cohesiveness. Workers could relate to one another through such corporate myths and the logo of the company is seen not just as another symbol. It has certain meaning to it, bringing the spirit of daring and risk in Enzo and Baracca to the fore and serves as a source of inspiration to members of the Ferrari corps. Such are the effects of stories or corporate "legends."[10]

After examining the corporate culture of Ferrari, it is evident that it has a power culture with the boss heading the way, reflecting the paternalistic streak in Italian management. Although not to the extent of absolutism during the time of Enzo, nevertheless the basic foundations are there for an authoritative and decisive leadership. However, this is combined with a task culture as Ferrari has different components of operation (e.g., the F1 and production teams) and has spread its branches to other countries (e.g., the US). These small workgroups work through networking arrangements with relative autonomy from the headquarters in Maranello.

Corporate and international strategies

Strategies are generally policies and moves made with objectives in mind, and various objectives of Ferrari are spelt out here. During the years after its inception, Ferrari needed to establish its own reputation as a racing giant and to bring fame to its name. With that in mind, Enzo made several strategic moves in this direction.

Early days: developmental initiatives
First, when he was at Alfa Romeo, Enzo came up with the "Ferrari Idea" in which gentlemen drivers were organized into a team so that it would be easier for them to compete in motor races. This brought about a relatively specialized team, and it was of a highly professional standard in its day. Established drivers like Nuvolari and Campari were brought

into the team. They helped in training Ferrari's own fledging students, who included Bravio, Tandini, and Moll. This improved the standard of the team substantially. Second, Enzo started the tradition of constant innovation in engines, with his adoption of the V12 twin-six engine when everyone else was moving out of such production, including the only company producing it at that time, Packard Co. Italy was in ruins, with survival and rebuilding of utmost concern, not motor cars and engines. His investments in engines paid off when Ferrari started winning many races at a later stage. Subsequently, the attention on engines and constant upgrading of its technology contributed to more victories on the race tack, putting Ferrari at the forefront of automotive technology. The third significant move made by Enzo was shifting his operations into the riskier job of specializing in the making of sports cars. The machine tools section of the business was scrapped, thus all its energy was now on the development of Ferrari motor racing automobiles. This brought prominent drivers into the team, including Luigi Chinetti, a specialist in endurance races and who was instrumental in making Ferrari well known in the US, at present its biggest customer (Rogliatti et al., 1990, p. 18). Also with specialization in motor cars, Ferrari could improve on its cars and focus on aspects such as quality and safety. Fourth, Ferrari built on its reputation as a car whose power and strength could win competitions, and at the same time enabling ordinary drivers to drive them on public roads. This was achieved through racing, and during those days, it was a good way to advertise cars. Ferrari's first customers were all amateur racing drivers and these races helped explore the motor racing world which included finding new customers (Rogliatti et al., 1990, p. 18). This was continued until international racing rules stipulated that racing and ordinary cars have to be differentiated. The last strategic move made by Ferrari was in consolidating its image as a car wanted by many, but not available to everyone. This was done through skilful public relations activities and setting purposeful criteria: a small number of cars were produced for customers carefully chosen. These customers would have to be able to drive very fast hence adding to the number of Ferrari victories, and make an impact in terms of publicity, e.g., film directors, actors, royalty and famous industrialists (Rogliatti et al., 1990, p. 19). Famous people like Ingrid Bergman, the Shah of Persia and Prince Bernard of Holland paid visits to the Ferrari factory in Maranello, thus serving this end well for the company.

The combination of these initiatives by Enzo led to Ferrari being well-recognized and dominant in the racing scene, and with the future of the company in mind, expansion of its facilities to increase production and expand its sales volume was the main concern, thus the enlargement and modernization of the Ferrari factory and output expansion. Enzo wanted to see his enterprise continue and besides expansion, continued emphasis was placed on other aspects as well. One was Ferrari's dominance in the world of motor car racing, and in this respect it fared pretty well, winning a number of World Drivers' and Constructors' titles from the 1950s to the 1980s. Another aspect was the continuous upgrading of practices and technologies for the automobiles. A significant step was taken in 1960 with the adoption of rear engines for Ferrari cars in the Formula One and Formula Two races. Before, Enzo was adamant in adhering to the principle that "it was the ox that pulled the cart and not the other way round," but he was gradually convinced otherwise. Also, Ferrari started to place importance on partnerships and dealings with other companies. This started with the 1951 meeting between Enzo Ferrari and Battista Pininfarina, who brought his son Sergio along, at Aosta between Maranello and Turin. This was known as the "Consular Treaty" in Italy (Lehbrink and Schlegelmilch, 1995), and thus Pininfarina started designing Ferrari cars and provided the bodywork.[11] This brought style and shape to the cars which were, up till then, not visibly different from others, integrating design into the strength of the cars and thus making them more endearing. Other collaborations with designers like Marichello ensued, and the acquisition by Fiat later would further ensure the financial survival of Ferrari. Lastly, reaching out to other markets was another primary concern. Ferrari started to sell cars internationally through a distributor network, with only one distributor per region. The most important was the US market, and Chinetti was the first Ferrari distributor, selling cars to Ferrari's key clients (Braden and Roush, 1982, p. 71).

By this time, Ferrari cars have attained a uniqueness which enhances its reputation as a car desired by many but possessed by few, with its image as a sports car firmly entrenched. Sergio Pininfarina remarked that "a Ferrari car is stylish, has personality, is elegant, and has speed and power, with advanced technology and fine craftsmanship" (Rogliatti et al., 1990, p. 80). However, from the 1970s to the 1990s, detrimental factors such as the oil crises of the 1970s, trouble with trade unions and terrorist attacks by the Red Brigades ensued. This culminated in the market slump of the 1990s, which arguably did not affect Ferrari sales much since production actually increased. But costs were rising, and with so many problems encountered, the company needed restructuring and rejuvenation. This was largely achieved under the leadership of Luca di Montezemolo.

CURRENT SITUATION: FERRARI'S PRESENT ACTIVITIES

At present, Ferrari has a set of strategies with aims to develop the company further. This can be classified into two broad sections, the first of which caters to the needs and wants of consumers, and the second is finding other niches and improving on its overall operations.

When it comes to customers, Ferrari has three definite strategies. The first is a targeting strategy which has been used since the time of Enzo. Currently, Ferrari cars are sold on invitation only; not just anybody can buy a Ferrari car. According to Ritson (2003), the company is using one of the biggest secrets of marketing, which is nobody ever made money by trying to sell to everyone. Profitability is thus ensured by selling to a specific group and not wasting resources on other customers who are not in this group. For Ferrari, this group consists of rich, powerful and the famous people, most of whom are not greatly affected by economic cycles. Furthermore, customers may even be rejected despite being in this targeted group if they bring disrepute to Ferrari's brand name (Caplan, 1988). Thus sales are rarely influenced by broad macroeconomic fluctuations. The second factor is that of pricing: Ferrari cars are very expensive and people pay more for the quality and exclusivity of the cars than for its mechanisms and usage. That is why a Ferrari car can be considered an economic luxury good; if prices are too low, there may be less demand for them. Such high price tags also reflect the premium people are willing to pay for personal service and confidentiality, for example, a Ferrari Enzo is sold at US$600,000 each, and production is limited only to 399 cars. People buying such cars would only go for them if they are exclusive and priced reasonably high enough to warrant this image. The last factor considered is that the signalled quality and exclusivity of high-end Ferrari cars would spill over to other Ferrari products or lower-end cars. Here is a public relations strategy which can bring in greater profits and perpetuate the brand name in many ways.

When people associate higher-end Ferrari cars like the Ferrari Enzo with exclusivity and high quality, other Ferrari cars like the 355 GTS, priced at US$90,000 each, could also derive the same image from them. Thus pricing does not just generate revenues; it also has a signalling effect which can help boost sales of products bearing the same brand and in this department, Ferrari can be said to have met with much success (Ritson, 2003).

Expansion, diversification and research are the other three important areas in which Ferrari has explored in order to maintain its position as a luxury brand name and international racing powerhouse. The expansion here is different from those of the past; now there is expansion of operations into other areas. For one, Ferrari has already expanded its Ferrari Museum, building an interactive theme park for games and activities which revolve around the theme of living the Ferrari experience (Jewkes, 2002). Another move was made to open a chain of stores, and it is planned that five or six stores would be opened based on the first flagship store already established in front of the Ferrari Museum. Two of them are planned for the US cities of New York and either Los Angeles or San Francisco, while the rest would be located in Germany and Japan. Other considerations include investing in theme parks through joint ventures in the US, and going into the hotel industry. Other areas of operation—with merchandising and licensing royalties in terms of Grand Prix T-shirts, watches, caps etc., being the main emphasis (Larner, 1998)—have rapidly expanded on their own and will continue to do so for some time (Jewkes, 2002).

The revival of Maserati was a major investment which Ferrari acquired from Fiat. It was important in its diversification strategy. Maserati cars are now being revved up to cater to sports cars customers who cannot afford Ferrari cars, but still want to own cars associated with the Ferrari name.[12] Maserati had been faltering in recent years, especially in the US market where it has a reputation for poor quality. Furthermore, the US market is very competitive in the sports car segment, with established players like BMW, Mercedes and Audi dominating the scene (Edmondsen et al., 2002). The Ferrari car is seen as a true sports car, while the Maserati may not have the same appeal and image. Maserati did cost Ferrari US$115 million in the past four years, although analysts believe that Ferrari could turn this investment around as they see Maserati's image as that of an "uncut diamond" which could restore its sparkle if handled with care. In fact, Maserati has performed quite well, with its presence increasing from 29 countries to 36. Sales have improved, especially in the UK which saw a 65 per cent increase from 1999 levels. Finally, another strategic move made by Ferrari is in the area of research. For the first time in its history, Ferrari recently funded a US university, Wayne State University, to conduct research on its highly competitive and confidential racing car technology (Lai, 2004). The university established a formal scholar exchange program with China's Tsinghua University and strengthened ties with European automotive research centres. For Ferrari, this represents a three-way flow of information and ideas on automotive research. It also allows the usage of the state-of-the-art Spray and Combustion Laser Diagnostics Laboratory in the university for experiments. It enables Ferrari to reach out to the Chinese automotive market which is expected to be the world's largest in the next decade. Strengthening its hand on technology, inflow of new ideas and concepts, and a better understanding of the Chinese market could prove beneficial to Ferrari's future operations.

Ferrari has put in much effort to find new niches for itself. There is the possibility, though, that all these may turn attention and resources away from its most prized asset, the Formula One racing team. This is still one of the major advertising avenues for the company, contributing immensely to its reputation and image. Ferrari's dominance in F1 is now under threat from other teams like McLaren and Williams-BMW, with its margin of victory shrinking from 129 points in 2002 to just 14 points in 2003.[13] Furthermore, customers' needs and wants change over time. To maintain its position in the up-market segment, more effort needs to be placed in handling consumer relations. The formula of choosing customers has worked well. But these customers have evolving tastes which would have to be looked into. Neglecting this aspect may prove costly in so lucrative a market. Also, heavy investments in alternative ventures like Maserati involve risks which include dilution of Ferrari's brand image, especially with the former's relatively poor reputation in the US market. All these must be handled with care if the initiatives made can be of much help in further developing Ferrari as a corporation, and as a brand name.

INTERCULTURAL CORPORATE COMMUNICATIONS

It is not surprising that a company of Ferrari's stature has links all over the world. Interest in it is high, and inter-corporate relationships litter its history, providing a basis for work on intercultural corporate communications. It is shown how Ferrari interacted and worked with other companies, and how the degree of such activities vary. In this chapter, three different degrees are analysed. There is a deep relationship in terms of acquisition of Ferrari shares, a medium level relationship in terms of dealers and distributors of Ferrari cars, and a relatively loose relationship in terms of sponsorship of the company. Intercultural corporate differences derive from diversity in styles of business, varied management methods, and differing levels in understanding each other's cultural differences. It is noted that with a deeper relationship, the importance of intercultural deviance also increases, potentially leading to situations whereby the relationships are either strengthened, or strained.

Mergers and acquisitions: the cases of Ford and Fiat

Looking at mergers and acquisitions, there were two major episodes in Ferrari's history. In 1963, Ford was close to acquiring the then SEFAC which had financing problems. Enzo Ferrari infuriated Henry Ford at that time for dismissing the deal at the last moment, and the acquisition attempt by Ford Motors was foiled. Later, Ford unleashed its own racing cars, competing with Ferrari in various races in the US (Lehbrink and Schlegelmilch, 1995), but was relatively unsuccessful in denting the latter's racing dominance. What essentially brought the acquisition to a standstill was Ford's refusal to allow Enzo a free rein in the competition department, which was his personal domain.[14] However, it was probably the right decision, as Ford and Ferrari belonged to two rather distinct national cultures which spillover onto the business climate. In terms of styles of business, the American way synonymous to Ford has always been assertive, since the competitiveness of the US market is very high. Sales are vigorously sought while in Italy, this level of aggressiveness is not very widespread. For Ferrari, sales volumes are seldom the main concern, as customers are selected. The mass production of the US is quite incompatible with the Italians at Ferrari, who value internal efficiency and quality. In terms of management and methods, the Americans and Italians have clear hierarchies, although the top executives in the former earn far more than those in the latter. Many things are laid out, regulated and differentiated in the job scope of US workers, while in Europe, things are not so clear cut. Job security, however, is important in Italy, especially in a climate of *clientelismo* and familial ties, while the US corporations are more impersonal and workers more individualistic (Hickson, 1997), thus job security is never really an issue. Lastly, it can be said that at that time, there was little understanding of each other's cultures. Enzo's insistence on keeping his competition portfolio and Ford's refusal to let him do so in the event of a merger was a case in point. The Americans saw profits and finance as the main indicator of how a corporation was run (Hickson and Pugh, 1995), and could not fathom Enzo's emotional attachment to his racing department. Conversely, Ferrari was not inclined to be absorbed by a company which sees itself just as a profit making venture. Continuity in its name and independence of operation were more important than profit maximization. Thus, cultural antagonism at the very beginning led to the breakdown of Ford's acquisition.

After looking at a failed acquisition, the successful purchase of Ferrari by Fiat's Agnelli family in 1969 serves as a good source of comparison. Fiat is the largest Italian automobile maker, with a market share of 36 per cent of cars bought in the country (*BBC*, 2002b). The acquisition by Fiat helped Ferrari earlier and kept it solvent when it experienced major problems, notably the injection of capital by Fiat in the early 1990s to boost Ferrari's finances when it was close to bankruptcy. This is the style of business in Italy. There is a certain propping up of companies having close ties with one another. This attitude toward other corporations cannot be found in places of cut-throat competition like the US. Fiat and Ferrari's management and methods are also similar; both being Italian companies, familial ties and *clientelismo* are important and the personal touch of leaders like Gianni Agnelli and Enzo Ferrari led both sides to a better understanding of each another. This was continued even after Enzo's death, with Agnelli letting the Ferrari family have a continued stake in the company, and personally inviting the current Ferrari CEO to take over. He also invited Michael Schumacher to join the Ferrari F1 team. Thus Fiat was instrumental in Ferrari's "drive" back to the top of F1 (*BBC*, 2003). Currently, Fiat is experiencing financial problems and an onslaught from its creditor banks (*The Age*, 2002). To help ease over Fiat's difficulties, Ferrari took over the loss-making Maserati car group and Fiat's Ferrari shares were sold in June 2002.[15] Substantial profits from selling up to 34 per cent of these shares helped

Fiat to some extent, and the company is recovering. However, Ferrari prefers to have more flotation of its shares, which could be used to reward key staff and keep the best people in their team. Furthermore, Ferrari enthusiasts would find this very appealing (*BBC*, 2002a). Last of all, there is much understanding between Ferrari and Fiat. The autonomy of Ferrari is reflected from the absence of its results on Fiat Auto's balance sheets. It is not seen as just another component of Fiat, but as a more specialized partner/subsidiary (World Markets Research Center, 2003). Furthermore, it is recognized that with Ferrari's fortunes rising and Fiat's declining, and with the paternalistic streak of Italian bosses, it would be best to keep Ferrari autonomous from Fiat. The markets they cater to are also different, with Fiat producing ordinary consumer automobiles while Ferrari is in the sporting scene and caters to the luxury car market. This mutual understanding and avoidance of cultural antagonism has worked well for both sides throughout the years, although Fiat is under pressure to be more profit-oriented after losing 24 per cent of its domestic market over this time period.[16]

Dealerships and distribution: the North American market

Intercultural considerations are of lesser importance when it comes to the medium level, specifically the relationship between Ferrari and its dealers and distributors in the international markets. In fact, styles of business, management and methods are of less relevance, considering the fact that Ferrari produces cars and exports them to its distributors. However, cultural antagonism can still be a big problem if not handled properly. One good example is Ferrari's relationship with its dealers in the North American market, where it is known that the American dealers, being individualistic and profit-oriented, neglect supporting Ferrari's image as a racing giant.[17] Ferrari places great emphasis on good service and getting to know customers, including participation in racing which is important in upholding the company's reputation. The North American dealers, however, are seen as non-committal to the sporting element, thus contributing little to Ferrari's technical and racing development. Thus, the company is prepared to reduce the number of dealers authorized to operate in its North American market, since 80 per cent of its revenue is generated by only 30 per cent of the dealers (Vukson, 2003, p. 152). However, for Ferrari to be successful in attaining such objectives, the company would have to look into the culture of the dealers in North America and come up with perks or penalties that can direct them to achieve such goals. Reducing dealerships is one thing. A better understanding of the cultural mechanisms at work should yield better solutions.

Sponsorships: Vodafone

The third tier of intercultural relationship, which is the least embedded within cultural threads, is manifested in the sponsorship of the company. Here, Vodafone's sponsorship of Ferrari would be studied.[18] Cultural differences in terms of style of business, management and methods, and even cultural understanding are not the main considerations of this relatively simple relationship; Vodafone provides funds for Ferrari, while Ferrari helps in the advertising of Vodafone, which is the world's largest telecommunications company. Vodafone recognises Ferrari's potential in the immense media coverage of F1 racing, which can expose its brand name to a worldwide television audience of 360 million people for each race (*The Times 100*, 2003). The image of Ferrari as triumphant in racing, of good craft and excellent technological capabilities further strengthens its appeal to Vodafone. In fact, Vodafone has a well-mapped sponsorship strategy with Ferrari at the fore: Ferrari, along with other sponsors, act as an ambassador for the Vodafone brand. Tangible links are established between products and services Vodafone provides and the Ferrari brand. There is a website linkage between the two corporations, providing updated information on F1 results and the latest versions of telecommunication devices (*The Times 100*, 2003). To further strengthen its association with Ferrari, Vodafone also provides a range of value-added services in its sponsorship package, e.g., having Ferrari logos on Vodafone mobiles. Ferrari also benefits from this deal, through financing and some forms of limited advertisement in the telecommunications market. It must be noted that share acquisition and network management are not involved here. Thus there is little impingement on internal operations within both companies. Intercultural conflicts are kept to a minimum despite constant interaction and communication in this relationship.

Associations with major corporations like Ford, Fiat and Vodafone are possible due to Ferrari's wide appeal and international recognition.

These are due to its reputation as a prestigious and exclusive carmaker, the trust placed in the quality of its cars, the elegance and design which is identified with the "Made in Italy" tag, and in its racing supremacy in F1.[19] With international demand high for only 4,000 Ferrari cars per annum, the company continues to be a magnet for investments and cooperative deals.

CONCLUSION

After an extensive study of the company, it appears that the business culture of Ferrari is very much tied to the national culture of Italy as a whole, although familial association is relatively weaker. This is mainly due to its acceptance of leaders and people out of the immediate Ferrari family in positions of power and decision making, although the element of *clientelismo* is still strong. The strategies that Ferrari uses today have already been largely formulated in the past. Decisions to choose customers, limit production, and improve technological capabilities were already practised in the early years, although newer initiatives like public relations, diversification, and active expansion into other areas are now part of Ferrari's overall plan. Intercultural corporate communications with other major companies depend on the level of the relationship and the cultural differences between them, with deeper relations and greater cultural differences leading to a deterioration in communications, potentially leading to a breakdown in the relationship.

Ferrari's business culture is rather unique, but at the same time influenced by the settings in which it developed. Post-war Italy is still a fragmented nation, and Ferrari's roots in Maranello remain very strong since everything began there and its cars are still only produced in that town. Emulating Ferrari's success will not be easy, in part because of its unique culture, in part also due to its entrenched position in the hearts and minds of most Italians and Ferrari fans around the world. The strength and cohesiveness of the brand name, its dominance of F1, its reputation for quality and elegance in design, and its exclusivity render Ferrari with the strongest association to anything quintessentially Italian. This "connection" and its dominance on the racing track are the pillars supporting its corporate culture, and continue to be the main anchors of Ferrari's success.

ENDNOTES

1 For more details, see Bryant (2004).
2 This was later repealed. Titles awarded by Mussolini's regime are no longer recognized.
3 Enzo's company was named Auto Costruzioni Ferrari at that time. For the sake of simplicity, it would be known as "Ferrari" in this paper.
4 Other than racing, Ferrari's achievements were recognized with other awards. Examples include the European hill climbing championship in 1962, the world speed and endurance challenge in 1965, and the international sports prototype constructors' championship in 1967.
5 The Agnelli family is Italy's version of the Kennedy family in the US, owning famous names such as Fiat Auto and Juventus, Italian football's Serie A champions.
6 The F40 is one of the most sought after Ferrari cars of all time.
7 As Di Montezemolo mentioned in *BusinessWeek* (2002), "You have to enjoy driving."
8 Such captains included Gianni Agnelli ('I' Avvocato), Carlo de Benedetti ('I' Ingegnere) and Silvio Berlusconi (Sua Emittentza). The former has since passed away, while Berlusconi is presently Italy's Prime Minister.
9 In Ferrari History, it is said that Enzo had an eye on "building a nice, profitable empire" of his own.
10 Stories can be told through various actors in a cultural network, for example, storytellers, priests, gossips, whisperers, spies and cabals. See Deal and Kennedy (2000) for more details.
11 It was a meeting between two "stubborn old men," both famous for being difficult in negotiations.
12 The models of Maserati cars include the Spyder and Quattroporte.
13 Here a comparison is made between the points awarded in the 2002 and 2003 F1 constructors' championship.
14 Note that Enzo Ferrari earlier broke away from Alfa Romeo due to the same reason, epitomizing the need for Italian bosses to control fully what they deem as their corporation's most important activities and practices.
15 For more details, see *World Markets Research Centre* (2003).
16 Fiat used to control 60 per cent of the Italian domestic car market.
17 For more details, see Braden and Roush (1982, p. 71).
18 Another important sponsor for Ferrari is Shell, the Anglo-Dutch oil company.
19 Reputation and trust are the pillars of successful corporate governance. See D'Alessandro (2002) for more details.

REFERENCES

Pat Braden, and Gerald Roush. *The Ferrari 365 GTB/4 Daytona*. Santa Ana; London: Newport Press; Osprey, 1982.

Terrence Deal, and Allan Kennedy. *The New Corporate Cultures: Revitalizing the Workplace after Downsizing, Mergers and Re-engineering*. London: Orion Business, 1999.

David J. Hickson. *Exploring Management across the World*. London: Penguin Books, 1997.

David J. Hickson, and Derek S. Pugh. *Management Worldwide: The Impact of Societal Culture on Organizations around the Globe*. London: Penguin Books, 1995.

Geert Hofstede. *Cultures and Organizations: Software of the Mind*. London; New York: McGraw-Hill, 1991.

Hartmut Lehbrink and Rainer W. Schlegelmilch. *Ferrari*. Koeln: Konemann, 1995.

Gianni Rogliatti, Sergio Pininfarina, and Valerio Moretti. *The Ferrari Idea*. Tauris, 1990.

William B. Z. Vukson. *Political, Structural and Technological Change*. Toronto; Ontario: G.7 Report, 2001.

John Andrews. "The lessons of history," *The Economist*, 1993, vol. 327, issue 7,817: pp. SS4, 3 pages.

Brian Caplan. "Subtle art of selling to the super-rich," *Asian Business*, vol. 24, no. 9, September 1988: pp. 45–7.

DG Employment and Social Affairs. "Ferrari-Maserati Group," *Best Workplaces: EU 2003*, Brussels: Conference Report-Award Ceremony, March 22, 2003: p. 16.

Stephen Jewkes. "Ferrari steers onto new roads," *Europe*, issue 418, July/August 2002: p. 19.

Monica Larner. "Those high-end Italians are revving up again: Ferrari, Ducati, and other makers are pulling out of the pits," *Business Week*, issue 3,600, October 19, 1998: pp. 138–9.

Mark Ritson. "Italian Stallion has proved itself a master of marketing strategy," *Marketing*, June 5, 2003: pp. 16–8.

WEBSITES:

BBC (2002a) "Ferrari 'plans theme parks'" in http://news.bbc.co.uk/2/hi/business/1879011.stm, March 18.

BBC (2002b) "Fiat to float Ferrari" in http://news.bbc.co.uk/2/hi/business/198696/stm, May 14.

BBC (2003) "Legendary Fiat Head Dies" in http://news.bbc.co.uk/2/hi/business/2690265.stm, January 24.

Bryant, James (2004) "Ferrari SpA." in http://www.hoovers.com/ferrari/—ID_59581—/free-co-factsheet.xhtml

BusinessWeek online (2002) "Luca di Montezemolo" in http://www.businessweek.com:/print/magazine/content/02_23/b3787609.htm?gb, June 17.

CarNet "Ferrari's figures" in http://www.carnetnews.co.uk/news/story425.html

D'Alessandro, Stephen (2002) "Making Corporate Governance Programmes a source of Strategic Competitive Advantage-Part 2" in http://www.mbo.com.mt/mbo.nsf/perspectives/Making+Corporate+Governance+Programmes+a+source+of+strategic+competitive+advantage

Edmondsen, Gail, Tierney, Christine and Welch, David (2002) "Ferrari's New Wheels" in http://www.businessweek.com/magazine/content/02_02/b3765116.htm, January 14.

Edmunds.com (2002) "Manufacturer Histories: Ferrari" in http://www.edmunds.com/reviews/histories/acticles/65322/article.html, June 17.

Ferrari History in http://home.clara.net/nigelk/index1.htm

Lai, Ming Chia (2004) "International Automotive Powertrain Exchange Program: Mechanical Engineering" in http://studyabroad.wayne.edu/global/Grants/faculty%20grant%20recipients.htm

The Age (2003) "Fiat's Agnelli family struggles for power" in http://www.theage.com.au/articles/2003/01/12/1041990180590.html, January 13.

The Times 100 (2003) "Vodafone" in http://www.thetimes100.co.uk/file/41/vodafone.doc

World Markets Research Center (2003) "Italy- Vehicle Market/Industry" in http://www.worldmarketsanalysis.com/wma_sample_pages/site_pages/WMASampItalyVeh.html

CHAPTER 11

As Solid as Steel: ThyssenKrupp, the Rise and Fall of Two Steel Dynasties

ALBRECHT ROTHACHER

INTRODUCTION

The interwoven story of the Krupp and the Thyssen in their parallelism displays an almost fatalist sequence. Built up by work-obsessed founding fathers in the heydays of German industrialization in the nineteenth century, and carried on by the more able of their sons, they survived the losses of WWI, the hyperinflation of 1923, the world economic crisis of 1929, WWII, and Allied Occupation. After post-war recovery with its strong demand for coal and steel, at one point generational decadence set in. Family fortunes were rescued into foundations, and the steel business restructured and merged to cope with tougher competition, new technologies and post-industrial patterns of demand.

Among the two dynasties Krupp is the older one, its steel business preceding Thyssen's by half a century. Their industrial role ended after five generations with the death of Alfried Krupp von Bohlen und Halbach in 1967, those of the Thyssens after three generations with the death of Fritz Thyssen in 1951.

THE KRUPP DYNASTY

The Krupp steel dynasty began with a false start. Originally the Krupps had been a wealthy merchant family in Essen hailing from the Netherlands (then spelled "Kruipe"). Friedrich Krupp (1786–1826) however, was less attracted by trading in colonial goods and local real estate, but rather fascinated by the possibilities of cast iron production. Napoleon's continental blockade held out the promise to develop Germany's iron and steel production as superior British competition was kept away.

Aged 20, Friedrich Krupp invested his inheritance into building a steel mill. He was not interested in producing the usual blacksmith products like pans, kettles, sheaths and nails, but rather in heavy steel casts, for which however at the time, there was no market. Being more of a visionary, he invested heavily in an oversized production site, even when orders had dried up. When relatives were unwilling to lend him further, he was obliged to sell his town house and other real estate and to move into a shack close to his empty plant with his young family.

Dishonest business partners, lengthy lawsuits, work accidents and time consuming duties as a town counsellor in Essen distracted Friedrich Krupp from more systematic market efforts. Although the quality of his new cast iron products found praise, commercial success eluded him. Aged only 40, Friedrich Krupp died of a lung disease in poverty. In spite of sizable debts, his widow Therese and his 13-year-old son, Alfred, continued his steel mill, then manned by seven workers. Against all odds, the company survived. Its steel cylinders were of superior quality. The German customs union helped to expand markets. A steam engine replaced the unreliable water mill for the supply of energy.

Already in 1836, Alfred Krupp established the first elements of its corporate social security system: a fund for mutual help in case of illness, invalidity and death for employees. In 1838, aged 26, Krupp travelled to England to study the British steel industry. Ten years later, he bought out his relatives, and was able to run his company alone.

At the London World Exhibition of 1851, a Krupp gun made of cast steel won a gold medal. During the Paris World Exhibition four years later, a Krupp steel exhibit spectacularly crashed through the wooden floor. Large export orders to Russia and Egypt followed. The beginning railway boom fuelled his business, in particular his invention of the single cast railway tyre, which unlike the pieces welded together so far, did not break.

Krupp steel quality also helped to win military procurement orders for artillery pieces to the Prussian state, which in turn helped Germany to win the 1870/1 war against France and to regain German unity.

A self-confessed workaholic and autocrat, Alfred Krupp in 1853, then aged 41, married a girl, Bertha, 20 years his junior. Less than a year later, their first and only child, Friedrich Albert Krupp was born. Their marriage was soon in trouble with his young wife rather visiting spas than the expanding steel works of Essen and the newly acquired collieries in the Ruhr to whom her husband seemed married instead.

When in 1882 Alfred Krupp objected to his son's engagement to a noblewoman, Bertha Krupp left him. The lonely patriarch then resided alone in a famous castle-like residence called "Villa Hügel" in Essen with its 220 rooms, until his death in 1887, from where he ruled over a workforce of 21,000 people. He strove for technical perfection in production, but also insisted on social benefits, like decent company-financed housing and healthcare for his hardworking employees at the same time.

Aged 34, his son, whom the old Krupp had always viewed with suspicion, took over. Although frequently sick when young, Friedrich Albert Krupp during his 15 years at the helm built the huge Rheinhausen steel mills, expanded into shipbuilding in setting up the Germania shipyard in Kiel, and acquired the Gruson Steelworks in Magdeburg. At the time of his death in 1902, Krupp had 43,000 workers. Unlike his father, Friedrich Albert did political lobbying. He cultivated the emperor, Willem II, and supported his naval expansion program, which incurred the wrath of then young anti-militarist Social Democratic Party. Antagonised by the rough and tumble of political controversy, he retreated to the Mediterranean island of Capri, where he was rumored to have been seen in the company of young boys. Once a Socialist paper revealed the scandal, Friedrich Albert Krupp died under unexplained circumstances, presumably by his own hand.

His only daughter Bertha inherited the whole company. As Europe's richest heiress, at age 20, with the Emperor present, in 1906 she married the diplomat Gustav von Bohlen und Halbach, who until 1943 managed the firm on her behalf. He was a tough taskmaster and a stern accountant.

Krupp, which had produced guns and submarines during WWI, was hit by the 1919 Versailles Treaty provisions. 100,000 of its 170,000 employees of 1918 had to be dismissed. In the post-war recession, orders for civilian steel products were few. The government in Berlin had little money to pay for the goods ordered by the French and the Belgians to be delivered for free as war reparations. Although initially not interested in politics, in 1923 he and other Krupp directors were accused of endangering the security of the French Occupation forces. Condemned to 15 years in jail and to a fine of 100 million Reichsmark by a French military tribunal, he was released after seven months. Thirteen Krupp workers were shot by the occupant.

His eight children were born during 1907–1922. They were brought up in the strict Prussian fashion of the day—however, not by their own parents, but by professional educators on Villa Hügel. One of the sons died as a baby, and two fell as young men in WWII.

Unlike other companies, Krupp did not finance the rise of the Nazis. But once they were in power, followed instructions after 1934 to convert back to armament production: tanks, artillery pieces, warships and submarines. By 1942, 42 per cent of all production was for the war effort.

In 1943, Gustav von Bohlen und Halbach retired. He was succeeded by his oldest son, Alfried Krupp, then aged 37, who helped by a special "Lex Krupp"—in line with the founder's provisions—inherited the entire company undivided from his mother Bertha.

Alfried Krupp had studied engineering, worked for a while in Dresdner Bank, and during 1936 was part of a sailing team, which won a bronze medal at the Berlin Olympics. In 1938, he became director of Krupp's armament division. Since 1943, Essen and the Krupp works became targets of massive Allied bombing. One third of the production sites were destroyed entirely, one third heavily damaged. Of what was left intact, 75 per cent was removed by the Allies as reparations during 1946–51. As his 70-year-old father Gustav was too ill to stand trial, the US arrested Alfried and some Krupp directors instead in April 1945. A US occupation court tried them in 1948 for assorted war crimes, like having contributed to a war of aggression, having used resources of occupied lands, and for having used forced labor.

He was sentenced to 12 years' imprisonment with his property confiscated. After a total of six years in jail, he was granted amnesty by the US High Commissioner and his property restituted (to the extent that it still existed). One of his brothers, Harald was kept by the Soviets in captivity as a POW until 1955.

It was only in 1953 that Alfried Krupp reassumed the command of his companies, whose steel was now mainly processed into locomotives and car engines. Alfried left the management of the Krupp works to a trusted general manager, Berthold Beitz, who as an assertive self-made man notably developed Krupp's steel exports to the Communist East.

As Alfried, who was married briefly twice, had only one son, Arndt, who was more of a playboy prominent in the scandal sheets, he left his fortune to a foundation in his name. Its chairmanship was assumed by none other than Berthold Beitz until 1989. Alfried Krupp von Bohlen died in 1967, aged only 60. His son Arndt, born in 1938, died in 1986, a victim of his own eccentric lifestyle. For not working in the company and for foregoing his inheritance, worth more than DM5 billion, in 1968 he had accepted annual gratuities of DM2 million, then considered scandalously high in frugal post-war Germany. Having grown up with his divorced mother, he had no identification with the Krupp name and tradition, and wasted his allowance away.

In 1992, other members of the family—descendants of Alfried's brothers—tried to gain control of the foundation. Yet, their claims were rejected by a regional court in Essen in 1999.

THE THYSSEN FAMILY

There are many parallels between Thyssen and Krupp—not just those caused by the cycles of boom and bust, of working as competitors in the same sector in the same region, by armament orders, war destruction and post-war purges—but also curiously in the generational sequence of austere founding fathers, striving sons, a decadent third generation (in Krupp's case: also fifth generation), the transfer of family fortunes into a holding foundation, and the takeover of both companies and foundations by professional management—until ultimately both Krupp and Thyssen were fully merged in 1999.

August Thyssen (1842–1926) started much later than the Krupps. With an inherited capital of 8,000 Thaler, in 1867 together with four Belgian partners, he set up a small steel mill in Duisburg. Four years later in 1871, he founded his own steel business into which his father and his brothers and sisters also contributed their capital. A new drilling and extraction system developed by Thyssen began to revolutionize coal and iron ore mining. As mining needed lots of water, he set up new water works. Redundant gas produced in the cokeries he used in large distance heating systems—equally produced by Thyssen. When August Thyssen needed finance, he bought shares in the right banks. With a forceful personality and a strong business acumen, he soon developed a vertically integrated enterprise: with mines for coal and iron ore, to milling of iron and steel and their further processing and trading, thus placing himself well to satisfy the booming demand for steel products following German unity after 1871. He had learned his management skills as a junior officer in the military. Like most founding fathers of the era, he thought little of delegation, was a stern disciplinarian, stingy to the extreme, uninterested in status symbols (except for purchasing a castle, Schloss Landsberg—

today a corporate seminar and guest house—where he lived alone), and as an incurable workaholic had an unhappy family life. His wife left him in 1885, and two of his four children sued him for a fair share of their inheritance in 1920. When his brother Joseph died in a work accident in 1915, he had lost his only confidant.

When August Thyssen died in 1926, his oldest son Fritz (1873–1951) inherited 38 per cent of the capital and the CEO command of the steel works. The other children, mostly married into nobility, were either paid out and given smaller plants to develop their own business, like his brother Heinrich. The others let Fritz Thyssen manage their shares.

The Thyssens played politically controversial roles. August Thyssen early in WWI advocated fairly aggressive German war objectives, but after the war, seemed to side with Rhineland separatists. His son Fritz, who was antagonized by the Communist insurrection of 1919 and by the heavy-handed French occupation of the Rhineland of 1923, during which he was arrested and fined, was more of a right wing patriot. In return for (subsequently broken) promises to re-establish the monarchy and to set up a corporatist state, he even financed Hitler's rise to power. Fritz broke, however, spectacularly with the Nazis in 1939 and wrote open letters to warn the world of their aggressive designs. Having fled to France, he was captured in 1941—first to be put into a mental asylum, then into a concentration camp, with his property confiscated. After liberation, he was rearrested again by the Americans as a suspect war criminal, but acquitted by a German tribunal in 1948.

After eight years in jail, Fritz Thyssen soon died in 1951, aged 78. He left his restituted fortune to his wife, Amelie, and to his only daughter Anita. They were subsequently sued by other relatives, who felt shortchanged over their shares in the company.

Both resided mostly in Argentina and were persuaded by the Thyssen management and the German government to put their shares into a foundation dedicated to promote science and research. A few years later the ladies disapproved of spending decisions taken by foundation managers of their former money. They and two grandsons tried to regain control in 1988—alas too late. Both the Fritz Thyssen Foundation and the Thyssen AG, Germany's largest steel producer, had shifted out of the family's control.

Still one sideline of the Thyssen family continued to produce headlines—mostly of the embarrassing kind in the tabloids. Aided by his inheritance, Fritz Thyssen's brother Heinrich Thyssen-Bornemisza

(1875–1947) had built up his own diversified business empire of banks, gas and electricity companies, shipyards and mining interests. His father's small, but exquisite collection of Rodin sculptures he expanded into an extensive art collection, which in the 1930s he moved to Switzerland. His son, Hans Heinrich (1921–2002) earned most his father's wealth and perfected the art collection, sharing his time equally between women (five of whom he married) and purchases of art works. In the end, against many competing bids, he sold Europe's probably finest collection of classical and modern classical paintings to the Spanish state, which now exhibits these treasures in a special museum in Madrid. Probably egged on by his fifth wife, Hans Heinrich ("Heini") then sued his own son Georg (of his first marriage) and most of his managers to regain a larger share of the revenues accrued in the stakes in international banks, mining and brewing interests united in a Bahamas-based family trust, which he however, had already handed to his children earlier. One of them, Francesca Thyssen Bornemisza in 1993, had abandoned her party girl image and married Karl von Habsburg Lothringen, a short term MEP and grandson of Austria's last emperor.

The costs of the trial quickly amounted to some 130 million Euros. for both sides, with Hans Heinrich, now seriously ill, giving a series of embarrassing interviews insulting his relatives and previous wives. In the end, a few weeks prior to his death, an amicable solution was found and the trial adjourned.

Whilst the dynastic dramas took their toll and stole the media limelight, the companies and their management were working—fairly undisturbed by family interventions. Within Krupp, Berthold Beitz was in charge during most of the post-war era. In Thyssen, it was Dieter Spethmann. Both ruled in close cooperation with the big private banks and with the trade unions, which in Germany's steel industry traditionally enjoy a strong statutory position—manning half of the supervisory board and supplying the companies' director of personnel ("Arbeitsdirektor").

Thyssen in the 1950s and 1960s strove to regain its position as a vertically integrated steel producer. In 1954/5, coal mines were reacquired, followed by the purchase of four large special steel, flat steel and steel tube makers in the Ruhr area, thus allowing rationalized economies of scale.

By the mid-1960s, Thyssen had become Europe's largest raw steel producer, and globally stood at the 5th rank. In 1969, it also established its own sales organization, the Thyssen Handelsunion AG, which subsequently diversified from steel trading into other building materials, industrial and real estate management and project management. With the Mannesmann AG, Thyssen in 1969 agreed on a division of labor. Mannesmann was to produce the pipes, and Thyssen to focus on rolled steel. In 1973, Thyssen purchased Rheinstahl AG, which helped further downstream processing activities for a wide range of steel products.

Krupp, which in 1945 had lost the Gruson Works in East Germany and its shipbuilding interests, the Germaniawerft, due to Allied dismantling and expropriation, even more forcefully went into steel processing in the 1950s and 1960s. Already in 1961 in Brazil, engine parts were produced. In Germany, the Atlas-Werke, makers of heavy engines were purchased. All coal-mining interests were transferred into the Ruhrkohle AG in 1969. Special steel makers were acquired subsequently. With a 25 per cent capital participation of the Iranian state, in 1976 a remarkably stable shareholder joined (although it was first represented by the Shah, then by the mullahs).

THE MERGER

Talks of a merger between Krupp and Thyssen date back to 1978, when Deutsche Bank and the IG Metal trade union ventured the idea. First, however, Krupp merged with Hoesch AG to cope with overcapacities in the early 1990s. Out of 105,000 jobs, some 40,000 were lost in the name of synergies and of focus on core businesses.

The merger between Krupp and Thyssen then went in stages: In 1983, close cooperation was agreed upon. In 1997, Krupp/Hoesch with 12 billion euros of turnover, the smaller partner compared to Thyssen (with 17 billion euros turnover), forced the issue with the help of friendly bankers sitting on both supervisory boards. First, flat steel production was merged. Protests of employees against an initial hostile takeover were followed by talks of a merger of equals with two legal headquarters (Duisburg and Essen)—while the real administration was in Düsseldorf—and promises to maintain jobs. With 186,000 employees at the time of the full merger in 1999, Thyssen Krupp still employs the same number. Today they are almost evenly spread over carbon and special steel production (26 per cent), automotive parts; chassis and body mostly (22 per cent), elevators and escalators (16 per cent), mechanical engineering, machine tools and production systems (16 per cent) and IT, material building and industrial services (20 per cent).

To cope with high indebtedness—which in 2002 still exceeded its proper capital by 42 per cent—ThyssenKrupp divested a series of special steel, welding, transportation services and recycling businesses during 2003.

Still with an annual production of 16 million tons, ThyssenKrupp remains one of the world's largest producers of steel and continues as the world leader in special steels. In spite of all vicissitudes of history and generational succession, the merged company has thus remained faithful to the visions of its two founding fathers.

REFERENCES

Lothar Gall. *Krupp Der Aufstieg eines Industrieimperiums*. Berlin: 2000.

Thomas Rother. *Die Krupps*. Frankfurt: Campus, 2001.

Thomas Rother. *Die Thyssens*. Frankfurt: Campus 2001.

Horst A. Wessel. *Thyssen & Co. Mülheim an der Ruhr*. Stuttgart, 1991.

http://www.thyssenKrupp.de/

Kurt Hornschild. "The attempt by Krupp/Hoesch to take over Thyssen—German business as usual?" *DIW Economic Bulletin*, April 1997.

Ernst Schwarz. "Arbeitsplatzabbau bei der fusionierten Thyssen Krupp Stahl AG." *World Socialist Website*, October 20, 1998.

CHAPTER 12

Nestlé: A Reliable Cash Cow Feeding the World

ALBRECHT ROTHACHER

For the world's largest producer of mostly dried powdered beverages and prepared food, who today follows the exceptionally unexciting "good food, good life" slogan, Nestlé has gone through a remarkable helter skelter of global public perceptions. It was founded in 1866 by a German pharmacist, Heinrich (later "Henri") Nestlé, who had emigrated to Vevey in Switzerland. There he invented an infant feeding formula replacing nursing mother's milk in order to save babies. One hundred and seven years later, the company found itself at the butt of a virulent US-led boycott campaign, claiming probably against better knowledge: "Nestlé kills babies," as on occasion the infant formula in some developing countries was mixed with untreated unsafe water. It took Nestlé more than one decade of stringent quality controls, strict adherence to WHO guidelines, consumer education and PR to convince the more accessible NGOs to abandon their first effective anti-globalization boycott.

Although after-ripples of the campaign are still to be felt in the loony fringe of anti-globalizers, if anything, the campaign has strengthened Nestlé's already stringent quality controls, ultra correct product and nutrition information policies and a slick studiously-friendly corporate image—just the right things to do in a sensitive market like global foodstuffs, where overfed consumers, given the right media campaign, can easily be misled to react hysterically.

As the world's largest food processor, Nestlé today has 260,000 employees working in 490 factories in 84 countries producing and selling some 6,000 brands, some of which, like Nestlé, Milo, Kit Kat, Perrier, Maggi, Friskies, Carnation and Buitoni, are among the world leaders in their segment, with a total turnover of £60 billion.

Nestlé's corporate history is quickly told. As mentioned, Nestlé started out with a pharmacist's wish to help mothers, who were unable to breastfeed. Heinrich Nestlé's infant formula in 1866 was a dried powder mix consisting of milk powder, malted cereals and sugar. The novelty of the process was to preserve the nutritional components of this "infant flour" during dehydration.

The pictogram of his family name, a little nest, was suitably made the corporate logo of the new "Farine Lactee Henri Nestlé SA," located in his pharmacy in Vevey in the French-speaking Southwest of Switzerland. Remaining childless, Nestlé sold his company at age 61. In 1905, it was merged with the "Anglo-Swiss Condensed Milk Company," which had been found by two Americans, brothers Charles and George Page, in the town of Cham, back in 1867.

In the depression following WWI, Nestlé, then already an international company, almost went bankrupt. It was saved after shedding some 20,000 jobs—the largest and only mass lay-off in its corporate history. In 1926, Nestlé entered the chocolate business by absorbing the troubled Swiss makers Peter, Kohler and Cailler and the German Sarotti. In 1938, the first soluble coffee, Nescafé, was invented. Relatively unscathed by the war, in 1946 Nestlé owned 107 factories in all five continents. The main product lines then were sugared condensed milk, infant food, chocolates and instant soluble beverages.

1n 1947, Nestlé bought Maggi, a German maker of dried soups and concentrated condiment mixes. During the 1950s, Nestlé did not purchase any further companies, but expanded ten-fold through internal growth on all continents. For 1960–74, again a multitude of companies were purchased in the sectors like canned food, ice-cream, frozen foods, mineral water, restaurants and California wines. The objective was to diversify the range of products, to master new technologies beyond drying, and to gain access to new promising markets. Nestlé's turnover grew from 4 billion Swiss francs (1960) to 17 billion Swiss francs (1974).

In 1960, Crosse & Blackwell, a British maker of canned soups and beans was bought, followed in 1963 by a participation in Libby, McNeil & Libby, which produces canned food in the US. In 1976, Libby became a fully-owned subsidiary. In order to enter the ice-cream sector, France Glaces, Jopa (Germany) and Delase (Spain) were bought. For frozen foods, Findus was taken over, which then was mainly active in the UK and in Scandinavia, as was Stouffer in the US. The yoghurt business was entered via a minority participation in the French Chambourcy Company. In 1968, Nestlé moved into mineral waters as a minority shareholder in Vittel (20 years later expanded to full ownership), through the purchases of Deer Park (US), Allan Beverages (Canada) and Blaue Quellen [Blue Springs] (Germany). Later in 1992 Perrier was bought.

In order to diversify further, Nestlé in 1970 set up "Eurest," a joint venture with Wagons Lits to operate railway dining cars, and bought a controlling stake in the Australian Cahills restaurant chain and in the Beringer Wineyards in California. Closer to its core businesses in 1971, Ursina Franck, a Swiss dairy and infant food producer was purchased. Transcending food and drinks, Nestlé in 1974 even bought a minority share of 25 per cent in L'Oreal, the French hair care and cosmetics company with no prospects for synergy, but for healthy growth and fat profits.

Still, the tendency to diversify into all directions in many global markets instilled a sense of drift and reduced profitability. Bureaucratization, that inevitable disease of administrations left to their own devices and with money to spend, had crept in. Three levels of management approval were needed just to issue a press release, for instance.

Amongst the Swiss shareholders (none of them permitted to own more than 3 per cent of the shares) the call for a strong guiding hand at the top of Nestlé became louder. It found its object in the charismatic straight talking boss of Nestlé's operations in Germany, Helmut Maucher. As a son of a dairy foreman, Maucher had been born in 1927, in the village of Eisenharz in the pre-Alpine region of Allgau in southwestern Bavaria. He joined Nestlé immediately after graduating from grammar school with a traineeship in the local dairy, then already owned by Nestlé. Working in Nestlé's German headquarters in Frankfurt, he did his MBA on the side at Frankfurt University. In 1980, he was called to join Vevey headquarters as one of the three executive directors and subsequently promoted to CEO and (since 1990) also chairman of the board—a uniquely powerful position permissible under Swiss corporate law. The proud Swiss do not usually relish the thought to work under German bosses, and Maucher later happily told the story of how he, during lunch breaks escaped from corporate HQ to eat in a local Vevey pub for a quiet lunch on his own from time to time. When the waitress asked him: "Are you from Nestlé?" Maucher replied in the affirmative. When she queried: "How do you manage with this German in charge?" he answered: "No problem. It is me." The objective was to build Nestlé into the world's largest food company (reached in 1996) by achieving world brand leadership in a limited range of focused sectors (frozen foods, ice-cream, mineral water, chocolate snacks, soluble drinks, including instant coffee, condensed milk, and later breakfast cereals and pet food). He divested off non-core restaurants and vineyards, and strengthened Nestlé's focus further by targeted acquisitions. Maucher's biggest early purchase was that of Carnation Company in 1985, for the then extravagant sum of $3.5 billion. As Maucher later reported, this was likened by Neue Zürcher Zeitung as "Management by Kanguru" (big jumps with an empty wallet). This jump opened the US market for dairy products, processed food and pet food.

Part of the deal was the German "Glucksklee" brand for condensed milk. A series of roast coffee companies, like Dallmayr in Germany, in Canada, Spain and Sweden was also taken over. In Germany, Herta, a producer of prepacked cold cuts was bought during 1984/7. In 1988, Rowntree Mackintosh, the world's fourth largest producer of chocolate snacks was bought, as was Buitoni Perugina, Italy's leading pasta and third largest food maker. In 1990, a joint venture with General Mills was set up to enter the cereals market. For proper marketing, a branding agreement was concluded with the Disney Company to use its characters exclusively on Nestlé cereal packs (and as freebies within). In 1992, Maucher bought Perrier, a French national treasure, and in 1993, the famous Italian Gelati Motta, and Alpo in 1994.

During his 15 years as CEO, Nestlé's turnover grew from 28 to 60 billion Swiss francs. The share value multiplied seven-fold. Later, Maucher described his acquisition experiences: "We had to strengthen chocolates. On the [European] continent, Nestlé had a tradition of pralines and bars, but was nowhere in the market for youth and lifestyle, the fun articles from Mars and Rowntree (A different source quotes Maucher as saying: 'In chocolate, Nestlé missed the part of the world that belongs to Coca-Cola and rock 'n' roll').[1] Mars was not available hence we went for Rowntree. We soon discovered that Jacobs had already purchased 25 per cent. Thus a bidding war started between Jacobs and Nestlé, with nobody really knowing what the other had just offered. In the end, a lot of money was spent, but it was worth it. We had the choice between selling some Cailler chocolate bars or more than 200,000 tons of Kit Kat, as we do today. Perrier was different, but also very interesting. People had laughed at me because of water. But 10 years earlier than others, I knew that consumers would abandon soft drinks and alcohol. Water means health and magic. With Perrier, we would get into competition with Danone, which was owned by Antoine Ribond. I telephoned him and we met. Then it was very easy. He has access to all political channels in France. Without him and the blessings of the French government, Nestlé could have never gotten Perrier. I was criticized at the time for the purchasing prices of my acquisitions. That was 'short-termism.' But the time which has passed since has proven me right."[2]

Maucher was famous for giving plain spoken straightforward newspaper interviews, which made for a good informative read, but which must have made the PR spin doctors of the food giant cringe.

In anti-new technology Germany, he advocated the use of genetically changed foodstuffs to improve the world food situation and to reduce pesticide use. He also asked for reduced regulatory and tax burdens in Germany, which in his published view was the last country in Europe he would consider for new investments. He called people living on welfare and unwilling to work "prosperity rubbish." This was surely perceptive, but badly received in the leftist magazine to which he gave the interview.[3] In another interview, he observed that German resourcefulness had perhaps turned into a fairy tale. Societies in decline had become irrational, overly protective and lazy, with the work ethic and families disintegrating. Contemporary Germany in his view shared 90 per cent of these characteristics.[4]

With its frequency of acquisitions and multitude of very conservative national and regional tastes—from chocolates to coffee—and well-established consumption habits, Nestlé wisely gave its national managers, subsidiaries and brand managers a lot of leeway and managerial autonomy. Maucher's successor, Peter Brabeck, shares this approach. US corporations tend to see Europe as a homogeneous market, but in fact, consumer tastes vary between countries: "The emotional link to the local consumer is extremely important in our business. That is why it remains a fragmented industry and that is why we try to stay as close as possible to local consumers."[5]

Maucher himself had de-bureaucratized the central administration in Vevey. The less personnel evaluations and job descriptions, the less frustrated and the more entrepreneurial were his people, he observed. Local and branch managers were empowered to operate freely within widely defined principles. Instead of managing by central edict, Maucher and Brabeck managed by travelling around, by observing local practice and by talking with management and co-workers. A lot of efforts go into management training. The well-reputed Institute of Management Development (IMD) in Lausanne is based in part on a predecessor institution co-founded by Nestlé.

The ambition of Maucher and Brabeck is to keep headquarters in Vevey mean and lean. Three vice-presidents have regional responsibilities: for Europe (40 per cent of turnover), the Americas (40 per cent), and the rest of the world (20 per cent). There are also functional responsibilities for strategic sectors, like for dairy products, coffee/drinks, chocolate/confectionary, ice-cream, processed food, pet food and food services. Mineral water is run from Paris.

The Austrian Peter Brabeck-Letmathe (1944–) is CEO since 2000. He studied economics in Vienna and ran various Nestlé country operations in Latin America, before being groomed by Maucher for succession. His vice-presidents and their deputies, hail from countries like the UK, Mexico, Belgium, Spain, Australia, Germany, Sweden, the Netherlands, Canada and the US. In difference to US food multinationals, all of Nestlé's senior management have a strong, varied international professional and educational background. Switzerland, which accounts for less than 2 per cent of Nestlé's turnover, is no longer represented among senior executives, except by Rainer Gut of Credit Swiss as chairman of the supervisory board.

R&D is a central HQ function. The Nestlé Research Centre and various product development centres also deal with quality management, packaging/engineering, industrial performance, environmental regulations, and agricultural practice. The strategic department deals with consumer trends and translates them into concepts for leadership decisions. This does not only apply to convenience food and the right size of packages and servings—reflecting shrinking family sizes, less home cooking and more frequent snacking. It also refers to the transfer of certain nationally developed products to other markets—like the spread of the US born coffee creamer "Coffee-mate" to the rest of the world.

Decisions on the introduction, production and marketing of certain products are taken not by HQ, but at the regional or national level. Within a given strategic context, local plants are fairly autonomous in their production decisions. Remaining core functions of the HQ ("center"), apart from strategic and policy decisions, are basic financial decisions, notably on important investments and their financing, guidelines on branding, setting up quality control systems (Total Quality Management), coordination between markets, including the international trade of Nestlé products, the supply of technical and marketing experts to support subsidiaries, the direction of central research and the coordination of decentralized research facilities, as well as the development of international leadership personnel.

As Maucher puts it: "It is important to feel and to comprehend trends quicker than your competitors. Unilever, for instance, has the same quality of professional people like us. They have the same marketing instruments and know the same market research. They have a long tradition in technology. Everyday they make a better margarine or a better ice-cream. Where are we different? In the fact that we have a few people with more visions, who have the power, the quality and the drive to implement these visions. In all other regards, our differences are marginal."[6]

With this minimalist HQ role, Nestlé appears more like a network organization with the center playing the role of a mediator and proactive holding. While this may appear as dangerously wishy-washy, Maucher always assured that personal responsibilities were clear. He abolished Nestlé's traditional collective leadership, and, like his successor, made sure that the leading team had a boss for strategic decisions, like key acquisitions and brand management with whom ultimate responsibility rested, namely himself.

When Peter Brabeck took over in 2000, the world food market had changed due to the conclusion of the Uruguay Round. Trade in foodstuffs was now much easier, allowing economies of scale in production by supplying neighboring markets as well.[7] Some 115 smaller plants were closed, and cost savings in production mostly ploughed back into advertising and promotions. The rationalizing effect was strongest in the pet food sector, where different national taste buds play less of a role. Some marginal activities like running a fishing fleet in Norway, growing peas for Unilever and low-margin businesses like commodity frozen food and processed tomatoes were also discontinued.

With continued profitability, Brabeck has the means to go after the coveted No. 1 or No. 2 world rank for his strongest brands. The concept is relatively clear-cut. Nestlé has a handful of global brands at the apex, followed by a greater number of regional brands, and then hundreds of local products of only national appeal. In water, for instance, the global brands are Perrier, Vittel and San Pellegrino. Regional waters are Contrex in Europe, Arrowhead in the US, and Nestlé Pure Life in emerging markets.

During 1985/2000, Maucher spent some of $26 billion for acquisitions. In his first two years as CEO, Brabeck's purchases amounted to $18 billion alone. First it was Ralston Purina ($10.3 billion), a pet food maker, then ChefAmerica ($2.6 billion) a frozen snack producer, followed by Häagen-Dazs and Schöller ice-cream (Germany) and Dreyers (US). As the *Economist* observed, Nestlé has a reputation for smooth merger integration. It leaves local management in place.[8] Its global pet food operations are now run from Ralston's hometown of St. Louis (similar to mineral water from Paris).

"Long-termism" continues to guide Nestlé's policies. It survived one decade of losses in China and South Korea, and did not pull out of Russia during the 1998 crisis. In all three it is now highly profitable, in Russia as a market leader for chocolate, coffee and ice-cream. With economic and demographic growth in the emerging markets, every decade some 500/800 million people are added as mid-income consumers of industrial foods. This in Nestlé's view is reason enough to hold on to a steady successful course.

ENDNOTES

1. *The New Internationalist*, 275, 1996.
2. Free translation from Helmut Maucher "Die Zeit hat mir recht gegeben" *Finanzinfo. ch. archiv*.
3. Helmut Maucher. "Gentechnologie—dazu stehen wir." *Der Stern*, 47, November 14, 1996.
4. Helmut Maucher. "Bequemlichleit, Sicherheitswahn und Genussucht." *Die Zeit*, 36, 1996.
5. *Business Times*, March 21, 2000.
6. Free translation, in: Friedhelm Schwarz. *Nestlé: Macht durch Nahrung*. Bergisch-Gladbach: Bastei Lubbe. 2003, p. 33.
7. "Interview: Peter Brabeck, Nestlé." *Financial Times*, April 8, 2002.
8. *The Economist*, August 31, 2002.

CHAPTER 13

Alltech: Irish Know-How in the New World

FRANK BRADLEY

At the Annual Sales and Marketing Meeting held in Dublin, Ireland, in February 1999, Dr Pearse Lyons, President of Alltech Inc. set a target for company worldwide sales to increase from $100 million to $500 million by 2008 and he wondered how this target might be achieved. During the symposium the company introduced new animal feed products and promoted existing products to key feed industry executives. Dr Lyons considered research to be the cornerstone of the company's success; about 15 per cent of annual revenues were being re-invested in R&D. Innovative marketing and sales techniques, largely based upon the concept of "Marketing through Education," also facilitated Alltech's rapid international expansion, but whether they would be sufficient to expand sales five-fold was the challenge facing Alltech.

Large competitors had begun to enter the market and imitate Alltech's product range and its unique business formula. As these large competitors, especially companies such as Bayer and Elanco, entered the market senior managers feared that Alltech's competitive advantage might be eroded. The company had to rethink its strategy to further differentiate its offering to stay ahead of the competition. Alltech's six regional sales directors believed they needed five or six new products, each of which would be capable of producing additional sales of at least $50 million. The company had identified a concept of a rotating six-product focus, known as the "Big Six," which between them were expected to produce sales of $500 million a year. In April 2000, the rotating Big Six were Bio-Mos, Sel-Plex, Sil-All, Fibrozyme, Bioplexes and Mycosorb.

As the company grew, the issue of direct control over sales and distribution, and the corresponding costs of establishing a dedicated presence overseas, had become increasingly important. Issues of cash flow and capital for expansion inevitably arose in management discussions which created new management issues for the company. The sales directors and the marketing director also wondered if they had the organizational structure or sufficient managers of the caliber required to increase sales five-fold in eight years. One director remarked that the company vision would require them to "think outside the box". Another matter of concern was how the company should respond to recent scares in the food industry. At the start of the new millennium Alltech faced many challenges which Dr Lyons acknowledged: "how can a corporation cope in a world of ever changing challenges, ever changing rules, a world that wants everything and wants it now? A world where today's winner is tomorrow's nobody." He was also aware of the very public attention being paid to his industry—"No industry is under more scrutiny than our feed industry, yet few industries respond more slowly."

ORIGINS OF ALLTECH

Established in 1980 with a capital investment of $10,000 in Lexington, Kentucky, USA, Alltech Inc. specialised in producing natural ingredients for the animal feed industry. Some 65 per cent of sales were outside the Continental USA. In 1995, the company employed nearly 250 people and had offices in Austria, Brazil, Chile, the Czech Republic, France, Germany, Great Britain, Hungary, Ireland, the Netherlands, Peru, Poland, Portugal, South Africa and China. By 1999, employment had reached 600 worldwide. In 1994, Alltech had sales of $36 million; $84 million in 1997; and was expected to exceed $100 million in 2000.

The main driving force behind Alltech Inc. was Dr Pearse Lyons whose scientific and entrepreneurial business skills helped to develop the company into a significant competitor in the international animal nutrition market. Lyons completed his primary degree in biochemistry at University College Dublin, Ireland followed by a Master's Degree in brewing technology at the British School of Malt and Brewing in Birmingham University, UK, where he also completed a PhD in the chemistry of yeast. Subsequently, he spent four years as research manager in Dublin with Irish Distillers Ltd., producers of most Irish whiskey brands and later to become part of Pernod Ricard. He then returned to England as general manager with Biocon, a young company producing additives for the brewing industry. He spent a further four years setting up a similar operation for Biocon in the US.

In 1980, when the fuel alcohol business took off, stimulating demand for advice on the setting up and operation of distilleries, Dr Lyons launched Alltech Inc., initially selling his personal services as a process consultant to gasahol producers. In the early stages, it was a low-budget operation, partly funded by family members. Simple manufacturing techniques were used in Alltech and equipment was bought second-hand. Much later, Dr Lyons recalled that the company's philosophy was "do it quickly and do it well—our motto is to be first with the isues and first with the solutions." This attitude to risk was reflected in his frequent references to a quotation which he attributed to Wayne Gretsky, the great ice-hockey player who retired in 1999: "Let's go for it, you miss 100 per cent of the shots you never take." For Lyons this meant "we want to have a corporate structure flexible enough to change quickly and willing to take chances." For this reason Dr Lyons wished to keep the company private—"we'll be 20 years in business in 2000 and I like being able to make decisions quickly. I intend staying private for the flexibility and speed of decision making that it allows."

ALLTECH INC.: THE EMBROYNIC YEARS

While the development of the fuel alcohol industry in the early 1980s enabled the company to establish and function in the early years, Dr Lyons believed that it had no long-term future. The industry was based on unbridled enthusiasm and government subsidies, both of which could vanish at any time. Managers were appointed whose function was to maintain, and if possible, increase the fuel alcohol area of the business, while Dr Lyons directed his attention toward developing new market opportunities. Using the cash flow generated from the initial sale of ingredients for fuel alcohol, Alltech began to divert its interests to areas which would not be influenced by world politics or by energy prices.

The company became a pioneer in the development, manufacture, application and support of biotechnology for livestock and poultry production. By the end of the 1980s Alltech's sales of animal feed ingredients including yeast cultures and extracts, enzymes, organic minerals, biologically-active proteins, flavors and direct-fed microbials were increasing by an average of 25 per cent each year. Alltech's initial business was to supply yeast cultures, enzymes and other additives to the alcohol fermentation industry. Having recognized that the ingredient requirements of the livestock feed industry could be produced through fermentation Dr Lyons decided to enter the animal feeds industry in 1983.

The motivation for Lyons to consider the animal feeds industry rested in the belief that yeasts, certain bacteria and enzymes could help animals utilize their food more efficiently thus lowering the cost of meat production. Other companies in the US were already involved in this market sector but lacked good scientific data. Yeasts and enzymes appeared to have a beneficial effect but the mode of action was not understood. The view at Alltech Inc. was that the future for these products lay in better research. Alltech Inc. understood fermentation, yeasts and enzymes and had access to university colleagues who carried out research in that field. Research enabled a range of technically innovative products for improving animal nutrition to be produced. Using the slogan "Doing things Naturally," a whole new range of feed additives began to take shape. At the time, existing customers for animal feed products were located close to the operative fuel alcohol industry, there were few other "bio-chemical" companies in the area, and farmers had begun to use yeasts for dairy cows and bacteria for silage.

The success of the company was not immediate, and it was fortunate that the demise of the fuel alcohol industry did not occur in the predicted two to three years, but rather over a five-year period. During this time, fuel alcohol sales still represented over 50 per cent of Alltech's revenue and it was not until the fourth and fifth years of operation that the animal feed sector began to dominate. Animal feed revenue steadily increased from $100,000 in 1980 to $3 million in 1985, $13 million in 1990 and $33 million in 1994 when feeds represented 90 per cent of total sales. By 1998, animal feeds represented 95.5 per cent of sales. With changes in the industry and in the beer market the company has since then regained its interest in alcohol products. In 1999, Alltech acquired a brewery in Kentucky and had begun to develop its own beer brand, Kentucky Ale.

ANIMAL FEED ENVIRONMENT IN 2000

In recent years animal agriculture has come under increasing public scrutiny. The public had become very concerned about the impact of intensive animal production on the environment, antibiotic resistance in human bacterial pathogens, and the need for plentiful food at affordable prices. The public had also been asking lawmakers to enact regulations to address these concerns. Industry analysts pointed out that the continuing goal of agriculture was to produce cheap food while consumers increasingly sought safe food and protection for the environment. In 1998, the European Union voted to ban the use of sub-therapeutic concentrations of four antibiotics in livestock feed. It already had prohibited the use of genetically modified organisms (GMOs) in food animal production. In the late 1990s, consumer trends indicated strong interest in antibiotic-free, low-fat, salmonella-free, organic and functional foods e.g., high selenium pork. This was seen by the industry as a move to natural alternatives. According the Dr Lyons, "some of these laws are not grounded in science. The real question is: how does science convince an audience already both skeptical and ignorant of science?"

From 1997, livestock and poultry producers in Denmark, for example, were not permitted to use feed-grade antibiotics as growth promoters in animal feed. So serious was the ban, that research on the use of sub-therapeutic concentrations of antibiotics in animal production had been greatly reduced. Commentators believed that this may have been due to a realization by the pharmaceutical companies that the ban would be made permanent. The Danish food industry appeared to be searching for non-antibiotic growth enhancers to replace antibiotics: "There will always be a need to examine the effect of other growth promoters and substances, which must be able to replace antibiotics with similar results or possibly improve performance," according to Dr Christian Bønsdorf Petersen of Denmark's National Poultry Advisory Office.

FOOD INDUSTRY SCARES

The recent scares and scandals in the food industry raised many issues for all participants in food production. One such scandal involved dioxin, a toxic compound being mixed into rendered animal fat which was distributed to 12 feed mills in Europe and subsequently added to 16 million kilograms of poultry, pig, dairy and beef rations in Germany, France and the Netherlands. Most commentators concluded that consumer confidence was at an all-time low—not only could the consumer not depend for food safety on the feed industry but neither could they depend on governments.

An additional nail in the coffin of consumer confidence arose when a German TV report in 1999 revealed that sewage sludge, including animal and human waste and animal parts, was fed mainly to poultry and pigs in

France. As a result Tesco, Asda, Somerfield and other supermarket chains boycotted French products. Consumers looked to supermarkets for answers and in the apparent absence of the feed industry acknowledging its role, accepting responsibility and proposing changes, a number of independent food safety authorities began to appear as well as a major international supermarket consortium which included Marks and Spencers and Sainsburys. In January 2000, the European Union established the EU Food Authority to coodinate food policies for consideration by the EU Commission. In the words of David Byrne, European Commissioner for Health and Consumer Protection: "in the minds of the citizens of Europe, safety is the most important ingredient in food."

In light of these trends, Alltech's aim—according to Catherine Keogh, Alltech's Worldwide Marketing Director—was "to forge the company's identity through an immutable image of a natural supplier— a farm-to-fork traceability supplier." How precisely the company should respond in the face of recent scares in the food industry was a cause for concern in the company. Alltech did not wish to be a vocal advocate for the cause as that might be perceived as attempting to profit from the hardships of competitors and the fears of customers. At the same time, Alltech did not wish to alert major competitors such as Monsanto to its carefully cultivated marketing patch.

Many feed manufacturers were beginning to view biotechnology-based natural feed ingredients as natural alternatives to additives such as antibiotics and synthetic growth promoters. According to Dr Power, Alltech's European Director of Research, "the awakening by the agricultural industry to the natural approach to food production was the principal driver in the rapid sales growth of Alltech products which are natural animal feed additives."

ALLTECH PRODUCTION FACILITIES

A site on 40 acres of farmland at Nicholasville, Kentucky, was identified in 1984 to accommodate a new production facility which would serve as a showpiece for Alltech Inc. The new facility consisted of offices, laboratory and manufacturing plant, set in attractive landscaped gardens which also contained a research farm constructed in the style of a Kentucky horse farm, and a 4,000-square feet Biotechnology Research Laboratory. The headquarters in Kentucky occupied 65,000 square feet and plans were in progress to triple its size by 2003 at a cost of $9 million.

Although Alltech Inc. was headquartered in the US, the company had offices and production plants throughout the world. By the middle of 1999, it had sales and distribution facilities in over 70 countries—including recently opened offices in Venezuela, Croatia, Slovakia and Kenya. In 1998, Alltech commissioned three new production facilities at Turtle Lake, Wisconsin, Cape Town, South Africa and Serdan, Mexico. The Turtle Lake facility had two evaporation systems and two spray driers with a combined annual capacity of 20,000 tons. As a result of this new venture, Alltech's North American production capacity was tripled. In early 1999, Alltech purchased two plants in Alexander in Canada from Nestlé which augmented its drying capacity.

In South Africa Alltech had refurbished it production plant near Cape Town. This facility also housed a fermentation system for producing lactic acid bacteria and reactors to produce non-corrosive mold inhibitors. The plant also manufactured Mycosorb. A growing number of producers and feed manufacturers in Kenya, Zimbabwe, and Nigeria were beginning to incorporate Mycosorb in their animal feeds. According to Alltech's regional director for Africa, Nick Smit, a new project for the South African plant would include "the installation of a new high-density fermentation system to produce diet-specific yeast cultures—which were expected to enhance the feeding value of African forages and raw materials."

Alltech's plant in Hungary was designed to produce bioplexed trace minerals for customers in Hungary, the Ukraine and the Baltic states. In 1998, Alltech also added fermentation and blending capabilities to its plant in Serdan, Mexico. According to Dr Gladys Hoyos, Director of Alltech-Mexico, the Mexican plant would supply customers with ingredients more efficiently. One of the major products of this plant was De-Odorase. Livestock producers around the world were beginning to add De-Odorase to feed to minimise odours.

ALLTECH BIOSCIENCE CENTRES

The company's own research facilities, referred to as Bioscience Centres, fuelled international expansion through the identification and production of a succession of new products over a relatively short time scale. In the early years, research was carried out for Alltech by some of the world's leading research institutes and universities, as well as in their own laboratories. The North American Bioscience Centre at Nicholasville,

Kentucky, as well as a European centre at University College Galway, Ireland, were established in 1991. These centers were established as a way of competing with other larger companies and to provide a clearly defined Alltech facility. A third centre in Beijing was opened in late 1995. Research and Development expenditure was estimated at over $4 million in 1996 with $0.3 million dedicated to the new research center in Beijing, $2.5 million to Nicholasville and the remainder to Galway. By the end of 1999, Alltech had established Bioscience Centres in Nicholasville, Kentucky, Beijing, and at its new European Headquarters in Dunboyne near Dublin.

The Alltech Bioscience Centres provided young scientists, pursuing higher degrees at universities, an opportunity to work directly on industry research projects. Each centre had 12–15 scientists working on projects proposed and funded by Alltech's partners. With the opening of the centre in Beijing, there were 45 full-time researchers in Alltech Inc.

In April 1999, Alltech Inc. announced the appointment of Dr Karl Dawson, Professor of Animal Science at the University of Kentucky, as Worldwide Director of Research. Professor Dawson also had responsibility for the student researchers. The company believed that in order to achieve its anticipated growth during the following five years it would require 40–100 additional postgraduate students to work in its Bioscience Centres. In 1999, research projects in the Bioscience Centres included efforts to discover enzymes to reduce animal production costs, organic trace minerals to reduce the impact of intensive animal production on the environment, alternatives to antibiotics, procedures for mycotoxin control, and novel concepts in protein nutrition. According to Dr Lyons, Alltech Inc. was also interested in other product categories such as crop protection, enzymes for food processing, natural minerals for humans, and natural herbs for humans.

ALLTECH PRODUCT RANGE

Alltech products were built around the theme of maximizing efficiency of animal production whilst minimizing pollution. Products had to be "ACE Friendly"—friendly to the Animal, the Consumer and the Environment (ACE). The ACE program, first developed in 1983, was soon imitated by a number of competitors. By 1999, Alltech manufactured nearly 150 feed ingredients and combination products, all of which were ACE friendly.

The first animal feeds product developed by Alltech was Yea-Sacc (1026). Yea-Sacc was a yeast product used to increase milk, beef and poultry production. Yea-Sacc typically was used at 10 grams per head per day by dairy cows, i.e., 3.6 kilograms per dairy cow per year. In the US alone, there were 10 million dairy cows in the mid-1990s and thus a potential market of 36 million kilograms ($100 million) of product. Yea-Sacc was the most widely sold yeast culture in the feed industry worldwide. It was soon joined by other biotechnology-derived feed ingredients.

De-Odorase which reduced smells associated with animal production was the single most successful product since Yea-Sacc. De-Odorase utilized natural plant material and waste degrading enzymes, effectively reducing ammonia and other noxious gases by 50 per cent. It could be added to feed or directly to lagoons, slurry pits or other waste treatment systems. In addition to its odor-controlling ability De-Odorase increased litter size in the sow, possibly by reducing blood urea nitrogen (BUN) concentrations. Despite Yea-Sacc and De-Odorase's continued growth and expansion, Alltech Inc. recognized that the key to long-term stability was product diversification—to have new improved products constantly challenging existing products. In 1995, the company produced 45 different products. Total plant capacity was three times production. Alltech grouped its product range into four categories: animal feed supplements, enzymes for animal feeds, animal biological regulators and mycotoxin binders for feed additives. These core products were the result of harmonising the multiple skills in fermentation, hydrolisis, blending and marketing possessed by Alltech.

SELLING AND MARKETING OF ALLTECH PRODUCTS

In May 1999, Alltech Inc. opened its new European marketing headquarters in Dunboyne, near Dublin. According to Catherine Keogh, the concept of housing the Bioscience and Marketing Centre in one building was an innovative approach which would maximize the synergy between conceptualization and development of new products and their commercialization. "With research and marketing functions running side by side, the Bioscience and Marketing Centre concept was designed to enhance communication, thereby eliminating unnecessary timelags," according to Keogh. At a cost of $3.5 million, the new state-of-the-art facility was seen by commentators as a major vote of confidence in the Eurpean market. The principal function of the marketing people was to be the communications nerve centre of Alltech by providing up-to-date information, generating in-house videos, promotional and other marketing materials, and by coordinating marketing plans. The 25,000-square feet development, built to ISO 9000 standards and housing 50 staff, also included a separate quality control and development laboratory.

In earlier years, Pearse Lyons had observed that feed manufacturers could be assisted on the technical side, to understand mode of action of feed additives, and also on the marketing side by providing a range of promotional aids, free of charge, under the manufacturers' own name and logo. A team of 10 brand managers served the US market, supporting either the distributors or local sales people. In addition, area and country sales managers supported efforts in Europe, Southeast Asia and Latin America. These managers, generally, possessed a higher university degree in animal nutrition and had fluency in English and at least one additional language pertaining to their geographical area. The sales people sold and supported the products, and also attended professional meetings as delegates or as speakers. After 20 years in business Alltech still maintained a relatively flat organizational structure with a number of areas such as research, marketing, production coordination and corporate media supporting regional sales efforts.

ALLTECH SYMPOSIUM AND LECTURE TOUR

A fundamental aspect of the company's marketing strategy revolved around the Alltech Symposium which was designed as a vehicle to educate both researchers and farmers and, at the same time, promote the Alltech product range. The company has hosted the Alltech Symposium every year for increasing numbers of research scientists, nutritionists and feed company representatives at various international locations. The concept of "Marketing through Education" was developed in response to what Lyons called the "hunger for knowledge" in the animal feed industry. The Alltech Symposium had become a focal point for those involved in the application of biotechnology in the feed industry. As recorded by a New Zealand feed compounder, a delegate at an Alltech Symposium:

> they charge top of the range prices, but it is the technical support that you get in return that puts them on top.

Education of the customer and the food consumer was a major foundation of Alltech's business philosophy. The company's annual Symposium on Biotechnology in the feed industry was one of the most popular technical meetings in the industry according to Catherine Keogh. The symposium attracted more than 800 professionals from around the world each year. Alltech also hosted five lecture tours each year—European, Middle Eastern, and African; Latin American, Asia Pacific and North American University. According to Keogh, "the purpose of the tours was to share technical and industry information with individuals who may not have the resources or time to attend technical conferences outside of their region."

In 1999, there were 850 delegates at the US Alltech Symposium which cost $800,000 while the European Lecture Tour started in Dublin on February 15 and concluded five weeks and 28 cities later in Breda, the Netherlands. According to Deirdre Coleman, PR of Alltech Ireland, "the number of attendees averaged more than 150 per stop. In Hungary the turnout was tremendous—340 feed industry professionals attended the one-day technical meeting. Attendees in Breda represented more than 60 per cent of the Netherland's total feed production." In addition to lecture tours, Alltech offered technical courses, such as the Dairy Short Course, Equine School and Pig Nutrition Conference. "Participants at the travelling Nutrition School were particularly interested in Bio-Mos mannan oligosaccharide—largely because of the EU antibiotic ban, Sel-Plex organic selenium and Mycosorb/MTB—100 esterified glucomannan" according to Coleman. The latest developments in animal biotechnology were available on Alltech's website (http://www.alltech-bio.com/).

A Far Eastern lecture tour was launched in 1993 and visited 11 countries, while the Latin American tour visited 10 countries. In 1999, the tour included 15 and 12 countries in these two regions respectively. By late 1999, no other company operating in the feed industry had attempted to emulate Alltech's marketing formula; according to Lyons: "even if they do, Alltech has a 20-year head-start".

Papers presented at the symposium were published in a hardcopy textbook entitled *Biotechnology in the Feed Industry*, at a cost of about $100,000. The net effect for Alltech Inc. was an explosion in international sales. Lyons was proud to say that:

> the proceedings in hard back form now adorn the shelves of many nutritionists around the world.

The company also produced the *Alltech Feeding Times* which kept customers informed on product development, company news, sales incentives and promotion programs in 16 languages. Dr Lyons believed that proprietary publications and events are more effective and less costly than standard advertising and PR activities. In general, language did not pose a problem since most scientists could read and work in English. As the company was engaged in producing science-based products, cultural factors were thought not to prevent effective marketing communications. The company translated all its sales literature into local languages.

ALLTECH'S MARKETING CHALLENGE

Aidan Connolly, vice-president North America—Corporate Accounts, believed that the core marketing approach for Alltech was "to build a brand which means creating a mutually acknowledged relationship between Alltech and the buyer which would transcend isolated transactions or specific individuals." He admitted that this would be a difficult task but he noted that companies in non-commodity businesses, especially consumer products firms, that had adopted this approach had achieved superior and sustainable share and price premiums, even in the most adverse of markets.

Alltech Inc. acknowledged the challenge created in the context of what some commentators considered "public hostility"—a hostile media, hostile and angry consumers and a difficult legislative environment. In 1998, headlines in general media coverage often referred to "Frankenstein Foods" as in the GMO debate or in connection with the many and extensive BSE outbreaks or the imminent banning of feed antibiotics in the EU. There was much more confusion in the media and Alltech was straining under the difficulty of communicating its message accurately but it was judged as an opportunity by company management.

CUSTOMERS FOR ALLTECH PRODUCTS

It was clear to Aidan Connolly that Alltech customers, especially the producers and farmers, sought specific benefits focused on technical expertise. He believed these benefits could be interpreted as the value accruing to customers as a result of consistent and reliable products and services focused on a customised and knowledge based application. Consistency and reliability, he believed, stemmed from Alltech's ability to understand the customer's position in the value chain while customization allowed the company to charge a premium. But most importantly, according to Connolly, Alltech provided knowledge-based customized services that required a very deep involvement in the customer's operations.

US yearly manufacturing capacity of animal feed had reached 160 million tons of feed in 1998. There were 70 companies capable of producing 45 million tons of animal feed in 525 mills. These companies had the capacity to mix about 27 per cent of total US feed potential for pigs, cattle and poultry. At the time there were no large feed integrators. An additional 750 million tons of feed was manufactured in firms or mixed on farms worldwide. It would be reasonable to expect, according to Keogh, that the additional feed ingredients market would accept a $1 premium for each feed tonne thereby providing a potential worldwide market of $750 million for this sector alone.

In the US, the top 25 broiler producers slaughtered 112 million birds each week. Some of these producers were very large; the top three slaughtered 51.45 million birds each week. In 1998, the top 50 pig producers were responsible for 2.6 million sows or about 52 million pigs. Typical usage rates for Alltech products was 1 kg per tonne feed.

ALLTECH COMPETITION

Competition in the animal nutrition market was intense. Declining livestock numbers had resulted in excess animal feed production capacity in many countries. Consolidation among feed mills had reduced the size of the customer base for the companies supplying nutritional additives. It was estimated that the number of feed mills in the EU had declined by 45 per cent to around 4,300 in 1990, and half of these were expected to close by the end of the century. In both Europe and the US, much of the market was served by a relatively small number of very large feed companies, e.g., Hoffmann-LaRoche (Switzerland), Rhone-Poulenc (France) and BASF (Germany). According to Lyons,

> the total feed additive market is dominated by the likes of Cyanamid, making antibiotics and steroids, and we don't compete with them but we are looking to the second market, like enzymes which are naturally occurring, like our silage

additives. We reckon that there is no other company offering the whole range of products as we do.

Within the enzyme, yeast and innoculant sectors, Alltech Inc. was ranked as a market leader. Alltech's main competitors included Finnfeeds (enzymes), Kemin, and AgriAmerica (similar product range to Alltech), Diamond V (yeast) and Charles Hansen (silage innoculants) (Exhibit 1). With the exception of AgriAmerica and Charles Hansen these companies were similar in size to Alltech—sales in the $30 million to $60 million category.

Feed manufacturers had begun to move into higher-value specialist products, such as vitamins, amino-acids, enzyme feed additives and prescription diets for pets. Alltech executives believed that animal

EXHIBIT 1 Profile of Alltech Inc.'s Competition

Kemin

Ownership:	Private
Employees:	135
Locations:	US; Belgium; Singapore
Product focus:	Mould, antioxidants, enzymes
Sales:	$45 million (US: $20 million; Europe: $15 million; Mexico: $2 million; Latin America: $2 million; Other countries: $6 million)
Manufacturing:	Three plants worldwide

Diamond V

Founded:	1943
Ownership:	Private
Employees:	80
HQ:	US
Distributors	Hong Kong, UK and over 30 other countries
Distribution:	Company sales staff and manufacturer representatives
Product focus:	Yeast Culture, Deem (Live yeast lactic acid)
Sales:	$20 million (95 per cent to feed manufacturers, 5 per cent to producers)

EXHIBIT 1 Profile of Alltech Inc.'s Competition (cont'd)

Finnfeeds

Ownership:	A division of Cultor
Employees:	60
Sales Subsidiaries:	UK, Finland, Chile
Distributors:	Singapore, US, Spain, Russia, Holland, Malaysia, China, Hong Kong
Product focus:	Enzymes (Avizyme, Prorzyme)
Sales:	$40 million

Albion Laboratories

Founded:	1956
Ownership:	Private
Employees:	45
HQ:	US
Distribution:	Sales staff and distributors
Product focus:	Organic minerals (Metal Animo Acid Chelates)
Sales:	$5 million (50 per cent international)
Manufacturing	Three plants

Zinpro

Founded:	1971
Ownership:	Private
Employees:	40
HQ:	US
Distribution:	Direct sales and distributors
Distributors:	Mexico; Bolivia; Holland; Japan; Taiwan; New Zealand
Product focus:	Organic minerals (Avaltimine: Zinc, Copper, Iron, Manganese, amino acid complexes)
Sales:	$12 million
Manufacturing:	One plant

nutrition products had considerable potential for further growth in the future, particularly with increases in research and development funding. The adoption and development of new production technology and biotechnology appeared to have been slower in the feed and feed supplements industry compared with that seen in the vaccine and pharmaceutical sectors.

ALLTECH INC. SALES IN PRIMARY MARKETS

Most of Alltech Inc.'s $100 million sales were in developed country markets; 29 per cent in North America and 28 per cent in Europe in 1998 (Exhibit 2). In these markets, the company had achieved significant market shares. In the newer markets, Alltech Inc. was well established having attained substantial sales and dominance in terms of market share. According to Lyons, Alltech controlled 40–45 per cent of the world yeast culture market, 20 per cent of the enzyme market and 30–35 per cent of

EXHIBIT 2 Alltech Worldwide Sales in 2000

Selected Products	Sales Forecast ($ million)
Biomos	8
Bioplex	10
Deodorase	5
Moldzap	5
Mycosorb	10
Sel-plex	6
Silall	6
Vegpro	5
Yeasacc	20
Alcohol (incl. enzymes)	10
Enzymes (animal feeds)	7
Other products	8
Total	100

Region	Sales Distribution (%)
Europe	28
US & Canada	29
Latin America	24
Asia Pacific	19
Total	100

the minerals market, including their own Bioplex development which recently came off trial at University College Dublin and at other locations.

Alltech held a 30 per cent share of the US market for natural animal feed additives. Europe ranked as its second largest market where its share was also 30 per cent. Latin America was Alltech's next most important market, 50 per cent. In South East Asia, a region emerging from a general economic crisis, Alltech's share was generally lower. Company expectations were not necessarily to increase market share; efforts were devoted to increasing the size of each of these markets. The total market in the Southeast Asia was expected to grow by 20–30 per cent each year over the following few years and to account for one-third of the company's revenue by 2005.

Alltech management expected total company sales in 2000 to reach $150 million: $20 million from enzymes; $18 million from mineral products; $2 million from the horticultural group; $3 million from human food products; $10 million from alcohol products and the balance from animal feed ingredients.

DISTRIBUTION OF ALLTECH PRODUCTS

Within the US, Alltech operated its own distribution while overseas it proved more cost efficient to appoint distributors in the early stages. Distributors were chosen carefully. The company attempted to locate distributors with the same philosophy as Alltech and they had to have considerable technical skills and links to universities. For Timm Neelsen, European distribution director, based in the Netherlands, distributors were partners and had to be willing to meet the challenge of helping to brand the company and the product. According to Lyons, "young, energetic hungry companies with superior technical skills and devotion to products" were the kind of companies sought. In order to ensure that Alltech products were not forgotten among portfolios of products, companies were encouraged to ensure visibility of products through a uniform Alltech marketing program, and to be mirror images of Alltech Inc. The company had always been careful in selecting and cultivating distributors. For distributors or clients, Alltech prepared a marketing program including videos, literature, sales training, etc., to make it easier for the company to increase market share while at the same time, increasing recognition of Alltech products among customers. The marketing program was often provided free of charge provided the Alltech logo featured prominently. According to Neelsen:

> your channels compete with you for the heart and soul of the "true customer." "Customer" is often used to describe the channel but frequently "competitor" is more accurate.

Following its success in the US, Alltech Inc. looked to export markets for business opportunities. The first market tested was Spain. A group of entrepreneurs, all with similar backgrounds to the founder of Alltech, was identified as possible representatives for the company in Spain. Using Alltech marketing techniques, the Spanish company became Alltech's first partner outside the US. Excluding the UK and Ireland, overseas markets were supplied through companies referred to as "partners" because of the way products were marketed using Alltech's house style and marketing ideas, translated into the appropriate language. By 1995, Alltech was able to harness the efforts of all its 34 partners worldwide, drawing on their experience and knowledge of markets, products and competition, to enable the company to compete with large multinationals.

In Spain, Mexico and New Zealand, Alltech encouraged young entrepreneurs to go into business on their own. Alltech assisted these companies by providing products at a low cost or no cost which enabled the entrepreneurs to get their critical first tranche of cash flow. Alltech did not retain any financial interest in these companies. The Alltech "A" featured strongly in all advertisements and promotional items, and incentives were offered to encourage clients and distributors to join in co-operative advertising. In Spain, for example, Alltech assisted a local entrepreneur in the establishment of a new business. Alltech, in 1994, enjoyed over $1 million in sales to this distributor and the brothers developed a network of 10 regional agents serving the Spanish market.

In addition, Alltech encouraged some distributors to become involved in expansion into new markets. For example, the Austrian market was served by a joint venture between the Swiss distributor and Alltech. Similarly, the Portuguese market was served by a joint venture between Alltech and the distributor, Probasa, in Spain. It was Dr Lyons's intention, eventually, to service overseas markets directly by setting up overseas offices to ensure a complete focus on Alltech products. When distribution arrangements performed well, Alltech accepted whatever system is in place but when the distribution channel was not satisfactory the company would establish a sales subsidiary. Alltech executives believed that distributors should know their local market and financial system.

BUSINESS STRATEGY 2000–2005

Sales reached $36 million in 1994 and exceeded $45 million in 1995. By 2000, sales had reached $100 million and a target of $500 million was established for 2008. Pearse Lyons believed that while this was a challenge, the Big Six—Alltech's blockbusters, as he called them, would deliver the required level of sales. Senior Alltech managers believed the company possessed a number of competitive advantages which would continue to contribute to its success—it was a private company which did not pay out dividends, it had only one shareholder which facilitated rapid decision-making, it was research and near market driven, and it had a well educated staff.

Lyons believed that Alltech had developed a unique, tangible source of value—technological and bioscientific support for the animal feed industry. "We provide specific application bio-science to end-use which we believe is an integrated and differentiated source of value which is difficult for competitors to copy—but it's not where you start that counts, it's where you choose to finish." For the founder and president of the company the "Alltech blockbusters" which would take the company to its sales target included products such as Fibrozyme, Bio-Mos natural growth promoter and Sel-Plex organic selenium.

In order to achieve the sales target, production of new products at lower costs, exploitation of new opportunities and marketing through education were each strongly emphasised throughout the company.

To achieve the first ambition meant supporting the Bioscience Centres in order to concentrate on the generation of new products, faster and at a lower cost than competitors. In seeking new opportunities young managers were encouraged to take advantage of new business opportunities as they arose allowing them to demonstrate their abilities as capable managers. Marketing through education implied a continuation of the company's program using its European, Far Eastern and Latin American Lecture Tours as marketing tools—the Alltech Symposium. The company reputation had been built around these tours and through them, their products had gained market acceptance.

According to Alltech Inc. executives, the future of the company would likely be dictated by its ability to maintain a high level of energy, enthusiasm and team spirit, by beating the opposition in regard to marketing innovation and by maintaining a steady stream of new innovative products. In the 1999 European Lecture Tour, Dr Lyons stated that:

> by continuing the strategy of market-driven research and by constantly fighting to close the gap between the laboratory and the marketplace, Alltech Inc. hoped to continue to provide the industry with new innovative products addressing the problems which face or are likely to face the industry.

CHAPTER 14

Haribo: The King of Jelly Bears

ALBRECHT ROTHACHER

Haribo stands for "Hans Riegel Bonn." It is a classical German "Mittelstand" success story of a family-owned SME producing niche products, sticking to it and going global. With $1.5 billion of sales (2000), it has become the world's fourth largest maker of sugar confectionary.

The company was started in a basement in Bonn's suburb of Kessenich as a husband/wife sweatshop in 1920. The founder, Hans Riegel Senior, was born in 1893 in a village nearby. With just elementary schooling, he had already worked for years in factories producing liquorice (then considered a pharmaceutical product) and sweets in the region. Having returned from WWI as a decorated NCO (Non-commissioned Officer), he decided to get married and to gain professional independence. As hyperinflation raged in Germany, the 27-year-old invested all his savings in two sacks of sugar and began to cook candies in a rented backyard shack together with his young wife.

The Riegels distributed the daily output by bicycle directly to retailers. At the same time, they systematically expanded their business by distributing free samples to new customers and collecting orders on return trips. Soon younger brother Paul joined. The company's speciality was to melt gum Arabic with changing ingredients into a multitude of funny shapes of jelly babies. In 1922, during a series of trial and error experiments, almost casually the jelly bear ("Gummibär"), Haribo's contemporary flagship product was born. Production was still done in heavy manual labor. By 1921, the number of employees had grown to eight. As daily production had increased to above hundredweight, bicycles were no longer sufficient for delivery. In 1923, a car was proudly purchased and in 1924, a proper small factory was built to be expanded gradually year by year for enlarged production, storage and garages—all on one large site. In the tradition of German family-owned companies, Riegel's house was adjacent permitting the owner to continually supervise production, delivery and overall management. Private and corporate lives were clearly intertwined. As the company was located in the heart of easygoing Rhineland, marketing successes were regularly celebrated in corporate parties, which involved the entire workforce and their families as part of a localized patriarchal corporate culture.

The product range had expanded to a large assortment of liquorice products, soft jellies, foam sugar products and pharmaceutical applications like menthol and eucalyptus drops and liquorice imp. Aided by a then modern advertisement campaign and a simple memorable slogan "Haribo makes children happy," which actually rhymes in its German original "Haribo macht Kinder froh." The catchy evergreen slogan has been in use ever since. As exports began to develop to Northern Europe and to the US, so did global sourcing for spices, condiments, fruit extracts and glucose.

When WWII broke out in 1939, many of the company's 270 employees, including the owner's two young sons, Hans Junior (born 1923) and later, Paul (born 1926) were drafted for military service. During the war, corporate expansion stopped. With the shortage of sugar, production was shifted to pharmaceutical food supplements. As liquorice soothes nerves, the throat and the stomach, and reduces the feeling of hunger, it was given in large quantities to coal miners in the nearby Ruhr area. While Bonn, like most German towns, was flattened by Allied carpet-bombing, Haribo's factory in Kessenich miraculously escaped intact. Yet the occupation of the plant by US troops, which ordered production to stop, was too much for its owner. Aged only 53, Hans Riegel Senior suffered a heart attack and due to the non-availability of medical care died in March 1945. His widow Gertrude, aided by his brother Paul, now had to fend for herself when production was allowed to resume in September 1945, until her sons were either released or escaped from French POW camps during 1946. Like many survivors of the war generation, the experience had hardened the sons to assume managerial responsibility at an early age.

The two brothers practised a clear division of labour. Hans Junior, the older of the two, was the marketing genius in charge of commercial matters and clearly played the lead part in the company. He also studied economics on the side and in 1951, earned a PhD with a study of the world sugar industry. His brother Paul, a trained engineer, was in charge of the technical aspects of production and innovated a sizable number of productivity enhancing and cost-cutting technical improvements of the production process. Matching their business and technical minds and different temperaments, they formed a lifelong highly successful partnership based on clear complimentarity. Their mother Gertrude was remarried in 1948 to the owner of a hat shop in Bonn. Until her death in 1973, she played the role of senior advisor in the company ("Senior Chefin") without being involved in day-to-day management. A sister, who was disinterested in the company, was compensated for her inherited share in 1957 upon marriage. In the 1950s, she then ran a movie theatre in Bonn, until the crowds stayed away in 1961.

In 1952, the first major innovation was achieved in inventing the now venerable "gold bear." Instead of being made of expensive gum Arabic, it was produced from gelatine and sugar, which apart from being cheaper, had the advantage of tasting better given the right mix of ingredients and condiments, which—like with Coke—remain a closely guarded corporate secret. A marketing breakthrough was achieved in 1961 by introducing handy pre-packed see-through plastic bags for the most popular mixtures, of which at any given time, some 250 different kinds were sold worldwide. Any product, which no longer sold well, was quickly taken off production and replaced by newly developed items.

With the advent of affluence, both brothers indulged in a fast-paced lifestyle of hard work and hard play. Already in the early 1950s, they introduced badminton as a new sport to Germany. In 1953, Haribo build the "Hans Riegel Halle," which specialized in badminton games and dominated the German Badminton Association. Their products benefited from this sporting association, until in 1988, Haribo's sponsorship was suspended following some acrimony of the sort, which occur on occasion between volunteer sports clubs and their powerful sponsors, who are sometimes perceived as overbearing.

Already in the 1950s, Dr Hans Riegel start his collection of foreign luxury cars, including Cadillacs, Ferraris and Lamborghinis—then a rarity in post-war Germany. He moved on to helicopter and Cessna piloting and regularly went hunting in Austria and Africa. His brother Paul did motorboat racing and was an accomplished horseman and marksman, who participated in international sports competitions. In the wild 1960s, when both were in their forties, Hans, who was only briefly married, acquired the reputation of a playboy with a rapid sequence of opulent parties and expensive publicity stunts. They may have served to give Haribo confectionary a more carefree fun image, but probably reflected more the war generation's wish to make up for its lost youth. His brother Paul was more of a family man. His oldest son, Hans-Jürgen, who since has been groomed for succession and who manages Haribo France successfully, was born in 1954, followed by three surviving children to a second wife.

In 1958, in an important symbolic step, the local competitor "Keitgen & Meier" was purchased. It had been the company in which their father had apprenticed some 50 years earlier. During the 1960s, Haribo's commercial expansion into France and the Netherlands was followed by the acquisition of local sweets and liquorice factories. By 1970, Haribo had grown to 1,500 employees and could claim to be the world's largest producer of liquorice. Its market share for liquorice in Germany alone stood at 90 per cent. For fruit jellies, it was 70 per cent. In 1976, Hans Riegel decided to phase out all non-brand production—even at the expense of market share. The marketing focus was to be on Haribo led by its "gold bear" flagship.

Only "Maoam," a chewing sweet, and "Vademecum," a chewing gum, which were later purchased and are both distinct from jelly and liquorice products, thus are permitted to remain as separate major brands.

The product range itself has become quite impressive: colourful gummi-worms and rattle snakes, alphabet letters, chewy lime frogs, sugar-coated "fruit salads," grapefruit, peach, raspberry and cherry gummi candies, hamburger looking candies, sugarless gummi bears, happy "Cola bottles," gummi crocs, sugar-coated gummi apples, and similar delights. But none of them was allowed to outshine the "gold bear."

Since the 1970s, advertisements and promotions were done in a big professional fashion. During the soccer world championships of 1974, Haribo received endorsements in TV commercials by leading German players like Gerd Müller, Sepp Maier and Franz Beckenbauer. Subsequently, popular children series on German TV, like the Bee Maja, were linked in commercials to Haribo products, a strategy that usually, but not always worked. Also a lot of merchandising was undertaken, with Gold Bears on T-shirts, coffee cups and umbrellas: all more of PR value then a source of great profits.

Still, the company continued to grow happily and healthily, multiplying its employee numbers at regular intervals: 1970—1,500 people, 1980—3,000 and in 2000—6,000 people. In the 1990s, a uniquely successful promotional partnership was entered into with the popular German talk show master, Thomas Gottschalk, who somehow manages to represent eternal youthfulness and good humor across the generations. His honorarium for biting into gold bears in funny prime time commercials amounted to some €1.5 million,[1] but certainly was well worth it. But the company also honored well-worn historical local promotion schemes, like exchanging huge amounts of oak seeds and chestnuts collected by kids for sweets at the factory gates during certain autumn days at the ratio of 10:1. This generous scheme had been introduced by Riegel Senior to feed the game of his Austrian hunting grounds in the 1930s. Although mainly of nuisance value to today's employees, it is still being continued for fear of annoying kids and their parents in the greater Bonn area.

There are differences of tastes even within in Germany. The South has a sweeter tooth, and the North is more into liquorice. However, reflecting the even larger culinary and linguistic diversity of Europe, beyond the borders of German speaking Europe, different avenues had to be pursued for effective marketing. As 60 per cent of turnover are achieved abroad mostly in Europe,[2] a sophisticated differentiation is needed for a fickle segment like pre-teenage confectionery consumption.

In France over the years, three family-owned industrial confectionery makers were bought up. Their origins went back up to 1838. Although strongly in need of modernization in production, packing and marketing, their traditional brands had to be maintained and cared for if the investment was to have any value. These are the hard liquorices "Zani" and "Zanoid," the soft liquorices "Zigotê" and "Cocobat," the sugar-coated jellies "Dragibus" and "Teles"—which are uniquely popular in France and Belgium—as well as strawberry-flavored marshmallows like "Tagada," "Chamallows" and "Dulcia," and the peppermint products of "Ricqles." In the three modernized factories in Marseilles, Uzes and Wattrelos, some 700 people are employed. In Uzes, Hans-Jürgen Riegel, head of Haribo France and designated successor built a "Musee du Bonbon" documenting Haribo's and the European confectionery sector's history in an old water mill. His modernist octogenarian predecessor generation had not wanted this tourist attraction on German soil.

As the "Tour de France" proved elusive with its inflated sponsorships, Haribo France opted for a more economical second rated "Haribo Classic" bicycle race, where it at least could play first fiddle in a less crowded field of sponsors. So far the strategy worked with market leadership in most production segments. In Belgium in 1996, Dulcia Sweet Lines were purchased near Antwerp, which—in difference to their name—produced the more acidic sweets popular in Belgium.

Along the Belgium and Dutch seacoast, pop music trucks are used for noisy Haribo product promotions, including public dancing and silly kissing competitions to conquer the teenage market.

In the UK, where coco-flavored liquorice is popular, a liquorice maker called Dunhills producing the famous black "Pontrefacts Cakes" had been purchased already back in 1972. In the UK, the sponsorship of the "London Towers" basketball team is seen as the right avenue for promotion.

In Spain, like in the rest of Southern Europe, more "fruity" tastes prevail. Here since 1995 from a factory in Gerona (Catalonia), the entire market of Southern Europe and Lain America is being supplied with sweets of the right taste.

In Turkey in 2001, a medium-sized sweets maker, Pamir Gida Sanayi, was taken over. As befitting a Muslim country, its gelatine for jelly production is chicken-based (not pork as for the rest), and hence suitable for export to the rest of the Muslim world.

In Austria, the purchase of Panuli Bonbon in Linz in 1988 is since used to supply Eastern Europe from this well located production base.

Closer to home after the German unification, Haribo soon in 1990 bought the run-down VEB Westsachsen (WESA) sweets maker, modernized its facilities and retrained its 120 employees, thus producing gold bears for the East German market.

The pattern of overseas expansion is fairly straightforward: first, there is market penetration, followed by the set-up of a fully-owned marketing subsidiary. Then there is either local production or the friendly takeover of a local family-owned company, which produces in line with local tastes. Obviously, Haribo makers know that in some markets, the Germanic gold bears simply do not sell well. Similarly, in terms of promotion schemes and target groups, overseas subsidiaries are allowed considerable leeway. Although products are marketed worldwide, with some forays into China and Japan, Haribo's marketing and production has been fairly Eurocentric.

Dr Riegel, the aged patriarch in Bonn, so far has shied away from tackling the notoriously difficult and expensive US market head on. Since 1982, a distribution company exists in Baltimore, which yielded some successes in niche marketing, but, in the absence of real marketing push and a crucial US production base, lacked critical mass. Plans for a facility in Pennsylvania are underway, but have not been implemented yet. Surely, once the gold bear has been made and found acclaim in the US, the path to the rest of the world will be free. True to popular form Haribo has already begun to sponsor NASCAR stock car racing in the US. Stock car-shaped gummi candies are already out for sale.

Since close to 60 years has Dr Hans Riegel managed, owned and successfully built up his war-ravaged inherited company. Little wonder that his views, strokes of a genius as well as idiosyncrasies, are law in his company. Having had the experience of usually having been right, reportedly he takes ill to people who contradict him or question his decisions. On occasion, ill-intentioned counsellors gain his confidence, like a senior accountant, who back in 1993 was caught having pilfered some €7 million effortlessly from the company's unaudited accounts to finance a suspiciously luxurious lifestyle.[3] Autocratic regimes, with often unpredictable likes and dislikes, usually invite courtiers who dispense with selfish advice. Haribo seems no exception. Yet also equally difficult as generous at times, the 81-year-old Hans Riegel still maintains an amazingly sure and safe grasp about the longings, habits and tastes of his main customers, who are mostly more than seven decades his junior. This is indeed a unique achievement, which a more professional management will have difficulty following.

ENDNOTES
1   Bettina Grosse de Cosnag, *Ein Baer geht um die Welt*. Hamburg: Europa Verlag. 2003, p. 173.
2   3SAT. *Boerse Magazin*. January 30, 2004.
3   Grosse de Cosnac, op. cit., p. 192.

CHAPTER 15

Chupa Chups: The Lollipop Company

ALBRECHT ROTHACHER

When Enric Bernat Fontlladosa died aged 80 on December 27, 2003 at his home in Barcelona, Chupa Chups, the company he founded 45 years earlier in 1958, had become the world market leader of an unlikely commodity—lollipops. With a brand awareness of between 82 per cent (China) and 100 per cent (Russia), and marketed in 170 countries, it had easily become Spain's best-known international brand (*BBC News*, December 12, 2003).

Enric Bernat was born into a family of well-renowned confectionary makers in Barcelona. His grandfather had already opened a successful sweets shop there, which soon was supplied by its own small factory in which six children, including Enric Bernat's father worked. In his teenage days, the factory was bombed and destroyed during the Spanish Civil War. In 1939, his father returned to rebuild the factory. He also became director of production in the confectionary company, which produced "Galletas la Gloria" (cookies of glory), in which he became a major shareholder. His 16-year-old son, Enric, was in charge of selling the biscuits directly to retailers. Soon he added sweets to his sales portfolio, inter alia as the local agent for La Suiza Renye. For a while, he also became a sales manager in a larger food and confectionary company until in 1950, aged 26, Enric Bernat set up his own small confectionary factory, Productos Bernat, in Barcelona. In 1951, he married Nuria Serra, the daughter of another Barcelona confectionary maker. Their three sons, Xavier, Ramon and Marcos manage Chupa Chups as president and vice-presidents respectively today.

In 1954, Domingo Massanes, a family friend, asked Bernat to revive Granja Asturias, a struggling apple processor with 200 different apple-based candies. Bernat accepted, but as an honorarium for a turnaround requested 50 per cent of shares and of profits. The company must have been seen as hopeless as these most generous stock and bonus options were accepted. One year later however, the Asturian apple processor wrote black figures and Bernat owned half of it. He then presented a radical restructuring plan. Granja Asturias should produce one product only to benefit from mass production and abandon all 199 others. His co-owners Massantes I. Gran were not convinced, but three years later in 1958 sold out to him.

Some market research (which then famously did cost him only Euro 300) had shown Bernat that two-thirds of sweets were consumed by children under 16. But the sweets were not made for children. Invariably they were too large or rectangular. They kept them in their hands, which soon soiled their clothing. To make both children and their long suffering mothers happy, Bernat wanted his sweets to be eaten like "with a fork." Thus in 1958, the lollipop was born, which was to be his one and only product for a long time. A wooden stick was soon replaced with a plastic one.

After some trial and error, the name Chups was invented. Then a jingle was put on the market, with a chorus singing "Chupa Chups" (lick the Chups). Consumers began calling their lollipops thus and the company followed.

As a skilled salesman, Bernat insisted on direct marketing to the sales outlets. He set up a distribution company in Zaragoza. With a fleet of Seat 600 cars, which were all decorated in highly visible youthful Chupa Chups designs, all outlets in Spain were regularly supplied. The sales staff was trained in eight-day seminars. The photos in the corporate literature show earnest dark suited middle-aged Spanish salesmen somewhat uneasy in their first encounter with the youthful leisure culture they were henceforth to embody. More seriously, they had to deliver, display and invoice their product, all in one visit.

Distinctly packaged stand-alone displays—close to the cashier or at the main sales counter were preferred, thus favoring impulse sales. The sales price was prominently shown as one peseta (today: one cent), which then bought one newspaper. The lollipops did not come cheap, hence represented a special treat. The price was also popular with shopkeepers, as it did not require the return of small change. In order to encourage impulse buying, the wrapped Chupa sets were put within reach of children's hands—then a novelty. The company reimbursed shopkeepers for all lollipops "lost" in the process. Originally offered in seven flavors (strawberry, lemon, chocolate, coffee, mint, orange), today the range has grown to 40, including chilli for the Mexican market.

In 1969, Bernat had none other than Salvador Dali redesign the somewhat stale Chupa Chups logo. According to *fama*, the great man in less than one hour on a piece of newspaper sketched the brand name into a daisy logo. In a gently modernized form, this distinctive, globally recognizable brand mark is still in use on all packing, lollipops wrappers, PR and store displays.

Chupa Chups today also aims at the youth market of the 16–25 age group. Hence an image of fun, hip and irreverence is developed, with youth celebrities in sports, fashion, music and Hollywood, like Ronaldo, the Spice Girls, Madonna, Michael Jackson, Giorgio Armani *e tanti quanti* endorsing the product and sucking it in public. Russian cosmonauts on a MIR station in 1995 also took their turn. Color, themes and messages, including a slick website, mercilessly exude permanent happiness and optimism. New flavors, a sugar-free version, packaging and gimmicks are added and tried non-stop.

With its lifestyle image in mind, co-branding for youth products is done for perfumes (Coty), dental care (Unilever), eyeglasses (Indo) and shoes (I.D. Line). An interesting case of brand extension is the Chupster, an ice-cream cum lollipop jointly developed and marketed with Unilever.

Sponsoring is done for brand enhancing visibility, like high speed sports (motorcycle racing, skiing, skating, horse riding), the local FC Barcelona, but also fashion shows, film festivals, rock concerts, the Mardi Gras, and the Berlin Love Parade. For corporate respectability, business schools in Spain and Switzerland are supported, as are NGOs engaged in development work.

Chupa Chups' international marketing started in the 1970s targeting Germany, Italy, the US, Japan and Australia. In 1980, a US subsidiary was established—although to this date a market share of only 5 per cent and a brand awareness of 16 per cent was achieved on this notoriously expensive market—followed by more successful subsidiaries in Germany (1982) and the UK (1983). Although the modernized plants in Villamayor (Asturias) and in Barcelona remain the main global production centres, in the 1990s, the new emerging regional export markets are served from new plants in St. Petersburg (1990), Shanghai (1994), Toluca/Mexico (1997) and Sao Paulo/Brazil (1998).

Annual output now stands at 3.8 billion units, which makes 0.7 lollipops per planetary inhabitant per year. Market share in Russia is highest at 92 per cent. The global market share (by value) is estimated at 30 per cent of the lollipop market.

Chupa Chups maintains a series of joint marketing agreements and partnerships; Cadbury in Australia, Morinaga in Japan, Tingyi in China, Van Melle in Germany, Haribo in Austria, Spain and Italy, Adams in Russia, etc. As a result, Chupa Chups has access to one million sales outlets worldwide (by comparison Coca Cola, the world's consumer product leader has four million). Direct distribution is still the leading channel in Spain (87 per cent). But in most other countries, more modern wholesaling is used.

In a marked departure from his single product success story, Bernat in 1994 permitted the launch of their "Smint," sugar-free mini-mints for the adult market. They are sold in colorful one-at-a-time plastic dispensers. As the pastilles are meant to refresh one's breath, their slogan is fairly blunt: "No Smint, no kiss." Clearly young adults are the target market. A few flavors are said to have additional health benefits, like peppermint preventing cavities, and liquorice soothing the throat. It is portrayed as an attractive, sociable and dynamic brand with refreshing and healthy qualities. Rather high-income urban consumers are targeted, a different crowd than the lollipop kids.

In a remarkably short time with heavy advertising and merchandising investments, global brand awareness was created, with sales now in 80 countries and a market leader role in the field of mini-mints. There is also a fair amount of co-branding, like with leading hotel chains and BMW. Using Chupa Chups global distribution network, the Smints' sales now stand at 120 million euros per year, representing a respectable 30 per cent of total corporate turnover.

Total sales of Chupa Chups are at 415 million euros (2001), 90 per cent of them achieved in export markets. The company's consolidated average growth rate during 1992–2001 stood at 27 per cent per annum, which is remarkable given the overall slow growth nature of the global market for sugar confectionary of 2–3 per cent per annum. During 2002, there was a minor fall in turnover (–2 per cent), and the number of employees was cut by 15 per cent to 1,700. Following a reorganization, the family holding EBF was set up, which now controls the Chupa Chups company, and owns the trademark and the company's real estate. EBF is jointly owned by the widow and the five Bernat children. As such, the empire of lollipops looks healthier than its products.

REFERENCES

Rory Lambert. *1958: The Year Chupa Chups was Born*. Barcelona: EBF SA. 1998.
Chupa Chups Corporate Brief. The Chupa Chups Group. Barcelona: 2002.
Leading Brands of Spain. Madrid: Brands of Spain Forum. 2003.
Sergi Sabout. "EBF, los Bernat mas alla de Chupa Chups." *Expansion*, March 20, 2004.

CHAPTER 16

Born by Committee: Baileys

FRANK BRADLEY

After more than two decades of rapid growth and market expansion into more than 130 markets worldwide, the dedicated Baileys marketing team in Dublin, working with other teams located in key markets around the world, believed that the time was ripe to benchmark the strategic development of the brand and to provide it with an evolving strategic focus to ensure continued success for the company. Baileys had always been the world's No. 1 cream liqueur brand and since 1985 had been the No. 1 liqueur. In 2000, Baileys became the 12th largest selling premium spirit brand in the world.

During the 1990s emphasis was placed on the behavior changes the brand was seeking to effect in consumers. Some senior executives in the company thought that insufficient emphasis was being given to communicating the emotional benefits of the brand. Bailey's management sought greater emphasis for the brand's emotional benefits. According to Frank Fenn, Baileys chief executive: "many brands try to own emotional benefits but fail because they don't root them in product and brand truths. Baileys has an advantage in this area because it does root its emotional benefit of indulgent pleasure in very strong brand truths—delicious taste."

For many years Baileys had been a very successful value-creating brand in the United Distillers and Vintners (UDV) portfolio. Despite its success, the marketing team toward the end of 1998 believed that the issues of consumption frequency and relevance needed to be addressed and they decided to commission a series of research studies. As was the case with many liqueurs, some consumers tended to reserve Baileys for holidays, family gatherings, romantic dinners and certain other special occasions. Research in a number of markets seemed to indicate that these occasions reflected stuffy attributes and values and not the youthful emphasis required. Research also identified frequency as an issue to be addressed—consumers did not drink Baileys often enough! According to Aldagh McDonagh, marketing director at Baileys at the end of the 1990s, this was the role of marketing communications, directed by a strong and clear positioning statement for the brand. McDonagh also believed that although Baileys was the No. 1 liqueur[1] brand, the company had to continue influencing and adapting to evolving consumer behavior in all major markets to ensure the maintenance of its premier position.

MOVING FORWARD: THE NEW FOCUS

According to the company, Baileys drinkers by the mid-1990s had become younger and more affluent—in the 21–35 age group with a 55–45 per cent female–male split. Volume consumption by core users was reported as light. In the UK, for example, the average consumer enjoyed two glasses of Baileys a month whereas worldwide, consumers drank one bottle a year on average. Addressing this issue the company embarked on a number of new advertising campaigns and brand extension strategies.

Market research revealed that many consumers viewed Baileys as a late-night winter drink or a special occasion tipple. In order to boost consumption, the company launched advertising campaigns aimed at modifying these images. Baileys was also promoted as a "summer drink" through the *Baileys on Ice* campaign and its use in Irish-style coffees had also been encouraged. While the *Baileys on Ice* campaign had been very successful in promoting the brand, particularly new ways in which to use it, the campaign also pointed to considerable variation in consumption of the brand across markets and across consumers in specific markets. To reinforce the *Baileys on Ice* theme, in 1994, the company signed a deal worth $8 million to sponsor the World and European figure ice-skating championships for five years. In 1994, 270 million viewers around the world watched these championships.

Reassessing the positioning of Baileys

Given that a substantial proportion of total yearly sales of Baileys occurred during December, with the Christmas week accounting for 27 per cent of annual volume, advertising and promotion activities were heavily concentrated in this period. In the UK alone, a nation-wide advertising campaign worth $4 million backed the brand in November–December 1994. The key issue for McDonagh was what might inspire consumers to form a continuing relationship with Baileys? The consumer planning function set out to:

> identify and validate the most motivating, relevant and salient international brand positioning for Baileys, one that would unite the most motivating expression of Baileys' core values with a growing universal need and motivation.

To effect a behavior change in all major markets, according to McDonagh, it was necessary to begin with how people think about themselves and the brand. In the past, the positioning had focused on behavior among friends and how Baileys facilitated this, rather than on any inherent indulgence in the product itself. It was essential, she argued, that any new "positioning be relevant for 25- to 35-year-old men and women, as our primary market and, to a lesser extent, to consumers less than 25 but above the legal drinking age, our secondary target." From the extensive research available she concluded that there were a number of aspects of the Baileys brand, each of which had strengths and weaknesses in terms of consumer motivation. The planning team faced the test of discovering for the brand, propositions capable of exciting consumers and hence enticing them to drink more. The research also showed that Baileys was seen as belonging to two categories—spirits and indulgence products. Specifically, the research showed that for all liqueur brands the following were among the top 10 perceptions of consumers:

- liqueurs taste good, are good gifts, and good for guests
- users are smart, intelligent and know what they want and are sociable
- liqueurs are nice to give to people who often are gourmets/connoisseurs and enjoyed in the company of close friends where laughter and having fun is a feature
- consumers bought these products primarily at Christmas, during holidays, for after dinner by the fireside, as a night-cap or for a romantic evening

The company wished to ensure a clear brand personality and imagery. It was argued, therefore, that the Baileys brand positioning needed to be revised. It was the view of respondents in the research that the brand's image or personality should become sharper, even with a bit of edge. Some research studies had indicated, moreover, that the brand was slightly old-fashioned and safe, bordering on the boring, but "nice." Baileys was still considered *The Original Irish Cream Liqueur* based on a unique recipe of quality ingredients providing the user with a warm, delicious taste and an appealing aroma.

The overall issue facing the brand, however, was one of regular consumption. From the research, McDonagh noted brand awareness was very high in Europe which gave rise to very high brand conversion rates and core consumers appeared everywhere to buy into values associated with the Baileys brand.

In Italy and the US, while consumers appeared to have very traditional views of the brand, they had much weaker links to it. Was this due to a lack of knowledge about the brand among consumers, McDonagh wondered? She believed that alcohol brands with which consumers felt a link tended to focus more on image building, personality and emotion. Liqueurs in general, she believed, were perceived in functional terms, partly because they were very different from each other functionally compared to, for example, vodka brands.

New geographic focus

From 1996 to about July 1997, Baileys' sales growth in the US was limited by a downturn in chain-market business in California and a continuing lack of development in many of the Southern states. Costs to all firms in the industry had increased due to high exchange rates and rising production costs. Many Irish cream liqueur companies were unable to implement price increases in 1996 due to the need to maintain a price-value ratio relative to major competitors such as Kahlua and the other value creams. The brand vision in US, according to McDonagh, was to become the No. 1 imported cordial/liqueur among US consumers. Sales of Kahlua stood at 1.2 million cases in 1996.

In an effort to increase sales, one option that was considered by the company was to strengthen its position in key emerging markets such as Mexico, China, India, Japan, the former Soviet Union and Brazil—markets, which were expected to offer the best opportunities for double-digit growth. In 1998, Baileys sales to these six markets were worth $25 million and the company hoped to quadruple that figure in the following five years. All profit recouped in the six countries over the planning period would be re-invested in these countries. The company expected to continue using television advertising in Russia, Brazil, Mexico and Japan. While heavy investment in these emerging markets was risky, R & A Bailey believed it was justified by the presence of growing middle classes in these markets.

Eastern Europe would also continue to be a focal point. According to Martin Cuppage, the manager responsible for the region, Eastern Europe was "a viable market," although its full potential would be limited by the lack of discretionary income. While the level of brand awareness was very high in these developing markets, liqueur companies were emphasizing product education by hosting parties, holding seminars and making presentations in addition to advertising heavily.

In addition to these opportunities, the planning team at R & A Bailey & Company Ltd. also acknowledged that nearly 12 per cent of all Baileys' sales occurred in duty-free outlets. As duty-free sales had been eliminated within the European Union in June 1999, in compliance with EU directives, the company planned to replace these sales in other duty-free markets globally.

New consumer focus

The dominant product attributes perceived in the US for Baileys among core users were Irish whiskey and cream, texture, complexity of flavour, the Baileys bottle and presentation pack, natural ingredients, the Original Cream Liqueur and low alcohol. The company emphasized the delicious taste, nature and compatibility with the body and lifestyle, and accessibility to a tasty premium beverage. Research indicated that users consumed Baileys also because it was desirable, rewarding and provided casual pleasure. The brand was perceived as playful, engaging and surprising. All the research carried out in the US, however, pointed to weak relevance among occasional/infrequent users. Frank Fenn realized that the continuous limited consumer conversion to core status would restrict volume growth, which would mean that Baileys would continue at a disadvantage to its key competitor Kahlua. The research also showed that Kahlua users interacted with their brand more than Baileys users i.e., they were more frequent users of their favourite brand.

The key issue in the US was to widen usage occasions and frequency of Baileys occasional consumers by more relevant advertising communication, increased frequency of advertising message to consumers, more on-trade promotions to project a more relevant image and usage for the brand. The planning team was not averse to considering the creation of product extensions, which would stretch equity into new categories such as desserts, chocolates, and shakes.

A coffee-cream idea already had considerable tangible market support. From research completed as far back as 1995, McDonagh noticed some new trends among US consumers which might affect the fortunes of the Baileys brand. In that year, sales of coffee-cream liqueurs reached 1.5 million cases, mostly Kahlua (71 per cent), Arrow (11 per cent), Kamora (6 per cent), Tia Maria (1 per cent) and all others (11 per cent). The research also showed the new trend in coffee taste spreading to other spirit categories, including vodka (Stoli Coffee); tequila (Patron XO Coffee); cream liqueurs (Kahlua Royale and Carolans Coffee); Amaretto (Café di Amore); Sambuca (Obio Caffe). There were other important coffee trends—in the previous five years new coffee introductions increased by 45 per cent while coffee houses/bars had grown at rate of more than 30 per cent. During the same period, branded coffee sales increased by 25 per cent and Starbucks sales had increased by 60 per cent.

CREATING A NEW PRODUCT CATEGORY

During the development of Baileys Original Irish Cream Liqueur in the early 1970s, David Dand was Managing Director of Gilbeys of Ireland, the sister company of R & A Bailey. Dand, born in Dublin in 1932, joined Gilbeys in 1958 from the position as Dublin area manager with the Bulmers Cider Company. In 1968, he assumed sole responsibility for Gilbeys of Ireland, a traditional importer of wines and producer of gin. Gilbeys was founded by the two Gilbey brothers in the mid-1850s on their return from the Crimean War. They had noticed that there was a new market opportunity in selling good wines to the emerging middle classes. In 1858, a year after establishing in London, the Gilbey brothers opened in Dublin where for most of the next century Gilbeys of Ireland continued to operate as retailers selling all products under the Gilbey label. A wholesaling business was added, and in Ireland two relatively small brands emerged: *Redbreast 12 Year Old Irish Whiskey*, the fills supplied by John Jameson of Dublin and *Gilbeys Gin*, later to become a well-established brand of gin in Ireland. In the early 1970s, Gilbeys acquired the agency for *Courvoisier Cognac* and on his return from a visit to the US, where he acquired the franchise for *Smirnoff Vodka* for Gilbeys, one of Dand's first decisions was to switch company emphasis from gin to vodka.

Consumer trends in alcoholic beverages

In the early 1970s, the US was the largest volume market for spirits followed at a great distance by Germany and Japan. A notable feature of the international beverage market was the importance of word-of-mouth communication, international travel, and duty free sales, especially for new alcoholic beverage products.

In Western markets, there was a trend towards lighter alcohols due to changing tastes and to very heavy taxation on the heavier alcohols. Other trends included the more stringent application of the drink driving regulations, the increased popularity of dining out and the growing importance of younger people and women with preferences for lighter alcohols. More significantly, the proportion of Americans drinking alcohol was declining, from 70 per cent in 1980 to 65 per cent in 1985. This was expected to fall to around 60 per cent by 2000. Observing these trends, Sam Aaron, President of Sherry-Lehmann Inc., a leading Manhattan retailer, said:

> It is a sociological phenomenon. Part of it is the caloric content of what people are drinking, but taste is the critical factor. It will continue and we will move more and more in the direction of European drinking habits.

Alcoholic beverages in Ireland

Liqueurs in Ireland had been viewed traditionally as after-dinner drinks for women and posed no threat to the major spirits sector. Liqueurs were considered luxurious and priced accordingly. Until the advent of *Irish Mist*, liqueurs in Ireland were imported. John D. Sheridan, author and satirist, illustrated the point in an essay about the exotic bottles, which adorned the shelves of local pubs in Ireland:

> They contain liquids of varying hues—bright green and dark orange, golden honey and deep chocolate. And their labels bear names, which conjure up dreams of foreign romantic places Cointreau, Grand Marnier, Drambuie, Tia Maria and many more. They are liqueurs.

Many pub owners believed that due to high prices, low margins and slow turnover, selling liqueurs could make little real profit. As a result, consumers also found liqueurs to be very poor value for money, sold at inflated prices and in minute measures. Even though liqueurs were attractively packaged they were usually placed on high shelves and therefore relatively inaccessible to the barman. Referring to this practice, Frank O'Brien, an acute observer of the public house scene in Ireland, noted:

> Once the dusting of the retrieved bottle was complete the liqueur glass had to be found. Consequently, only the tough skinned or attention-grabbing consumer would be enticed to call for a brand of liqueur in the majority of Irish licensed establishments.

For these reasons and because of the small size of the Irish liqueur market, Irish alcoholic beverage manufacturers had traditionally looked toward the export market to absorb most of their output; 98 per cent of the production of *Irish Mist* was traditionally exported. Considerable quantities of beer and spirits had been exported each year from Ireland.

New product development: a cream liqueur

In early 1971, a committee of senior managers in Gilbeys of Ireland was formed with the express objective of becoming a "think-tank" which would scan the environment for business opportunities. As the company's own experience and knowledge was confined to the alcoholic beverages sector, a uniquely Irish drinks product reflecting Ireland's heritage and unparalleled agricultural tradition was considered appropriate. After much deliberation, the "think-tank" eventually came to realize that whiskey and cream together would be a unique product, a uniquely Irish combination that would also remain within the scope of the company's range of experience.

The possibility of a market for a pleasant-tasting light liqueur was attractive for three reasons. First, in the liqueur market, alcohol content was discovered to be a less significant factor in determining preference. Since Gilbeys could reduce alcoholic strength to a minimum acceptable level, for a liqueur, without significantly affecting consumer response, a new liqueur product could be offered at a highly attractive price while at the same time increasing the profit margin. A company executive remarked at the time that consumers purchased liqueurs for their taste, not for their alcoholic content. Second, it was believed that consumer reaction to new drink types would be relatively quick and heavy expenditure on media advertising would not always be necessary in the early stages if the product were unique. Third, most established liqueurs, e.g., Benedictine, Drambuie, and Grand Marnier, had a low "use up" rate (the speed at which a drink product is consumed); they were high proof, more difficult to drink and therefore took a long time to be consumed. Gilbey's idea was to produce an instantly palatable liqueur that invited rapid consumption.

While the product concept was relatively simple and manageable, the chemistry proved to be a very difficult issue to resolve as whiskey and cream do not mix naturally. Experimentation in Gilbeys of Ireland succeeded when a combination of whiskey, cream and a complex mixture of flavours with hints of chocolate, coffee and vanilla were discovered which passed the initial taste tests. To keep the product fresh, each cream molecule was coated with whiskey during the blending process when the grain spirit and chocolate and vanilla flavours were added. It took a long time, however, before the recipe was perfected and the difficulties associated with bulk production and shelf life were satisfactorily overcome. In the late 1990s, similar issues emerged again as the company began to consider how to cope with the much-increased production to satisfy market demand. The technology associated with pasteurisation created challenges for the production team and many issues had to be resolved.

Once the technical problems of producing a cream and whiskey mixture were solved, the Gilbeys of Ireland new product team began work on the brand name, image and packaging. The results of the initial research, which was arranged around focus groups through International Distillers and Vintners' (IDV) network in London and New York, were mostly inconclusive, although there was reasonable evidence that consumers liked the taste of the new product. These first tests of the product did not make the decision to continue testing in the UK any easier. In early 1974, with much anxiety, the decision was made to install a pilot plant in Dublin with a total annual capacity of 25,000 cases.

Deciding the brand name

The brief for the development of the brand name, prepared by David Dand, was that:

> It should be Irish without being stagy and that it should be easy to say in almost any language. It had to be legally protectable, capable of easy identification and one had to be able to differentiate the brand strongly from any competitor.

The initial investment was $15,000. Numerous ideas were tried and finally *Baileys Original Irish Cream Liqueur* was chosen. The overall image of the brand had to reflect the unspoilt, natural environment of Ireland and Irish heritage. Parallel to the off-shelf development of the product and the brand name, a specialist firm was hired to develop bottle packaging to match the image the company had for the new product.

Baileys Original Irish Cream Liqueur was a high-priced, high quality, low alcohol (17° proof), Irish product aimed at international markets in developed and developing western type economies with substantial populations and stable political systems. The product was initially targeted at the female 25–45 year age group over a widening social scale consuming the product at home. In late 1981, David Dand, Chairman and Managing Director of R & A Bailey & Company Ltd., recalled that the original objective established for the brand was:

> to position the brand as an original high quality liqueur type of drink with a solid Irish heritage, having a much wider consumer franchise than any other liqueur, thus establishing an entirely new drink sector synonymous with, and epitomized by, Baileys.

Launch of *Baileys Original Irish Cream Liqueur*

On November 26, 1974, *Baileys Original Irish Cream Liqueur* was launched in Dublin having cost in the region of $40,000 to bring to production and $15,000 to launch.

The new product was test marketed in the Netherlands and UK in 1974, and subsequently launched in these two countries and Denmark. Gilbeys of Ireland, through its subsidiary, the newly established R & A

Bailey and Company Ltd, sometimes operated through agents but normally channelled the new product through national distributors to regional wholesalers and then to retailers. In making the channel decision Baileys management placed the emphasis on being able to work closely with the local expertise of exclusive agents which was similar to the traditional way used by liqueur companies. Control over the promotional activities of national distributors and the channel in each market was, however, held by Baileys. Though the company was part of a much larger international group, all R&D, investment, production and marketing costs were borne by the Irish company.

The company organized a series of tasting sessions in the outlets where the product was available since, according to a senior company executive, the image desired for the product was one of antiquity it was inappropriate that the consumer should discover it through the broadcast media. Rather, consumers should feel that they had discovered something that had always existed. This strategy was extremely successful. Tasting sessions complemented by trade press advertising followed by heavy consumer advertising were to remain the cornerstone of the Baileys international market entry strategy throughout the world. The extensive tasting program continued through 1977 supplemented by the first advertising campaign featuring a public house as the setting. Research subsequently showed that the product was consumed at home, typically by women over 25 years old having purchased in off-licence establishments. Subsequently, the advertising setting was changed.

In 1975, 19,000 cases were sold, by 1980 sales had increased to 1.45 million cases, by 1990 sales had reached 3.5 million cases and 4.2 million in 1997. By 2003, sales were expected to reach five million cases. By early 1981, Baileys was selling to more than 30 countries and territories worldwide, by 1995 it was 120 and by 1999 it was 130.

Brand communications in the early years

The company attempted to ensure that the taste message, already discovered to be very powerful, was clearly brought out and emphasized in all its communications. Some examples of Baileys advertising themes in various international markets at the time illustrate the point:

- "the cream is real, the whiskey is real, only the taste is magic"
- "Ontdek de fijnheid van het ongerepte stoere Ierland"

- "Decouvrez la douceur tendre de la rude Irlande"
- "Irish Cream har kommit till Sverige!"
- "El gusto magico de Irlanda"
- "Original Irish Cream. Med aegte irsk whiskey"
- "Original Irish Cream schmeckt: so echt nach Cream, so recht nach Whiskey, so sehr nach mehr".

Furthermore, the blend of whiskey and cream in the brand enabled the company to claim that the:

> heritage of Baileys derives naturally from the history and traditions of Ireland, long renowned as an agricultural country with some of the finest dairy products in Europe and a parallel tradition of whiskey.

Initial market acceptance

Target annual sales of 50,000 cases in the three years following launch were forecast. Previous market research had shown indifferent results and industry experts disliked the drink. In a more rigorous market research test, using paired outlets; sales volume was encouraging but not outstanding. In regard to sales expectations, Keith McCarthy-Morrogh, at that time Gilbeys of Ireland marketing director, recalled:

> we were looking for a sideline which would be new, distinctly Irish, and which would develop, after about three years, into something which would sell about 50,000 cases a year.

Sales took off almost immediately and exceeded the 1,000-case mark in Ireland during the following year. For the senior management team, the taste of Baileys was the fundamental reason for its success and it was taste which the company believed distinguished the brand from all other spirits and imitators. As David Dand remarked at the time of the launch in Dublin, the brand:

> offers the consumer the potency and sophistication of a liqueur, while remaining a most moderate drink.

A universal appeal for Baileys was first recognised by management in 1975–6 when they noticed that the product was selling well in the stores in a number of US Air Force bases in Germany. Noting this male segment a senior Gilbey's executive at the time stated:

> this endorsement for the product is essential in ensuring credibility as an alcoholic drink.

Immediately on entering the German market, Baileys faced competition from *Chantre Cream*, a local "me-too" product sold at a much lower price. Baileys entry to the Australian market resulted from an accidental meeting between David Dand and the local Grand Met distributor who agreed to take an initial shipment of 400 cases. Baileys was an immediate success especially in rugby clubs where it was reported that after a game, cold and exhausted players consumed the product "by the neck."

Throughout the late 1970s the demand for the product constantly outstripped supply and the company invested over $1.5 million in new production facilities including a range of large tanks, additional manufacturing plant, a new bottling line, extensive new warehousing and office buildings. The under-capacity problem was an important factor behind the company's decision to delay entry into the US market until 1979. David Dand recalled:

> we couldn't enter the American market immediately simply because we did not have the production capacity to satisfy anticipated demand.

In addition, Baileys management believed that they had to acquire significant experience and a reputation on international markets before tackling the lucrative US market. At that time the US was the world's largest market for liqueurs accounting for 4.3 million cases or approximately one-third of total world imports; a further 37 million cases were manufactured in individual countries for local consumption. By the late 1980s, the longer-term objective for the brand was to develop through the liqueur market into the mainstream drinks market. The key indicator to market selection, however, was that markets had to have a proven track record in their demand for international liqueur brands.

By 1979, liqueur exports from Ireland had reached almost two million cases; 35.4 per cent of which was sold in the UK; 18.6 per cent in the US and 11.3 per cent in the Netherlands. It is estimated that liqueur consumption in the US reached 18.25 million cases in 1980, of which 27 per cent was imported. Consumption of liqueurs in the US market was estimated at 0.75 litres per person per year. Other significant markets in terms of per capita consumption were Belgium, Italy, the former West Germany, France and Canada. In 1976–8, Baileys produced 1.59 million cases of which 95 per cent was exported.

By mid-1995, Europe had become Baileys largest market accounting for 51 per cent of sales, North America for 30 per cent, duty-free outlets for 12 per cent and the remaining 7 per cent divided among the emerging markets of Asia, Africa and Latin America. The company's medium-term strategy was to establish Baileys in the six key emerging markets—the former Soviet Union, China, India, Japan, Brazil and Mexico—and persuade existing consumers to use more Baileys.

ORGANIZATIONAL CONTEXT AND STRUCTURE

In the mid-1990s the worldwide spirits drinks industry was dominated by Guinness's United Distillers, Grand Metropolitan's IDV, Seagram Spirits and Wine Group and Allied-Domecq's Hiram-Walker. In 1997, Guinness and Grand Met merged to form Diageo thus bringing International Distillers and Vintners and United Distillers together to form United Distillers and Vintners (UDV). The Big Three continued to rationalize production, reduce head-office staff and purge the portfolio of weak brands. Some of the cash saved was diverted to marketing and sales-force support for flagship brands. By the end of the 1990s it was believed that growth for brands would come from new markets in Eastern Europe, Russia, the Far East and Latin America.

Strength in distribution

IDV was a strong force in marketing and distribution of whiskey (most Scotch brands, J & B Rare and Black Velvet Canadian Whisky), gin, vodka, rum and liqueurs, not only in the UK but also in several other countries. Before the merger of Grand Met and Guinness two large spirits groups dominated the industry: International Distillers and Vintners on the Grand Met side, the ultimate owners of R & A Bailey and Company and United Distillers on the Guinness side. IDV had ranked a close second to Guinness's United Distillers with the corporate roots of its various predecessor firms going back to the early seventeenth century.

IDV was formed in 1962 from the merger of W & A Gilbey and United Wine Traders, which brought together the production knowledge of the former with the marketing skill of the latter. The new company inherited an impressive but unstructured portfolio of long-established prestigious brands in various stages of international maturity. In the late 1970s, IDV was still little more than a loose confederation of different operating companies bound together by history but with little co-ordination of direction. There was no corporate view on branding and little contact between R & D and Marketing.

At an IDV planning meeting with sceptical senior executives and chief executive officers of subsidiary companies held in York, England, in 1978, the R & A Bailey and Company marketing team presented its international marketing plan for the then emerging *Baileys Original Irish Cream Liqueur* brand. The marketing team reviewed the brand's performance, already on the market since 1974, and optimistically discussed the possibility of a five-year sales forecast of one million cases per year. A director of R & A Bailey and Company later recalled that at that stage sales were running at somewhere between 0.60 million and 0.75 million cases each year. The strength of IDV had rested upon its small brand portfolio and, in particular on its famous whisky brand J & B Rare.

Responding to retailer power

Retailers had become very powerful and by the late 1980s were beginning to show their muscle in various ways. One outcome of this was the polarization of country markets into strong brand portfolios facing strong retail chains. As the latter internationalized they were expected to threaten margins. In the late 1980s and throughout the 1990s there was a pronounced trend away from "on-trade," i.e., in pubs and bars, towards supermarket sales. The price differences between branded whiskies and private label had grown in some cases to £3–£4 a bottle in the UK.[2] In the recessions of the late 1980s these premiums were very difficult to maintain. As a result own label whiskey sales in the UK had grown to about 20 per cent of off-trade sales. A similar pattern was evident in France for white rum and in Germany for gin. During the recessions consumers questioned brand price-value. According to Ned Sullivan, CEO from 1991 to 1995, the Baileys brand price-value was also affected, "the price-value relationship has got to be taken into account, whether you are selling a $16 brand or a $10 brand."

As a result of these trends major brand owners had increasingly sought to acquire control of wholesale distribution channels rather than to rely on competitors to distribute their brands where they had no national marketing presence. In Europe the Big Three—Diageo, Seagram and Allied Domecq—had acquired their local wholesalers. By consolidating distribution the drinks industry hoped to improve its bargaining position. In the US, legal restrictions prevented drinks companies from owning distribution or retail outlets—a three-tier system of manufacturer, wholesaler and retailer existed and no firm could operate in more than two tiers. Consequently, an importer would have to use different distribution channels depending upon the state.

Brand management in UDV

In the early 1990s, IDV and UDV began to emphasize a new context for their beverages based on the insight that consumers were "drinking less but better." At the time of the merger the IDV top three brands, Smirnoff, Baileys, and J & B Rare accounted for about 80 per cent of profit contribution. Smirnoff was outselling J & B Rare by a factor of 3:1. At the time it was the world's largest selling vodka and second largest spirit brand. Sales of Baileys were reported to be slightly more than 20 per cent of Smirnoff sales and growing rapidly. Other well known brands in IDV's portfolio were Gilbeys Gin, Malibu, Piat D'Or, Croft Sherry, Black Velvet Whisky, and Amaretto Di Saronno.

The basic strategic business unit (SBU) in IDV was defined by a single portfolio national or international sales-force, with closely related marketing specialists supported by administration staff. These SBUs existed as independent businesses or were grouped into National Marketing Companies (NMCs) with responsibility for a portfolio of brands in a country, e.g., Paddington in the US. Alternatively they might be grouped into International Brand Companies (IBCs) with responsibility for one or more brands worldwide under the control of an International Brand Director, the custodian of the brand who was responsible for its performance and development on a worldwide basis. R & A Bailey and Company Ltd. was an IBC. The central concept of the SBU was that it should enable UDV to benefit from the advantages of being small within a large corporate structure.

A clear matrix structure was implied in these arrangements. It was expected that creative tension and conflict would arise between the International Brand Directors and the National Marketing Companies but these conflicts were expected to be resolved by pragmatic compromise to optimize the IDV position. Unresolved conflict was to be referred upwards with the Director making a case based on brand profitability and the Company basing its case on local profits in the territory.

PRODUCT PLATFORM AND BRAND PORTFOLIO

In the early 1990s, the world's major liqueur companies were testing global markets with a series of new offerings, hoping to identify or initiate new consumer trends. One significant offshoot of the liqueur business was the pre-mixed cocktail. Responding to the decline in after-dinner drinking, drinks companies shifted emphasis from supplying traditional sipping liqueurs to producing ingredients for long drinks and cocktails favoured by trendy young consumers. "Digestif" drinking was traditionally, and continued to be, an important sector for Baileys but the emphasis was changing: "the whole advertising and positioning of the brand, particularly over the last six or seven years, has worked to give it more mainstream appeal" said Ned Sullivan in late 1994. It was an ambition among the senior executives of the company that Baileys would become a mainstream drink. The chief executive, Frank Fenn, believed the company had a clear role to play in this evolution. For Fenn, buyer perceptions were learned and it was the company's job to influence the evolution of perceptions in a way that competitors could not easily imitate—"the Baileys brand strategy plays a defining role in this evolution which can have enduring consequences," he added.

International brands may have dominated the liqueur category's top 10 list, but local traditional liqueurs still played a major role in many key markets, particularly in Europe. In Germany, the world's second-largest liqueur market, four of the top five brands were essentially local brands, with Berentzen Cream leading at one million cases. In Spain, France and Italy, three of the top five liqueurs in each market were local brands. These markets offered a major opportunity for international brands to draw sales from local products.

One of the most dramatic changes for the liqueur sector occurred in Scandinavia. In Sweden, the high prices for international spirit brands and fine wines were reduced dramatically in 1992 when the taxation structure for wines and spirits was changed from a value-based system with an alcohol-by-volume (ABV) calculation. While virtually all premium spirit brands stood to benefit, the low-to-mid-strength products experienced the most dramatic price cuts. The retail price for a half-litre bottle of *Baileys Original Irish Cream Liqueur* fell from 147 Swedish kronors (US$19.11) to 83 Swedish kronors (US$10.79)—a 45 per cent price reduction. One of the three greatest challenges at IDV was to take advantage of the opening up of the Scandanavian drinks market. Even with more competitive pricing, brand building in Scandinavia was expected to be difficult, with wide-ranging restrictions on alcohol advertising. Thus, sales effort to the trade was critical in Scandinavia.

Baileys Light and *Baileys Gold*, other extensions and brand alliances

R & A Bailey and Company's first product extension sought to address diet concerns. *Baileys Light* was launched in the North American market in 1992. According to Ned Sullivan:

> we picked up in our tracking studies that there was an opportunity for a *Baileys Light*. What it has done is appeal to a slightly different segment of the market—consumers of light products and occasional users.

The objective for this brand extension was to re-attract lapsed (tried but not in the previous year) Baileys users and to hold and maintain current users who had acquired health and fat concerns. In a test market, *Baileys Light* held strong promise in the US. That, according to sales people in the company, used in conjunction with *Baileys the Original* could be a winning combination to increase the brand's overall market share and increase sales. It was noted that there were approximately 200 million adults in the US who were potential consumers of Baileys—the Original or Light. Approximately 31 per cent of these people were aware of *Baileys Light* but had not tried it, 14 per cent were lapsed users of Baileys, while occasional users accounted for 7 per cent and the brand was unknown to 46 per cent.

McDonagh was aware, however, that the product formulation of *Baileys the Original*, based on 50 per cent less fat and 33 per cent fewer calories, did not reflect the growing consumer trend toward fat-free food and drink. She was also aware that the extension had low brand awareness and research suggested that the packaging should be further differentiated from that used for *Baileys the Original*. McDonagh also believed that it might be worth considering delivering on the "100 per cent guilt-free indulgence." Consumer feedback in the US in late 1999 indicated that *Baileys Light*, at 50 per cent fat-free, was a sub-optimal proposition for consumers. Toward the end of the 1990s, there were no plans to expand the distribution of *Baileys Light* beyond the North American and duty-free markets. It was subsequently removed from the US and duty-free markets.

Around the same time, *Baileys Gold* was introduced, exclusively for the Japanese domestic and duty-free markets. It featured the familiar brand flavours but incorporated a 10-year-old Irish whiskey adding an extra touch of mellowness for the whiskey-conscious Japanese consumer. Major emphasis was placed on developing sophisticated packaging for this version of the brand. *Baileys Gold* was partly a response to the Japanese desire for luxury and the importance of gift giving in that society.

In the early 1990s, the company decided to experiment with brand alliances believing that there were benefits in linking the functional and symbolic attributes of its brand with others to enhance consumer value. Around 1993, Baileys chocolates were produced under licence by a well-known Dublin chocolatier. In 1995, Baileys teamed up with the premium ice-cream brand, Häagen Dazs (another Grand Met brand, now also part of Diageo) to produce Baileys flavored ice-cream. Extensions into the food sector were expected to expand the market for Baileys as it was believed that people would likely be reminded of Baileys after tasting the chocolate or ice-cream version.

A new brand: Sheridans

In 1992, R & A Bailey & Company Ltd launched a new stand-alone cream liqueur brand, Sheridans. The ultimate aim was to produce another major spirit brand, not just in Ireland, but worldwide. Sheridans was the first global product to be introduced by R & A Bailey since the launch of *Baileys Original Irish Cream* in 1974. Over $2.5 million was invested by R & A Bailey to produce a tailor-made production line for Sheridans dedicated production team. Two other spirit-based liqueur products were introduced in the 1980s, *Demitasse* and *Penny Royal*, neither of which met company requirements on profitability or market share and so were withdrawn.

Sheridans was a unique double spirit comprising a white top tasting of creamy vanilla floating on a dark body of liquid tasting of rich coffee chocolate (sometimes referred to as a "Guinness look-a-like," in liqueur form). The white spirit was 17 per cent alcohol and was made of fresh cream and Irish spirit. The dark was 26 per cent alcohol and composed of a select Irish spirit infused with natural chocolate and coffees. The bottle was considered by Pat Rigney, the brand director for Sheridans at the time of the launch, to be one of the brand's greatest assets and an integral part of the brand's personality. It was really two bottles in one, two adjoining bottles, individually capped, containing 500 milliliters of dark spirit and 250 milliliters of white. In 1994 the company introduced a smaller 350-ml. version to stand alongside the 750-ml. bottle.

In its first year alone, Sheridans sales exceeded 100,000 cases and estimates for the future were very high. Sales of 500,000 cases a year was the long-term target. Sheridans sold more than many established brands in duty-free outlets worldwide and in many of the 20 countries where it was available including the US, Germany, the UK, Spain, Australia, New Zealand and Canada. In 1995, in Ireland it ranked second only to Baileys as the country's best selling liqueur. According to Rigney, Sheridans was unlikely to join Baileys as a multi-million case seller—"Sheridans will not be another Baileys in terms of volume—it will be a niche premium brand."

Sheridans was promoted as a premium brand with an image and price to match; it was 30 per cent more expensive than Baileys. Of particular satisfaction to the company was the fact that the new product appeared to have expanded the liqueur market rather than take consumers away from Baileys. For example, in Ireland, 10,000 cases of Sheridans were sold in 1992, its first year on the market, compared to 40,000 cases of Baileys in its first year.

Value brands: *Emmets* and *O'Darbys*

In addition to the Baileys and Sheridans brands the company acquired two well-known liqueur value brands, Emmets and O'Darbys, in the portfolio as a result of the company's 1991 acquisition of R & J Emmet & Company Ltd., for $5.5 million. According to Ned Sullivan "the acquisition of Emmets has been financially very good for us—strategically it got us into a segment of the market which we could not enter with Baileys. In the US, Baileys is $18 a bottle, Emmets is $12 a bottle while O'Darbys is $8 a bottle." The company did not advertise its two lower-priced brands, relying instead on the price incentive and occasional in-store promotions.

While Baileys and Sheridans targeted the high end of the market, the R & J Emmet & Company brands aimed at the lower end. R & J Emmet & Company brands catered to the cost-conscious consumer. The brands were maintained as separate entities. Production of Emmets continued in the Bailieboro plant in Co. Cavan, Ireland, about 90 minutes drive northwest of Dublin, rather than being consolidated with Baileys production in Dublin. As Ned Sullivan pointed out:

> Baileys bring 1,800 trade buyers and their sales teams to Ireland every year to visit the factory. Can you imagine their reaction if they saw Baileys coming down one production line, and Emmets coming down an identical line beside it?

While neither Emmets nor O'Darbys have been introduced in the UK, it was likely that if they were, each would be targeted at wrestling the No. 2 slot from Carolans, a competitor of Baileys. In 1994, sales of Emmet Classic reached 300,000 cases a year while O'Darby Irish Cream sold 280,000 cases. Dubliner Irish Cream, an Emmet brand extension, was popular in Italy where sales exceeded 50,000 cases, while Bananas 'n' Cream (an extension to the Emmet line) sold 60,000 cases in the Canary Islands alone.

BAILEYS OVERALL PERFORMANCE

R & A Bailey and Company had recorded considerable success in the 26 years since it launched *Baileys Original Irish Cream Liqueur*. By 2000, Baileys was the No. 1 cream liqueur brand by over three million cases and the No. 1 liqueur brand, selling over four million cases in 130 countries worldwide. Baileys was the No. 13 premium spirit brand in the world, the No. 1 selling liqueur and the No. 5 selling spirit in duty-free shops. According to estimates from investment analysts Lehman Brothers, as reported in the trade press, Baileys made a profit of about $3.60 on every bottle in 1994. Other trade sources suggested a gross profit in excess of $5 for a litre bottle. Either estimate made Baileys the most profitable non-aged spirit in the world.

Baileys accounted for 40 per cent of the milk consumed in Ireland and required 40,000 cows to maintain the cream supply and the brand represented about 55 per cent of total Irish spirits exports. Over 90 per cent of product ingredients and packaging were sourced in Ireland and the company employed 400 people directly while there were 4,000 people in directly related employment.

ENDNOTES
1. In the US and Canada, liqueurs are sometimes known as cordials.
2. Exchange rates were:

1981:
US$1 = £Stg 0.42;
£IR 0.53;
DM 1.96;
Yen 203.31;

1995:
US$1 = £Stg 0.66;
£IR 0.64;

2000 (April):
US$1 = £Stg 0.63;
£IR 0.86;
DM 2.15;
Yen 106.33.

CHAPTER 17

Tsingtao Brewery: China's Newest Multinational

JUSTIN TAI WEI CHUEN

INTRODUCTION

Tsingtao Brewery is probably the best known Chinese brand after Haier outside China.[1] In fact, the brewery is now 101 years old and still going strong. Based in the country with the world's largest population, Tsingtao is set to be one of the major players in the international beer market. Currently, it is the largest brewery group in China, accounting for 12.1 per cent of its domestic beer market (*Euromonitor*, 2004). The world market has also been an arena where Tsingtao has flourished, as it reached its goal of being amongst the top 10 brewers globally in 2002.[2] It is interesting to note that the Chinese government has formed a strategic alliance with the world's largest brewery, US giant Anheuser-Busch of Budweiser fame, in which by 2010, the former would retain only 30.6 per cent of its stake in Tsingtao while the latter would acquire up to 27 per cent (*Euromonitor*, 2004). This is probably an unprecedented move by the Chinese side in its bid to privatize one of its own State-Owned Enterprises (SOEs), amongst which Tsingtao can be counted as one of the very few success stories. This may prove to be a great move on the part of its American partners, who after all, would have a huge stake in a company which has tremendous potential and is experiencing a significant growth in profit margins (e.g., from 6.1 per cent in 2000 to 8.4 per cent in 2002). Despite the SARS outbreak and its impact on Beijing and Guangdong—the two regions which form the core of Tsingtao's demand—the outward-looking brand is going to open up further to the world market, potentially offsetting its future dependence on the local Chinese market. For now, the strategic focus of Tsingtao is to continue its aggressive acquisition program domestically, to form more alliances with foreign breweries in product development, and to establish licensing agreements with foreign brewers to open more overseas markets to its brand name. Also, it has various brands under its name; with its core brands being Tsingtao the original lager and Tsingtao Premium, which is a classic premium lager.

Tsingtao beer has always held a unique place in the history of Chinese beer drinking. For one, it is believed to be the first beer made in China and its factory has always been part of the itinerary for Communist Party leaders visiting the city of Qingdao. It is even said that one of the pioneers of the Long March and former senior Politburo member, the late Marshall Ye Jianying, wrote a poem for the beer, exulting it in comparison with another Chinese favorite, plum blossom wine. Thus, after the 1979 opening-up of China, Tsingtao has been competing hard with other breweries throughout the country to keep alive its tradition of being China's premium beer. At one point of time, Tsingtao Beer actually accounted for 90 per cent of beer exports from the mainland (Thomson, 1988). After years of development, the company has gained joint stock company status, being listed on the Hong Kong and Shanghai stock markets since 1993. It also has various subsidiaries in places like Nanjing, Harbin, and Hangzhou, dealing with the production, distribution, sales and domestic trading of its beer products. At present, the brewery produces exclusively in China, having up to 50 plants spread across 17 provinces within the country, and maintains a worldwide marketing network, exporting to 40 countries in Asia, Europe and North America (*Euromonitor*, 2004). Its annual capacity of production currently stands at over three million tons, and competition in the domestic market is intense, with the likes of China Resources Beverages and Beijing Yanjing Brewery not far behind. International competition comes from established brands such as Carlsberg, although Tsingtao has already overtaken major brands like Kirin in this context. In any case, with China now being the world's largest beer market,[3] and with Tsingtao's dominance in this country which is experiencing one of the highest levels of economic growth in the world today, the company is on the ascendance with respect to its operations and goals in further developing and consolidating its position as one of the top breweries in the world.

DETERMINING THE "TSINGTAO CULTURE"

It is clear that the brewery is one of the most important and prominent companies in China today. Thus, an analysis of the company in terms of its corporate culture would help outsiders understand the inner workings of a mainland Chinese company. In fact, with China's impending rise, future dealings with such companies are unavoidable. This chapter aims to offer different perspectives on Tsingtao's operations and bring about a greater appreciation of its corporate culture along with the national settings it works in. Corporate culture can be seen as the culture of an organization, which Geert Hofstede defined as the patterns of shared values and beliefs that over time produce behavioral norms adopted in solving problems (Middleton, 2002, p. 6). As a company with a century-old history, Tsingtao has developed a unique culture of its own. With that in mind, we can see how this culture is manifested in the structure of the brewery and its operations.[4]

History and ownership

Tsingtao was born in 1903, six years after the colonization of the city of Qingdao by the Germans in 1897. It was set up against the backdrop of a chaotic era, in which the Qing Dynasty endured the foreign invasions after the Boxer Rebellion of 1900. German businessmen, in partnership with British investors, started the company. It was first known as Tsingtao Company Stock of the German Beer Corporation. In those days, all the equipment and raw materials needed were imported from Germany. In fact, German investors may have started the brewery to cater to the demand for beer by German troops stationed in the city (Landler, 2000). Hence, German influence can still be felt there, with the original brewery still situated across the street from a park where German soldiers once lived. The stone houses located near the brewery have steeply slanted roofs and there is purportedly some resemblance with Bavarian architecture. This is further accentuated with the recent building of an ersatz German village on the outskirts of town by the company for the annual Tsingtao International Beer Festival.[5] The Germans held onto the ownership of Tsingtao until they were run over by the Japanese in WWI. Reflecting the fate of its city, Tsingtao was soon controlled by the Japanese. The company was under the administration of the Japanese throughout the most tumultuous times in Chinese history. At first, the Japanese were ceded the city of Qingdao through the Treaty of Versailles in 1919. However, in 1922, the city was returned to Chinese rule, but with the invasion of China by Japan in 1937, the Japanese reoccupied Qingdao in 1938. After WWII, Tsingtao was run by the Kuomintang government for a short time. With the Communist victory in 1949, the Chinese Communist Party took control of the company and placed it under state jurisdiction. It is still officially an SOE to this present day.

The ownership of Tsingtao by the Chinese government sums up its emphasis in terms of production. It is still very much constrained by the state, and has been in public hands for much of its history. Even the German investors who started the company were probably financed by the German government at that time, well-known for its advocacy of state-sponsored capitalism since the time of Bismarck. Hence, the company still subscribes to the ideals of Chinese socialism, epitomizing the concept of *suoyouzhi* which entails the public ownership of all means of production with the state acting as its custodian (Hickson, 1997, p. 312). This would blur the lines between owners and employees, bringing about lesser accountability, which is endemic in most Chinese institutions. *Suoyouzhi* was brought to another level with the Chinese government's attempt to shift away from the model provided by the Soviet Union toward even greater mass participation, resulting in the Great Leap Forward (1958–9) and the Cultural Revolution (1966–76). This was only abandoned to a relatively large extent with Deng Xiaoping's rise and his efforts to open China up to the world in 1979. Thus, Tsingtao was finally given the opportunity to explore the beer market and to realise its ambitions.

However, the fortunes of the company have not always been very smooth. After further boosts of reaching out to the international market with more export contracts to Japan and Indonesia in 1988 (Thomson, 1988), Tsingtao listed its shares on the Shanghai and Hong Kong stock exchanges in 1993. As it was the first SOE to do so, the parties involved painted a rosy scenario, with many investors being upbeat about the prospects of these red chips doing well.[6] However, by 1994, Tsingtao had lost the confidence of such investors as foreign breweries were making inroads into the Chinese market, which up till then, was very much protected by high tariffs and barriers to entry (*Business Times* Singapore, 1994). Even the then chairman, Mr Zhang Yadong, had to be held accountable for the company's lacklustre performance. He had to resign from two of his three posts in the company, that of chairman and general manager, ostensibly to relieve some of the burden and concentrate on his work as Tsingtao's Communist Party committee secretary (Lee, 1994). The brewery went through a rough decade, with intense foreign competition from the likes of Foster's, Carlsberg and San Miguel, rising costs of raw and perishable materials like barley bringing about greater losses, and also rising competition from local breweries which were producing cheap beer catering more to common drinkers compared to Tsingtao's premium status on the mainland (Landler, 2000). In 1996, there was actually a 9.6 per cent decline in net profits (Lucas, 1996). With the company in need of restructuring, the leadership of Tsingtao, at the behest of then Chinese Premier Zhu Rongji, appointed Mr Peng Zuoyi as general manager. He went on a "crusade" to save China's flagship beer brand, mainly through revamping senior management and buying up local breweries. Hence, the decline was arrested somewhat in 1997, when the company managed to announce modest improvements in sales and marked increases in profits through the imposition of rigorous cost controls and retrenchment of workers, presumably cutting the underemployment experienced in Tsingtao and inherent in most SOEs (Harding, 1997). By 2000, the company had largely recovered and became the largest brewery on the mainland, with its market share increasing from 2.8 per cent in 1998 to 5.2 per cent in 1999. This was mainly due to strategic acquisitions and mergers with local breweries, although this also involved increasing marketing expenses (*The Asian Wall Street Journal*, 2000).[7] In the meantime, foreign breweries were retreating from the Chinese market as they found that the premium segment in which they competed accounted for less than 7 per cent of overall beer sales. The volume was not sufficient for them to continue operations. Hence, brewers such as Foster's and Lion Nathan decided to reduce their presence on the mainland.[8] With Anheuser-Busch being one of the few remaining foreign brewers still going strong in the Chinese market, Tsingtao decided on creating a strategic partnership with the US company.

At present, Tsingtao is expanding, with further acquisitions of local brewers expected and more strategic alliances formed. It has broadened its export market to around 40 countries, and with China's accession to the World Trade Organization (WTO), Tsingtao took this opportunity to do what no other mainland company has ever done before. It managed to enter Taiwan's beer market, where at one point it actually held a 16 per cent share of the market.[9] The brewery has also reached an agreement with Asahi for exclusive rights to the sale of Tsingtao Beer in Japan. The company has also started negotiations with other investors and brewers in South Africa and Europe, with the goal of actually establishing interests in these regions. Therefore, it is clear that Tsingtao would not go the way of most SOEs in China. In fact, the company aims to be one of China's biggest multinational companies. With the results it has achieved so far, the brewery seems to be looking strong and going in the right direction.

Size and structure

Tsingtao has always been the largest brewery in China. When it was a full-fledged SOE, there were many administrative layers for decision-making. This was in line with the general form of Chinese industrial governance, in which there are two parallel hierarchies working at the same time; that of the administration and of the Communist Party. In addition, the administrative structure itself had two lines leading to two bureaus, the local functional and industrial bureaus, both operating with regards to regulatory, technical, advisory and administrative purposes (Hickson, 1997, p. 314). The political control of the party is evident with another layer embedded into these structures, contributing to the bloated bureaucracies of the SOEs. Tsingtao was no exception, and with the opening up of China, the company has streamlined its administration and there is now a solitary and implicit political hierarchy evident at the management level. There is only a supervisory committee at the apex with an advisory role, along with a culture center/political affairs headquarters and a labor union involved at the lower hierarchies (see Tsingtao Brewery Group website). The "dual system" of having party "arms" placed at all hierarchical levels hindered enterprise consolidation and reduced enterprise autonomy, thus with the structure less rigid, increased efficiency and productivity has helped Tsingtao consolidate its position as China's leading brewery. It has also enabled Tsingtao a relatively free rein in terms of forming alliances with foreign companies and acquiring other local brewers, enabling the formation of a critical mass for the company to operate with economies of scale. In most cases, Tsingtao's reforms replicate China's open-door policy, with the effects of improvements in economic incentives and efficiency, correction of its industrial structure, and more effective exploitation of its comparative advantages very apparent as both country and company develop (Lin *et al*, 1996).

Technology

Although beer making is not exactly a high-technology engagement, the development of Tsingtao does entail rapid technological progress as Chinese industries are in general very backward due to China's 30-year isolation.[10] Here, the importance of Tsingtao's alliance with Anheuser-Busch is highlighted. The latter's US$182 million contribution will be used by the brewery to upgrade its existing plants in China. Tsingtao would also be able to gain marketing, production and technological expertise from this association with the US super-brewer, enhancing its technological capabilities and competitive edge (*Euromonitor*, 2004). Furthermore, Tsingtao has also linked up with the Japanese brewer, Asahi, which would provide the company with the newest production equipment. In addition to such operative measures, the development of products is another important area in which Tsingtao is focusing on. The introduction of draught beer for the first time in the brewery's history has led the Tsingtao Beer Science Research Center to invest RMB68 million in finding ways to resolve technical problems associated with the lack of pasteurisation during the production of this new product. Also, since 2002, the company has embarked on the development of different beer flavours, of which green tea beer, bitter lemon beer and chrysanthemum beer are more prominent (*Euromonitor*, 2004). Thus, in technological terms, Tsingtao is moving at break-neck speed compared to other breweries around the world, since it really has much to catch up with.

Goals, objectives and values of the organization

A company has to have its own set of values and beliefs to make it unique as a corporate culture (Deal and Kennedy, 2000). Here, Tsingtao has espoused several dominant ideals which it believes are essential for the company to do well. This list consists of a core concept in bringing about an enterprising company which serves the society well; the attainment of an enterprising spirit striving to pursue excellence and going beyond their own capabilities; the creation of a world famous brand with an international first-class enterprise; manufacturing products which are elegant and of good taste; and having a style of operation which is efficient, serious and cautious (see Tsingtao Brewery Group website). The company also has a tradition of excellence with regards to beer making and its other products. This began with the gold medal it won in Germany's

Munich International Expo in 1906. Tsingtao Beer won seven national gold medals and was also a three-time champion of the International Wine Meeting held in the US. Other accolades include a gold medal for the Singapore International Drink Exposition in 1993, the 23rd International Gold Star for outstanding enterprise and quality in 1997, and its listing as one of the top 10 most influential companies in China in 2000. In 1999, Tsingtao was also the only Chinese company listed amongst the top 50 famous brands of Asia. Such a tradition of honorifics and good standing is rare for Chinese companies, and Tsingtao has certainly proved to be resilient in this aspect.

Also, the company aspires to be a Multi-National Company (MNC) representing China on the world stage and competing with other MNCs which are based in the US, Europe and Japan (see Tsingtao Brewery Group website). With such an ambition spelt out, it can be said that Tsingtao has attained a limited status as an MNC, at least with respect to the beer market. But it is still some way off from being a globally recognized MNC in the same league as big names such as Japan's Toyota, the American giant General Electric, and Unilever from the Netherlands.

The business environment

The Chinese economy is in the process of reform, with liberalization, privatization and economic decentralization taking place in most sectors. For the beer industry, Tsingtao has experienced its fair share of the effects of these reforms. The different stages of reform include profit retention and enterprise incentive schemes; the double-track price system and alleviating market distortions; the slow relaxing of financial constraints and independence of operations from the state; implementing the contract responsibility system; and auxiliary adjustments in factor allocations (Fan and Nolan, 1994). All these are taking place in the context of Chinese national culture, which emphasizes respect for age and hierarchy, orientation toward groups, the preservation of "face," and the importance of relationships (Hickson, 1997, p. 323). These are, in turn, congruent with the basic teachings of Confucius, who advocated observance of unequal relationships, using the family as the prototype of all social organizations, behaving virtuously towards others, honoring education and hard work, and being moderate in all things (Lewis, 2002).

Respect for age and hierarchy mainly stems from the Confucian concept of rite and propriety, placing people in different social hierarchies and epitomising unequal relationships, which include that of ruler and subject, father and son, etc. Also, the importance of the extended family in China encourages the development of a strong collectivist tradition and group orientation. Hence, the family is the model of all social relationships, e.g., the state is supposed to be benevolently autocratic, maintaining a patrimonial presence with respect to society at large. The "face" issue is a matter of pride and recognition of a person's social standing and position, with both *lian* and *mianzi* important. This can explain the salience, to the Chinese, of the impressions others have of them, and as observed by Hickson, this emphasis seems to be of a far greater significance compared to any other national culture. Another critical aspect of Chinese culture is that of *guanxi*, referring to the quality of personal relationships which are external to immediate familial ties. This can be established when there is at least one fundamental characteristic common between persons, e.g., in terms of birthplace, lineage, surnames, alma mater, or belonging to the same organizations.

Hence, in such a setting, there is a standardization of sorts throughout society and within the business culture. However, there is also a measure of flexibility with the process of reform taking place and the use of personal relationships, which has traditionally helped Chinese companies tide over difficult times. These include bank loans to SOEs, whose company leaderships normally have ties with local or central government officials. Thus, in a system of flux but with an ironically fixed culture, the internal dynamics are adaptive, although tensions involved could not be ignored.

The people

When it comes to the workers and management, it is thought that both parties are in a relatively harmonious relationship as the labour union is officially part of the senior management. Also, Tsingtao is quite explicit in its description of the ideal employee and management images it wants to project. For ordinary workers, it is dedication to their work. Managers are expected to serve the brewery well, keep things in order, do their best for employees, and be morally strict with themselves. The company also has a set of conditions which it hopes its employees aspire to meet. These include the aim of maximizing shareholder profits, adapting to market conditions, providing faster and more convenient service, maintaining good quality, searching for talent based on ability and intelligence, developing from a high start-point and expanding through lower cost, keeping brand superiority and preserving Tsingtao's leading status, and be sensitive toward saving resources and environmental protection (see Tsingtao Brewery Group website).

It is unknown if such criteria are really enforced and implemented by the company. However, such personnel goals are deemed attainable in the Chinese context, as there is a tendency for relatively strict adherence to authority and social status. This is very much a Confucian tradition at work, and with most of the activities involved being that of mass production in beer products, the standards are well-aligned to what the company really needs at this moment; harmonious relations between managers and workers, along with a sensitivity toward domestic and foreign consumers. The importance of the people working there and following the company's direction when it comes to human resource (HR) development and interpersonal relations could be an area of greater focus in the future, as most MNCs have rather sophisticated HR practices.

Evaluation of Tsingtao's corporate culture

It is obvious that Tsingtao has a fundamental power culture in a bureaucratic context. In its history, it has been in public ownership with the state providing much of the directives. Also, the environment is conducive to one centralized power source as the Chinese are the epitome of Confucian values, emphasizing unequal relationships, family orientations and even patrimonialism.[11] However, there are elements of role culture firmly embedded within the systemic operations of the company, since it is a large company with a Communist legacy of bureaucratic control still very much evident. Its high investments in technology and the speed of its development would make such processes more mechanical and enhance the role orientation within the company structure. Furthermore, the goal of pursuing growth needs increased systemisation of its business developments, and the procedures described for proper application by its employees show the role-culture trend that is in process. However, there is little place for task or personal cultures in Tsingtao. In the case of the former, the company works as one big unit with centralized command instead of small workgroups, whilst for the latter, the charisma of its leaders is not an issue. Thus, the power and role culture orientations for Tsingtao are very strong, and vital to its current operations.

TSINGTAO'S STRATEGIES FOR ITS FUTURE DEVELOPMENT

After determining the culture of Tsingtao, it is imperative to see how this culture contributes to the implementation of the company's strategies in its quest for success. It was clear that in the earlier days, especially under the direct control of the government, the brewery's output and operational details were planned and laid out by the authorities. When China started opening to the outside world, Tsingtao had a limited strategy of banking on the support of the state and tapping on the recognition of its brand by overseas Chinese communities (Thomson, 1988). However, such moves are insufficient for Tsingtao to become an internationally recognised brand name. Thus, it started listing its shares on the Hong Kong and Shanghai exchanges, being the first mainland Chinese enterprise to do so in Hong Kong. Along with this, there is the aggressive takeover of various other breweries scattered across the country.

All these have been effective to a limited extent. Hence, the company has more ambitious plans in the pipeline for further development. Tsingtao's strategies are currently two-fold; one emphasizing on internal operations, and the other on external affairs (*Euromonitor*, 2004).

On the internal operations of the company, Tsingtao will continue acquiring more local breweries. In fact, it is through this strategy that Tsingtao managed to regain its penultimate position in the Chinese beer market (*The Asian Wall Street Journal*, 2000). The increase of operations from only four plants in one province to 46 brewing plants and three malt production facilities in 17 provinces would only grow with more Chinese state-run breweries failing. However, it is noted that at present, 30 per cent of Tsingtao's brewing operations are experiencing financial difficulties, with another 30 per cent just managing to break even. This is a concern which needs to be addressed sooner or later, since the collapse of even parts of its overall production could be fatal to a company still finding its way around in a more liberalized environment. The brewery is also looking at strengthening its ties with Anheuser-Busch, and the latter's enormous investment in Tsingtao would be used to finance various upgrading projects, including those of its plants and technology. This is expected to increase Tsingtao's capacity by 100,000 to 150,000 tons per annum. Furthermore, this linkup would also provide an avenue for Tsingtao to gain more technological and management expertise from its US partner. Tsingtao also has 14 sales offices spread across China, and there could be more of such offices opening up as the company seeks to consolidate its peak position as China's top brewer. The company has even embarked on expanding its markets beyond beer and lager; it entered the Chinese wine market in December 2002 with its Kai Xuan range of wines (*Euromonitor*, 2004). Domestic wine production is said to be ranked as the seventh most profitable industry in China at present, with sales estimated to grow by 56 per cent over the next five years or so. However, this diversification project is not the brewery's top priority, as it wants to concentrate on its comparative advantage in beer production. Thus, the growth of Tsingtao's wine production would proceed, albeit with less fervor compared to its more immediate interest in developing the beer segment of its overall operations.

In terms of external affairs, Tsingtao is looking to other regions to expand its brand name and international market share. Negotiations with investors in South Africa and Europe were initiated in March 2003, as the brewery wants to further its interests in both regions. Such a move would help widen its market reach, as both South Africa and Europe are huge markets. It is also noted that Tsingtao Beer has a German flavour which could find a measure of resonance in both these areas. Moreover, Tsingtao is seeking to brew its beer under license outside China for the first time in its history. In fact, the company is expecting to launch production in its new brewery in Taiwan by July 2005 (Dickie, 2004). Speculation that the company is currently discussing options with an unidentified brewer in Southeast Asia in pursuit of this objective has now been confirmed. The *Financial Times* reported that by the end of 2005, the production of Tsingtao Beer would be contracted to a Southeast Asian brewer and hence, the brewery would be able to produce beer at a substantial amount for beer markets in Malaysia, Singapore and Thailand, along with other countries in the region (Dickie, 2004). This is yet another potentially vast market for Tsingtao, and the production of its beer under licence in this region would reduce transportation costs significantly, with considerable gains in operating profits. In addition to this, there is the agreement with Asahi in the summer of 2002, stipulating that the Japanese brewer would get exclusive rights to sell Tsingtao beer in Japan. The beer would be produced in a plant in Shenzhen where Tsingtao and Asahi had produced Asahi Super Dry since 1999. Once again, access to another lucrative market beckons Tsingtao, and with its cooperation with a local Japanese brewer, the success of this agreement should help the company gain a future foothold in Japan's large market.[12] Besides these new overseas settlements, Tsingtao has also secured the renewal of its earlier agreement with Barton Inc. its US distributor, with the contract expected to run till 2005 (*Euromonitor*, 2004).

Hence, with old agreements upheld, and new ventures forthcoming, Tsingtao's external operations look set to continue in its quest for growth and development. This would go along with China's economic liberalization, enhancing Tsingtao's chances in competing in a beer market which, admittedly, is rather stagnated outside China. Tsingtao is also increasingly run like a privatized company, with its shares listed in 1993 and the Chinese government would have only a 30.6 per cent stake by 2010.[13] Thus, with both internal and external measures in place, Tsingtao would be on course to becoming one of China's flagship companies with international brand recognition and a larger share of the global beer market. If the expansion strategy succeeds, Tsingtao's presence in regions like Europe, Africa and Southeast Asia would be strengthened. For a brewery with the desire to mature into a true MNC, such strategies are perhaps unavoidable, and would prove to be of great challenge to a company which has been in state care for much of its history.

INTERCULTURAL EVALUATION: USING THE HOFSTEDE MODEL

Since Tsingtao is set to expose itself more to outside competition, its various agreements could be assessed in cultural terms, with an examination on whether such settlements could succeed in the long run. Clearly, there is a further need to analyze the cultural implications of its strategies. Thus, using Hofstede's work on corporate attitudes in a cross-cultural setting, a better understanding of Tsingtao's operations and its future projections would suffice. Hofstede (1991) spelt out the mechanism for such an analysis, looking at the power distance or degree of authoritarianism, predictability or uncertainty avoidance, individualism versus collectivism, masculinity versus femininity, and the Confucian dynamics involved (long-term versus short-term orientations). Here, different sets of intercultural experiences would be studied along with Hofstede's model, with particular emphasis on

Tsingtao's acquisition of local breweries, its partnerships with foreign companies, and its expansion into foreign markets through means such as brewing under licence outside China.

Acquisitions of local breweries

Tsingtao's acquisition spree of late is quite staggering in quantity, with 1999 being a year in which the brewery bought up 15 other breweries situated in the eastern, southern and central parts of China at a price of US$58 million. These breweries were mostly SOEs in their own right and were steeped in debt, hence with their acquisition, Tsingtao actually added US$5 million in liabilities from its expansion plans (Wonacott, 2000). Of course, for Tsingtao to compete effectively, the critical mass to be attained would require continued engagements in such high-risk and potentially loss-making ventures.

Comparing the corporate cultures of such SOEs with that of Tsingtao, it is clear that there should be little conflict as the latter itself is an SOE. In terms of power distance, SOEs in China, and in most other parts of Asia, are very hierarchical, with respect being shown to persons of authority or seniority (Hickson and Pugh, 1995, p. 154). The high power culture nature in Chinese management means that top managers tend to make decisions in a top-down approach. The authoritarian distance is probably attenuated with China's history of centralized control, thus participation from employees at the lower levels is not as apparent. The management of uncertainty in China is linked with its management of time, in which there is a patient, unhurried attitude which allows business negotiations to develop gradually (Hickson and Pugh, 1995, p. 168). This helps to manage uncertainty, not necessarily avoiding it, and most Chinese are thought to be relatively tolerant of such ambiguities. Once again with its Communist legacy, SOEs are probably not as tolerant in this respect as their overseas cousins, but it is expected that China's enterprises would move in this direction with the liberalization process in place. In terms of individualism versus collectivism, SOEs are very Chinese in this respect; society and business are collectivist with an important familial or personalistic element firmly attached to them. The high value of *guanxi* in Chinese society is integrated in its business processes and SOEs are no exception. In fact, Tsingtao's success in its acquisitions could be attributed to its famous brand name. Local brewers probably feel that association with China's premium beer company would enhance their own development. For the aspect of masculinity versus femininity, China's SOEs are placed in the middle of the continuum. This means that they are placed between being result-oriented and competitive, to being caring toward society and adhering to social obligations. As China develops further, it is expected that the former aspect would dominate to a greater extent, although as essentially state-run companies, the femininity factor would not be totally abandoned. Lastly, in terms of Confucian dynamics, Chinese enterprises always hold a longer term view of doing business, with personal relationships and market share more important than short-term profit-seeking. Hence, long-term relationships are sought, and this is essential even at the employee level, where job security is prized and employee loyalty is highly valued and seen as necessary (Hickson and Pugh, 1995, p. 169).

Since Tsingtao and its acquired local brewers are all SOEs, all these characteristics are mostly in harmony with one another. Hence, it is expected that the brewery will continue its inland expansion, with the only limitation being that the Chinese government will not allow a monopoly in its premium beer market due to its vested interests in other major Chinese brewers like the Beijing Yanjing brewery.

Partnerships with foreign companies

As mentioned earlier, Tsingtao's partnerships with foreign brewers such as Anheuser-Busch and Asahi look promising. In the former case, the US giant is increasing its stake in Tsingtao, while the latter is to have exclusive rights to selling Tsingtao Beer in Japan. However, cultural discrepancies between Tsingtao, Anheuser-Busch and Asahi could not be discounted, as all three cultures are very dissimilar in various aspects.

In terms of power distance, Tsingtao probably has the highest authoritarian distance amongst the three. Although similarly hierarchical, Asahi implements a uniquely Japanese process; the *nemawashi* and *ringi* procedures; which, in a way, ensure that the lower stratum gets their share of participation in the decision-making process by means of consensus-seeking measures (Hickson, 1997). The American brewer is also not as top-down as Tsingtao in its management, with flatter hierarchies and teams formed to engage in operations. For managing uncertainty, the Chinese are quite apt at it as their concept of time is that things cannot be rushed, and must be done well in order for operations to be completed on time. For the Japanese, they would prefer to avoid all uncertainties. This is manifested in their culture of consensus-seeking (Hickson and Pugh, 1995). The Americans, however, can relish uncertainty as a challenge. Since time is money, they tend to rush things through. This is not exactly uncertainty avoidance, but more of not wanting to waste time. With respect to individualism and collectivism, the Chinese and the Japanese brewers are expected to be very collectivist. Both cultures involve job security and employee loyalty, although for the former, this was due to the system itself being explicit about such management of its workforce. For the Americans, society is very individualist, and hence, in this manner, there could be potential conflicts with their Chinese partner, which is, above all, an SOE with social obligations. For the masculinity/femininity spectrum, Tsingtao is thought to be the most feminine due to its status as an SOE, while Asahi is expected to be more result-oriented, although the welfare of its employees is still important. Anheuser-Busch, as a typical American company, is profit-driven and result-oriented, and hence is expected to fall on the masculine side of the spectrum. In all, this links well with the Confucian dynamics involved, with the Chinese and Japanese companies looking at things from a long-term perspective, with market share and personal relationships being the focus. The American company is more short-term-oriented, centering on profits and immediate gains. One further factor to consider here in the comparison between the three cultures is Francis Fukuyama's differentiation of high trust and low trust cultures (Middleton, 2002). The low trust culture in China would make personalistic and patrimonial relationships very important, further accentuating the *guanxi* element in Chinese business. The relatively high trust nature of Japanese and American business cultures is due to the greater confidence and effectiveness of the established public institutions. Hence, Tsingtao is expected to be largely subject to the *guanxi* factor, whilst Asahi and Anheuser-Busch deal more along legalistic lines.

It is clear that the disparities in cultural discourses may hinder and disrupt the development of business ties between Tsingtao and Asahi, along with the agreement between Tsingtao and Anheuser-Busch. The many differences can make these settlements daunting in implementation, with Anheuser-Busch expecting to have a greater say in the management of Tsingtao, while Asahi's operations in Japan would be closely monitored by the Chinese brewery. Conflicts may arise, but with common objectives of greater profitability and increasing market share for all sides, the potential for these agreements to succeed is great. The initial stages could see the ironing out of intercultural differences, and with time, there should be greater confluence in operations, although the various unique cultural characteristics on all sides will not be lost.

Extending brewing operations outside China

Tsingtao's attempts to extend the brewing of its beer products outside China are exceptional as the brewery has never produced beer outside its mainland stronghold. As these arrangements would be carried out mainly through licensing agreements with investors in South Africa, Europe and Southeast Asia, the level of intercultural conflict should not be very great. The effects of differences in power distance, uncertainty management and avoidance, the comparisons between individualism and collectivism, masculinity and femininity, and "long-termism" versus "short-termisim," are not expected to feature much in the operational aspects, although the negotiations would see much intercultural exchange between Tsingtao and its foreign investors. As these measures involve the alignment of goals and prospects for all parties involved, the practicality displayed by most of the different cultures should be able to overcome the distinct cultural disparities at play. Hence, in this respect, as long as the negotiations are made with a degree of understanding of each other's culture, disparate business styles and management methods, the future operations under licensing agreements should go on smoothly, with investors selling Tsingtao products without too much interference from the company. Conversely, the company could benefit from having its brand name perpetuated to other parts of the world and reap substantial profits from such licensing agreements. Thus, the various aspects of intercultural conflict would apply only to a limited degree if Tsingtao is to allow its foreign licensees more leeway in operations in their own countries. Whether this will actually happen due to Tsingtao's power culture inclinations is uncertain. Yet there there seems little choice but to grant more autonomy as foreign markets require localized expertise in terms of marketing, advertising and management.

CONCLUSION AND ANALYSIS OF TSINGTAO'S POTENTIAL

After analyzing the cultural aspects of the company, a summation of its strengths, weaknesses, and prospects is needed. In terms of its strengths,

Tsingtao is the largest brewery in China, which is also the largest beer market in the world at the moment. China itself is the fastest growing economy in the world, and this could only work to the company's advantage. The Tsingtao brand name is undisputed, at least in China, and its image as a premium brand enables it to sell beer at premium prices. Furthermore, it has strategic alliances with established brewers like Anheuser-Busch and Asahi, and through such arrangements, the potential for improving on its operations through importation of expertise is enormous. Other factors which contribute to Tsingtao's strength is its intensification of research and development, the brewery having the best distribution capabilities in the Chinese beer market, and its acquisitions of local breweries, notably the acquisition of the Shaanxi Baoji Brewery in 2003, making Tsingtao the dominant beer producer in the Shaanxi region with up to 85 per cent of the market share (*Euromonitor*, 2004). All these are in tandem with Tsingtao's status as an SOE with the state providing critical support, since the company is seen by the central government as one of its flagship companies with the potential to "represent" China in the MNC arena. Thus, the brewery's advantages are huge, and it should become more than a formidable force in the international beer market. It may even have the potential of displacing more established brands such as Carlsberg or Heineken, since it has already dislodged several others from the pedestal.

However, Tsingtao also has weaknesses which could hinder its development into a full-fledged MNC. First, the packaging is very old-fashioned and has not changed since the 1950s (*Euromonitor*, 2004). This may have some nostalgic value, but in fashion-conscious markets, such packaging can only reduce its appeal. The company's website also needs an overhaul, with many articles still missing and the standard of English being relatively poor. The company's marketing efforts have not been very voracious. Many have heard of the brand, but people in general do not know much about Tsingtao Beer, nor have they seen it in stores outside China. Tsingtao's products also do not have consistency in taste and flavor between those produced in its various factories. Evenness in this respect is essential if the company wants to expand operations abroad. At present, Tsingtao's overseas ventures are hindered by the lack of licensing agreements. Thus its exports still encompass very high transportation costs. Along with the high costs involved, Tsingtao's status as a premium beer also affects its pricing power on existing products, which remains weak despite improvements through better product mix. Lastly, Tsingtao's local acquisitions have reduced its profitability. Its investments in new breweries have not been sufficient to maximizing their efficiency. Thus, despite the many advantages Tsingtao has, the huge cache of problems inherent in the company could prove decisive in its future operations.

Despite such concerns, the prospects for the company look rosy for the near future. Under the stewardship of its former president, Mr Peng Zuoyi, during the days of reform, and with its current chairman Mr Li Guirong and general manager Mr Jin Zhiguo at the helm (Perliski, 2004), the company is in a position to grow stronger and develop further. Tsingtao is in the world's largest beer market, with China overtaking the US in 2002 for the first time. Also, beer volumes are expected to grow in China by 35 per cent per annum, and Tsingtao is probably the best placed company to exploit this imminent growth. Hence it is expected that the company will continue to be the country's largest brewer for a long time to come. Its current market share in China may be small. This is because many local manufacturers dominate the beer market in China through protectionist measures, as legally, there remains the prohibition in sales of beer outside its provinces of origin. The ongoing liberalization of China's economy should increase Tsingtao's share well beyond the current 12.1 per cent it now holds. Also, with the consolidation of its position in the Shaanxi region and southern China through the buying up of the Huashi Beer Group Co. this would boost Tsingtao's production, especially in South China with projected increases expected to be over one million tons. All these go along with its strategic alliance with Anheuser-Busch, the implementation of its modernization program, the company's commitment to expanding its global influence, and the setting up of licensing agreements with foreign brewers. Thus, Tsingtao is on the way to becoming the quintessential Chinese MNC, and for other Chinese companies with similar ambitions, the likely role model to follow in the near future.

ENDNOTES
1   The brewery would be referred to as Tsingtao and the city, Qingdao.
2   It was ranked 9th, ahead of the Japanese brand Kirin and just behind Denmark's Carlsberg.
3   China superseded the US recently in terms of volume for beer consumption. See *Euromonitor* (2004) for more details.
4   Here, Charles Handy's work on organizational culture would be used for the analysis. See Handy (1993) for more details.

5   The Tsingtao International Beer Festival is held annually on the 17th of August and runs through 17 days of festivities in the city of Qingdao. This is modelled after Germany's famous Oktoberfest in Munich. Last year, in 2003, Tsingtao celebrated its centenary during its 13th beer festival.

6   Red chips are stocks of SOEs, which are still owned and controlled by the Chinese government regardless of the stock holdings involved.

7   One good example was Tsingtao's purchase of the Langfang Brewery in 2000, improving its access to China's Northern markets and increasing Tsingtao's own beer production by 100,000 tons. See *Companies and Commodities* (2000) for more details.

8   The former is an Australian brewer, while the latter is from New Zealand.

9   However, with the current strained ties between mainland China and Taiwan, especially after the 2004 Taiwanese Presidential Election, the uncertainty generated by this event could adversely affect Tsingtao's standing in the Taiwanese market.

10 China's seclusion from the international arena was due to the Communist victory in China's civil war and the subsequent Cold War between the democratic West and Communist East.

11 Patrimonialism captures the essence of paternalism, hierarchy, responsibility, mutual obligation, family atmosphere, personalism, and protection in the Chinese context. See Hickson (1997) for more details.

12 The importance of breaking into the Japanese beer market cannot be underestimated, since Japan has the second largest economy in the world behind the US.

13 As mentioned earlier, this is along with Anheuser-Busch's acquisition of 27 per cent of Tsingtao shares. This move is unprecedented as China's SOEs seldom give up more than 50 per cent of their shares to non-state institutions.

REFERENCES

Carrie Lee. "Tsingtao Chairman decides his cup has overflowed." *South China Morning Post.* July 26, 1994, p. 1.

Charles Handy. *Understanding Organizations.* London: Penguin Books, 1993.

"China's Tsingtao Brewery buys Langfang Brewery to win northern markets." *Companies and Commodities.* May 23, 2000.

D. J. Hickson. *Exploring Management across the World: Selected Readings.* London: Penguin Books, 1997.

D. J. Hickson, and D. S. Pugh. *Management Worldwide: The Impact of Societal Culture on Organizations around the Globe.* London: Penguin Books, 1995.

Geert Hofstede. *Cultures and Organizations: Software of the Mind.* London; New York: McGraw-Hill, 1991.

Greg Perliski. *Tsingtao Brewery Company Limited,* 2004. http://www.hoovers.com/tsingtao/—ID__43060—/free-co-factsheet.xhtml.

James Harding. "Cuts strengthen Tsingtao results." *Financial Times,* August 22, 1997, p. 21.

John Middleton. *Culture*. Oxford: Capstone Publications, 2002.

Josephine Ma. "Tsingtao steps." *South China Morning Post*. March 1, 1997.

Louise Lucas. "Companies and finance—Asia Pacific—higher costs drag Tsingtao to surprise 9.6 per cent fall." *Financial Times*. April 17, 1996, p. 37.

Mark Landler. "Tsingtao outsells intruders even as it courts Anheuser." *New York Times*. July 20, 2000, p. 1, column 2.

Mure Dickie. "Companies Asia-Pacific: Tsingtao looks beyond China for growth," *Financial Times*. April 28, 2004.

Peter Wonacott. "Asia Focus: Tsingtao is thirsty to reclaim its title—beer maker embarks on an acquisition blitz—buying spree comes as foreign brewers in China retreat", *The Wall Street Journal Europe*, July 21, 2000, p. 30.

Qimiao Fan, and Peter Nolan. *China's Economic Reforms: The Costs and Benefits of Incrementalism*. New York: St. Martin's Press, 1994.

Richard D. Lewis. *When Cultures Collide: Managing Successfully across Cultures*. London; Naperville: Nicholas Brealey, 1999.

Robert Thomson. "Here's to Tsingtao Beer and its efforts to sell to the world." *Sydney Morning Herald*, May 27, 1988, p. 14.

"Stock recommendation: Tsingtao loses edge as high barley costs bite." *South China Morning Post*. February 25, 1996.

"Tsingtao blames higher costs for slump." *Reuters News*. August 28, 1995.

"Tsingtao Brewery ahead". *Financial Times*. August 23, 1996, p. 20.

"Tsingtao Brewery Co. Ltd." *Euromonitor*. April, 2004.

"Tsingtao Brewery confident no fund raising needed until 1997." *China Securities Bulletin*. June 4, 1996.

Tsingtao Brewery Group website, http://www.tsingtao.com.cn/

"Tsingtao Brewery reports rise in net production in '99—firm is now largest beer maker in China—company intends to boost market share this year." *The Asian Wall Street Journal*. April 19, 2000, p. 15.

"Tsingtao loses favour in China beer market." *Business Times* Singapore. July 8, 1994.

WGuides.com, 2004. http://www.wguides.com/city/648/city_history.cfm.

Yifu Justin Lin, Fang Cai, and Zhou Li. *The China Miracle: Development, Strategy and Economic Reform*. Hong Kong: The Chinese University Press, 1996.

CHAPTER 18

Harrods: Making it Big

CHUA YI FEN

HARRODS IN SHORT

In the heart of London, in a place called Knightsbridge, stands a majestic building that is reminiscent of a palace. But a palace it is not, rather, the product of an enterprising young man who made it big. The immense proportion of the building astounds the ordinary passer-by, the window displays tease the minds of what lies within, the Edwardian décor seeks to impress and attracts the tourists. A man decked out in green finery stands ready to greet one beyond the glass doors.

Upon entering, one is overwhelmed by the huge Food Hall to the Grand Staircase in the centre of the room. Further explorations of the interior allow one to feast one's eyes on the opulent jewellery department, the toy kingdom to the authentic reproduction of the Egyptian experience. From daily necessities to the most luxurious indulgence, it is all there for your choosing. *Omnia Omnibus Ubique*—Everything, (for) everyone, everywhere. What you want, we provide. So goes the motto of the store. This is Harrods.

THE HISTORY

The building shows little resemblance to what it was nearly 150 years ago, in the year 1853. It used to be only a single-room, flat-roofed terrace house with a modest garden in front, which was owned by Charles Henry Harrods, who specialised in tea and grocery. A shrewd businessman who practised the policy of "no credit purchase" and "lowest price in London," his profit was almost guaranteed. In 1853, upon retirement, he sold the shop to his son Charles Digby Harrods at the price of £500, firm in his belief that one should work for one's needs.

Digby was an efficient and energetic young man who was ambitious to build up the business. He continued in his father's tradition of cash on purchase. He was strict with his staff but fair. As his shop continued to gain recognition from the local gentry and villagers alike, profits soared. By 1871, Digby was taking in £1,000, which was 50 times what his father had earned. The staff at the shop amounted to 16. Tremendous demand for delivery service prompted him to purchase a single-horse carriage. In 1874, he was able to purchase two additional premises next to his store. Harrod's stores were born. Van delivery began. By now, the modest grocery store was selling perfumery, medicine, stationery, china and glass in addition to its traditional goods. The story may have ended here, but for the great fire in December 1883.

The fire that broke out at Harrods' store has significance for the present Harrods. The fire destroyed the entire premises plus some. Digby was at this time in the midst of preparing for his customer's orders and in view of the accident, wrote a letter to each of them apologising for the inconvenience caused and promised that their purchases will not be delayed by more than a few days. At the same time, Digby took up a temporary counter at a nearby shop to conduct his business. Rebuilding of the stores was in progress and the new premises were opened in 1884. For the first time, Digby allowed credit accounts to be opened; touched by his customers' loyalty, among them was Oscar Wilde. The new premises were three floors high with at least 13 departments ranging from simple groceries to a saddlery and stable. Harrods was on its way to become the splendor of today.

It is not known if Digby married. It is however said that "the building of the new store had taken a lot out of him" and "he was inclined towards retirement." His father, the firm's founder, died shortly after in the year 1885 and he decided to sell the store. Henceforth Harrods was to become a floated limited liability company. His last task was to train a general manager to take over the reins. Upon the recommendation of his friend, Edgar Cohen, a certain Richard Burbidge was employed. Digby thereafter retired for good and moved to Somerset and later Sussex, where he died in 1905 at the age of 64. By this time, Harrods' reputation was already made.

When Richard Burbidge took over the reins, he was even more industrious than his predecessor. His reign was recalled in vivid detail by two measures he took. First of all was the expansion of the Harrods' store to "occupy the entire island site." This was by no means an easy feat. It took him 20 years to fulfill his dream. To start with, there were still a number of private residences and some commercial concerns on the site.[1] These include a long process of lease acquisition and rebuilding. The purchase and construction of the acquired building was linked with a series of share issues which created controversy.

Some residents or shop owners were not willing to give up their premises, especially since the area was fast becoming the fashionable part of London. An example[2] cited was a Mrs DeCoster, who refused to give up her drapery shop to Burbidge, until several years later, when she finally gave in to his demands. Naturally, this meant an increase in drapery sales for Harrods! At the same time, Burbidge wasted no time in acquiring the slum areas behind the store. This had the added effect of upgrading the entire area and removing the "slum impression," boosting the area's popularity, an effect not foreseen and not intentional, but nevertheless, a consequence that turned out well.

Second was his adoption of a policy of consideration for his staff. Never in the history of Harrods was this practised and formalised. Certainly Burbidge's measure came even before the implementation of the *Shop Act* (Dale, 1981). For the first time in British retail history, staff training was extensively provided and opportunities for upgrading presented. Not least was the introduction of shorter working hours from 12 hours to eight, and a day off! Burbidge was a man who firmly believed that a well-rested employee is a productive worker. In addition, recreational premises were also built for the staff and activities held to forge a closer relationship between the boss and the Harrods family. His measures paid off and in the year ended January 1910, Harrods was earning £210,092 a year.

The success of Harrods during his reign surpassed all time. Indeed, he was said to be the architect of the store's rise to the status of a national institution (Callery, 1991). It was during his time that Harrods first royal warrant was received, stating Harrods as the furnisher and draper to the Queen of Norway, who was Princess Maud before her marriage, daughter of Princess Alexandra and Edward VII.

Sixty years of Burbidge's dynasty was brought to an end, when Hugh Fraser from the House of Fraser, a large company dealing in retail stores, managed the acquisition of Harrods. The acquisition, known as the 1959 battle, passed down as a legend due to the heated confrontation between three interested companies: Debenhams, House of Fraser and United Drapery Stores. Despite Debenhams's fortunes, it eventually lost out to Fraser and a new era begun for Harrods. With Fraser holding court as chairman, Robert Midgley was appointed as managing director. His contribution and practice of "housekeeping" became part of his contribution to Harrods' tradition. He was a strong advocator of the belief that the retailer's job is to display goods in a way that attracts the attention of anyone who passes by. With the approval of Fraser, Harrods underwent a revamp and a face-lift. He succeeded in bringing about increased business for Harrods.

And so developed Harrods slowly into the store we know today. Harrods was indeed fortunate to have such an industrious line of chairmen and managing directors, who had contributed to the evolution of organization culture and values held by Harrods today; a line that started with Charles Henry Harrods whose £20-a-week's-taking grocer's shop was by the mid-1980s taking in a third of a billion pounds annually (Dale, 1981).

EVERYTHING FOR EVERYONE EVERYWHERE

Perhaps the greatest secret behind Harrods' success was its ability to deliver an assortment of goods under one roof. Recall the motto of the store *Omnia Omnibus Ubique* and the impressive conferment of the title and telegraphic address "Everything, London." Indeed, Harrods lives up to its reputation. There is no shortage of incidents and stories regarding the store's ability to deliver. Perhaps this can be best described by borrowing the words of customers and staff.

> When we were children and lived in the South of France, our Nurse was known as Harrods, because she could always produce whatever anybody needed. (a woman born in the Edwardian era)

Actress Dame Sybil Thorndike was interviewed on tour in Calcutta and was asked for her religion. "Church of England," she replied. "Oh, like Harrods," came the response, "your religion supplies everything for everybody."

Staff recalled fondly the alligator purchased by a woman named Beatrice Lillie as a Christmas present for Noel Coward, which Harrods promptly delivered. In 1967, the self-proclaimed King of Albania instructed Harrods to send an elephant to Ronald Reagan, then governor of California, as a gift. The 700-pound elephant was later donated to the Sacramento Zoo. Another spoke of the hospital built for Queen Elisabeth of Belgium in 1914 upon request. Within days, medical supplies and equipments was brought across the channel and a 640-bed hospital was set up, headed by Herbert Costa, manager of the Building and Electrical Departments. He later received the Cross of the Ordre de Léopold II from the grateful Belgian King.[3]

The retail business is highly competitive. As more shopping avenues open up and more retailers and shop owners enter the scene, Harrods must work even harder today to attract and retain its customers. New goods are constantly offered as Harrods keeps up with the trends, from the latest technology gadgets to the newest therapy treatment. New departments are nearly monthly occurrences in the store, the latest being the Egyptian Hall. As the younger members of society become the greatest spenders of our times, the stores opened up new lines of apparel to meet their needs such as more affordable yet fashionable and quality street clothes, and even provided entertainment, engaging local pop groups like Boyzone and Westlife to perform in the store.[4]

The current chairman, Mohammad Al-Fayed, is very much the person behind these undertakings. Dedicated to the store and despite having no background as a retailer, Al-Fayed has a great vision for making the store a dazzling place. His investment, valued at £250 million, is on par with that of the Edwardian heyday. In fact, to him, retailing is like theatre,[5] that is alive and exciting and whose purpose is to entertain.

THE ORGANIZATION

Having had a line of industrious and far-sighted chief executive officers necessarily provides a strong foundation for Harrods' success.[6] But to manage and create a store such as Harrods cannot just be the job of one man. Both the Harrods and Burbidge's dynasties have long practised a philosophy of blending quality goods with excellent service, as well as a practice of patriarchal concern for the staff (Callery, 1991).

As early as the days of Charles Henry Harrods, Harrods staff was treated fairly albeit under strict and autocratic rule. Henry himself was a firm follower of the "stick and carrot" policy. Fines were meted out for offenders like late arrivals and poor service while rewards in the form of praises and bonuses were given out to the efficient worker. Finally, Richard Burbidge's policy of consideration for the employees like shorter working hours and day-off contributed to the fairness practised at Harrods. Staff communications were held frequently and staff activities like weekend outings, inter-department sporting competitions, annual dinners, also for the first time in England history, education and self-improvement courses held in-house, that includes languages, business skills and presentations.

Even till today, staff training and the encouragement of learning is practised. For example, not so long ago, Harrods staff was encouraged and made to attend drama courses as part of their skills upgrading.[7] The drama courses were to provide role-playing courses that the staff can relate and react to, for the purpose of knowing how to behave in challenging situations that may arise between an employee and a customer, in addition to body language and voice projection skills. Not only that, the company also offers grants to employees interested in pursuing new qualifications that are related to the business such as management, product technology and languages, conducted by Harrods in collaboration with the Open College, under the in-house career training scheme or the executive training scheme.[8]

The staff is also expected to display detailed product knowledge, familiarity with the layout of the store and also to advise customers in the event that a particular good or brand may not be found in Harrods. The Green Men, stationed at the front of the store, must even know the external surroundings of the store in the event that customers lose their way. They must also be prepared to flag a cab for customers who are in need of it.

Harrods is pretty much a product of the British culture. This is not only true of its major product, Harrods Tea, which is a direct consequence of British tea culture, but also of its management. The most apparent comes in the form of power holder and gender issues. At Harrods there is a strict hierarchy and the chairmen are known as much for their fair but high handed and autocratic manner in which they treat their staff. Nowhere this was more evident than at an event commemorating Richard Burbidge's 14 years as chairman. A medallion was commissioned for this affair, and the top and bottom management was expected to purchase the silver or bronze versions of the coins, in accordance with their ranks.[9]

On the gender issue, the first break came in the form of Ida Fowle in 1917 and later, Dorothy Pendleton in 1927 (Callery, 1991) and Martha Wikstrom in 2001, the first female managing director. Currently, the only female on the board is Anne-Marie Verdin,[10] who is the director for communications and marketing. On closer inspection, it can be seen that these reputed women in Harrods are reflective of the general attitude towards career opportunities in Harrods. It is likely that they are placed in departments requiring a soft touch like staff recruitment, training and marketing and other personal touch duties like acting as a spokeswoman.

Harrods chairmen are also known for their dedication to their work and they are firmly integrated in the daily workings of the store, whether through mingling, inspection or even carrying out customer service duties themselves. It could be that since Harrods has only one major store till as late as 1983, this is not impossible to conceive of.

CONTINUITY AND CHANGES

Harrods has come a long way since 1853. What are the traditions preserved ? What has changed and what are the plans for the future? The procession of chairmen from Harrods to Al-Fayed has anchored firmly to the store motto and values of provision of quality goods and services, trying their best to meet up to their reputation of having the ability to supply anything from the cradle to the grave. The Food Hall and Tea Rooms are direct throwbacks to the roots of Harrods, and have never been shifted in its 150 years from the ground floor, recognizing its origins as a grocery. Staff training remains one of the active policies of all time. Royal patronage is destined to be a regular issue of interest at Harrods, beginning with the issue of royal seals in 1956 and ending with the controversy surrounding Princess Diana and Dodi Al-Fayed's deaths in 1998 and the momentous event of losing the royal warrant of Buckingham Palace in 2000, which it had held since 1956.[11]

Harrods also continues to add services to enhance the overall experience. The Harrods Bank which was set up in 1890 at the Banking Hall, remains to this date, and is currently dealing with Harrods accounts of millions pounds held by customers with Harrods. The Exports department also continues its tradition of dealing with international goods coming in and out of Harrods. In recent years, new services like Harrods Travels and Harrods Casino are added. There are also plans for a Harrods Hotel and a tourist information centre, which caters to the increasing attraction of Harrods to visitors in London.

Continuity is accompanied by changes, necessary for the survival of Harrods at present and in future. Most important is the transformation of Harrods from pure shopping to entertainment shopping. Under Midgley, merchandise display was introduced as part of the Harrods culture. This is brought to a greater height under the current chairman, Mohammad Al-Fayed. While many retailers baulk at having to spend more than the necessary money for marketing and advertising, Harrods put its entire heart into this affair. No expense is spared to market a new line of goods, or to improvise the décor of an existing department and to the display of goods. Indeed, visitors to Harrods can spend the entire day in the store, experiencing the ultimate visual experience. As a visitor once remarked, "A day in Harrods is like being in a museum without the stifling quietness."

The rise of Harrods has been accompanied by the patronage of royalty and the fashionable upper class of British society, as visible in its four royal warrants and the departments that strictly cater to functions and parties and to the dressing of the debutantes' coming out ball. Contemporary British society, while still unconsciously heeding the class dictates of the old century, nevertheless cannot afford to ignore the rising middle class and the young high-spenders. Harrods therefore has to adapt to meet the requirements of this new class of spenders and customers while not losing its reputation as the fashionable place to shop in. Keeping in tune with the new generation was the introduction of new apparel in clothing, accessories, simple furniture and electronic gadgets, as well as the occasional appearance of a local pop group and entertainers.

In addition, as opposed to the strict adherence to a "One Harrods" policy, Al-Fayed after his ascension, has embarked on a series of expansions, beginning with the opening of an outlet in Japan in 1983, followed by the Heathrow store, and stores in Frankfurt, Singapore (in 1993) and in Kuala Lumpur airport in 2000. Harrods' expansion is one shadowed by the need to protect its quality and prestige (Dale, 1995). Many outposts of international companies, through outsourcing, often "result in exploitation of the brand's name, like Gucci or Pierre Cardin, and have to buy back licences, a trap, which Harrrods wishes to avoid," so said a spokesman for Harrods.[12]

Although Harrods expands, new outlets are never of the same great scale as that of Harrods Knightsbridge, the flagship. These outlets are directly responsible to the headquarters in London. This is to ensure the simultaneous marketing of Harrods internationally while ensuring the name of Harrods Knightsbridge remains secure. In November 1999, Harrods also started an online shopping site[13] and conducted virtual shopping experiences so as to deal directly with international customers interested in shopping with Harrods that way.

CURRENT AFFAIRS

Harrods is not without its pitfalls and to omit them is surely misrepresenting the picture. The hottest recent speculation lies in its ability to survive in this cutthroat world of retail competition. Undisputedly a high-priced shopping affair, it has the tendency to attract more tourists than the local, serious shopper. As such, Harrods' profits are fluctuating despite the face-lift and the effort placed in the presentation of the store. Analysts are of the opinion that extraordinary presentations make up for modest results, says Christopher Dawson, a London analyst with Management Horizons.

There have been concerns that the costs of putting a premium on store appearance and spending nearly $300 million in renovations are stretching the ability of the store to bring in profits. This is a concern that should not be underestimated. While true that selling a single exotic item at Harrods is equivalent to making a big profit, it is wise to keep in mind that these are not regular events. Truly, Al-Fayed should also heed the subtle warning that "the 11 million people drawn by Harrods' showmanship each year don't all spend"[14] and "more likely we will walk away with nothing today."[15]

To top it all, the organization is also shaken by multiple resignations and sackings. The most recent being Martha Wikstrom, who has been managing director for only two years from 2001 to 2003. All this has increased speculation over Al-Fayed's management and the state of the company, fuelling rumors of failing financial performances and possibility of Harrods selling out.

AFTERTHOUGHTS

The story does not end with this chapter. The literature of Harrods will surely continue to grow. Its growth has not been a path littered with flowers, but a story of unfailing determination, ambition and pride in the face of momentous events like the rise and change of dynasties, along with controversial takeovers,[16] world wars, recessions and boom, bomb scares and of course the great fire of 1883. Each event, each change shapes the Harrods we know today and it will continue to develop to suit the climate while preserving its quality and service to the world. As Mr Al Fayed claimed with pride, "Harrods will be here for ever." Having traced the development of Harrods, this writer sincerely wishes for its success in the face of recent uncertainty, and hopes for a conclusion befitting a legend of a fairy tale.

DEDICATION
This chapter is dedicated to my parents, Joey, Joe and RX.

ENDNOTES
1. Dale (1981). The freehold to public houses were difficult to come by at that time since there was no Property Bureau at that time and purchase of property tended to be a lengthy process between the owners and the buyer, at times with a middleman. Some of them include a line of private houses along Hans street, which is now the front of Harrods.
2. Callery (1991). There was no stated reason to the eventual surrender of Mrs DeCoster.
3. See *Harrods Knightsbridge: The Story of Society's Favorite Store*.
4. *Music Week*, July 15, 2000, p. 26.
5. Helliker (1993).
6. There was an exception to every rule however. Between the time of Digby's retirement and the employment of Richard Burbidge, there was no general manager in line for succession and two floor managers, William Smart (ground floor) and William Kibble (sales) were considered potentials by the newly formed Board of Directors, headed by Alfred Newton. Smart was eventually chosen as the new general manager. Within two short years, the shop's fortunes began to slide and sloppiness and inefficiency permeated the store. The directors and Cohen persuaded Digby to return and put affairs in order and to search for a competent replacement, which turned out to be Burbidge.
7. *Human Resource Management International Digest*, vol. 10, issue 4, 2002, pp. 21–3
8. Merrick (1996) and Harrods Online.
9. Callery (1991), p. 99.
10. Hoover's Online: The Business Information Authority, 2004.
11. Marc (2000) and Cheng-Chua (2000). The royal warrant is an official designation granted to businesses, declaring their goods to be of quality fit for kings. Harrods has become prestigious having held four such warrants over the century. The loss of seal is rumored to be an act of reprove against Mohammad Al-Fayed's claim in court that Princess Diana and his son were killed by a palace conspiracy.
12. Blackhurst (2001).
13. Conttrill (2000).
14. Still, it is claimed that tourism accounts for 20 to 25 per cent of sales. See Annoymous (2002).

15 Helliker (1993). Quoted from a businessman from Wiltshire, by the name of Mark Lovett, who was waiting near the ladies' room for his wife.
16 Lohr (1989) and Wallace (1994). The famous takeovers are the acquisition by the House of Fraser in 1959 and the takeover by the Al-Fayed family in 1984. The latter caused a furor of news and speculation about the legitimacy of the takeover by the Al-Fayed family and also led to some scandal in the Tory parliament.

REFERENCES

Bruce Wallace. "The year of sleaze" in *Business Source Premier*. November 14, 1994, vol. 107, issue 46, pp. 80–2.

Chris Blackhurst. "A brawl in Knightsbridge" in *Management Today*. October 2001, pp. 70–4, London.

Christina Cheng-chua. "The EuroConsumer: A taste of royalty" in *Business World*, June 27, 2000, pp. 1–3, the Philippines.

Eirmalasare Bani. "Harrods to open first outlet at KLIA July 29" in *Business Times*. July 24, 2000, p. 1, Kuala Lumpur.

"Harrods" in *Marketing*. August 1, 2002, p. G23, London.

Harrods Online at http://www.jobs2jobs.com/Profiles/Harrods/.

Harrods Online at http://www.harrods.com/.

Hoover's Online at http://cobrands.hoovers.com/.

Human Resource Management International Digest, vol. 10, issue 4, 2002, pp. 21–3.

Jamie Doward. "Business and media: Blow to Fayed as Harrods 'star' leaves" in *The Observer*. April 13, 2003, p. 1, London.

Ken Conttrill. "Harrod's virtual line" in *Traffic World*. June 2000, vol. 262, issue 11, p. 19, Washington.

Kevin Helliker. "Retailing: Harrods: Grandeur comes at grand cost" in *Wall Street Journal* (Eastern edition). December 1, 1993, p. B1, New York.

Marc Champion. "Prince Philip to venerable Harrods: Take the seal off the venerable door" in Neil Merrick. "Open all hours" in *People Management*. December 12, 1996, issue 25, pp. 32–3.

Music Week. July 15, 2000, p. 26.

Sean Callery. *Harrods Knightsbridge: The Story of Society's Favorite Store*. London: Ebury Press, Random Century Group, 1991.

Steve Lohr. "Brawling over Harrods" in *New York Times Magazine*, October 8, 1989, p. 632, New York.

Tim Dale. *Harrods: A Palace in Knightsbridge*. London: Harrods Publishing, 1995.

Tim Dale. *Harrods: The Store and the Legend*, 2nd Edition. London: Pan Books Ltd, 1986.

Wall Street Journal (Eastern edition). January 14, 2000, p. A13, New York.

CHAPTER 19

Nomura: A Tale of Greed and Money?

ALBRECHT ROTHACHER

Scandals and bad publicity are no strangers to Nomura's gruff securities salesmen. For decades, they start their careers as freshmen peddling securities orders for Nomura in gruelling door-to-door visits, following ever more exacting sales targets. In a very un-Japanese way of the survival of the fittest, only the toughest rise to the top. Nomura's corporate warriors even managed to make a lasting negative impression on the world's second toughest business people, the brokers at Wall Street. Little surprise therefore, that Nomura having risen to become Japan's largest securities house found itself involved in a great number of scandals ranging from insider trading, support for corporate greenmail and dealings with gangsters and shady politicians in Japan,[1] to asset stripping in post-Communist Prague.

Tokushichi Nomura, the founder of the house of Nomura was born the illegitimate son of a leading Osaka samurai, the keeper of Osaka castle, in 1850. At the age of 10, he became an apprentice to a moneychanger in Osaka, then Japan's main commercial centre, who at the same time acted as a rice broker, a line of business which often was commercially very successful but considered crooked by respectable society. In 1872 after his adoption, Nomura inherited his master's shop, which he subsequently renamed Nomura Shoten. In 1878, he joined the Osaka Securities Exchange. Still for the next hundred years, bank loans and bonds, not share issues, would be the main supplier of capital to Japan's industries. The stock market was considered to be a gambling den dominated by hustling rice traders.

While Tokushichi Senior shunned the stock market, his son Tokushichi, born in 1878, was less shy. He joined Yasuhiro Shoten, a young stock-trading firm run by his brother-in-law in 1896 as an apprentice at the height of the stock market boom following the victorious First Sino-Japanese War.

Soon the lure of easy riches became too strong for young Tokushichi. He took ¥500, then a small fortune, from the company's safe and purchased speculative stocks. Promptly he lost everything, including subsequently his job. He then retailed stocks for his father's company by visiting clients in Osaka on his bicycle with stock market news at hand. Some of them however, turned out to be untrue and resulted in his father compensating irate customers. This aggressive approach to retailing was to become Nomura's trademark for the century to come.

During three years of compulsory military service in an engineering corps, Tokushichi Junior was finally disciplined and knocked in shape. Decommissioned in 1902, he became a general manager in his father's business, dealing with his passion: analyzing the stock market and retailing shares to the firm's customers. His brother, Jitsusaburo traded in copper, silver and gold. In his view money changing, which was increasingly handled by banks, had no future for his company. During the Russo Japanese War of 1904/5, which led to another stock market boom, Tokushichi Junior managed to persuade his resistant, but often drunk father to accept Nomura's transformation into a stock broking firm. Nomura soon specialised in getting insider information from Mitsui Bussan, the trading arm of Mitsui, and from Nippon Yusen, its shipping arm on early business successes—which helped its newly formed research unit to identify sure winners (Alletzhauser, p. 44). During bear markets, notably the crash of 1907, the fame of Nomura's forecasting skills travelled. His father, however, died in 1908, refusing to accept his son's brave new world. During WWI, Nomura rightly anticipated plentiful of Allied procurement orders and invested heavily into Japanese shipping lines.

In the interwar years, the Japanese economy was dominated by the *zaibatsu*, family-owned conglomerates, like Mitsui, Mitsubishi, Sumitomo, Yasuda and Suzuki. They were mostly traditional businesses whose dynamism during the Meiji period was rewarded by bargain-priced offers of publicly developed companies. As theirs was older money, the *zaibatsu* families looked down upon the *nouveau riches* like the Nomura, who made their fortunes during the stock market speculation of WWI. While most *zaibatsu* were eager to invest and to benefit from Japan's colonial expansion into China, Nomura was more interested in tropical commodities. The company bought a rubber plantation in Borneo and set-up trading offices from Hanoi to Singapore. In 1918 also the Osaka Nomura Bank, the forerunner of today's Daiwa Bank, was founded. In 1922, Tokushichi set-up a family-owned holding, Nomura Gomei ("Nomura Partnership") to control *zaibatsu* style, the bank, the trading company (Nomura East Indies) and other interests.

In 1927, following the Wall Street crash, the banking panic spread to Japan, where soon the over-indebted Suzuki *zaibatsu* collapsed. When the banking panic began to threaten his own Osaka Nomura Bank based on unfounded rumors, Tokushichi began to dispense of his personal cash and liquid assets to quell his depositors' panic–ultimately with success.

Like Mitsubishi and Mitsui, Nomura in the aftermath of the crisis used its bank for leveraged purchases of wounded *zaibatsu* assets like those of Fujita *zaibatsu* with its mining, railways, banking and forestry and life insurance empire at fire sale prices (Alletzhauser, p. 77). The deposits of his bank were used to buy the shares, which subsequently were used as collaterals to borrow funds for further purchases.

In 1928, Tokushichi aged 50 was appointed by the Emperor to the House of Peers, probably because he was one of the best tax payers in the country (Ibid., p. 80). Although in principle opposed to the military's Manchurian and Chinese aggressive ventures, Tokushichi kept a low political profile, and continued to focus on the expansion of his Nomura *zaibatsu*—with Nomura Bank, Nomura Securities and Nomura East Indies (which began in 1917) at its core.

It was very Kansai-centric—away from the political corridors of power in Kanto. Even today, the successor companies of the Nomura *zaibatsu*'s components—Daiwa Bank, Cosmo Securities, Osaka Gas, Nomura Construction and Shikobo have their headquarters in Osaka.

Like in many elite families with their fast-paced lifestyles, tragedy struck frequently. His brother Jitsubaburo died of pneumonia in 1919. His second son, Tokio, was killed in a freak accident, when a train hit the car he was driving in 1928. Together with him was Daisuke Kuhara, heir to the Nissan *zaibatsu*, who also died. Two years later, Jitsusaburo's oldest son was killed by an avalanche while skiing in the Japanese Alps.

His oldest and only surviving son, Yoshitaro was more culturally inclined and after a year of study in the UK indulged full-time in the leisured lifestyle of the upper British classes replicated in Japan. He set-up the Nomura club in which *zaibatsu* executives would mimic the moves and habits of London's club land.

Although all surviving and able male family members were drafted into senior management positions, Nomura had to rely increasingly on hired hands ever since the pre-war days. The two most influential among them were Tsunao Okumura, a good-natured Epicurean character, and Minoru Segawa, a hard driving cholerical go-getter. Both rebuilt Nomura Securities after the war and charted its growth well into the 1970s.

During the war itself, Nomura made money through commissions by placing Japanese war bonds. It also developed successfully investment trusts, pooling clients' money for stock market investments. Nomura's properties in rubber and palm oil plantations and refineries in Borneo and Sumatra were run according to procurement needs issued by the military, and thus became non-performing assets, only to be lost permanently after the war.

Japan's military planners were obsessed by the notion of economies of scale and attempted forcible mergers in most economic sectors. Nomura Securities did only narrowly escape this consolidation move. At the same time, after the Battle of Midway in 1942, Nomura's Research department predicted defeat, and the company discretely prepared for the inevitable. It began selling stocks on its own account, hid the evidence and stashed away the proceeds.[2]

Yet the war related stress began to take its toll in January 1945. Tokushichi Senior died of a heart attack. Six months later after the destruction of their Kobe mansion, his oldest son and heir who had long been sick, equally passed away. For a few months, his oldest son, 12-year-old Fumihide Nomura, was to become the titular head of the family and the *zaibatsu*.

When the war ended, the Nomura *zaibatsu* controlled Japan's eighth largest bank (Nomura Bank). Nomura Life Insurance was ranked fifth. Nomura Trust and Banking was No. 6. Nomura Securities was the market leader in investment trust sales. Osaka Gas, which it also controlled, was one of Japan's largest utilities. Caught by their own war propaganda, which held big businesses in Japan responsible for the Pacific War and its war crimes, the US Occupation authorities ordered the dissolution and expropriation of Japan's 14 leading *zaibatsu*. The owner families were all to be purged and their properties confiscated. Given the complexity of the *zaibatsu* structures and hidden assets, the implementation of this vulgar Marxism was left to the Japanese themselves. This allowed the *zaibatsu*-owning families at least to keep their seemingly worthless forest property for which the US Occupation officers did not care.

Soon, former *zaibatsu* companies started purchasing each other's shares to protect themselves against takeovers and to re-establish their cooperation under a *keiretsu* (grouping) umbrella, with a cross-holding ownership pattern, which has become typical of Japan's capitalism to this day.

The fragments of the Nomura's surviving personal portfolio were secretly assembled in Nomura Construction. Yet reassembling the full Nomura *zaibatsu* as a *keiretsu* (unlike Mitsubishi or Sumitomo) was no longer possible after the Occupation ended. Daiwa Bank was controlled by fiercely anti-*zaibatsu* management and set-up its separate circle of corporate influence. Equally Osaka Gas and Nomura Life (later renamed Tokyo Mutual Life Insurance) went their own way.

For the post-war reconstruction of Nomura Securities, the political contacts of its new president, Tsunao Okumura (1948–59) proved helpful, notably his friendships and special treatment of PM Shigeru Yoshida and Finance Minister (later PM) Hayato Ikeda, as Okumura even in times of scarcity would treat them to geisha parties in Kyoto and bottles of Hennessy in Tokyo, and possibly more importantly would finance their election campaigns.[3] The result was a fairly unregulated untaxed market for securities on which securities companies could thrive—often based on insider trading and creaming off their customers.

In 1953, Nomura reopened its New York office (closed in 1936). Soon it could place the Toshiba shares, which GE wanted to shed, into friendly Japanese hands, like in those of Mitsui Bank. For the rest, Nomura's bridgehead at Wall Street during most early years had difficulties breaking even. Native recruits left quickly once they discovered that their career prospects in Nomura's hierarchy were fairly truncated for foreigners.

Starting in 1982, Nomura began hiring foreign graduates of prestigious US and UK business schools for their standard career stream. Instead of being given responsible junior tasks befitting young MBAs, they were locked up in Nomura's run down dormitories in Funabashi and subject to the habitual boot camp treatment cum lectures. Quickly these youngsters rebelled, took their stay in Japan as a paid vacation and turned their dormitory into a fraternity house. Even more disciplined later generations left soon.[4]

In Japan, like in the early days of Tokushichi Nomura Senior, 100 years later the retail of share placements is still done by polishing door knobs and visiting customers in the style of Tupperware and Yakult ladies (in Germany the publishing and insurance giants Bertelsmann and Allianz grew big similarly by peddling book club memberships and life insurances in door-to-door sales). An aggressive—or often simply desperate—sales force was able to push almost any recommendation of the month to its 200,000 corporate and five million individual clients, thus effectively recycling Japan's high domestic savings back into the economy.

The performance of Nomura's sales force is closely monitored, with individual and branch offices' sales objectives always surpassing past performance. Every three years staff is promoted, demoted or relocated without prior warning. Nomura's pay is good and during the bubble years of asset inflation until 1992, in spite of a dubious reputation the company ranked very high on desirability scale of university graduates. Nomura throws its young recruits fairly soon into the deep end of the corporate crocodile pool. Hardly trained, the young trainees are told to fill their quota of collecting the business cards of new customers and to follow them up with phone calls to place orders. Often they are told not to return to the office or to their corporate dormitory until targets are reached. In despair, many turn to relatives to reach their commission objectives. There are however, even limits for kind hearted rich uncles to the extent to which they follow their 22-year-old nephews' sales pitch of the day. After having survived three years of stock market lectures and gruelling street retail lessons in the business school of hard knocks, the Nomura trainee is gradually transformed into a self-confident battle-hardened sales professional, able and willing to perform effectively by the rules of hard work and hard play of corporate Japan. Nomura also hires young women. But their function is essentially to be pretty and graceful, to serve tea and to cheer up the worn out corporate warriors, until they get married to one of them, in which case she will show understanding for his long hours of work and customer relations.

Information, especially when from insider sources, is a precious commodity in stock broking. In Nomura, it is controlled by its powerful trading manager. According to Alletzhauser, it is passed on first to senior executives (for stock purchases in the name of close friends and relatives), then to influential politicians, followed by friendly institutions, until it finally reaches the Nomura retail salesman (Alletzhauser, p. 206). Sometimes organized crime (*yakuza*) figures are being helped out.

This is not without risk. When deals turn sour, *yakuza* do not take kindly to losses. They either beat their hapless Nomura account manager to death[5] or insist on full compensation from the firm.

As Nomura's market share in 1981 hit a glass ceiling of 15 per cent, it set-up a subsidiary, Kokusai Securities, as a nominal competitor and a de facto dependent ally. Kokusai had the added advantage of being a depository for burnt-out Nomura sales staff and management on pre-retirement packages. It was little surprise then that Kokusai's profits and dividends remained poor. Its main function was to push Nomura's market share to 20 per cent. Every Monday, Kokusai and other smaller Nomura affiliated brokers, like World, Itogui, Takagi, Ichiyoshi, Taisei, Nichiei and Sanyo Securities received instructions which stocks and sectors Nomura intended to push,[6] with the first mover advantage going to Nomura itself. Its sell/buy recommendations then became almost self-fulfilling prophecies—for the desired period of time. By the mid-1980s, when money seemed to grow on trees, Kokusai's profits as Japan's fifth largest securities house also grew by leaps and bounds based on commission earnings from ever more frothy paper deals of hugely inflated assets.

Apart from being a stockbroker, Nomura's role in the often murky world of Japanese high finance is manifold. When in the early 1980s, the rich owners of Japan Sightseeing, Shintaro Sasaki and his son, Eitaro Itoyama, also an LDP Diet member, with the support of Ryoichi Sasakawa, a shadowy wire puller of the rightist fringe and the master of motorboat racing in Japan, tried to take over Yomiuri Shimbun, Japan's largest and conservative newspaper, Nomura came to the rescue of the befriended Yomiuri Holding and yielded to the greenmail.[7] Worse, Nomura in 1985, probably not the first time (and surely not the last), felt compelled to pay gangsters (*sokaiya*) specializing on corporate blackmail.

Political goodwill was bought by allocating share issues to politicians and then to drive up the prices through "strong buy" recommendations and clients' purchases, while allowing politicians to cash in while prices were still riding high.[8]

During the summer of 1991, it became public that Nomura had compensated 49 corporate clients, including gangland fronts illegally to the tune of ¥26 billion (US$220 million).[9] In repentance, Chairman Setsuya Tabuchi (Nomura President 1978–85), and President Yoshihisa Tabuchi (1985–91) both resigned. Setsuya Tabuchi was removed from his prestigious vice chairmanship of Keidanren.[10] The new President

Hideo Sakamaki pledged that Nomura would change its ways and stop sponsoring organized crime.

Six years later in May 1997, he was arrested for having done just this almost since the day he had assumed office. Ryichi Koike, a powerful *sokaiya* had purchased Japanese securities companies stock courtesy of a generous loan by Dai-Ichi Kangyo Bank (another corporate chieftain to resign in disgrace) and threatened Sakamaki with disrupting the next shareholders' meeting—which would represent a nightmarish loss of face to the consensus-driven cowards in Japanese senior management. Sakamaki met Koike in person in April 1992. As a result, the shareholders' meeting passed in sweet harmony. Subsequently during 1993, Nomura paid Koike ¥320 million (US$3 million) into a special account.[11]

Sometime later, in 1995, trouble was looming again. Nomura was to announce its first ever loss and at the same time wished to rehabilitate the two disgraced Tabuchis (no relations) by reappointing them to the Board. Koike was paid ¥39 million (US$400,000) for his cooperation to ensure a smooth general meeting. With Nomura's relapse and Sakamaki locked up (he received a suspended jail sentence later), respectable business at home and abroad abandoned the tainted company in droves. "Is it really that surprising if you find your fund manager is dealing its profit into organized crime?" a Hong Kong investment manager was quoted.[12] High losses on Russian debt and on the US commercial mortgage market did not help either.

At the same time, US and European competitors were moving into Nomura's home turf, notably advising on the sale of Nippon Credit Bank, on the IPO (initial public offering) of NTT Docomo and highly profiled M & A activities in Japan[13] and to gain access to Japan's $10 trillion household savings and her $2 trillion pension fund market.[14] Merrill Lynch for this purpose bought up the remnants of collapsed Yamaichi Securities and its branch network in 1998. At the same time, Nomura's stepbrother, Daiwa Bank let it be known that it would terminate all of its international operations and revert to the role of a Kansai-based regional bank in Osaka.[15] It had earlier made financial history when an unsupervised rogue currency trader, Toshihide Iguchi, had lost US$1.1 billion at their New York branch. Daiwa then accepted a US$340 million fine for its attempt to hush the affair.

Meanwhile, in the Czech Republic Nomura cheaply bought a controlling stake in the sizable, but poorly managed Investment and Postbank (IPB) in March 1998. They had promised the Czechs that they would restructure the bank, retrain the staff and clear its backlog of unserviced debts. In reality, however, Nomura was only interested in IPB's large industrial holdings, consisting inter alia of the big Radegast and Pilsner Urquell breweries and in luxury hotels in Prague, which like an asset raider it sold expensively, while letting the undercapitalized bank go against the wall.[16] After a massive run on the bank, the Czech state renationalized IPB and ended its expensive adventure with Nomura. The *Financial Times* called Nomura's behaviour as "falling short of the standards expected of a major bank."[17]

When talk was rife about a foreign takeover of Nomura, its management in despair picked an unusual character, Junichi Kjiie, then a 51-year-old economics PhD-holder from the University of Chicago, who had spent most of his working life with Nomura in New York and Zurich—not typical leadership material for the company. Quickly dismissed as a powerless egghead, Kjiie in a sustained effort managed to turnaround against all odds. The old slash-and-burn culture was abandoned. Suspected *yakuza* accounts were discontinued, and public trust gradually regained. In Mergers & Acquisitions, Nomura leads the field again in Japan, with foreign competitors scaling back operations. It also market leads in investment banking services and in mutual bond funds in Japan. Its retail operations even became profitable with US and Australian bonds sold to interest-starved Japanese clients.[18] A subsequent moderate rally of the Nikkei helped to put Nomura's rebound profitability on a more sustainable footing. As a result, Kjiie's successor Noboyuki Kaga already feels emboldened to announce plans to venture abroad in force again.[19]

There is certainly a moral tale to Nomura's aggressive rise from humble beginnings, its hubris and falls in 1945 and in 1997, and its chastened recovery. Surely the company's fate also stands for the strengths and weaknesses of corporate Japan and its management culture.

ENDNOTES
1   Al Alletzhauser. *The House of Nomura*. London: Bloomsbury. 1990, p. 272.
2   Alletzhauser, p. 109.
3   Alletzhauser, p. 147.
4   Alletzhauser, p. 227.
5   Ibid., p. 207.
6   Ibid., p. 214.

7   Alletzhauser, p. 272.
8   Ibid., p. 289.
9   *Japan Times*, July 18, 1991.
10 *Japan Times*, July 2, 1991.
11 Kenji Hanyu. *TBS News/Foreign Press Centre*, June 16, 1997.
12 Tim Healy. "Nomura Securities Reels from a Trading Scandal." *Asiaweek*, March 21, 1997.
13 Gilian The. "The Eclipse of Nomura." *Financial Times*, July 1, 1999.
14 Brian Brenner. "A Big Stink Speeds up Tokyo's Big Bang." *Business Week*, July 7, 1997.
15 *BBC News*, October 25, 1998.
16 Albrecht Rothacher. *Im Wilden Osten*. Hamburg: Reinhard Kraemer Verlag. 2002, p. 209.
17 *Financial Times*, June 22, 2000.
18 Brian Brenner. "Nomura Comeback." *Business Week*, April 7, 2003.
19 "Makeover for Nomura." *Bloomberg*, July 31, 2003.

CHAPTER 20

Saatchi & Saatchi: Make, Break, Lost and Found

TERRY TAN

INTRODUCTION

In the world of advertising now, there are two companies with the name Saatchi, Saatchi & Saatchi and M&C Saatchi, rather surprising, considering that the name Saatchi is not common. How then did two companies end up having the same name? This chapter will give a brief run through of the history of Saatchi & Saatchi: how it started, how it exploded into an advertising world, how it almost hit rock bottom, and how, subsequently the advertising empire saw two Saatchis.

HISTORY

Humble beginnings

In 1967, a young man by the name of Charles Saatchi set up a small creative consultancy firm with his friend Ross Cramer. Charles, the second son of an Iraqi-Jewish textile businessman had met Ross while both were working at the American-owned Benton & Bowles, Charles as a junior copywriter and Ross as a senior art director. The duo later moved to Collett Dickinson Pearce, one of London's most dynamic agencies then, where they created their first controversy. Having been given an assignment for Ford, the duo created an ad that used Ford's competitors (namely, Jaguar, Rover and Mercedes) as a comparison. Such an ad, known as a "knocking copy" was at that time forbidden by Britain's Institute of Practitioners of Advertising (the ban was subsequently lifted). After a year at Collett Dickinson Pearce, the duo was headhunted by another agency, John Collings. But their tenure there was short. The duo did not get along with the boss, Andrew Blair, and so quit after six months, deciding this time, to set up their own creative consultancy, Cramer Saatchi.

It has to be clarified that a creative consultancy is not the same as an ad agency. Whereas a creative consultancy is called in by other companies on an ad hoc basis, to help in the generation of ideas, ad agencies however have fixed commercial clients. Ad agencies buy air and media space, get ideas (with the help of creative consultancies) and produce ads.

Cramer Saatchi started off with five staff: Cramer, Saatchi, Jeremy Sinclair (a copywriter), John Hegarty (whom the duo had met earlier at Benton & Bowles and again at John Collings) and a secretary. At the beginning, they refused to do work directly for commercial companies, only getting jobs through ad agencies, as a sort of goodwill. But a stroke of pure luck was to hit them soon, in the unlikely venue of a school, and they were to accept their first direct commercial client.

MILESTONES
Bagging the HEC contract

One of the biggest names ever, and probably the company (if it can be called one) that kicked off the start of Cramer Saatchi's meteoric path was the Health Education Council (HEC). Cramer, while picking up his child from school one day, had met a woman whose child was in the same school. As it turns out, the woman was working for HEC, and told Cramer that the HEC might need some creative consultation in designing posters and brochures. Cramer Saatchi was thus contracted by the HEC. Their work, starting at first as simply designing posters and brochures, later progressed to newspaper campaigns as the HEC realised it could afford more advertising expenses. One of the most famous works by Cramer Saatchi, which people still remember, is the pregnant man ad they did for the HEC. Sinclair one morning decided that having a pregnant woman in a pregnancy ad would be boring. Instead, by putting a man who appears to be pregnant, and including a tag line that said, "Would you be more careful if it was you that got pregnant?" the controversial ad became the most talked-about ad in London within weeks and gave Cramer Saatchi the international exposure it needed.

As the company got more successful, Charles too got ambitious. Not wanting the company to remain a small creative consultancy, he decided to turn the consultancy into a full fledged ad agency. His decision was fortified by the HEC and also the Citrus Marketing Board of Israel's desire to hire Cramer Saatchi as their ad agency. With two big names offering their contracts, this was indeed a good time to expand. But to this suggestion Cramer wasn't very keen. As such, he decided to leave the company. Charles Saatchi, who had all along been concerning himself with the creative side of the company, now needed a business brain to take the place of Cramer. That was when Charles decided to rope in his younger brother, Maurice Saatchi.

Maurice Saatchi, the third out of four brothers, had graduated with first class honors from London School of Economics in 1967, and was then working as a junior executive at Haymarket, the publishing company that published *Campaign*, a magazine for the advertising industry people. It was in Haymarket that Maurice got to know many people and got closely linked to the people at *Campaign*. At the same time, Maurice also witnessed how Haymarket's boss, Michael Heseltine, was constantly on the lookout for established magazines to acquire. His technique in buying up companies would, as we will later see, be taken up by Maurice. Maurice's early connection with the admen's magazine would also prove to be instrumental in Saatchi & Saatchi's rise and fall later on. In 1970, when Maurice joined his brother, the now full fledged ad agency was to be renamed Saatchi & Saatchi.

Compton backing

A few years into Saatchi & Saatchi's establishment, the Saatchi brothers started their wild ambition of acquiring companies. Although they successfully acquired small companies like George J. Smith, Brogan Developers, and E. G. Dawes, many bigger companies still eluded them, for nothing more than the fact that Saatchi & Saatchi was still considered a small, albeit dynamic upstart. But all this was to change in the year 1975.

S. T. Garland Advertising, established in 1928, by Sidney Garland, had been an independent company until 1960 when New York's Compton Advertising decided that it wanted to establish a base in the UK, and bought 49 per cent of the S. T. Garland agency, thereby establishing S. T. Garland as Garland-Compton. At the same time, Compton Advertising was also to control a new company called Compton UK Partners which would have total control over the new Garland-Compton.

Garland-Compton was looking for dynamic new blood in the old and possibly stagnant company. A list of companies was considered, excluding Saatchi & Saatchi. One had the most potential. That was the Kirkwood Company. But toward the end of negotiations, Kirkwood decided that it didn't want to risk the possibility of their own young company being dragged down by the inertia of the giant and pulled out. While discussions with the Kirkwood Company fell through, by a stroke of luck, Maurice had called Ron Rimmer, Garland-Compton's managing director to poach him over. Rimmer however set up a meeting between Garland-Compton and Saatchi & Saatchi to discuss a merger. At the end of 1975, a deal was made. Charles would sell his company to Compton for 36 per cent shares of the new enlarged group. Compton in New York would now own 26 per cent, down from the 49 per cent[1] it previously owned. The rest belonged to shareholders. This merger was hugely significant, as this gave the brothers a new vault of wealth to continue their buying spree. Although more accurately a merger, the Saatchi brothers insisted that the name Saatchi & Saatchi remained in the enlarged group name. The name Saatchi & Saatchi Garland-Compton emerged. But more often, the public would conveniently drop Garland-Compton from the tedious name and identify the group as simply Saatchi & Saatchi. With more money now to play with, and a bigger name to back them up, Saatchi & Saatchi had leaped exponentially from a small upstart to a dynamic and strong group. It now has not only the resources but also the reputation to start their voracious acquisition appetite.

Thatchy & Thatchy

We do owe them everything, Charles and I.
When Mrs Thatcher hired us, nobody had ever heard of us. Certainly not in America. That election victory in 1979 was the basis of our international—particularly US—expansion. She was so respected in America that if she thought we were good, we were good. She made us.
– Maurice Saatchi[2]

In 1976, Saatchi & Saatchi Compton Ltd.'s client list would include names like British Leyland, Schweppes, Brutus Jeans and Gillete-Braun (for whom they successfully propelled Braun's new electric shaver into second position in the dry shaver industry in just one year). Saatchi & Saatchi were getting very big clients, and they managed to hold on to Procter and Gamble (one of the biggest clients at that time) and Rowntree Mackintosh accounts as well. All these heavyweight clientele boosted their reputation, and was to be a lead up to one of their most influential clients yet, the Conservative Party's Margaret Thatcher.

In 1978, the Conservatives enlisted the help of Saatchi & Saatchi to promote themselves. The Conservatives had, for the elections to be held in 1979, a daunting task of winning the seat back from the ruling Labour Party. Director of communications, Gordon Reece, decided to employ an advertising agency to promote the Conservatives, very much like how producers would promote their products. This was, back then a rather unheard of tactic as political parties had till then only employed the use of volunteers to promote themselves. With Saatchi & Saatchi's creative flair, and their pioneering use in UK of knocking copy, the Labour party was in for a hard time indeed. Tim Bell, their media director, was put in charge of the account. Many famous ads were produced for the Conservatives. Their tactic was simple, to attack the opposition, devalue their stance, erode their confidence and reputation. The most famous of all was a poster that showed a long never-ending line outside an unemployment office. The headliner said: "Labour isn't Working, Britain's Better Off with the Conservatives." This ad immediately gained popularity, equalled only by the pregnant man ad.[3] That year, the Conservatives won the election by a relatively small 5.2-per-cent margin. This win was enough to establish the name of Saatchi & Saatchi worldwide as a household name and as the Conservative's agency, as "Thatcher's Admen."[4] It also won them the interesting nickname of "Thatchy & Thatchy."

This was to be a milestone in Saatchi & Saatchi's path, changing from local ad agency to an international force to be reckoned with.

In 1979, Saatchi & Saatchi Garland-Compton, the main advertising wing itself, excluding the main holding company, reached the top position with declared billings of 67.5 million pounds.[5] Within a short span of nine years, the young upstart of a company whom some people had mistaken to be a Japanese hi-fi company, and others an Italian company, had taken over long time industry leader of 20 years, J. Walter Thompson.

Saatchi's bad patch

Throughout most of the 1980s, Saatchi & Saatchi was to continue its acquisition spree. From the initial plan of acquiring ad agencies, the brothers' appetite got bigger and started acquiring marketing, public relations, market research and management consultancy companies to name a few. By 1986, they would have spent close to $461.5 million on acquisitions. It was also then that the company had grown so big that it had to be split into two units: communications services and consulting services.[6]

In 1987, the brothers made a laughing stock of themselves when they tried to buy over a bank. The brothers aimed for the fourth largest bank in Britain, Midland Bank. At that time, the bank was in a bad shape with a lot of trouble with third world loans and bad investments. Meetings were held in secret between Maurice and Midland's chairman, Sir Kit McMahon. But the meeting didn't go well. McMahon was not satisfied with what Maurice had to offer. And he didn't feel that Midland's customers would want such a dynamic and lively company to join it. He felt that Midland's customers wanted the bank to be as stable and as uneventful as possible. News of the failed takeover leaked out, and very soon, for the first time, the brothers were being ridiculed by industry members.

In 1988, Saatchi & Saatchi's reputation took a slight dip. Unable to raise funds through shares offering, but yet, still greedy for more companies, the brothers resorted to issuing Europreference shares which earned them $316 million. The terms of the purchase stated that by July 1993, if the price of the stock did not rise to above the original price of 441 pence, the company would have to buy back all the shares from the public at the original price plus a 20 per cent bonus. This potentially set the company up to pay more than $300 million if the stock holders exercised the right.[7]

1989 marked a very bad year for the Saatchis. In that year, not only did the ad industry on the whole suffer a slight contraction (spending was to increase to only 3.8 per cent in 1990 as compared to double digits in the early 1980s[8]), Saatchi & Saatchi itself also, for the first time declared a fall in profits. Maurice himself had announced at the annual general meeting that for the first time after 18 years of consecutive profit growth, they were not going to be able to meet profit expectations.[9] At the same time, the increasing cost of the brothers' acquisition spree had worn down whatever dwindling profits the company was making. Shrinking profits, acquisition sprees, plus the fact that the company could possibly owe the public $300 million in four years' time finally forced the brothers to admit that things were getting out of hand and that someone was needed to get things back in order.

New blood, old body

Help came in the form of Robert Louis-Dreyfus as chief executive and Charlie Scott as finance director. And the first thing Louis-Dreyfus did was to demand that Charles and Maurice not interfere with his rescue package. Reluctantly they complied.

After studying the company, it was decided that the company needed to cut costs very badly. Louis-Dreyfus made many changes, including firing people (up to 6,000 were laid off) and cutting top management pay. Even Louis-Dreyfus himself drove a modest Peugeot 205 company car.[10] He also implemented performance-related incentives and took away huge fixed salaries which would give no incentive for management to work hard.

Louis-Dreyfus also realised that to be the biggest was no big deal. The company had to focus on its core competency, advertising. Thus, the consultation wing of the company had to go. By 1991, he had sold off 10 out of 12 consulting companies.

Yet another problem lingered: the Europreference share issue. As of 1989, the Europreference share price was hovering around 90 pence. Louis-Dreyfus had to somehow pull it up to the original price by 1993. A restructuring plan was hatched by Louis-Dreyfus, which involved converting the Europreference shares into common shares, and the bigger shareholders would get seats on the board. Bank facilities were increased for Saatchi & Saatchi, and bank loans were extended. In 1991, the plan was approved, and for the first time sine 1989, the company was according to Scott, "on stable financial footing."[11]

But two most pertinent demands from Louis-Dreyfus to wrest the company out of the red was that firstly, the company move out of the Berkeley Square location, and secondly, that the name Saatchi & Saatchi not be used so widely. Louis-Dreyfus made the first demand because that prime location at Berkeley Square was costing the company far too much money and although was huge enough to house more than

60 people, only housed less than 10 people. The 14,000-square feet office space costing £64 per square feet was just too extravagant. The second demand came about because people were associating all the companies that Saatchi & Saatchi plc owned. Although the main advertising wing was doing well, the other arms were not. As such, the reputation of the advertising wing was being pulled down.

But the two brothers were not to budge on those two important issues. The Saatchis absolutely refused to entertain any mention of moving out of Berkeley. The posh environment represented the image they wanted to portray. Leaving it for a cheaper location would look bad on them. They also refused to lessen the usage of the name Saatchi & Saatchi, as they wanted their names to be in all the companies. Thus, after three years at Saatchi & Saatchi, Louis-Dreyfus left the company having improved its financial standing quite substantially. However, unable to weed out the two pertinent problems, the ailing company merely got a booster jab to cure the symptoms. The main illness of how the company was controlled, the spending (mainly the Berkeley Square location) and the overuse of the name Saatchi & Saatchi still remained.

Ousted by a Herro

In December 1994, Maurice Saatchi was asked to step down as chairman of Saatchi & Saatchi Company plc. Instead, he was offered the post of chairman of Saatchi & Saatchi Advertising Worldwide. A demotion in the eyes of Maurice. How did the founder of a company get asked to leave the very empire he set up?

The Saatchi brothers' nemesis came in the form of Wisconsin-born David Herro. Herro as a person will be discussed in a later section. We will here focus on Herro's role in ousting Maurice from chairmanship.

Young, successful and enjoying big cars and expensive lifestyles, Herro and the mutual fund he started, Oakmark International had by 1993, held a 10 per cent stake in Saatchi & Saatchi. In 1989, when Saatchi & Saatchi's stock landed in trouble, plunged some 93 per cent in value[12] and handed control over to Louis-Dreyfus, Herro, who had a penchant for buying garbage or under-valued stocks, started buying up Saatchi & Saatchi stocks, quickly becoming the largest shareholder.

With such a huge stake in Saatchi & Saatchi, Herro started keeping close tabs on the goings-on in Saatchi & Saatchi, specifically on the Saatchi brothers. Herro had invested only because he trusted Louis-Dreyfus's leadership. He knew that it had been the two brothers who had caused the company's downfall, and was very wary of them. When Louis-Dreyfus resigned in 1993, Scott took over, and immediately tensions started mounting between Scott the CEO and Maurice the chairman. Both were trying to get the other out of office. He wasn't happy at all with the two going public with their disagreements. More than that, he was worried that Maurice was going to kick out the very management that Herro himself had invested in. If that were to happen, the Saatchi brothers would be in control again, and that did not seem like a good alternative. After having sent letters to Maurice warning him to cooperate with Scott, only to have them ignored, Herro in 1994, then went down personally to London and met with Maurice for the first time. Such shareholder activism, where the investors actively exercise their right on matter of the company was rather unusual in the UK, but was common in the US. The meeting with Maurice, seeing how he led his extravagant life, only made Herro more determined to get Maurice out. More than that, he felt that it was very unbecoming of a chairman to try get his CEO fired via the public media. Herro thus decided to use his right as a major shareholder to garner other shareholders' support to get Maurice out of Saatchi & Saatchi.

On March 30, 1994, a board meeting was held that actually fired Maurice. But Jeremy Sinclair, who had stuck around all these years, begged them to give Maurice another chance. The decision was left up to the CEO, Scott, who decided to not fire Maurice. Apart from giving him the chance, they also knew that Maurice had links to many important customers, including Mars and British Airways.

Unsatisfied with the turn of events, Herro contemplated calling an Emergency General meeting to get Maurice out, but decided against it as he realised Maurice was up for elections soon.

The situation at Saatchi & Saatchi escalated through the year, with Maurice not only getting a pay cut, but a shorter contract as well. Still, Herro was not satisfied. An independent analyst, Suzanna Taverne, was asked to come in to study the company. She too found that the holding company, as Louis-Dreyfus had suggested, should take away the name Saatchi & Saatchi. With a holding company (Saatchi & Saatchi Company plc) that was not doing very well having the same name as the advertising wing (Saatchi & Saatchi Advertising) that was doing well, the reputation of the advertising wing would no doubt be pulled down and would be "endlessly problematic."[13] To that, Maurice was once again adamant. She also theorised that Maurice only wanted to own a big company and didn't really care for customer conflicts. She too concluded that Maurice was hampering the growth of Saatchi & Saatchi. With yet more proof at hand, Herro was determined to get his way.

On December 16, 1994, the board of Saatchi & Saatchi Company plc met on the sixth floor of the Whitfield Street office. Apart from the board members, attorneys and financial advisors were present. In a marathon eight-and-a-half-hour meeting, only one thing was on the agenda, to fire or not to fire Maurice Saatchi as chairman. In the end, only Jeremy Sinclair was left supporting one of two founding members of the advertising empire. As such, there was no choice but to get Maurice to step down as chairman. The board however knew that Maurice's name in itself was an asset to the company. Big names like British Airway's Colin Marshall and the Mars brothers John and Forrest Mars had sent formal letters in support of Maurice. Kicking Maurice out of the company totally would risk Saatchi & Saatchi losing these two big clients. They thus decided to offer Maurice the position of chairman of Saatchi & Saatchi Advertising Worldwide.

Saatchi vs Saatchi

Maurice decided not to take the offer of chairman of Saatchi & Saatchi Advertising Worldwide. Making his decision known on January 3, 1995, he went on to set up the New Saatchi Agency. Now housed in a modest office on Davies Street, not far from his beloved Berkeley Square location, the new building was cheap, noisy and tacky. Subsequently Sinclair, Kershaw and Muirhead (which the media termed the three *amigos*) also joined him in the New Saatchi Agency, and Charles followed suit on February 16, 1995. A whole chain of lawsuits followed. Saatchi & Saatchi plc sued Muirhead for $50 million, accusing him of breach of contract, misappropriation of confidentiality, proprietary documents, and breach of fiduciary responsibilities. They also sued Maurice, and the three *amigos*, accusing them of "a conspiracy to injure the business of the Group and against Maurice Saatchi for soliciting the other three."[14] Charles also sued Saatchi & Saatchi PLC for constructive dismissal, claiming that they had made his position as lifelong president intolerable by naming him in legal actions.

With the resignations of the three *amigos*, share prices fell as well, and reporters speculated that it was a ploy of the Saatchi brothers to devastate Saatchi & Saatchi's share price till it got low enough for them to buy it over.

Within days, the press coverage of the goings-on in and out of Saatchi & Saatchi reached phenomenal levels as reporters staked the agency doors for the latest news, giving second priority to even the Russian bombardment of Chechnya.[15]

The New Saatchi although having a rocky publicity start, had powerhouse clients. A day before Charles resigned, it was announced that Mirror Group Newpapers and Gallaher, after reviewing the situation, had awarded their accounts to New Saatchi. On 2 and 3 May 1995, British Airways and Quantas respectively gave the New Saatchi their much coveted accounts. The decision to award the account was a long and tedious one with many rounds of presentations starting a month before. In the end however, the New Saatchi, with its simple, clear and focused presentation, beat other competitors like Saatchi & Saatchi Advertising, J. Walter Thompson and Bartle Bogle Hegarty. The win was to be a very significant one. Having lost so many big accounts to New Saatchi, Saatchi & Saatchi had to think of a way out.

Tensions between the two companies had come to a head when both sides decided that continued tensions would only harm both parties, peace was the best way out. On May 16, 1995, representatives from both sides met including Sinclair from the New Saatchi and Wendy Smyth from Saatchi & Saatchi or Cordiant (the new name of the holding company as of March 16, 1995). The Saatchi brothers were not present. During the brief four-hour meeting, both sides expressed the intention of settling the lawsuits quickly out of court. As such, the Muirhead case was dropped as both sides had no idea why the case even came about, save to just rattle Muirhead. A lawsuit involving Charles and Maurice's pension fund from Cordiant was dropped provided the brothers do not seek any additional compensation. The case against the three *amigos*, attempting to prevent them from working for New Saatchi until their contract expires with Cordiant was dropped as they realized that UK courts favoured the welfare of employees and their right to earn a living. Such a case against the three *amigos* would only be in vain. With all the lawsuits dropped, New Saatchi had achieved its goal. Cordiant however had not. To protect their business, Cordiant signed a moratorium with New Saatchi, stating that the latter could not poach clients and employees from Saatchi & Saatchi Advertising and Bates Worldwide.[16]

One more item remained though. The name of the new company. This matter was only settled on May 20 after more than 20 hours of negotiation. The name M&C Saatchi was agreed upon after meeting a few demands set by the new chairwoman of Saatchi & Saatchi Advertising, Jennifer Laing. She demanded that the name Saatchi not be the first word of the company's name. Also, it could not start with the word new. There must be something in front of the name Saatchi and it should not be "new." Laing refused to budge on her demands and a court case would ensue if it wasn't met. Names like MC Saatchi, M&C Saatchi and M&C Partners were suggested, and finally M&C Saatchi was selected because Laing wanted as many words as possible in front of the word Saatchi. With more words in front of the name Saatchi, people would not be inclined to drop the front words and keep to Saatchi only. As such, M&C Saatchi was borne.

CORPORATE STRATEGY

Acquisition pattern

Saatchi & Saatchi throughout the years have been infamous for their appetite for acquisitions, buying up not only small companies, but big ones as well. Around 1978, they bought Hall Advertising in Edinburgh, O'Kennedy-Bindley and Hunter Advertising in Dublin and Collet Dickenson Pearce in UK. Between 1983 and 1985, Saatchi & Saatchi acquired Wong Lam in Hong Kong, Hayhurst in Canada, Campaign Advertising in New Zealand, McCaffrey & McCall in New York, and Gough Waterhouse in Sydney. They also bought up many other advertising companies in Britain, like Sharps Advertising. One of their biggest acquisitions was in 1986 where they spent a hefty $450 million buying over Ted Bates Worldwide with a client list comprising of big names like Mars, Colgate and Nabisco.[17]

Saatchi & Saatchi had a very unique acquisition pattern. They would only buy over companies if, firstly no other company was contesting the bid. Secondly, management remained in position. The purchase price would be paid off with an initial lump sum, followed by three- to five-year instalments that would be weighted against the company's performance. Funds for their acquisitions would come not from their own pockets, nor from the company's funds but by issuing shares.

The concept behind acquisitions of ad agencies came from Marion Harper, founder of Interpublic, who decided that companies should not be limited in growth by client limitations. In the ad industry, often a company cannot represent two clients who are competitors in the same industry, say Nike and Reebok for example. Marion Harper therefore came up with the idea of a main holding company owning many individually-run ad agencies. This way, the main company can generate profits from any client without infringing on privacy laws, as information would not be divulged between companies. The Saatchis likewise followed this model in their quest for size.

Image management

From the beginning, Saatchi & Saatchi's business strategy was to be in people's faces. The brothers were gregarious, showy and manipulative and they showed it. They didn't care for norms or industry codes of conduct.

For the launch of their full-fledged agency in 1970, the brothers put out an ad in the papers promoting themselves very much like how companies would promote their products. This was unheard of in the ad industry as ad agencies were there to promote products, not themselves. Although frowned upon by fellow admen, this strategy gained Saatchi & Saatchi much publicity and the practice was soon taken up by others.

Making bold claims was another of the Saatchi brothers' strategy. Newspaper reports of the new company stated that Saatchi had started his company with a million pounds of billings.[18] This of course was an exaggeration. In their controversial promotion ad, they also claimed to not follow the industry norm of 15 per cent commission on media advertising rates. Instead, Saatchi & Saatchi suggested charging clients 22 per cent of total billings. This novel way of charging however was never really implemented. The brothers also announced on various occasions, their plans to invest overseas in America and France, and that discussions were on the way. But these too never bore fruit, but it did have one effect, it made the people sit up and pay attention to this new company whom everyone now thought had international foresight and bucked trends.

It would not be an exaggeration to say that Saatchi & Saatchi paved the British ad industry's way out of the gentlemanly and inevitably non-dynamic mould that it had been so firmly set in.

The brothers were also extremely proud of their name. When Saatchi & Saatchi Company plc moved to the Berkeley Square location of Lansdowne House in June 1989, they only occupied the seventh floor, the top floor. But the brothers paid almost £70 million to put the name Saatchi & Saatchi on the main entrance to the building, thus making it seem as if they owned the whole building, when the main tenant was actually the pharmaceutical company, Glaxo.

Even in the dealings with Garland-Compton, the insistence of the brothers on having their name in the name of the new company also served to benefit them. The long and tedious name of Saatchi & Saatchi Garland-Compton was so frequently shortened to only Saatchi & Saatchi that in time, people mistook the two to be the same. Charles, who was usually picky when it came to the name of the company used in the press, conveniently let this mistake slip.

Saatchi & Saatchi also maintained their reputation of being the misfits of the industry. The usage of knocking copy was typically Saatchi. The ad industry in London, being a gentlemen's industry up till the 1980s, did not allow the mention of competitors to make one's products look good. But being inspired by American models of advertising, Charles Saatchi used it nevertheless with his Ford account.

Further inspired by the dynamism in the American ad industry where ad agencies would approach clients and fight for accounts, unlike the British way whereby ad agencies do not approach clients, but wait passively (and according to them, dignifiedly) for clients to approach them, Maurice Saatchi started cold calling companies. He would also approach potential clients during functions or gatherings, starting his pitch by first introducing himself, then saying, "Although you are probably very happy with your present advertising agency, I think we have found a way for you to make more money and sell more products."[19] When pressed for more details, Maurice would say nothing more than ask that they visit him at his office. This way of pitching would inevitably create doubts in one's mind, and the probability of getting better sales would lure them into the Saatchi office.

Charles was also very particular about what went to the press about the company. No one in the company was allowed to talk to the press. Charles was to have total control of such media relations. The most popular and well read press in the ad industry was at that time *Campaign*. Maurice's short stint at Haymarket, the company that owned and published *Campaign* would prove invaluable to Saatchi & Saatchi's close link with the relevant grapevines. Not to be forgotten is also the brothers' finesse at handling and manipulating the press. The brothers had a special ability to make each and every reporter from different magazines feel special, to make them feel like they are the most important to them and that the scoop was specially for them. Even during Maurice's "war" against Charlie Scott, Maurice aptly used the press to maim Scott. It had been said that a couple of days after Maurice sent an expense claim to the company for entertaining the press, a favorable report about Maurice or bad press about Scott would undoubtedly ensue.

Culture management

One wonders how Saatchi & Saatchi handled the different corporate cultures, especially when they so ferociously acquired companies from different countries and industries. How did Saatchi & Saatchi deal with the diverse corporate cultures?

The fact is they didn't. Much like how Charles was a collector of sports cars and art, the Saatchi brothers merely wanted to collect companies to make the main holding company big. They didn't really care for integrating the companies or running them. In fact, one of their conditions for acquisition was that the management was to remain. Each company would still operate as it had been. The other companies were viewed more as outposts than actual creative branches. Creative juices still came from London.

As such, Saatchi & Saatchi did not face any acquisitions problems of culture clashes at all. Decision making and management styles were left totally up to the company and their holding companies. Saatchi & Saatchi it seemed had no real interest in running them. By not enforcing a uniform culture throughout all the companies, Saatchi & Saatchi retained each company's individuality, be it in different industries or in different countries.

Good turned bad

Some of the brothers' business strategies seemed to work very well. In fact, at the point of implementation, it seemed like they had found the winning formula. However, these "winning formulas" would come back a few years later to haunt them, and in some cases even threaten to drag them into bankruptcy. Checks and balances were not put in place to keep them afloat.

Acquisition funding and payment

Saatchi & Saatchi had a unique way of funding and paying for their acquisitions. By issuing shares to the public, and getting the necessary funds from there, the brothers thus managed to raise enough funds to fuel their appetite and yet at the same time not draw into their own bank account. Acquisition contracts always also stipulated that an initial sum will be paid and the remaining to be paid over a period of three to five years depending on the performance of the company. Thus, Saatchi & Saatchi did not have to raise the full amount of the acquisition at one time. This method of acquisition worked very well, enabling the brothers to swallow many companies. It seemed that Maurice and Charles had found a winning formula.

Their method worked well for a while, especially when the company was riding high in public opinion between 1985 and 1987. But in 1985, after the ridicule of the failed Midland Bank acquisition, and the slowdown of the ad agency, public opinion of the wonder brothers fell. They were no longer able to raise the necessary funds for further acquisition through shares issue. At a loss, the brothers resorted to issuing Europreference shares as discussed above. And immediately, with the money raised from these shares, they went on to buy yet more firms. This set them up for potential bankruptcy.

Acquiring company after company all the way up till 1988 only meant that throughout 1991–3, the brothers would have to start paying up the remaining performance based instalments. Company funds were being depleted from firstly, all the acquisitions and secondly, the high cost of running the main holding company, Saatchi & Saatchi plc. This dragged down the financial stability of the company. Also, while having to worry about the instalment payments, Saatchi & Saatchi (specifically Louis-Dreyfus who was the CEO then) had to worry about pulling up the share price, otherwise, come 1993, they would incur another debt in excess of $300 million. This brittle situation was finally eased when Louis-Dreyfus and Scott implemented a rescue plan that converted the Europreference shares to common shares, increased bank facilities and extended bank loans.

Paying high salaries to keep the management also seemed like a good way to avoid culture clashes, but it inevitably led to the top management not having any incentive to work since they were already getting so much pay. This once again turned against the brothers.

Ignoring acquisitions

> Most of the people who sold the Saatchis their business never saw them.
> – Robert Louis-Dreyfus[20]

The Saatchi brothers had a peculiar habit. Being only interested in acquisitions for collection, once they had gotten the company, they would completely ignore it. And they were good at it. They would buy a company and never look at it again, instead, would move on and search for other acquisitions.

The people in the neglected companies grew to hate Saatchi & Saatchi, as the promise of having a strong holding company to lead them never materialized. Not only did it not materialize, they didn't even get to see the infamous brothers.

This hatred for the blatant neglect caused the company a lot of money. In 1989 when Louis-Dreyfus tried to sell off the consulting wing by selling the companies back to themselves, he was cursed at, not because of something he had done, but simply because he represented Saatchi & Saatchi, the company they despised. Peterson & Co., a company specialising in trial litigation advice would buy itself back for only $1 million, when Saatchi & Saatchi had bought them for $123 million three years ago. Other companies like Information Consulting Group and the Hay Group followed suit. In the end, after having invested more than 125 million pounds in acquisition for the consulting wing, Louis-Dreyfus could only get back 80 million pounds.

Synonymous name

Saatchi & Saatchi's insistence that their name be retained in all the companies they merged had, during the good times, a mutually beneficial, cumulative effect. Because the names of the companies were so long, this worked well, as all companies with the name Saatchi & Saatchi in it would be known only as Saatchi & Saatchi. Whenever the advertising wing gained some honor, the main holding company and all other companies under them would increase their reputation as well. The name Saatchi & Saatchi just kept getting more and more popular. They were synonymous with creativity and dynamism.

But such mutually benefiting relationships were a double-edged sword. When the company started to fall on bad times, although the main advertising wing was still doing well and earning healthy profits, the smaller companies in other industries were not. As such, the name of Saatchi & Saatchi started to get dragged through the mud. The reputation and business of the profitable advertising wing was being marred.

Also, as the years went by, people got used to Saatchi & Saatchi's shock tactics. No longer did they create controversy. Even if it did, it would get boring after a while, as everyone knew that that was just how the brothers were like. Even this novelty effect wore off, resulting in a loss in reputation.

Top-heavy management

As Saatchi & Saatchi got bigger, the brothers nevertheless handled the company like a small family business. The atmosphere at the main Saatchi & Saatchi companies was rather relaxed. Meetings were not conducted at the Saatchi & Saatchi Company plc office. Instead, the chairman and the directors would have meetings at the Royal Automobile Club, over beers and snooker. Profits were dwindling around 1988, but the paychecks of the executive directors continued to grow. Maurice's salary during that period grew 25 per cent to £625,000 from £500,000.[21] And in a show of affluence that the company could not afford, in 1989, Charles and Maurice moved the office from its Lower Regent Street office to the swanky Berkeley Square location.

PERSONAL TRAITS
The Saatchi brothers

The brothers together formed an insatiable duo. Hungry for collection, size and image, both propelled the company, but had to subsequently relinquish control.

Both, having come from an Iraqi–Jewish background, somehow always felt like outsiders in Britain. Eager to prove their worth, they were to climb to the top and treat everyone else like peasants. They created an air of superiority around them, and people had to fight hard to get their attention and favour. But once you fell out of favor with them, you ceased to exist in their eyes. Paul Bainsfair, an account executive with Saatchi & Saatchi had once been in the brothers' inner circle of friends. But the moment he resigned, "it was like I died," "if I saw either of them in the street, I would expect them to look the other way."[22]

The Saatchi brothers led a luxurious life. Not ones to scrimp and save, the company Saatchi & Saatchi reportedly spent £6.5 million annually on the brothers' expenses.[23]

The relationship between the two brothers was rather unique. Charles had a quick temper. And on occasion, it had been said, that he flung chairs at Maurice when he didn't understand concepts fast enough. "I can't believe we came from the same womb," Charles would sometimes scream at Maurice.[24]

Although having problems of their own, the two brothers never failed to put up a united front when dealing with the press and Charles remained fiercely protective of his younger brother's reputation.

The brothers truly transformed the way the advertising industry in Britain worked. Throwing out the gentlemanliness of the old admen, they broke all rules, including the knocking copy ruling and the taboo against approaching other companies' clients. They also started marketing their company the way they would market clients' products and approached clients for accounts. Having close relations with the press, they would also manipulate their information leakages to the press like never seen before.

Their disregard for customer feelings however cost them business. Buying companies and merging them, they placed clients competing in the same industry together in the same firm. It was one such case with Helene Curtis Industries' Finesse and Procter & Gamble that Saatchi & Saatchi was forced to quit the Helene account on the demand of the world's largest advertiser. Quitting the account cost them $90 million in billings.

Charles Saatchi

The elder of the two, the collector and the creative, Charles had been the one behind the creative edge of Saatchi & Saatchi. For a time, it was also Charles who drove the company. It was only when Charles started to take a step back from the company that Maurice became more vocal. Charles has been a collector since young, starting with Superman comics, to jukeboxes, cars, and then art. Along the way he also developed the habit of collecting companies with Maurice. Charles' art collection had at one point in time been estimated to be worth $250 million with over 800 works produced by more than 50 artists. Indeed, Charles' influence over the art world was so great that he has been used as a "seal of approval."[25]

Not only did he collect inanimate objects, Charles collected people as well, and paid a handsome price for them too. He often bought over people whom he thought were of talent, and employed them within his company. Amongst them was Jeff Stark. In 1984, Charles acquired a small but successful British ad agency, Hedger Mitchell Stark for £1.2 million. The main purpose of the acquisition was not for the company per se, but for Jeff Stark, a brilliant copywriter who used to work for Saatchi & Saatchi but left to start his own company. Charles love for cars also sapped the company's funds, as the company paid for the maintenance of his 17 cars.

As the company got bigger, Charles started getting more reclusive. Not wanting to meet people, he avoided public events, and never attended a single board meeting. When Herro came down to meet Maurice in London for the first time, Charles would hide behind the main door, and try to catch glimpses of the conversation.[26]

Maurice Saatchi

> A puppy that "craps all over the carpet then licks your hand."
> – Wendy Smyth, Saatchi & Saatchi plc Finance Director

The younger of the two brothers, Maurice had been recruited into the company as the business mind. As such, Charles would do the creative work while Maurice would be in charge of getting the clients.

The company spent a lot of money on Maurice as well. Apart from his high pay, in one year alone Maurice was chalking up taxi bills of $60,000. $50,000 was spent on a party thrown for the premiere of the movie *Damage*, based on the novel written by his wife Josephine Hart.

Maurice also spent a huge amount of money renovating his residence, Old Hall at Sussex. Hart reported how Maurice had spent a lot of money flooding acres of land just to get lakes to their home. This pride in living spaces would also translate into his obstinacy in not moving out of the costly Berkeley Square office. It was an image that he did not want to give up. Saatchi & Saatchi the company as well as the brothers had elevated themselves to a position of superiority. Anything less would not do.

Maurice also established himself as an excellent PR man. When the company started, he would cold call clients to get business. Never mind that these calls hardly turned into deals; it served to ingrain the name Saatchi & Saatchi into people's minds. At functions, he would approach clients with his famous pitching line which promised more sales. Maurice however refused to give further details, asking instead that they visit him at his office. It was against the rules to approach other people's clients, but rules neither applied to Maurice nor Charles.

Indeed, Maurice had a knack of breaking the rules. As aptly described by Wendy Smyth, he would step on your toes and later pretend like nothing happened and come to you, showering you with attention. And people fell for it, often forgiving him for the things he did. Thus was the charm of Maurice.

David Herro

A typical all-American boy, ambitious, disciplined, driven and not afraid of confrontations, Herro was a team player, who was in the running for a football scholarship till he got knocked unconscious during a game. In school, he had been given the nickname "FS," pronounced as Fess, an acronym for "Fight Starter." Herro was also considered trustworthy and could be counted on to keep his word.

An economics whiz kid, having graduated from the University of Wisconsin with a Master's in economics, he successfully launched many mutual funds for the Principal Financial Group in Des Moines and later for the State of Wisconsin Investment Board. It was with this impressive track record that the Chicago-based Harris Associates offered him the opportunity to start his own fund, Oakmark International.

Herro was a direct, hard hitting man. When he realised that the clashes between Scott and Maurice were escalating, he personally went down to London to meet Maurice. And ever since that meeting, Herro had been unimpressed by Maurice. In fact, it made him watch Maurice more. Herro's consistent doubts about Maurice, despite the latter's many efforts to work harder and for less pay, resulted in his persistent calls for general meetings to oust Maurice.

Clash of personalities?

For once, the Saatchi brothers had met someone who was focused, so focused in fact that he saw through all their slick smooth talking. Herro was very unlike the brothers in the way they conducted business. While the brothers would make false claims to the press and not deliver in the end, Herro remained true to his word, and he expected the same from others. Fully confrontational, Herro had no qualms about hitting through the brothers' masquerade and making them accountable for the pay they drew. The brothers on the other hand (especially Charles) would shy away from any sort of confrontation, and weave their way out of the situation.

Because his own mutual fund was heavily invested in Saatchi & Saatchi, Herro had a vested interest in making sure the company succeeded. He would relentlessly watch over the company, stepping in every so often to make sure things were on the right track. This could not be more different from the brothers. The Saatchis would acquire companies with the promise of a strong creative leadership, only to neglect them soon after.

Herro remained undeterred in his belief that Maurice was not doing the company any good. Herro's type of investor activism was also rather unseen in the UK although it was getting common in the US. This clash of cultures caught the Saatchis unawares.

THE TWO SAATCHIS NOW

Saatchi & Saatchi is currently being run by CEO Kevin Roberts and creative director Bob Isherwood. Still holding on to the old spirit that "Nothing is Impossible," Saatchi & Saatchi aims "To be revered as the hothouse for world-changing creative ideas that transform our clients' businesses, brands and reputations."[27] Indeed, with its emphasis on passion for the industry and its value on fresh ideas, it looks ready to conquer the market.

M&C Saatchi is still being run by Charles, Maurice, Sinclair, Kershaw and Muirhead. With six guiding principles including "Brutal Simplicity of Thought," "Creative Hard Sell," "Can Do Culture" and "Global Ideas"[28] amongst a few others, it is set to make a simple yet hard hitting mark on the global world again.

CONCLUSION

The Saatchi empire has indeed been a great one. No one can deny the strength at which the Saatchi empire came and took the world by storm. The brothers applied a rather unusual business concept, one that cannot be easily attributed to any one particular culture. They were neither straight-laced like the British nor confrontational like the Americans. At the same time, they had that air of superiority and grandeur akin to the British, and also the dynamism and showmanship of the Americans. But one thing for sure, the brothers formed an impeccable team, Charles contributing his creativity and Maurice complementing it with his business acumen.

Transforming the way the British advertising industry worked, Saatchi & Saatchi was to be a pioneer on many fronts. However, the force that propelled the Saatchi brothers to the empire could not pull them through the long-term business world. Buying too many companies around the world worked for a while to boost their image and strength, but in the long run, profits and losses caught up with them, and people started to see past the showmanship of the brothers.

The expansion and rampant acquisitions were fuelled by the brothers' creative synergies and not strategic business planning. They looked upon the business as a small privately run business, doing anything they liked with it. This led to a lack of concern for increasing costs, profit margins and most typically Maurice neglecting the consequences.

Maurice once told a bedtime story during a speech to his North American employees. The story was later interpreted by the employees to show Maurice's similarity with the scorpion. Maurice, like the scorpion would do what he wanted to do, mainly acquiring companies and would disregard the consequences with often fatal results.

> Once upon a time, there was a frog and a scorpion sitting by a river. The scorpion, wanting to cross the river, asked the frog for a ride. "But if I let you ride on my back, you will sting me and I will die," said the wise frog.
> "Not so," replied the crafty scorpion. "If I sting you, then you will die and sink and I will drown since I cannot swim."
> The frog invited the scorpion onto his back. Halfway across the river, the scorpion pricked the frog with his stinger. Mortally wounded, the frog looked back at the scorpion and said, "But now you're going to drown. Why did you do this?"

The scorpion stared at the frog and said, "Because I'm a scorpion. And that's what scorpions do."[29]

It is what they do, and they will continue to do it. After losing their hard-earned empire from 25 years of hard work, and now starting over again, only time will tell if the Saatchi brothers are indeed like the scorpion, doing what it is supposed to do with the eventuality of certain death.

ENDNOTES
1. Kevin Goldman. *Conflicting Accounts: The Creation and Crash of the Saatchi & Saatchi Advertising Empire*. New York: Simon & Schuster, 1997, p. 44.
2. Alison Fendley. *Saatchi & Saatchi: The Inside Story*. New York: Arcade Publishing, 1995, p. 59.
3. Goldman. *Conflicting Accounts*, p. 49.
4. Fendley. *Saatchi & Saatchi*, p. 59.
5. Philip Kleinman. *Saatchi & Saatchi: The Inside Story*. Illinois: NTC Business Books, 1989, p. 24.
6. Goldman. *Conflicting Accounts*, p. 74.
7. Goldman. *Conflicting Accounts*, p. 108.
8. Ibid., p. 106.
9. Fendley, *Saatchi & Saatchi*, p. 96.
10. Fendley. *Saatchi & Saatchi*, p. 104.
11. Goldman. *Conflicting Accounts*, p. 139.
12. Goldman. *Conflicting Accounts*, p. 161.
13. Goldman. *Conflicting Accounts*, p. 215.
14. Goldman. *Conflicting Accounts*, p. 266.
15. Fendley. *Saatchi & Saatchi*, p. 164.
16. Goldman. *Conflicting Accounts*, p. 296.
17. Kleinman. *Inside Story*, p. 69.
18. Goldman. *Conflicting Accounts*, p. 36.
19. Goldman. *Conflicting Accounts*, p. 36.
20. Goldman. *Conflicting Accounts*, p. 131.
21. Goldman. *Conflicting Accounts*, p. 109.
22. Fendley. *Saatchi & Saatchi*, p. 49.
23. Goldman, *Conflicting Accounts*, p. 109.
24. Ibid., p. 39.
25. Goldman. *Conflicting Accounts*, p. 148.
26. Fendley. *Saatchi & Saatchi*, p. 124.
27. Official Saatchi & Saatchi website, http://www.saatchi.com/worldwide/index1.html.

28   Official M&C Saatchi website, http://www.mcsaatchi.com/
29   Goldman. *Conflicting Accounts*, p. 224.

REFERENCES

Alison Fendley. *Saatchi & Saatchi: The Inside Story.* New York: Arcade Publishing, 1995.

Kevin Goldman. *Conflicting Accounts: The Creation and Crash of the Saatchi & Saatchi Advertising Empire.* New York: Simon & Schuster, 1997.

Philip Kleinman. *Saatchi & Saatchi: The Inside Story.* Illinois: NTC Business Books, 1989.

CHAPTER 21

The Chinese *Nouveau Riches* as Movie Moguls: The Stories of Run Run Shaw and Loke Wan Tho

STEPHANIE CHUNG PO-YIN

INTRODUCTION

Film-making is both a craft and an industry.[1] The hardest battles of the movie industry were always fought at the distribution and exhibition fronts. The French Pathe's studio and the major studios of Hollywood were well aware of this and developed an industrial structure of vertical integration that combined production, distribution and exhibition to dominate their markets.[2] In Asia (specifically in the Chinese market), the Cathay Organization and the Shaw Organization under the direction of Loke Wan Tho (1915–64) and Run Run Shaw (1907–) respectively represented two of the most significant attempts to adopt vertical integration into the movie industry. Modelling their operations after the Western industrial structure and managerial styles, the Cathay and Shaw enterprises have lent themselves readily to organizational analysis in an era of rapid globalization. Although both Shaw and Cathay adopted the studio system from the West, they retained the structure of the traditional Chinese family business. To a greater degree, these Chinese family-based business operations depended on the temperament of the families' patriarchs. The issues that surrounded the history of these two families, therefore, are profound indications of the era. By documenting the history of the two families/companies under their patriarchs, this chapter illustrates the transformation of a Chinese *nouveau riche* class in the frontier society of modern Asia.

THE MATRIX: SINGAPORE-HONG KONG-SHANGHAI

The rise of the Chinese *nouveau riche* class, such as the Loke and Shaw families, in Southeast Asia is closely related to the advance of the European colonial activities in the Far East starting from the nineteenth century. As far back as the middle of the eighteenth century, the Europeans had colonized a substantial part of Southeast Asia. These colonial activities had reshaped the region's political and economic landscapes.[3]

With the establishment of British colonial rule in Singapore (1817), Hong Kong (1841) and the foreign concessions in Shanghai (1843), a commercial corridor has gradually developed in maritime Asia. These three maritime cities gradually become the *frontier par excellence* for many European merchants. A large number of Chinese migrants were also attracted to settle there in search of luck and opportunity. The majority of these migrants were from such coastal provinces as Zhejiang, Guangdong and Fujian. The migration always appeared "in chain," with friends and relatives following each other to settle in particular locations. As a result, these Chinese migrants had cultivated a cohesive web of interlocking relationships, which often spanned several regions and countries in coastal Asia. These extensive commercial and cultural networks became precious business assets which made the Chinese merchants especially competitive in such frontier societies found in South China and Southeast Asia, where the legal and administrative infrastructures were relatively underdeveloped. The diverse social composition of this frontier society had provided the overseas Chinese with ample opportunity to benefit from business intermediation within and across the ethnic, language and social boundaries. The mediating role of the Chinese mercantile community soon filled up the gaps between conflicting cultures, institutions and economies.[4] The Chinese migrants, by providing a crucial contact point in a socially segregated society, had carved out a distinctive role in Southeast Asia and southern China. As will be seen, the Lokes and the Shaws are two of these intermediaries. Eventually, they extended their investments to movie industry.

GRAVITY OF CHINA'S FILM INDUSTRY: THE SOUTHWARD SHIFT

As early as the 1920s, Shanghai had become China's powerhouse in movie production. In 1937, when the cloud of the Sino-Japanese War was gathering, Shanghai capital quickly flew southward to Hong Kong where the movie industry found its refuge. This southward shift continued after 1949. Under a communist regime, China's film industry was placed under the strict political control/censorship that affected the importation and exportation of the material. With the closure of China's market after 1949, Southeast Asia had replaced mainland China and became the largest export market for Hong Kong movies.

The theatre business in post-war Southeast Asia was dominated by two major cinema circuits. They were: (1) Cathay Organization operated by the Loke Wan Tho family; (2) Shaw Organization operated by the Run Run Shaw family. Both families were migrant merchant houses that engaged in the movie distribution and exhibition industry starting from the 1920s. The Loke family was from Canton of the Guangdong Province and the Shaws were migrants from Shanghai of the Zhejiang Province. Their headquarters were set up in Singapore. However, after 1949, their theatre businesses were in crisis—as China and Taiwan had imposed heavy political restrictions on film exports; the film supply for Southeast Asia was quickly reduced. To supply their cinema circuits, the two families had to venture into film production. Hong Kong, the refuge for a large number of southbound movie talents from mainland China, became their ideal production base. To stabilize the film supply, the two merchant houses extended their investments to Hong Kong where they set up their film studios. A rivalry between the two companies gradually developed as competition grew intense, pushing the studio system toward new heights. Nevertheless, beneath Shaw and Loke's Westernised outlook, the two companies retained the structure of the traditional Chinese family business fundamentals. The boom and bust of the companies still relied very much on the longevities and personalities of the families' patriarchs.[5] To understand the post-1949 evolution of the two companies, we must start with the history of the two families.

THE SHAWS AND THE SHAW ORGANIZATION

Run Run Shaw is a typical Ningbo merchant. The patriarch of the Shaw family, Shao Xingyin (1867–1920), was of Ningbo origin. He went into the dye pigment business as a teenager and later set up his own firm. When Shanghai became a treaty port, he immediately extended his business networks there. He had 10 children, and among the surviving seven, four were sons—Runje (1896–1979), Runde (1899–1973), Runme (1901–1985) and Run Run (1907–). Growing up in Shanghai, the brothers received a Chinese education that included Western exposure. In the 1920s, Runje, the eldest of the brothers, had engaged himself in a wide array of profit-making ventures. In 1923, for example, he purchased a bankrupted theatre and reorganized it into a modern theatre. In 1925, he ventured into cinematic movie production. With a variety of readily adaptable cast members, scripts and costumes borrowed from the drama troupes working for his theatre, he set up Unique (Tianyi) Film Productions. Making good use of his family members, he established a division of duties among his siblings: Runje became a film director, Runde was the accountant, and Runme was responsible for distribution. Run Run, the youngest brother, also assisted in film marketing while studying full-time at an English school founded by the Shanghai Young Men's Association. They adopted the strategy of low budget-fast production operation and soon churned out several popular movies.[6]

In 1924, Runme (the third brother) went to Southeast Asia (Singapore) for business opportunities. In 1926, the youngest of the brothers Run Run Shaw also went to Singapore to assist his brother. However, the two brothers' endeavor in Singapore was not paying off as they wanted. The two young Shanghainese were isolated by the dominant Cantonese, Chaozhou, and Fujian immigrant communities. They were driven to operate a mobile cinema by taking Shaw films on the road. By 1930, they had managed to accumulate adequate capital to collaborate with a Penang-based tycoon and organised a cinema circuit which spread across Singapore, Kuala Lumpur, Ipoh, and Malacca. In 1930, the Shaw brothers were acquainted with Baba tycoon Ong Boon-tat. With Ong's assistance, the Shaws purchased the New World Amusement Park.[7] By the late 1930s, the brothers had purchased more than 15 theatres, two amusement parks and maintained an extensive outlet for Shaw movies.

In the 1930s, when sound movies were introduced to China, Cantonese films took Southern China and Southeast Asia by storm. The Shaws saw a golden business opportunity there and ventured into producing the Cantonese movie *White Gold Dragon*. The movie was made efficiently using a readily available script, costume, cast and songs from a Cantonese opera of the same title. It was extremely popular among the Cantonese communities inside and outside of China. Inspired by the easy success, the Shaws relocated their film production base to Hong Kong with an agenda to collaborate with more Cantonese opera singers active in South China.⁸ In 1934, the Shaws set-up the Hong Kong branch and in 1938; the company was renamed Nanyang Studio. By 1937, Shanghai was occupied by Japan and the movie industry was stagnant. When the war extended to Hong Kong and Southeast Asia in 1941, Nanyang Studio was confiscated by the Japanese troops. Runme and Run Run's theatres in Malaya also ceased operation. Then in post-war Southeast Asia, Runme and Run Run quickly expanded their cinema chains. By the mid-1950s, the brothers were operating more than 100 theatres and 10 amusement parks in Southeast Asia.⁹

THE LOKES AND THE CATHAY ORGANIZATION

Compared to the Shaws, the Lokes were more Westernised, had weaker connections to their home county and were a smaller family unit. Loke Wan Tho was the son of a wealthy Cantonese merchant named Loke Yew (1846–1917). Loke Yew was born to the Wong family. As an orphan, he worked for a businessman named Loke and assumed the employer's surname when he was seven years old. Later, he went to the Malay Peninsula as "a contract labor" and eventually founded his own provision store. It was at the time when the British, worried that a Westernised Siam might expand into the Malay Peninsula, colonised a substantial part of the archipelago to gain control of its rich tin reserve. Tax-farming and mining rights were also auctioned off to the Chinese migrants to help develop the virgin land. Loke obtained the rights and later ventured to operate over a dozen mines and ran rubber, coffee, coconut and pepper plantations along with cement and iron factories. He also opened a bank in Kuala Lumpur in 1913. Loke Yew had four wives and eight children, though interactions between households were limited. When he died in 1917 with an estimated estate of over (L) 10 million, the family business was placed under his third wife, who had one son and two daughters. The son was Loke Wan Tho.¹⁰

Loke Wan Tho was born in Kuala Lumpur in 1915. He received an elitist, European education in Kuala Lumpur before attending Chillon College in Switzerland when he was 13 years old. He gained his Bachelor Degree in Literature and History at Cambridge University in 1936, and later obtained his Master Degree in Economics at the London School of Economics. In 1940, Loke returned to Singapore and took over the family business from his mother. By that time, the Loke business empire included banks, rubber plantations, tin mines, real estate, catering, hotels, and entertainment.[11] When Japan invaded the Malayan Peninsula in 1942, Loke escaped to Indonesia. After the war, Loke returned to Singapore in 1945 where among other business ventures, he collaborated with the British firm J. Arthur Rank to distribute British films in Southeast Asia. The collaboration also saw the establishment of the International Theatre Ltd. in 1948. Within a few years, he had over 40 theatres in his cinema circuits.[12] To stabilize the film supply to fill his theatres' exhibition schedules, Loke founded the International Film Distribution Agency in 1951 and established a Hong Kong branch in 1953.[13] In 1955, Loke took over a bankrupt movie studio in Hong Kong, established a Motion Picture & General Investment Company (MP & GI) and began to produce movies for his theatres in Southeast Asia.[14]

THE CLASH: CATHAY VS. SHAW

Meanwhile, the Shaws' cinema circuit in Southeast Asia was run by Run Run Shaw, with films that were produced in Hong Kong by his elder brother. After Loke founded his film production base in Hong Kong in 1955, the Shaws' low-budget films, paled by comparison, were losing their market niche. To counterbalance Loke's MP & GI success, Run Run Shaw was desperate for a greater film supply. To achieve this, he relocated to Hong Kong in 1957. Run Run Shaw and Runme Shaw (the third brother) severed connections with Runde (the second brother), and in 1958, announced the founding of Shaw Brothers (HK) Ltd in Hong Kong. They also charted out plans to establish their own studio.[15] The Shaw studio was built in the Clear Water Bay, situated on 46 acres, with 15 sound stages, 16 location sets, three sound studios and staff who each work in three shifts of eight hours. An actor training program was also established to nurture actors and actresses and to create stars. Classes included set and stage exercises, make-up technique, Mandarin instruction and etiquette. The trainees' salaries were extremely low but those with potential were singled out and groomed for stardom. A head-on collision between Loke and Shaw seemed unavoidable.

Both Run Run Shaw and Loke Wan Tho transplanted to Hong Kong a Western studio system for producing, distributing and exhibiting movies. Managerial innovations were introduced to strengthen frontline monitoring from the central. Western management practices like mass production, annual production plans, script supervision and block distribution were also adopted. Several films were shot simultaneously to save time and expenses. Both MP & GI and Shaw adopted the Hollywood star system in their studios, orchestrating media contacts while controlling private lives and public images of their actors and actresses.[16] Departments for promotion were established and publishing arms were formed to produce official magazines to promote their films and stars.[17]

In the late 1950s and the early 1960s, there was a fierce competition between Shaw and MP & GI. The struggle pushed Asia's movie studio system to new heights, which produced a large number of movie talents for the Chinese cinema. When Shaw made epic movies like *The Kingdom and the Beauty* (1959) starring Linda Lin Dai which won numerous Asian Film Festival awards, MP & GI charted plans to headhunt Linda Lin Dai and other Shaw starlets. A fierce talent bidding war followed. In 1963, Shaw's *Love Eterne* made Ling Bo a superstar, MP & GI fought back with *Sun, Moon and Star* (1961) starring new-born star You Min. At the climax of the confrontation, the two companies were producing "competing versions" of the same movies based on similar story lines. For example, in 1961 Loke invited Eileen Chang, prestigious novelist in contemporary China, to return from the United States to refine the script for a film adaptation of the classic novel *Dream of the Red Chamber*. Immediately, Shaw rushed to steal the storm by shooting its version simultaneously in two studios. Eventually, MP & GI was driven to shelf its production.[18]

Even though both Shaw and Loke adopted Western practices of integrating production, distribution and exhibition in running their studios, the two companies had very different management styles and cultural outlooks. As Loke studied History and Literature at the Cambridge University, he tended to recruit personnel with a similar background to run his company. As he was remote-controlling MP & GI from Singapore, he had to delegate a high degree of autonomy to his studio's frontline production in Hong Kong. These key administration and production personnel were comprised mostly of repatriates who were familiar with Western practices. MP & GI's movies, therefore, were always filled with middle-class sensibilities, Western tastes and grand scenery. On the contrary, Run Run Shaw was a down-to-earth Shanghai businessman. Run Run Shaw had relocated his base to Hong Kong and was more aggressive and business-minded in running his businesses. When it came to recruiting "think tanks" to fight MP & GI, Run Run Shaw immediately looked to the Shanghai-educated circle for inspiration and assistance. Shaw's production personnel inevitably injected a lot of

Run Run Shaw's shrewd business calculations into its movies. They were the "gatekeepers" monitoring Shaw's frontline productions. To a great degree, the themes and aesthetics portrayed in Shaw's movies were tailor-made to meet the variant tastes, censorship policies and political inclinations of the markets in Taiwan, Hong Kong and Southeast Asia.[19]

By the 1960s, both Cathay and Shaw were run by centralized leadership, with Loke Wan Tho and Run Run Shaw as patriarchs. This practice had its strengths and weaknesses. When Loke and Shaw were both young and energetic, power succession was not a threat to the companies. As will be seen, Run Run Shaw's longevity has become a precious business asset, securing decades of stability for the Shaw enterprises. On the contrary, MP & GI enjoyed no such asset. On June 20, 1964, disaster struck MP & GI. While attending the 11th Asian Film Festival in Taiwan, Loke Wan Tho was invited to a sightseeing trip. On the return trip, the plane crashed, killing Loke and a host of MP & GI executives. The company plunged into chaos.[20]

The Lokes did not have the kind of close relationship enjoyed by the Shaw family. After Loke Wan Tho passed away, brother-in-law Choo Kok Leong was driven to take charge of the movie business. Choo, a specialist in agriculture, originally supervised Loke's rubber plantations. Different from Loke, Choo did not have a dream related to movies. Under Choo, Cathay's operation was scaled down and suffered drops in output and market share. Shaw, meanwhile, was expanding its production and exhibition business.[21] In 1971, Cathay's movie production arm was closed.

EXPANSION OF THE SHAW ENTERPRISES

In contrast to MP &GI's decline, Shaw was stepping up its productions. At its height, the Shaw studio had a stable of more than 500 members of resident contract staff including scriptwriters, carpenters, artists, sound records and cinematographers. Comprehensive training programs also hatched different species of movie stars feeding the various movie genres produced by Shaw. Post-production dubbing was introduced to shorten shooting time and to expand actor supply. A Publicity Department, under Raymond Chow, also orchestrated media connections promoting Shaw's stars and movies worldwide. As early as in the 1950s, Run Run Shaw had recruited under his wing a number of southbound migrant directors. They were mainly "men of letters" receiving solid classical Chinese learning from Northern China. Understandably, movies directed by these

Northerners were rich in northern flavor in their themes, cinematic images and aesthetics. As many of them were also admirers of Northern regional operas, the images they created in the movies also tend to be operatic, and the tone nostalgic, scholarly and elitist. Notable among them was Director Chang Cheh, who handpicked male actors Jimmy Wang Yu, John Chiang, Ti Lung and coined his label of *yang gang* (staunch masculinity) film genres. Chang's *One-Armed Swordsman* (1967), for example, had turned southbound actor Jimmy Wang Yu into a superstar. Chang's paramount status in the Shaw Studio was further consolidated. Chang's movies, with secure large budgets, were full of swift operatic images borrowed from Northern regional operas. Director Li Hanhsiang's *huangmei diao* (literally, Yellow Plum rhyme) musicals, adopted from operas popular in the Zhejiang region and stuffed with scholarly sentiments, took Hong Kong, Taiwan and Southeast Asia by storm. Director King Hu, inspired by Japanese samurai movies, also created a martial-chivalric genre for Chinese cinema. However, with the departures of these Northern directors in the late 1960s and the early 1970s, Run Run Shaw was driven to reorganize the hierarchy under his wing. Cantonese film talents such as Chun Kim, Chor Yuen and Lau Kar-leung were gradually appointed as film directors. With their Cantonese/local backgrounds, they recycled such traditional Cantonese legends as "Southern Shaolin" and "Kung-fu Master Hung Hee Kun" into popular movies. Cantonese opera and kung-fu also became their sources of inspirations in shooting action scenes.[22] The generational changes of these Northern and Southern directors had helped prolong the production life cycle of the Shaw studio.

Nevertheless, entering the mid-1980s, Shaw's model of vertical integration in movie production was formally dismantled—its cinema circuit ceased operation, its cinemas were leased to tycoon Dickson Poon's D&B circuit; its studio was also leased to Television Broadcasts Limited (TVB). Remarkably, while Run Run Shaw was retreating from the cinema circle, his influence on television industry was on the increase. Run Run's business vision had shifted—from cinema to television. Modelling on the old recipe of "vertical integration," TVB is a "reincarnation" of Shaw in the Chinese television circle.[23] TVB's Studio City, converted from the Shaw Studio in 1986, became the world's largest producer of Chinese-speaking TV programs. By the turn of the twentieth century, the proliferation of new exhibition outlets such as satellite television, pay-TV and DVD had also inspired Run Run Shaw to explore a new market—

a Galaxy Satellite Broadcasting Limited was set up in Hong Kong in 2000, and through which, Shaw charted out plans to open up the market in mainland China. Also in 2000, Shaw's film archive (with a collection of more than 760 movies) was sold to a Malaysian conglomerate for HK$600 million. In 2002, digitally-remastered Shaw CDs and DVDs were released by Celestial Pictures (with Shaw as its core shareholder). More than one million of these digital products were sold in 2003. Shaw movies had found a new channel to reach its audiences.[24]

CONCLUSION

We began with the observation that the transformations of Cathay and Shaw are manifestations of the life stories of movie moguls Loke Wan Tho and Run Run Shaw. The Shaws and the Lokes were families of migrants whose business operations were active in Hong Kong and Southeast Asia. Their life experiences spanned different adopted homes and cultural landscapes and they had become "mixing vessels" of things Eastern and Western, traditional and modern. Although both companies adopted the studio system from the West, they still retained their nature as a traditional Chinese family business. The longevity of their patriarchs, ironically, always determined the fate of the companies.

ENDNOTES

1. See, for example, Litman, Barry R., *The Motion Picture Mega-Industry* (MA: Allyn & Bacon, 1998), pp. 64–8; Vogel, Harold L., *Entertainment Industry Economics: A Guide for Financial Analysis*, 4th edition (Cambridge: Cambridge University Press, 1998), pp. 3–141.

2. On the history of these studios, see Puttnam, David, *Movies and Money* (New York: Vintage Books, 2000).

3. Davenport-Hines, R. P. T., & Jones, Geoffrey, *British Business in Asia since 1860*, New York, Cambridge University Press, 1989; Allen, G. C., and A. G., Donnithorne, *Western Enterprise in Indonesia and Malaya: A Study in Economic Development*, London: Allen & Unwin, 1957.

4. See for example, Chung, Stephanie Po-yin, "Surviving economic crises in Southeast Asia and southern China: The history of Eu Yan Sang business conglomerates in Penang, Singapore and Hong Kong," in *Modern Asian Studies*, 36:3 (2002), pp. 579–617.

5. Chung, Stephanie Po-yin, "A Southeast Asian tycoon and his movie dream: Loke Wan Tho and MP & GI", in Wong Ain-ling (ed.), *The Cathay Story*, Hong Kong Film Archive, 2002, pp. 36–51; Chung, Stephanie Po-yin, "The industrial evolution of a fraternal enterprise: The Shaw Brothers

and the Shaw Organization", in Wong Ain-ling (ed.), *The Shaw Screen, A Preliminary Study*, Hong Kong Film Archive, 2003, pp. 1–18.

6 See *Nanyang Year Book*, Singapore: Publication Department, *Nanyang Siang Pau*, 1939, p. 197; Chung Lei/Zhong Lei, *Wushi Nian Lai De Zhongguo Dianying* (50 Years of Chinese Cinema), Taipei: Cheng Chung Book Co Ltd, 1965; Tu Yün-chih, *Xianggang Yingye Fenxi Baogao: Shaoshi Yinhai Wushi Nian* (An Analysis of Hong Kong Film Industry: 50 Years of Shaw Cinema), Taipei: Crown Publications, 1978.

7 Runme Shaw, Tan Sri. *Pioneers of Singapore*, Oral History Project, January 1980 to February 1984, transcript no. b00059/03, National Archive of Singapore.

8 Lao Ji, "Shao Zuiweng Yu Xue Juexian" (Runje Shaw and Sit Kok-sin), *Panorama Magazine*, Hong Kong, no. 19, June 1975, p. 63.

9 See Lao Ji, "Shao Zuiweng Zhidou Lin Kunshan" (How Runje Shaw Outwitted Lin Kunshan), *Panorama Magazine*, Hong Kong, no. 20, July 1975, p. 61; "Xingma Diqu Xiyuan Wang Niaokan" (An Overview of Theatre Networks in Singapore and Malaya), *Southern Screen*, Hong Kong, no. 37, June 1957, p. 2.

10 Butcher, J. C., & H. W. Dick, (eds.), *The Rise and Fall of Revenue Farming: Business Elites and the Emergence of the Modern State in Southeast Asia*, London: Macmillan, 1993.

11 Loke Wan Tho Papers, National Archives of Singapore.

12 "Cathay's grand plan to build theatres," *International Screen*, vol. 7 (April 1956), p. 10.

13 "Bai Gung joins International," *International Screen*, vol. 2 (November 1955), p. 18.

14 "The grand and spectacular new Yung Hwa Studio," *International Screen*, vol. 5 (February 1956), p. 19.

15 See Lao Ji, "Shaoshi Xiongdi Wei He Fenjia" (Why the Shaw Brothers Split), *Tanxing*, Hong Kong, no. 1, April 1962, pp. 76–7; Lao Ji, "Shao Zuiweng Xuanlan Gui Pingdan" (Runje Shaw: From Heydays to Retreat), *Panorama Magazine*, Hong Kong, no. 21, August 1975, pp. 51–2.

16 "How MP & GI train three new actors," *International Screen*, vol. 76 (Feb. 1962), p. 27; "How is a good actor nurtured? Introduction to the MP & GI Actors Training Program," *International Screen*, vol. 111 (February 1965) p. 54.

17 See, for example, "Completion of a film," *International Screen*, vol. 23 (September 1957), p. 39.

18 "Each version of *Dream of the Red Chamber* has its merits," *Star Scouts*, vol. 1 (April 1962), pp. 73–4; "How MP & GI train three new actors," *International Screen*, vol. 76 (February 1962), p. 27; "How is a good actor nurtured? Introduction to the MP & GI Actors Training Program," *International Screen*, vol. 111 (February 1965) p. 54; see also Loke Wan Tho Papers, National Archive of Singapore, in the documents left by Loke are many clippings about Shaws, indicating that he paid lots of attention

to Shaws' activities; "The truth behind Shaws' rush into *Love Eterne,*" *Milkyway Pictorial*, vol. 57 (December 1962), pp. 5–6.

19 Interview record with Raymond Chow/Zou Wenhuai, Hong Kong Film Archive, Oral History Project, February 27, 1997.

20 Wong Chuk-hon, pp. 118–123.

21 "Lian Fuk Ming and wife visits Hong Kong to look after business," *International Screen*, vol. 120 (November 1965), p. 48.

22 Interview record with Ho Meng-hua, Hong Kong Film Archive, Oral History Project, November 21, 1997; Chang Cheh, "Shaoshi De Boxing: Xianggang Shi De Haolaiwu" (The Rise of Shaw: Hollywood in Hong Kong), in Chang Cheh, *Huigu Xianggang Dianying Sanshi Nian* (Looking Back at Thirty Years of Hong Kong Cinema), Hong Kong: Joint Publishing (Hong Kong) Company Ltd., 1989.

23 Run Run Shaw was shareholder of the Television Broadcasts Limited (TVB) since its founding in 1967. With the death of two of the largest shareholders, Andrew K. W. Eu and Harold H. W. Lee in the 1970s and early 1980s, Run Run Shaw became chairman of the TVB board in 1980.

24 Chung, Stephanie Po-yin, *A Century of Hong Kong Cinema and Television*, Hong Kong: Joint Publishing (Hong Kong) Company Ltd, 2004.

REFERENCES

Barry R.Litman. *The Motion Picture Mega-Industry*. MA: Allyn & Bacon, 1998.

David Puttnam. *Movies and Money*. New York: Vintage Books, 2000.

Harold L. Vogel. *Entertainment Industry Economics, A Guide for Financial Analysis*, fourth edition. Cambridge: Cambridge University Press, 1998.

International Screen. Hong Kong, 1958–1969.

J. C. Butcher, & H. W. Dick (eds.). *The Rise and Fall of Revenue Farming: Business Elites and the Emergence of the Modern State in Southeast Asia*. London: Macmillan, 1993.

Loke Wan Tho Papers, National Archives of Singapore.

Nanyang Year Book, Singapore: Publication Department, *Nanyang Siang Pau*, 1939.

Panorama Magazine, Hong Kong, 1959–1980.

R. P. T. Davenport-Hines, & Geoffrey Jones. *British Business in Asia since 1860*. New York: Cambridge University Press, 1989.

Runme Shaw, Tan Sri. *Pioneers of Singapore*, Oral History Project, January 1980 to February 1984, transcript no. b00059/03, National Archive of Singapore.

Southern Screen, Hong Kong, 1957–1980.

Stephanie Po-yin Chung. *A Century of Hong Kong Cinema and Television*. Hong Kong: Joint Publishing (Hong Kong) Company Ltd, 2004.

Stephanie Po-yin Chung. "Surviving economic crises in Southeast Asia and Southern China: The history of Eu Yan Sang business conglomerates in Penang, Singapore and Hong Kong," in *Modern Asian Studies*, 36:3 (2002), pp. 579–617.

Stephanie Po-yin Chung. "A Southeast Asian tycoon and his movie dream: Loke Wan Tho and MP & GI," in Wong Ain-ling (ed), *The Cathay Story*. Hong Kong Film Archive, 2002, pp. 36–51.

Stephanie Po-yin Chung. "The industrial evolution of a fraternal enterprise: The Shaw Brothers and the Shaw Organization," in Wong Ain-ling (ed.), *The Shaw Screen, A Preliminary Study*. Hong Kong Film Archive, 2003, pp. 1–18.

CHAPTER 22

Hello Kitty: A Silly Cat Earns a Lot of Money

ALBRECHT ROTHACHER

It may appear as strange at first sight that a chapter is written about the commercial success of the ultimate symbol of childishness, the Hello Kitty cat. Yet, as it has become big business not only in Japan, but also represents a cultural phenomenon of contemporary East Asian consumer societies, the interest appears perfectly legitimate. Of the $1 billion annual sales of Sanrio Corporation, the "Hello Kitty" icon generates half. None of the other 400 equally synthetic characters ("My Melody," "Baby Cinnamon," "Twin Star," etc) ever comes close.

Hello Kitty, a kitten without a mouth, is "small, soft, infantile, mammalian, round, ... non-sexual, mute, insecure, helpless or bewildered."[1] The cat is pure imagery. There is no "life story," nor any message. Part of the "culture of cute" (*kawaii bunka*), its post-modern infantile attraction is purely a projection in the eye of its beholders: a princess of purity to youngsters, an innocent playmate to young girls, and a childhood memory for young women, or simply junk in a sweet "cute" package for most of the rest of mankind.

In difference to US cartoon or animated film characters, the Sanrio products have more subtle forms, rounder features and pastel colours. The main market focus of the $17 billion character market in Japan is the 15–19 year olds, but easily stretches to women of up to 34 years of age, who—some 17 million of them in total—are increasingly single as they postpone marriage and, unlike in the West, face little societal pressure to grow up. Japanese teens find it *kawaii* (cute) to act immature, to use squeaky voices, and to act purposefully clueless. While in Europe and the US starting at age 12, kids face peer (and some parental) pressure to stop acting childish, there is no such thing in Japan. Women may act "cute," submissive and weak until their late 20s well into adult life. In commercially exploiting this market "Sanrio stumbled into one of the most ingenious formulas in the history of modern branding," Belson and Bremner rightly observe.²

The company's founder, Shintaro Tsuji, was born in Kofu in Japan's central rural Yamanashi prefecture in 1927. When he was 13, his mother died and his father also seemed to disappear. In a tough struggle for survival in wartime Japan—a formative school for many founder entrepreneurs which is missing today—he managed by selling self-made soap on the black market. Armed with a chemical engineering degree from a local university, Tsuji secured himself an administrative job with Yamanashi prefectural government in 1947. Yet already in the 1950s the restless youngster was asked to set up the prefecture's liaison office in Tokyo. Presumably bored by his bureaucratic work in 1960 he set up the Yamanashi Silk Centre in Tokyo with public funds as a private company. In 1962 he branched out into a non-silk product like rubber sandals, which for better sales he adorned by fixing a fruit design (strawberries mostly). When it sold well, as an early branding exercise Tsuji had put his fruits also on coffee cups, plates and other pottery.

Looking at foreign designs to be sold in Japan in the late 1960s, he acquired the licence to market Charles Schultz's Snoopy character in Japan. He also bought the right to sell Hallmark greeting cards and Mattel's Barbie dolls in Japan. However, the dolls proved too expensive with too many cheaper imitation dolls around and the Japanese did not quite take to the US habit of sending expensive X'mas cards. At the same time, cute designs on school stationery, school girl diaries and other fancy goods sold well.

As a dog (Snoopy) and a bear (Winnie the Pooh) were already in Tsuji's cute portfolio, he had Hello Kitty as a cat slapped on notebooks, pens and handbags as branded low-priced gift items for the adolescents market and started selling them in "Giftgate Shops" which later expanded into a chain. By 1973 he bought out his Yamanashi co-owners and renamed his company "Sanrio" (which in Japanese-Spanish is meant to mean: Three Rivers).

By the late 1970s Sanrio ventured into teenie magazine production and even produced an animated Hollywood film which earned Tsuji one proud Oscar but for his company brought only losses. Following the craze for theme parks, a park called "Puroland" imitating Disneyland indoors was opened in 1990 in Tama in suburban Tokyo, followed in 1991 by "Harmonyland" in rural Oita on Kyushu.

These theme parks are to promote the Sanrio characters (apart from Hello Kitty and her relatives, similarly aseptic characters like Strawberry King, Cheery Chum and Button Nose) and to make money with stage shows and dance contests. Tsuji now in his 70s, is said to visit them weekly for further improvements and to experience consumer feedback firsthand.

First marketing attempts in the US had failed. As the US did not take to dolls changing colour in hot bath water, remained unpersuaded to start gift-giving habits, and preferred low-cost items like T-shirts rather than expensive handbags, Sanrio's New York office had to close in the 1980s.[3]

In the meantime Japan's *zaitech* craze had also hit Tsuji at Sanrio. At the height of Japan's bubble economy he had ploughed plenty of corporate assets and borrowed money—¥170 billion to be exact—into stocks, real estate and *tokkin* funds, which after 1992 duly crashed. As a classic bubble phenomenon, Sanrio's value fell by 93 per cent in the mid-1990s.

During 1994–8 it had to absorb some $400 million stock exchange related losses. Only Kitty's surprise revival in 1999/2000 allowed Sanrio to clear some of its debts and to start paying dividends again. However, in 2001 Tsuji again fell victim to his stock market addiction and lost heavily once the high-tech dot com bubble burst.

Hello Kitty came to corporate rescue due to sudden endorsements by Japanese pop stars who publicly confessed their addiction to and admiration of the icon. In Japan's depressed 1990s it was only young single women who continued to spend—mostly on escapist consumerism as relative affluence allowed them to remain kids. Hello Kitty was a surprise symbol for these "moratorium people." In more general terms the branded items—which were put on 6,000 Sanrio products (produced mostly abroad in commission) and 16,000 licensed products, on which it earned royalties of some 3 per cent—served to put some whimsy and humor into an increasingly depersonalised mass consumption society. As a result in the 1990s a typical Japanese nuclear family was "brimming with cute items—from stationery to toilet items."[4] The popularity of pictograms in Japan should come as no surprise. Its *manga* culture alone counts for some $6 billion sales per year. Its animated video industry (Sega, Nintendo, Sony) now dominates the global videogame market. Hello Kitty as a precursor to Pokemon and Super Mario is based like its successors on folklore characters (and monsters) already around since ages—similarly as Disney had raided and cannibalized German fairy tales for story lines.

The revival of Hello Kitty hardly worked in the US and in Europe, but it was successful in East Asia: notably in Korea, Taiwan, Hong Kong and Singapore, where the "word-of-mouth" endorsement of Japanese pop divas was effective,[5] reflecting the appeal of Japan's pop culture among East Asia's youth.[6] Today some 17 per cent of Sanrio's revenue is generated outside Japan, mostly in the related pictographic cultures of East Asia.

Worries are strong that the tender icon will not survive the next whim of faddishness, given that there are manifest signs of over-extension: Hello Kitty stretching from stationery to credit cards, karaoke bars and Daihatsu cars. With its Asian location, counterfeiters are aplenty. In Shanghai alone some 95 per cent of Hello Kitty goods are said to be fakes.

Sanrio still rests less on marketing research but on the gut instincts of its founder Tsuji. At the same time, the character goods market in Japan is under demographic pressure. Since 1989 the number of high school students has fallen by 25 per cent (or by 500,000 out of 2 million). Cultivating infantilism among young women obviously has its societally self-defeating price. *Manga* certainly are a shallow derivative of Western pop culture—which already is shallow enough. Character goods mostly end up little used in waste dumps before long. They serve needs of instant gratification, of the fairly mindless pursuit of novelty, and of a "wrapping culture" which—like in Japan—values form over substance. It would be more than a miracle if a company pursuing these values did survive very long.

ENDNOTES

1   Ken Belson, and Brian Bremner. *Hello Kitty: The Remarkable Story of Sanrio and the Billion Dollar Feline Phenomenon*. Singapore: John Wiley & Sons, 2004, p. 11.
2   Op. cit., p. 5.
3   Op. cit., p. 93.
4   Op. cit., p. 18.
5   Op. cit., p. 166.
6   Ana M. Goy-Yamamoto. "Japanese youth consumption." *Asia-Europe Journal*, 2, 2004, 271–282, p. 279.

CHAPTER 23

Corporate Sponsorships in Asia and Europe

WEI SHEN

This chapter gives a brief introduction to the Corporate Social Responsibility (CSR) movement in Asia and Europe with special reference to the range of sponsoring activities offered by the multinationals in both regions. 46 firms[1] from two Asian countries and five European countries respectively were chosen and their sponsorship activities by category, funding format as well as publicity were compared. All of the sampled countries have shown their social commitment by sponsoring a wide range of community, national and international projects. Environment is the key subject here, while differences in sponsoring categories exist between Asian and European firms.

INTRODUCTION

Corporate sponsorship originates from the idea of ethical marketing and corporate social responsibility (CSR). CSR emphasizes the codes of conduct, business ethics for companies to become a valuable corporate citizen. The CSR movement has been backed by various public institutions, such as the United Nations, International Labor Organization and regional bodies like the European Union. Also, it has been widely perceived as an essential element of global corporate governance, in which private companies assume responsibilities that lie outside the scope of profits and shareholder values but perform tasks that traditionally have been considered as government responsibilities.[2]

Why sponsor?

All over the world, pressure groups, especially non-governmental organisations (NGOs), have pushed the multinationals to be accountable for their business impact on all relevant stakeholders. As a result, business leaders have widely accepted the general consensus of CSR and much of this is attributed to globalization. In the arena of globalization and global governance, companies are said to assume a leading role in the world scene and that they should join forces with different stakeholders including NGOs, governments and international organizations to rescue the planet, its people and to combat social exclusion and injustice.[3]

There is also commercial interest. According to research, 81 per cent of consumers agree that they are more likely to buy a product that is associated with a cause they care about, price and quality being equal.[4] 74 per cent of consumers think that it is acceptable for companies to involve a charity or good cause in their marketing. By giving sponsorships to different activities, companies benefit from positive brand building and enhancement, a unique emotional engagement with the consumers and therefore different from the competitors and their brands.

Limits and critiques

The effects of CSR are very much under debate. Many academic journals and publications argue that the nature of corporate sponsorship is of commercial and promotional purpose although generally recognising the societal positive effects as well.[5]

Classic economic theory from Adam Smith tells us that "there are no free lunches." Will companies eventually pass on the costs of corporate sponsorships to customers? Henderson (2004) argues "all these cost increases will impact on consumers" and worries about the attempts whether by business or government to lay down common norms and standards for all countries. In that sense, the CSR movement can lead to political and economic distortion, even possibly result in the "tragedy of commons," pressurised by extreme activists and groups. There are also concerns about the race-to-the-top among corporations, which is known as the "California effect."

In managerial thinking, it also challenges the traditional theory of division of labor. In Michael's (2003) neo-liberal school approach, he emphasizes the resources misallocation within the firm:[6]

> Staff time dedicated to activities (CSR/sponsorships) are essentially in the marketing function and also lead to the politicization of the organization.

Nevertheless, no one can deny the impact and contribution of CSR (sponsorships) in the ongoing large economic and social transformation in the interaction among different stakeholders, including governments, businesses and civil society.

METHODOLOGY

Sample firms

A total of 46 Asian and European firms were chosen for these studies. They are all within the top 50 of Forbes Global 500 list. The number of Asian corporations comes up to 16 dominated by Japanese companies, while the 30 European companies are spread widely in Germany, France, United Kingdom, the Netherlands and Italy. 10 different industries are represented, ranging from automobile to electricity and utility companies (see Figures 23.1 and 23.2).

Data sources
1. Annual Reports, available from all sample companies.
2. Explicit Corporate Social Responsibility Reports (also known as Sustainability Report or Social Report).
3. Internet search: a systematic search for web pages that made references to corporate sponsorship of events, activities of selected sample companies. The search engines used were Google and Yahoo.

Results

Sponsorship activities and events have been grouped into 11 different categories according to the program nature. By subject they are arts, children, environment, humanitarian aid, infrastructure, music, research, scholarships, sports, volunteer work and youth.

Analysis of sponsorship by category

Without doubt, environment is the No. 1 issue for becoming a responsible corporate citizen. All sample companies have raised their concern about the environment. Most companies have special reports on the environmental assessment of their production and commit

FIGURE 23.1 Sample companies in Asia and Europe

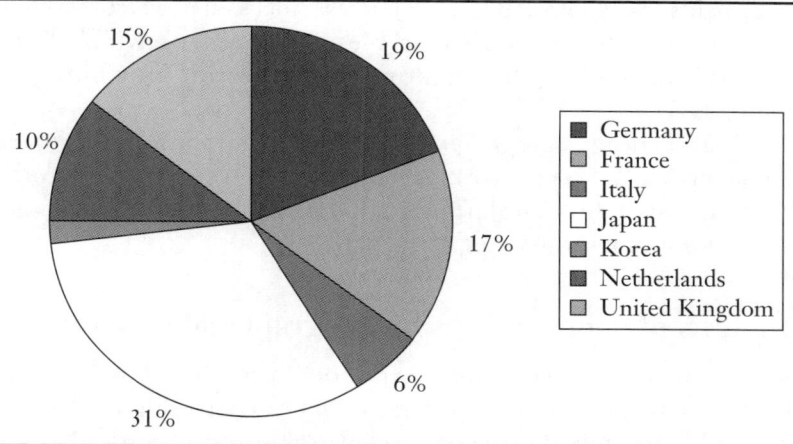

FIGURE 23.2 Sample companies by industries

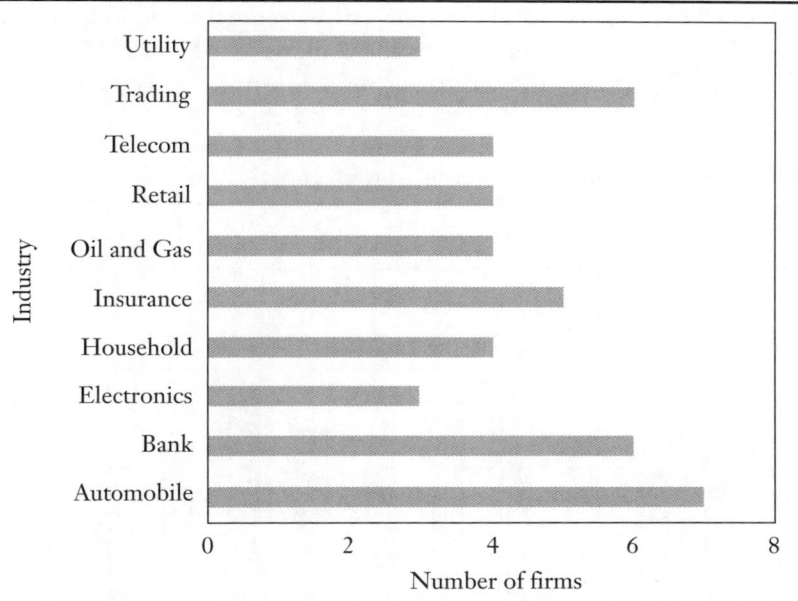

themselves by joining the UN Global Impact, supporting international agreements like Kyoto and last but not least focus on product recycling and use renewable energy. Companies also sponsor environmental research and projects like fighting desertification in China (see Figure 23.3).

Our leading categories receiving large sponsorships are Humanitarian (28, 6 per cent), Scholarships (27, 6 per cent), Research (21, 56 per cent), Arts (20, 4 per cent). Infrastructure and Volunteers are at the lowest sponsoring rates, (10, 2 per cent).

Analysis of sponsorships by geographical location

Besides environmental issues, with a rate of 81 per cent, scholarships are the most attractive destination for corporate sponsorships. 13 out of 16 sample companies in Asia offer scholarships to students. Other top categories are Humanitarian Aid, Music, Youth, Children, Research and Volunteers (see Figure 23.4).

In Europe, Humanitarian Aid occupies the second largest sponsorship category (67 per cent) after Environment, and followed by Arts, Research, Scholarships, Sports and Children (see Figure 23.5). Thus generally speaking, in Asia the sponsorship activities are more

FIGURE 23.3 Company sponsorships by category

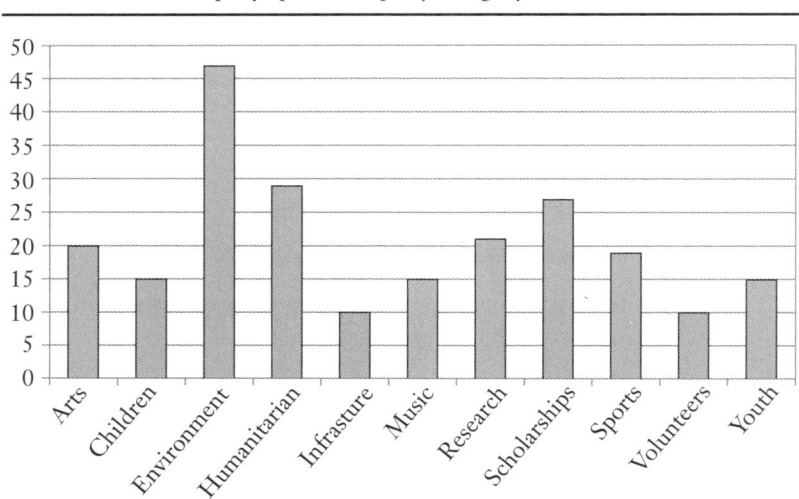

concentrated (59 per cent) while in Europe the activities are comparably widely spread over various categories (54 per cent).

Findings
Based on the data and results above, some interesting findings on the differences in sponsoring activities between Asia and Europe can be identified.

Comparison of sponsorships in Asia and Europe
In Asia, education is the sponsorship domain. Just as Samsung quoted, "Priority in human resources,"[7] scholarships are widely used as their partnerships with universities and academia and provide a useful access to the national and international talents. This kind of scholarship program also facilitates the international exchange of students. One good example is the grants for post-doctoral students from Korea to study in Japan offered by Toyota. Another interesting dimension of education sponsorship is that Japanese firms are very keen in organizing

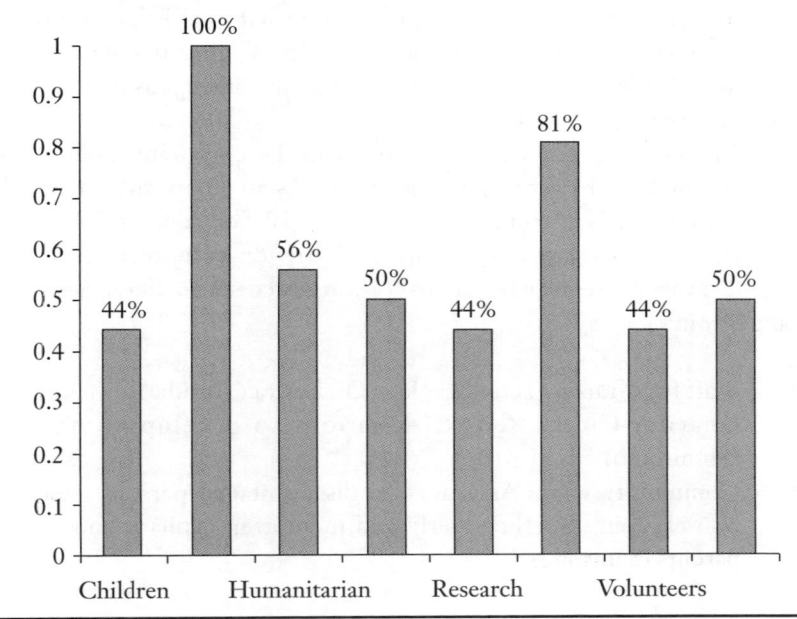

FIGURE 23.4 Top sponsorship category in Asia

FIGURE 23.5 Top sponsorship category in Europe

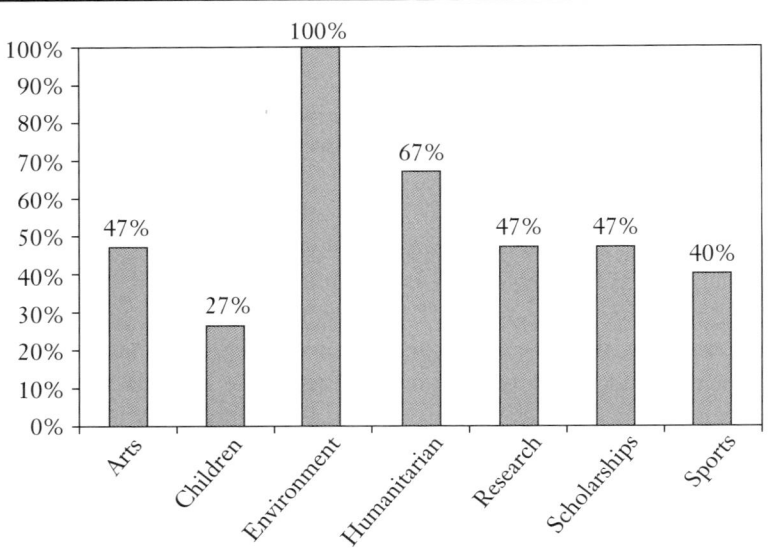

scientific contests, both at national and international level, and these usually come with generous prize contributions. Companies like Toshiba also invite students around world to conduct internships as part of their social contribution.

Interesting is the staff involvement in the corporate sponsorship activities in Asia. 44 per cent of the chosen Asian companies have their own staff initiatives compared to a mere 10 per cent of European companies. Many Japanese companies provide volunteer leave and organize various regular programs for interested staff. These activities range from:

- Staff fund-raising activities: Jazz Orchestra (Toshiba)
- Charity: Clothes/books donations to developing nations (Sumitomo)
- Community work: Assistance to disadvantaged persons (Itochu); housekeeping for the elderly and mentoring orphans and young parents (Samsung)

Most companies view the volunteer work as team-building exercises besides showing their commitment to the local community. Samsung furthermore supports family volunteering and gives awards to outstanding volunteers. Though most activities are carried out domestically, there is a trend of introducing the volunteer work worldwide by Asian multinationals. Again, according to Samsung, more than 61 per cent of Samsung employees around the world donate their time for worthy community services. Whilst volunteerism is increasingly seen as a key element in managerial development, Asian companies have established a well-developed tradition in their corporate cultures.

In Europe, humanitarian assistance is highly valued in their companies' philosophy. African countries are the biggest recipients of corporate development aid and some developing countries in Asia (i.e., Cambodia, China, Laos, Southeast Asian countries) also benefit from this scheme. The main categories funds go to are: HIV/AIDS, Human Rights, Public Health, and Social Issues (see Figure 23.6).

European companies also have a higher sponsorship rate in the Arts sector (Arts is not even listed in the top five investment category). This becomes even more obvious when it comes to countries like Italy, Germany and France, which have a long history of art and culture. All three Italian firms (Fiat Group, Generali Group and ENI Group) heavily invested in the arts and cultural heritage sectors. The main objective of these sponsorships is to broaden awareness of the arts and to enhance Italy's leadership in art and cultural collections.

FIGURE 23.6 Categories of sponsorship funds

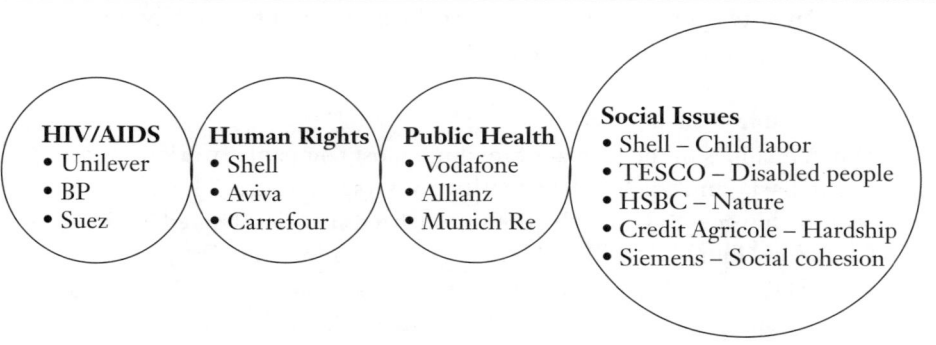

There is a wide range of activities on:

- Acquisition of art collections
- Restoration of art collections
- Restoration of real-estate property (such as heritage)
- Institutional support for leading organizations in the sector
- Exhibitions and co-hosting of special events
- Scientific research in arts subjects

Common features
Despite the different interests in some categories, Asian and European companies still share some common visions on getting involved with the community.

Funding category
- Research is a key funding area for both Asian and European companies (44 per cent and 47 per cent respectively). Companies support scientific labs, think tanks and researchers, boost international cooperation, close interrelation between research, education and training. It is also used as an enhancement of the communication among academia and the firm's own R&D teams. Many companies sponsor projects closely related to their operations, like Shell (environment, climate change), Carrefour (medical research) while Volkswagen and its foundation support a well-structured program (see Figure 23.7).
- The Sports category is very much within the national context. Companies usually sponsor their top-level athletics and national favorite sports or top scale of world sports event, e.g., Olympics, FIFA World Cup (see Table 23.1).

Sponsorship format
When it comes to the format of funding, most companies work both on event basis and with other institutions (see Figure 23.8). Much sponsorship goes to United Nations specialized agencies (United Nations Children's Fund–UNICEF, United Nations Joint Aids Programme–UNAIDS and United Nations Women's Fund–UNIFEM) and international organizations (World Wildlife Fund–WWF, Red Cross and Red Crescent).

FIGURE 23.7 Structure of Volkswagen sponsorshop program

```
                    Research
                     Areas
        ┌──────────────┼──────────────┐
   Thematic       International    Off the Beaten
   Impetus            Focus            Track
        │              │
    Societal        Persons &
   Challenges     New Structures
```

TABLE 23.1 Funding in sports category

Countries	Sports and Companies
Olympics Games	Sony, Samsung
France	Tennis (BNP Paribas)
Cycling	(France Telecom)
Germany	Soccer (Metro, Siemens, etc.)
Italy	Soccer (Fiat Group, etc.)
Japan	Baseball (Mitsui, Toshiba, etc.)
Korea	Soccer (Samsung), Asian Games, Olympics Games
The Netherlands	Marathon (ING Group etc.)
United Kingdom	Soccer (Vodafone etc.)
F-1 Racing	Shell (NL/UK), BP (UK) etc

Depending on the nature of the program, companies also collaborate with Non-Governmental Organizations (NGOs), such as Human Rights Watch and Amnesty International. Companies also sponsor specific events, which reflect the corporate identity and culture. These are mainly concerts, (film/music/sports) festivals, and youth summits. They also respond to current emergent events or crises. The tragedy

FIGURE 23.8 Funding format

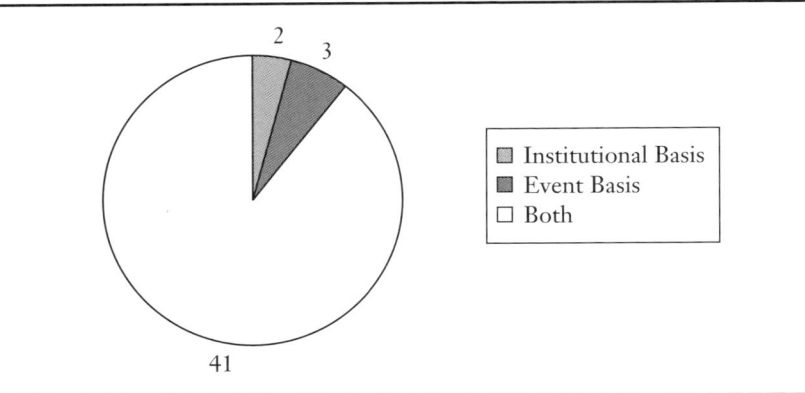

of September-11 in the US and the terrorist attack in Bali has lead to a number of initiatives from Japanese firms and Vodafone to sponsor charitable events in aid of the victims.

Furthermore, most Asian and European companies have their own named foundation to operate their sponsorship activities on the behalf of the companies. The rate of foundations in Europe is slightly higher than the rate in Asia (see Figure 23.9). Many companies have more than one foundation, and they are either centralized or based in the region with their own mandate in arts, culture, development assistance, education and similar aspects.

Public presentation
All Asian and European companies list their sponsoring activities on their websites or publish them in a separate social report, community or sustainability report. European companies are holding stronger positions in reporting as 67 per cent of the sampled companies have both online and print versions, a much higher average than the Asian companies' 12 per cent (see Figure 23.10).

CONCLUSIONS AND BEYOND

Looking at all 46 companies operating in Asia and Europe and their approaches to corporate sponsorship, one is happy to see all of them are

FIGURE 23.9 Companies with Foundations

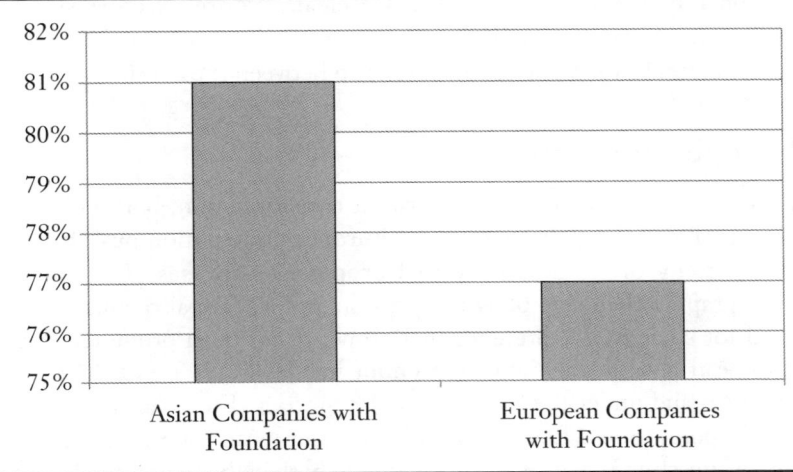

FIGURE 23.10 Sponsorship publicity

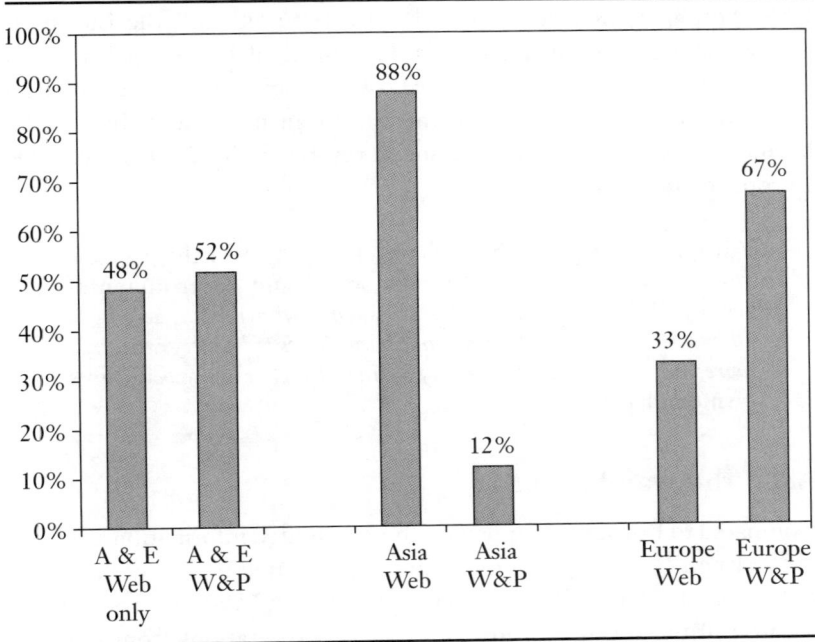

now investing in their social involvement and are trying to operate responsibly and ethically. There are clear favoured sectors such as environment, education and humanitarian aid for both Asian and European companies. However, there remains a gap between the continents.

Europe: an overview

Europe is currently undergoing crucial transformation, both politically and socially. Both globalization and European integration push forward the strategy of sustainability to European businesses. The current demographic challenge of aging, pension and welfare also enhances the need for strong CSR presence in Europe. It has been prompted at the European level at the Council Summit in Lisbon (2002) on CSR Best Practices and under the EU's initiative toward a "European Framework for Corporate Social Responsibility." Most European enterprises welcome this by investing heavily in diverse activities both in the region and beyond.

Europe has acquired a well-developed sponsorship system including an advanced reporting and monitoring structure, which is lacking in Asia. In the Netherlands, UK and France, there are special bodies in charge of CSR. Various CSR forums also play a role to enhance the European dialogue at political and social levels. The current debate in the European Parliament on a proposal on a EU-wide social and environmental reporting scheme is a result of the European movement. Just as the business network on corporate social responsibility in Europe, CSR Europe[8] comments:

> European Companies have come a long way over the past few years in recognising their own social and environmental responsibilities. *CSR (corporate sponsorships) have become a buzzword throughout Europe, and it continues to be integrated into more and more facets of everyday business life.* (italics are author's own emphasis.)

Asia: the way forward

Compared to European companies, there is limited information available in the English language on their sponsoring activities. Many think one of the reasons why CSR is popular in Europe and Western countries is because of the social pressure and societal expectations from the civil society there. This may also be true in view of the current economic situation in the Asian region. Besides Korea, Japan and a few others, most Asian countries are in the process of economic reform. Most of these new developing economies are capital-intensive and export-oriented, which sometimes neglect their social impact. However on the other hand, Asian societies also have unique cultures in religion and business. Social norms and values also apply to business, which encourage the sponsorship activities. CSR have been part of the corporate cultures in many advanced economies like Japan and Korea. One unique feature is the teamwork spirit in staff volunteerism.

However, globalization also plays an important role. Asian companies follow the trends to use sponsorship activities to enhance their brand building, the recruitment of young talents, and there is an increased awareness of the importance of corporate governance.[9] Like in Europe, Asian companies also like to institutionalize their sponsorship activities especially for those that operate internationally.[10]

Without doubt, Japanese and Korean firms have led the wave of corporate sponsorships in Asia. It has since spread to most emerging economies in the region. Globalization is inevitable, and so is the CSR movement. The Asia-Europe gap is diminishing, at least in terms of corporate sponsorships.

ENDNOTES

1. Forbes Global 500 list: http://www.forbes.com/2003/07/07/internationaland.html
2. Morten Ougaard. *The CSR Movement and Global Governance*. Copenhagen Business School, 2003, e-mail: mo.ikl@cbs.dk
3. David Henderson. "The case against Corporate Social Responsibility." Former Chief Economist at OECD in Paris, Visiting Professor at the Westminster Business School in London, Institute of Economic Affairs (IEA), 2004. http://www.abc.net.au/rn/talks/perspective/stories/s438527.htm
4. Chris Holmes. *Cause Related Marketing: The Game Plan, Cause Related Marketing Research Publication—The Ultimate Win Win Win Business in the Community*, ISBN 0-9480-6305-X, 2003.
5. *Business Ethics Magazine*, 2003, published in Minneapolis, also featured in Ougaard, 2003.
6. Bryane Michael. "Corporate Social Responsibility, an overview and critique", PowerPoint Presentation, Oxford University, 2003.
7. http://www.samsung.com/aboutsamsung/socialcommitement/ (accessed March 2004).

8   CSR Europe is a business driven membership network whose mission is to help companies combine profitability and sustainability, http://www.csreurope.org/
9   ACCA. *Responsibility in Business, Attitudes to Corporate Governance in China and South East Asia*. 2004, http://www.accaglobal.com/
10 Eleanor Chambers et al. *CSR in Asia: A Seven Country Study of CSR Website Reporting*. Nottingham University Business School, 2003, http://www.nottingham.ac.uk/business/ICCSR

REFERENCES

ACCA. *Responsibility in Business, Attitudes to Corporate Governance in China and South East Asia*. 2004, http://www.accaglobal.com/

Business Ethics Magazine. Minneapolis: Ougaard, 2003.

Bryane Michael. *Corporate Social Responsibility, An Overview and Critique*. PowerPoint Presentation. Oxford University, 2003.

Chris Holmes. *Cause Related Marketing: The Game Plan, Cause Related Marketing Research Publication—The Ultimate Win Win Win Business in the Community*. ISBN 0-9480-6305-X, 2003.

Eleanor Chambers, et al. *CSR in Asia: A Seven Country Study of CSR Website Reporting*. Nottingham University Business School, 2003, http://www.nottingham.ac.uk/business/ICCSR

David Henderson. *The Case Against Corporate Social Responsibility*. Former Chief Economist at OECD in Paris, Visiting Professor at the Westminster Business School in London, Institute of Economic Affairs (IEA), 2004, http://www.abc.net.au/rn/talks/perspective/stories/s438527.htm

Forbes Global 500 list, http://www.forbes.com/2003/07/07/internationaland.html

Jennifer N. Rosenberg, et al. *The Use of Corporate Sponsorship as a Tobacco Marketing Tool: A Review of Tabasco Industry Sponsorships in the United States, 1996–1999*. Boston University School of Public Health, 2003.

Morten Ougaard. *The CSR Movement and Global Governance*. Copenhagen Business School, 2003, e-mail: mo.ikl@cbs.dk

http://www.samsung.com/aboutsamsung/socialcommitement/ (accessed March 2004).

http://www.volkswagen-stiftung.de/ (accessed March 2004).

http://www.csreurope.org/ (accessed March 2004).

Contributors

Chua Yi Fen, BA (Hons), is a freelance writer.

Frank Bradley, Professor of Marketing, The Michael Smurfit Graduate School of Business, University College Dublin, Ireland.

Jason Alexander Villanueva, is an Administrative Officer, Human Relations Department, Singapore Airlines.

Justin Tan Wei Shen, Analysis Officer, Ministry of Defence, Singapore.

Lim Chee Hong works in Marks & Spencer International.

Stephanie Po-yin Chung, Associate Professor, at the Department of History, Hong Kong Baptist University, Hong Kong.

Wei Shen, MA, LLM, Research Assistant and PhD candidate, Department of Geography, Loughborough University, UK.

Index

A
Aaron, Sam, 206
Abdullah Ahmad Badawi, 38
Advanced Info Service Co. (Thailand)
 investment by Sing Tel, 34
advertising
 knocking copy, 264
AEG, 49–50
Agnelli, Gianni, 132, 144
Air France
 arrangement with BOAC, 94
air transport industry
 effect of WTC crash (September 11, 2001), 112
 great losses, 103
Aircraft Transport & Travel, 90
Al-Fayed, Dodi, 249
Al-Fayed, Mohammad, 247, 249–51
alcohol branding, 203
 "Big Three," 213–15
 changing trends in consumers, 206, 208, 215
 in Ireland, 206–7
 new markets, 213
Alfa Romeo, 130, 137
 split with Ferrari, 135
All-Japan Speed Rally, 118
Allan Beverages (Canada), 162
Allied-Domecq's Hiram-Walker, 213
Alltech Feeding Times, 179
Alltech Inc.
 Animal, the Consumer and the Environment (ACE) concept, 175
 Australian market, 185
 big six concept, 168, 186
 bioscience centers in Europe, 174–7
 biotechnology research, 170, 173
 competition, 168, 181–2, 187
 customers, 179–80
 distribution strategy, 184, 186
 expansion, 168
 generational succession, 16
 history, 169–70
 HQ in Kentucky, 173
 international presence, 169, 174, 177, 183–6
 Kentucky Ale, 171
 long term stability, 176
 marketing program, 184–5
 Marketing through Education concept, 168, 177–8
 organizational structure, 177
 products, 175–6
 R&D, 171
 sales target, 168, 186
 in South Africa, 174
 technical support, 177, 179
Alltech Symposium, 177–8
Amersham
 takeover by General Electric, 58
Anglo-Swiss Condensed Milk Company, 161
Anheuser-Busch, 222, 228, 232
Animal, the Consumer and the Environment (ACE) concept by Alltech, 175
animal agriculture
 genetically modified organisms (GMOs) ban, 172
 public scrutiny, 171–2
animal nutrition market competition, 180
Annual Sales and Marketing Meeting, Dublin, 168
Art Shokai, 118
Asia
 strength of business model, 19
 corporate sponsorship, 311–13
 financial crisis, 33, 69, 75, 77
Asian film industry, 289
Atlas-Werke, 158
Audi, 141
Australia's use of English language, 9

Auto Union, 130
Ayling, Bob, 108–9

B
Backman, Michael, 13
Baileys
    acquisitions, 219
    advertising strategy, 201–2
    brand image, 209
    duty-free sales, 204
    entrepreneurial creation, 16
    German market, 212
    international awareness, 203–4, 209–11, 213, 218
    launch of Sheridans, 218
    market acceptance, 210–11
    market leader, 220–1
    marketing strategy, 200–4, 209, 214
    product extensions, 217
    rapid growth, 200
    strategic development, 200
    US market, 21, 203–4, 212
Baileys flavored ice-cream, 218
Baileys Gold, 218
Baileys Light, 217–18
Baileys on Ice, 201
Baileys the Original, 509, 217–18
Baracca, Countess Paulina, 136
Baracca, Francisco, 136–7
BASF (Germany), 180
Battle of Britain, 96
Battle of Midway, 257
Bayer, 168
Bazzi, Luigi, 130
Beijing Yanjing Brewery, 223
Beitz, Berthold, 154, 157
Belgacon, 33
Bell, Arthur Graham, 23
Bell, Tim, 268
Benton & Bowles, 264
Bergman, Ingrid, 138
Berlin Love Parade, 197
Berlin Olympics (1936), 154
Bernat, Enric (founder, Productos Bernat), 195–6
Bernat, Marcos, 195

Bernat, Ramon, 195
Bernat, Xavier, 195
Bertelsmann losses in the US, 57
Bharti Group, India
    investment by SingTel, 34
Bio-Mos, 168
Bioplex development, 184
Bioplexes, 168
biotechnology
    in the Feed Industry, 178
Blair, Andrew, 265
Blaue Quellen (Germany), 162
BMW, 141, 198
BOAC-Cunard Ltd, 94
Bohlen und Halbach, Gustav von, 153
Bønsdorf Petersen, Dr Christian, 172
Bosch buy-out by Siemens, 57
boycotts of French food, 173
Brabeck, Peter, 166
Brabeck-Letmathe, Peter, 165
branding requirement for national images, 19
Branson, Sir Richard, 107
Britain
    conduction of meetings, 10
    recession (1989–92), 103
    use of English language in, 8
British Air Carriers, 90–2
British Airways
    British Caledonian (BCal), 105
    airline alliances, 105, 107
    Awards for Excellence, 101
    control of UK market, 104
    corporate culture, 101
    cultural transition, 16, 96–97, 101–2
    Employee Brainwaves, 101
    employee training programs, 100, 102
    expansion strategy, 105
    history, 95
    injection of entrepreneurialism, 18
    losses, 105, 107–8
    Managing People First (MPF) program, 102
    merger talks, 105–6

problems, 97–8
public company, 103
Putting People First, 102
reputation, 107–9
restructuring, 112
staff redundancies, 102–3
Total Quality Management (TQM), 101
virtual airline, 108
British Airways (BA), 90
British Caledonian (BCal), 105–5
British economic slump, 97
British Empire, 130
British European Airways (BEA)
air routes, 92
de Havilland Trident 1, 94
merger with BOAC, 95
travel packages, 94–5
British government
airline merger, 92
air service, 90–1
privatization, 98
support for national airline, 94
white paper, 94
British Marine Air Navigation, 91
British Overseas Airways Corporation (BOAC)
Air France, 94
air routes, 92
attraction to officer classes, 96
merger with BEA, 95
new cargo terminal, 94
South American operations, 93–4
British South American Airways (BSAA), 92, 93
British United Airways
merger with Caledonian Airways, 104
Buddhist Tenrikyo sect, 64
Buffet, Warren, 86
Bulmers Cider Company, 205
Burbidge, Richard, 244–5, 248
business cultures
complexity of, 8
strengths and weaknesses, 70

business styles
Geert Hosftede findings, 5
Business Week Global, 104
Byrne, David, 173

C
Caledonian Airways
merger with British United Airways, 104
Campaign, 266
Canada's use of English language, 8
Canadian Imperial Bank of Commerce, 86
Canary Wharf, 86
Caniato, Alfredo, 130
Caniato, Augusto, 130
Capital Group of Companies
ownership of SingTel, 23
Carlsberg, 223
Carnation Company, 163
Cathay Organization, 289
Cathay Pacific, 103, 110
Chang, Anthony, 88
Cheung Kong, 85, 87
Chief Information Officer (CIO), 26
China
attitudes towards law, 8
beer exports, 223
cause of corruption, 13
first paging network, 32
refugees from, 85
required business information, 10
Siemens joint ventures, 58
State-Owned Enterprises (SOEs), 222
China Resources Beverages, 223
Chinese Communist leadership, 88
Chinese management style, 235–6
Chinetti, Luigi, 138
Chow, Raymond, 88
Chung In Yung, 16, 73, 77
Chung Ju Yung (founder of Hyundai)
authoritarian control, 81–2
business ideals, 76–8
charged in court, 76

death, 69, 81
formed KDK Electronics, 73
initial businesses, 70
move into electronics, 73
relation with General Park, 71
retirement, 69
runs for President, 76
Seoul Olympics (1988), 75
set up United People's Party (UPP), 76
splits company, 80
Chung Mong Hun, 80–81
Chung Mong Ku, 80
Chung Sang Young, 81
Chupa Chups, 195
flavors, 197
generational succession, 16
international marketing, 195, 197–8
launched Smint (1994), 198
marketing and co-branding, 196–8
sales & distribution, 196, 198
sponsorship, 197
Civil Air Transport Subsidies Committee, 91
Civil Aviation Authority, 105
coffee-cream idea, 205
Cohen, Edgar, 244
Coleman, Deirdre, 178
Collett Dickinson Pearce, 264
Collings, John, 265
communication patterns
cultural variations of, 8
communication strategies
at Honda Motor Company, 125
company mergers, 4
competitive advantages
low cost airlines, 111
Compton Advertising, 266
concept of time
variation across business cultures, 10
Concept of Time, The
Geert Hofstede definition of, 6
Concorde, 95, 109

Confucian work ethic
relation to US, 11
Connolly, Aidan, 179
Consensus Orientation
Geert Hofstede definition of, 6
consolidation of SingTel's position under Sung Sio Ma, 32
contract-based employees, 27
contracts
attitudes towards, 8
corporate culture
British Airways, 101
Charles Handy definitions of, 2–3
definition of, 1
effect of short term financial goals, 3–4, 6
emotional distance between bosses and subordinates, 5
Ferrari, 133
Geert Hofstede parameters, 5–6
Geert Hofstede definition of, 224
globalization and, 5, 14
individualism vs. collectivism, 6
Information System approach, 26
Japan, 66, 121–2
masculinity vs. femininity, 6
merger and, 95–6
reasons for, 3
relation to mission statement, 1
SingTel, 24, 25, 27, 36–7
society as reflection of, 4
task-based, 96–7
threats to, 3
transformation of, 48
Tsingtao Brewery, 224, 228, 231–2
variations of, 1
corporate landscape, 15
corporate principals at Matsushita, 62
corporate social responsibility (CSR), 306–7
corporate sponsorship, 306
Asia, 311–13
Europe, 313–14
corporate structure
relationship to cultural concepts of leadership, 11

corporate survival, 15
corporate trust, 4
Courvoisier Cognac, 205
Coward, Noel, 246
Cramer, Ross, 264, 266
Cramer Saatchi, 265–6
cross channel air service, 90
Crosse & Blackwell
    buy-out by Nestle, 161
cultural and national differences, 35
Cultural Revolution (1966–76), 225
Cunard Steamship Company, 94
Cuppage, Martin, 204
Cutts, Robert
    interviews with Toshiba employees, 46

D
Daimler Airway, 91
Daimler Benz
    absorb AEG (1982), 50
Daimler Chrysler US losses, 57
Daiwa Bank, 258
Dalian Toshiba TV Co., 45
Dand, David, 205, 209
Dawson, Christopher, 251
Dawson, Dr Karl, 175
De Havilland's DH Comet 1, 93
De-Odorase, 176
Deal and Kennedy, 133
decentralization, 19
Deer Park (US), 162
Deng Xiaoping, 225
Deutsche Bank
    jobs in, 1
    loans to Siemens, 49
    US losses, 57
di Montezemolo, Luca, 132, 134, 140
    overhauled Ferrari, 132
dioxin's use in food, 172
Doko, Toshio, 42
DRAM production, 43
Dresdner Bank, 154
dualism
    at Honda Motor Company, 123–4
    Western meaning, 123

Dutch language, 9
Dutch KPN, 86
duty-free sales, 204

E
East Asian organizations
    family ownership in, 13
Easyjet, 111
Eddington, Rod, 109–110
Elanco, 168
Electrolux alliance with Toshiba, 44
enzyme market, 183
EU Food Authority, 173
Europe
    air transport market in, 104, 107, 110–11
    corporate sponsorship, 313–14
    deregulation of markets, 48
    end of public monopolies (1992), 51
    first submarine fiber optic cable to Singapore, 32
European business model, 19
European trends
    SingTel adoption of, 30
European Union, 135, 306
Excel (low-cost Hyundai car), 72

F
family
importance in Italian companies, 133
family rivalry
    within Hyundai, 69
    problems in successions, 81
Farine Lactee Henri Nestlé SA, 161
FC Barcelona, 197
Fenn, Frank, 200, 204, 216
Ferrari
    autonomy, 145
    capped production, 129
    ceremony, 135
    consumer targeting, 132–3, 138, 140
    corporate culture, 133, 137, 147
    cultural transition, 16
    family business, 133, 136

Fiat ownership, 18, 129, 133, 144
first car built in 1946, 131
Ford purchase of, 143–4
history of, 129–32
marketing and branding, 18
merchandising, 141
model types, 129
national pride, 129
near bankruptcy, 132
partnerships, 139
pricing, 140
quality, 140
racing, 134, 138–9
reputation, 138–9, 147
revival of Maserati, 141–2
shareholders, 129
sponsorships, 146
strategic moves, 137, 140–1, 147
US market, 141, 145–6
worker's loyalty, 134
worldwide sales, 129–30, 132, 139, 142–3
Ferrari, Enzo
Acerbo Cup win, 130
Alfa Romeo, 131
death, 90, 132
early jobs, 130
negotiations with Ford, 131
stories about, 136–7
Ferrari Idea, 130, 137
Ferrari logo, 136–7
Ferrari Museum, 141
Fiat
Ferraris autonomy within, 18
ownership of Ferrari, 129
purchase of Ferrari, 144
Fibrozyme, 168
Finland communication, 8
First Sino-Japanese War, 255
Fontlladosa, Enric Bernat, 195
food industry scandals, 172, 179
Alltech response, 173
bans, 178
German TV report (1999), 172–3
Forbes, 84

Ford
competition against Ferrari, 143–4
negotiations with Ferrari, 131
purchase of Ferrari, 143
foreign investments
as part of long term growth, 33
Formula One world championships (F1), 131, 135, 142, 144
Ferrari's success, 132, 134
McLaren, 142
Vodafone and Ferrari, 146
Williams-BMW, 142
World Constructors title, 132, 139
World Drivers Championship, 132, 139
Formula Two world championships (F2), 139
France
conducting meetings in, 10
Frankfurt University, 162
Fraser, Hugh, 245
French Chambourcy Company, 161
Fritz Thyssen Foundation, 156
fuel alcohol industry, 170–1
Fujitsu alliances
Hyundai Electronics, 74
Toshiba, 44

G

Galletas la Gloria (cookies of glory), 195
Garland-Compton
merger with Saatchi & Saatchi, 267
General Chun's coup, 73
General Electric (GE), 52
support deal with Toshiba, 42–3
takeover of Amersham, 58
General Park
assassination of, 73
Chung Ju Yung, 71
rise of Korea's economy, 73
generational succession
crucial timing, 17
differences between founder and children, 17

German customs, 152
German Grand Prix in 1935, 130
German industrialization, 151
German unity, 155
Germanic
   cultural modus operandi, 7
Germanic organizations
   management structure, 12
   required business information, 10
Germany
   attitudes towards contracts, 8
   concept of time, 10
   conducting meetings in, 9–10
   de-nazification, 50
   different regions, 192
   foreign representations and capital participation, 50
   government support of Siemens, 58
   hyperinflation, 188
   patents and overseas possession lost, post-WWI, 49
   production of first telephone systems (1877), 48
   public policies, 57
   social partnership, 51–2
   unity in 1990, 50
   use of language, 9
Gilbeys Gin, 205
Gilbeys of Ireland, 205, 207–8
Global Crossing
   bought by Li Ka-shing, 88
global expansion
   requirement for cultural knowledge, 14
globalization
   effect on national corporate culture, 18
   problems with, 5, 162, 168–9
Globe Telecom, Philippines, 34
GMO debate, 179
Go, 111
Gold Rush
   concept of time, 10
Gottschalk, Thomas
   partnership with Haribo, 191–2
Gran, Massantes I., 196

Grand Metropolitans IDV, 213–14
Granja Asturias
   revival, 195–6
Great Leap Forward (1958–9), 225
Gregg, David
   notes on Hyundai workers, 78
Gretsky, Wayne, 170
group identity
   at Honda Motor Company, 123–5
Gruson Steelworks, 153
Guinness' United Distillers, 213
Gummibär invented, 188
Gut, Rainer, 165
Guthrie, Giles, 94

H
Habsburg Lothringen, Karl von, 157
Haier, 222
Halske, Johann, 48
Handley Page Hermes, 93
Handley Page Transport, Ltd, 90–1
Handy, Charles
   definition of organizational cultures, 2–3
Hans Riegel Bonn, 188
Hans Riegel Halle, 190
Hansen Turbine Works of Gotha (Germany), 15
Haribo
   advertising slogan, 189
   commercial expansion, 191
   corporate secrets, 190
   definition of, 188
   distribution, 193–4
   exports, 189
   generational succession, 16
   gold bear invented (1952), 190
   Gummibär invented (1922), 188
   husband and wife, 188
   international tastes, 192–4
   Keitgen & Meier, 191
   local promotion, 192
   location, 189
   marketing, 190–1, 193
   product range, 189, 191–2
   production levels, 188–90

Tour de France sponsorship, 191–2
  VEB Westsachsen (WESA), 193
  World War II, 189
Harrods
  acquisition by House of Fraser, 245
  customer service, 247, 250
  employee training, 245, 247, 248–9
  expansion, 244–5, 250
  family ownership, 16
  fire in 1883, 244
  history, 243–6
  marketing, 250
  new premises, 244
  online sales, 250
  outlets, 250
  problems, 251
  reputation, 244, 246–7, 249
  royal patronage, 249–50
  royal warrant, 245, 249
  sale of, 244
  transformation of culture, 249–50
Harrods, Charles Digby, 243–4
Harrods, Charles Henry, 243, 246–7
Harrods Bank, 249
Harrods building, 243
Harrods Casino, 249
Harrods Hotel, 249
Harrods Travels, 249
Health Education Council (HEC), 265
Heathrow, 96
Hegarty, John, 265
Heinrich, Georg, 157
Heinrich, Hans, 157
Hello Kitty, 302–5
Henry Ford's manufacturing system, 124
Herro, David, 271–2, 284–5
Hideshiro Fujisawa, 119
hierarchical system
  old school companies, 26
Hisashige Tanaka (founder of Toshiba), 41
Hoffmann-LaRoche (Switzerland), 180
Hofstede, Geert
  1970 survey of IBM, 5
  analysis of Tsingtao, 234–5

Homestead Act, 10
Honda
  cultural transition, 16
  employee mottos, 123
  management mottos, 122
Honda Motor Company
  company philosophy, 117, 122, 126–7
  "complimentary principal," 126
  founders, 117
  huge success, 126–7
  management style, 117
  safety net, 125–6
  sales in USA, 126
  young leaders, 125
Honda R&D
  separate from Honda Motor Company, 123–4
Honda Technical Research Institute, 121
Hong Kong
  Japanese occupation, 84
  riots in 1967, 85
Hong Kong and Shanghai Banking Corporation (HSBC)
  offer to Li Ka-shing, 85
Hornbostel Silk Weaving Plant of Leobersdorf (Lower Austria), 15
House of Fraser's acquisition of Harrods, 245
human intercourse, 8
Husky Oil, 86
Hutchinson Whampoa
  downgrading, 87
  generational succession, 16
  offer to Li Ka-shing, 85
  sale of subsidiaries' shares, 87
Hyundai
  activities in East Asia, 75
  Asian financial crisis, 77
  benefits from Seoul Olympics, 75
  car manufacturing, 71
  collapse, 69–70, 80, 82
  Confucian values, 76
  construction business, 70–1
  cooperation with Mitsubishi, 72

core business philosophies, 69, 71–2, 79
corporate culture, 76, 78–9
corporate image suffers, 76, 80
entry into Middle East, 73
foreign investments, 71, 81
generational succession, 16
government grants, 71
Korean War, 70
R&D, 74
risk taking, 69
strikes, 75, 80
success, 69, 81
US motor market (1985), 72, 82
Vietnam War, 71
workers' treatment, 81, 72
Hyundai Electronics
alliance with Fujitsu, 74
Hyundai Engineering and Construction (HEC), 70
Hyundai Heavy Industries (HHI), 72–3, 78–9
Hyundai Motor, 72
Hyundai Resources Development Corporation, 75
Hyun Jeong Eun, 81

I
IBM
alliance with Toshiba, 44
Imperial Air Transport, 91–2
Inchon plant
moved to production of DRAM, 74
India's work ethic, 11
Infineon, 55–6
Infocomm Development Authority (IDA)
dispute with Sing Tel, 29
innovation of engines, 138
inquiry into airline competition, 110
Institute of Management Development (IMD), 164
Institute of Practitioners of Advertising (IPA), 264
Instone Air Line, 91
intercultural communications, 36

international beer market, 222
International Brand Companies (IBCs), 215
International Distillers and Vintners' (IDV), 208
International Labor Organization, 306
International Wine Meeting, 229
Ireland's use of English language, 9
Irish Distillers Ltd., 169
Irish Mist, 206–7
IT jargon in Toshiba, 41
Italian society, 136
Italian style of business, 144
Italian style of management, 135–6
Italy
attitudes towards law, 8
communication, 8
conducting meetings in, 9
growth of industry, 133

J
J. Walter Thompson, 268
Jaguar, 131
Jameson, John, 205
Jano, Vittorio, 130
Japan
attitudes towards contracts, 8
bureaucratic problems, 17
civil engineering projects, 45
communication, 8
conducting meetings in, 9
controlled competition, 43
corporate culture, 66, 121–2
economic crisis in 1929, 63
electronics market, 42–3
military expansion, 64, 255, 257
Peace and Happiness through Prosperity Institute (PHP), 67
replacement cycles of technology, 44
US occupation, 257–8
use of language, 9
zaibatsu, 14
Japan Machine and Tool Research Institute, 120
Japanese Communist Party (JCP), 42

Japanese economy, 255–6, 259
Japanese industries, 254
Japanese management, 121
Jitsusaburo Nomura, 255

K
Kahlua, 204
Keitgen & Meier
    purchase by Haribo, 191
Kentucky Ale, 171
Keogh, Catherine, 173, 176, 178
Kia, 71
Kim Dae Jung, President, 81
Kim Song Il, 81
King, Lord John
    adoption of American style practices, 98
    resignation, 105, 107
King of Plastic Flowers (Lee Ka-shing), 84
Kirin, 223
Kirkwood Company, 267
Kiyoshi Kawashima, 124
KLM, 103
Kokusai Securities, 260
Korea
    attitudes towards contracts, 8
    chaebol, 14
    economy, 79
    government support for companies, 74
    memory chips, 43
    strikes, 79
    working conditions, 73–5, 80
Korean War
    Hyundai construction, 70
KPN Telekom, 87
Kraftwerksunion
    sale by AEG to Seimens, 50
Krupp, 151
    Germaniawerft, 158
    Gruson Works, 158
    production of armaments, 154
Krupp, Alfred, 152, 154
Krupp, Arndt, 154–5
Krupp, Bertha, 152–3
Krupp, Friedrich, 151–3
Krupp, Friedrich Albert, 152
Krupp dynasty, 151
Krupp sites
    targets of Allied bombings, 154
Krupp von Bohlen und Halbach, Alfred, 151
Kuok, Robert, 88

L
La Suiza Renye, 195
Laing, Jennifer, 275
Lamsan family, 88
language
    cultural variations, 8–9
Latin America
    attitudes towards contracts, 8
    work ethic, 11
law
    attitudes towards, 8
Lawson, Nigel, 98
Lee Hsien Yang, 32
    approach to corporate management, 25
    Best Telecom Executive, *Telecom Asia (2001, 2002)*, 25
    education, 24–5
    SingTel, 22, 25, 34
Lee Hsien Loong, 24
Lee Kuan Yew, 24
Lewis, Richard, 6
Li, Richard, 88
Li, Victor, 88
Li Ka-shing
    business strategy, 84, 86–8
    Canadian Imperial Bank of Commerce, 86
    Canadian investments, 85
    dynastic empire, 88
    education, 84
    expansion of interests, 85
    Global Crossing, 88
    Hutchison Whampoa, 16
    joint ventures in mainland China, 85

King of Plastic Flowers, 84
   media ventures, 86
   net worth in 1996, 86
   promotion, 84
   real estate development, 85
   sale of Orange, 86
   takeover of foreign interests, 86
   third generation (3G) phone network, 86, 87
   US denouncement, 88
Lillie, Beatrice, 246
linear active
   Richard Lewis definition of, 7
liqueur market
   international brands, 212, 213, 216–17
liqueurs of Ireland, 206
Lockheed 10 Electra, 92
Loke Wan Tho, 289
London World Exhibition (1851)
   Krupp gun, 152
Louis-Dreyfus, Robert, 270–2
Lyons, Dr Pearse, 168–9
   Alltech, 170
   animal feed industry, 171, 172
   animal nutrition market, 180–1
   Biocon, 169
   motivation & beliefs, 171, 179

M

Maggi
   bought by Nestlé,161
Maglev, 57
Mahathir Mohamad, 36
Malaysia's relationship with Singapore, 36
Management Horizons, 251
Mannesmann
   purchase by Vodafone, 86
   purchase of Orange in 1999, 86
   takeover by Vodafone, 54
   work with Thyssen, 158
Maranello, 129
Mardi Gras, 197
marine
   definition of, 27

Marshal Ye Jianying, 223
Marshall, Sir Colin, 99, 107
   involvement with PPF, 101
   previous roles, 99
   statement in *Harvard Business Review*, 100
   training program, 100
   vision for BA, 101
   winning strategy, 99–100
Maserati, 131, 142
   revival by Ferrari, 141–2
Massanes, Domingo, 195
Matsushita
   alliance with Toshiba, 44
   batteries production in the 1930s, 63
   copes with economic crisis (1929), 63
   cultural transition, 16
   foreign employees, 7
   low cost production, 62
   order to cease operation (1945), 65
   US losses, 57
   workers' treatment, 62
Matsushita Institute of Government and Management (MIGM), 67–8
Maucher, Helmut, 162, 164, 166
M&C Saatchi, 264, 275
McDonagh, Aldagh, 201–3, 205
McDonald's Russian sales staff, 7
McNeil & Libby, 161
Mediterranean
   concept of time, 10
meetings
   conducting of, 9–10
Meiji government, 41
Mercedes Benz, 130, 141
Micron Electronics
   purchase of DRAM production from Toshiba, 45
Microsoft's alliance with Toshiba, 44
Middle East
   work ethic, 11
Midgley, Robert, 245
Midland Bank, 269, 279

minerals market, 184
mission statement (meaning), 1
Mitsubishi
    cooperation with Hyundai, 72
Mitsui bank
    ownership of Toshiba, 41–2
Mitsui Bussan, 255
mobile market
    flooded in 2000, 57
Mobile One (M1), 26
    price war with Sing Tel, 31
Modena, 129
Mong-joon acquires Hyundai Heavy Industries, 80
Monsanto, 173
Morita, Akio (Sony founder), 66
Morse code
    improvement by Werner von Seimens, 48
Motorola
    handsets for Three UK, 86–7
    joint venture with Toshiba, 42
multi active
    Richard Lewis' definition, 7
multinational enterprises
    deep rooted national values in, 6–7
Munich International Expo, 229
Murdoch, Rupert, 86, 110
Mycosorb, 168

N

Nakagawa Electric
    acquisition by Matsushita Electrics, 66
National
    market share, 63
National Marketing Companies (NMCs), 215–16
National Poultry Advisory Office, Denmark, 172
national pride (Ferrari), 129
natural monopoly
    definition of, 30
NEC
    handsets for Three UK, 86–7
Neelsen, Tim, 184

Nescafe, invention of, 161
Nestlé
    acquisitions of companies, 161, 166–7
    boycott of, 160
    corporate logo, 161
    cultural transition, 16
    decentralization, 19
    during Depression, 161
    entry into chocolate business, 161
    expansions, 161–3
    in Germany, 164
    globalization plans, 162–3
    history, 160–1
    international market, 165–6
    management style, 165
    managerial autonomy, 164–6
    public perceptions, 160
    successful internationalization, 19
    Swiss/German relations, 162
    turnover, 161, 163
Nestle, Heinrich, 160–1
Nestlé Research Centre, 165
New Saatchi Agency, 273–4
New Zealand
    use of English language, 9
News Corporation, 110
Nippon Yusen, 255
Nixdorf, Heinz (death, 1986), 55
Nixdorf Computers, 55
Nomura
    corporate trademark, 255
    cultural transition, 16
    hire of foreign graduates, 258
    history, 254–60
    Japanese corporate landscape, 18
    Japanese war bonds, 257
    New York office, 258
    salesmen, 254, 259
    scandals, 254
    specialization, 255
    yakuza deals, 259–61
Nomura Bank, 257
Nomura Construction, 258
Nomura family tragedies, 256
Nomura Life Insurance, 257

Nomura Securities, 257–8
Nomura Trust and Banking, 257
non-governmental organizations (NGOs), 306–7
North Korea threats, 75
Northern Guangdong
    source for many Chinese immigrants, 84
NTT DoCoMo, 86–7

O

Oakmark International, 271
Okamura, Tadashi, 46
Okumura, Tsunao, 257–8
One World Alliance, 107–8, 110
Optus
    acquisition by SingTel, 25, 34, 36
    relation to Telstra, 37
Orange
    sale to Mannesmann in 1999, 86
organizations
    acceptable behavior in, 1
Orlando, President Vittorio, 137
Osaka Gas, 258
Osaka Light, 61
Osaka Nomura Bank, 256
Osram, 49–50

P

Packard Co., 138
Page, Charles, 161
Page, George, 161
Pan Am, 91
Paris World Exhibition, 152
Peace and Happiness through Prosperity Institute (PHP), 67
Pearson, 86
Pell, Bennett, 23
people skills
    requirement of, 27
Pernod Ricard, 169
Perrier, 162, 164
personal digital assistant (PDA), 41
Philippines
    work ethic, 11

Philips
    alliance with Toshiba, 44
    venture with Matushita Electrics, 65–6
Pierer, Heinrich von, 58
    restructuring at Seimens, 53
    Siemens CEO in 1992, 52
Pininfarina, Battista, 139
Pininfarina, Sergio, 139
Porsche, 131
power distance
    Geert Hofstede definition of, 5
President Roh, 76
Prince Bernard of Holland, 138
Princess Diana, 249
Procter and Gamble, 85
Productos Bernat, 195
Putting People First (PPF) program, 100–1

Q

Qing Dynasty, 224
Queen Elisabeth of Belgium, 247

R

Rathenau, Emil
    support for AEG, 49
reactive culture
    Richard Lewis definition of, 7
Reagan, Ronald, 246
Redbreast 12 Year Old Irish Whiskey, 205
Reece, Gordon, 268
regional variations, 7
retail competition, 251
Rheinhausen steel mills, 153
Rheinstahl AG, 158
Rhone-Poulenc (France), 180
Ribond, Antoine, 163–4
Riegel, Gertrude, 189–90
Riegel, Hans Jr., 189, 190, 193
Riegel, Hans-Jürgen, 191
Riegel, Hans Sr., 188–9
Riegel, Paul, 188–9, 191
Rigney, Pat, 219
Rimmer, Ron, 267

Romania
  communication in, 8
Romanic language, 9
Romanic organizations
  management structure, 12
  required business information, 10
RAF (Royal Air Force)
  during WWII, 96
  landing strips in Africa, 90
Rueter, Edzard (Chairman, Daimler Benz), 50
Ruhrkohle AG, 158
Run Run Shaw, 289
Russo Japanese War, 255
Ryanair, 111

S
S. T. Garland Advertising, 266
Saatchi, Charles, 264, 266, 273, 282–3
Saatchi, Maurice, 266, 271, 283–4
  downfall, 272–3
Saatchi & Saatchi, 264
  acquisitions, 266, 269–70, 275–6, 279–80
  business strategy, 276–9
  cultural transition, 16, 18
  image, 277–8, 280–1
  lawsuits, 274
  merger with Garland-Compton, 267
  press reports, 273
  reputation, 269, 277–8
  restructuring, 270–1
  split, 272–3
Saatchi & Saatchi Compton Ltd.
  client list, 267–8
  and Margaret Thatcher, 268
Saatchi & Saatchi Garland-Compton, 268
Samsung
  alliance with Toshiba, 44
  leader in DRAM production, 74
Sanrio Corporation, 302–3, 305
  generational succession, 16
  theme parks, 303–4
  US market, 304

SARS outbreak, 28, 222
Scaglietti, 129
Schultz, Charles, 303
Schumacher, Michael, 132, 144
Schumacher, Ulrich (Chairman, Infineon), 56
Scuderia Ferrari, 130
  Societa Esercizio Fabbrische Automobili e Corse (SEFAC), 131
Seagram Spirits and Wine Group, 213
Segawa, Minoru, 257
Sel-Plex, 168
Serra, Nuria, 195
Shah of Persia, 138
Shaw Organization, 289
Sheridan, John D., 206
Sheridans, 218–9
Shinawatra Group
  investment in by Sing Tel, 32
Shinjin
  manufacturing of cars, 71
Shinkansen, 45, 57
Shintaro Tsuji, 303
Shop Act, 245
Short Company, 91
Siemens
  acquisitions in US, 55, 57
  Be Inspired campaign, 56
  Bosch buy-out, 57
  corporate cultural change, 19, 56, 58
  corporate image, 56
  corporate restructuring, 19, 49, 51–4, 58
  corporate takeovers, 54–5
  cultural transition, 16, 51–2
  deregulation of European markets, 48
  Deutsche Bank loans, 49
  electrical appliance maker in 1930s, 49
  family ownership, 48–9, 51
  foreign shareholders, 54
  fund managers, 54
  German government support, 58
  German reunification (1990), 50

Index

IT systems, 54
joint ventures in China, 58
Kraftwerksunion share purchase from AEG, 50
medical IT services, 53
new business in East Germany, 50
number of employees, 49
Osram share purchase from AEG, 49, 50
product development, 51, 57
profit & loss, 53, 57
public and semi-public clients, 50
sales in Germany, 57
semiconductor business, 55, 56
set up Telefunken with AEG, 49
strength of R&D, 57
strategic principle, 49, 55
takeover of Schuckert in 1873, 49
TGV and Shinkansen, 57
Toshiba joint venture, 42
Westinghouse buy-out, 54, 57
World War II participation, 49–50
Siemens & Halske, 48
Siemens, Herman von, 50
Siemens/Nixdorf merger, 55
Siemens, Peter von, 51
Siemens Schuckert, 49
Siemens, Werner von, 48–9
Sil-All, 168
Silicon Valley in Dresden, 57
Sinclair, Jeremy, 265, 272
Singapore
- attitudes towards contracts, 8
- first submarine fiber optic cable to Europe, 32
- free trade agreement (FTA) with USA, 24
- intercultural difference with Malaysia, 36
- Postal Department and Telecommunications, 23
- telecommunications market, 21, 23

Singapore International Drink Exposition, 229
Singapore Telecom International, 23
Singapore Telephone Board (STB), 23
SingNet
- Internal Security Department scanning of emails, 29

SingTel
- Advanced Info Service Co. (Thailand), 32, 33
- advertising expenditure, 31
- Belgacon investment, 33, 37
- Bharti Group (India) investment, 34
- communications services, 22
- company profile, 21–3, 29–30
- corporate culture, 24, 27, 28
- corporate image, 28, 33, 38
- corporate size, 21, 22
- corporatization in 1992, 23–4
- cultural transition, 16
- debt, 34–5, 37
- dispute with Infocomm Development Authority (IDA), 29
- employee training, 26–7
- expansion into foreign markets, 21, 23, 27, 31
- European assets, 32
- foreign revenue, 32, 37
- global infrastructure, 22
- Globe Telecom (Philippines) investment, 34
- Information System (IS) approach, 21, 26
- injection of entrepreneurialism, 18
- Internet market in Singapore, 23
- investment risks, 35, 38
- Lee Hsien Yang (President and CEO), 22
- Malaysia, 38
- market capitalisation, 22, 30, 32–3, 37
- MobileOne (M1) competition, 31
- mobile phones market, 22
- national differences, 35
- NCS purchase in 1997, 26
- Optus acquisition, 22–3, 25, 34, 36
- People's Developer Award from Singapore Productivity and Standards Board (PSB), 27
- regional expansion, 31, 33–4

revenue and profit strategy, 30 34, 35
Singapore Post (SingPost), 37
subsidiaries, 22
Telecom Asia recognition, 23
Telecom Service Provider for National Day Parade 2003, 28
Telkomsel (Indonesia) investment, 34
Temasek Holdings ownership, 23, 24, 28, 30, 33, 35–6, 38
The Capital Group of Companies ownership, 23
3G mobile technology, 38
Virgin Mobile joint venture (2001), 28
Yellow Pages, 38
SingTel Academy, 26
Slattery, Matthew, 94
Smallpiece, Basil, 94
Smint, 198
Smirnoff Vodka, 205
Smit, Nick, 174
Smith, Adam, 307
Snoopy, 303
soccer world championships, 1974 Haribo, 191
soccer player definition, 27
Social Democratic Party, 153
social infrastructure systems
 meaning of, 45
Soichiro Honda
 automated machines, 119
 built first race car, 118
 education, 117–19
 Honda Technical Research Institute, 121
 originality & innovation, 119, 122
 retirement, 125
 Tokai Seiki Heavy Industry, 118
Soichi Saba (President of Toshiba), 42
Sony
 alliance with Toshiba, 44
 comparison to Matushita Electrics, 66
 US losses, 57

Soviet Navy
 sale of equipment from Toshiba subsidiary, 42
Spain
 communication, 8
 conducting meetings in, 9–10
Spanish Civil War, 195
specialized positions
 procurement of, 27
Spethmann, Dieter, 157
Spinetta, Jean-Cyril, 111
sponsorship activities, 308, 310
Spray and Combustion Laser Diagnostics Laboratory, 142
Spyder, 129
Star Alliance, 110
Star satellite TV, 86
Starbucks, 205
StarHub, 26
 entry into fixed line market in 2000, 31
 MTV sponsorship, 28
Steers, Richard, 73
strategic business unit (SBU), 215
Style and Gender
 Geert Hofstede definition of, 6
Sullivan, Ned, 214, 216, 219
Sung Sio Ma, 32
Sweden
 communication in, 8
Switzerland
 attitudes towards law, 8

T

Taizo Ishizaka, 42
Tadini, Mario, 130
Takeo Fujisawa
 founder, Honda Motor Company, 117
 Japan Machine and Tool Research Institute, 120
 Mitsuwa Shokai, 120
 personal philosophy, 119, 120–1
 retirement, 125
 Soichiro Honda, 121
Takeo Kameyama, 65

Tashio Iue
    founder, Sanyo, 65
    leaves Matsushita Electric, 65
    Konosuke Matsushita, 61
Taverne, Suzanna, 272
Tei Adachi, 118
telecommunication infrastructure, 30–1
Telecommunications Authority of
    Singapore (TAS)
    merger with Singapore Telephone
    Board (STB), 23
telecommunications industry, 28, 30, 31
Telefunken, 49
Telkomsel, Indonesia
    investment by SingTel, 34
Telstra's relation to Optus, 37
Temasek Holdings
    ownership of SingTel, 23
TGV, 57
Thai Farmers Bank, 88
Thailand's work ethic, 11
Thatcher, Margaret, 98, 268
Thompson, Sir Adam, 105
Thorndike, Dame Sybil, 246
Three Mile Island accident (1979), 45
Three UK, 86–7
Thyssen, 151, 158
Thyssen, Amelie, 156
Thyssen, August, 155–6
Thyssen, Fritz, 151, 156
Thyssen, Joseph, 156
Thyssen AG, 156
Thyssen and Krupp
    cultural transition, 16
    merger, 155, 158–9
Thyssen Bornemisza, Francesca, 157
Thyssen-Bornemisza, Heinrich, 156–7
Thyssen Handelsunion AG, 157
ThyssenKrupp, 18
Tiananmen Square, 85
Time Optimised Processes (TOP)
    established at Siemens, 52
Time Warner
    alliance with Toshiba, 44
Tipo 12
    racing debut in 1947, 131

Tokai Seiki Heavy Industry, 118–9
Tokushichi Nomura, 254
Tokyo earthquake in 1923, 118
Tokyo Olympics, 1964, 42
Tokyo Shibaura Electric Works, 41
Toshiba
    alliances, 44
    brand image, 46
    cultural transition, 16
    debt, 41, 43
    desktop computers, 42–3
    digital TV, 41, 43
    domestic sales, 44–5
    employee dissatisfaction, 46
    expansion into electrical
    appliances, 41, 44
    DRAM production, 42, 45
    General Electric (GE), 42–3
    information technology (IT), 41,
    43
    invention of electrical rice cooker
    (1995), 43
    Japan crash in 1992, 41
    labor troubles, 42
    market leader in electronics, 42–3
    medical department, 45
    Motorola joint venture, 42
    old economy devices, 41
    outsourcing of manufacturing,
    45–6
    personal digital assistant (PDA),
    41
    post-WWII Japan, 41
    profits, 45
    R&D investment, 41, 43–44
    restructuring, 41, 42, 46
    Roberts Cutts interviews, 46
    semi-autonomous in-house
    companies, 46
    semiconductor development, 43
    set up of Shinkansen, 45
    Siemens joint venture, 42
    survival threat, 42
    target for Japanese Communist
    Party (JCP), 42
    thermal and nuclear plants, 45

Toshiba Kikai
  sale of equipment to Soviet Navy, 42
Toshihiko Yamashita (CEO, Matsushita Electrics), 66–7
Total Quality Management (TQM), 165
  at British Airways, 101
Touching Lives Fund (SingTel), 28
Tour de France
  sponsorship by Haribo France, 192
Toyota Motor, 117
trade unions
  establishment in Japan, 65
  in Korea, 74
travel packages, establishment of, 94–5
truth
  notions of, 8
Tsinghua University, 142
Tsingtao Beer
  cultural transition, 16
  German influence, 233
  strategic focus, 223
Tsingtao Beer Science Research Center, 228
Tsingtao Brewery
  Anheuser-Busch alliance, 228
  awards, 229
  branding, 222–3
  Chinese government ownership, 225
  corporate culture, 224, 228, 231–2, 236–8
  corporate structure, 227
  employee conditions, 230–1
  foreign partnerships, 236
  German influence, 224
  global market, 222–3, 225, 227, 229, 232–4
  history, 224–6
  Japanese ownership, 224–5
  Kai Xuan wines, 233
  local acquisitions, 235–6
  product expansion, 233
  strategic direction, 232–3
  technological advancement, 228, 232–3
Tsingtao Company Stock of the German Beer Corporation, 224
Tsingtao International Beer Festival, 224
23rd International Gold Star, 229

U

UN Global Impact, 310
Uncertainty Avoidance
  Geert Hofstede definition of, 6
United Airlines, 103
  alliance with BA, 105
United Distillers and Vintners (UDV), 200
United Nations, 306
United People's Party (UPP), 76
United Technologies
  alliance with Toshiba, 44
US
  air transport market, 111
  attitudes towards contracts, 8
  business model, 19
  communication, 8
  concept of time, 10
  conducting meetings in, 9
  denounces Li Ka-shing, 88
  largest market for spirits, 206
  plans to break up Siemens, 50
  Three Mile Island accident (1979), 45
  use of English language in, 8
  work ethic, 11
US Department of Transportation, 107
Uslan (Hyundai City), 74

V

Vancouver Expo, 86
Vanda, 87
VEB Westsachsen (WESA)
  purchase by Haribo, 193
Versailles Treaty (1919), 153
Victor Company
  acquisition by Matsushita Electrics, 66
Vietnam War
  Hyundai, 71

Villa Hügel, 153–4
Virgin Atlantic Airlines, 107
Virgin Mobile
    SingTel joint venture, 28
virtual airline, 108
Vittel, 161
Vodafone
    purchase of Mannesmann, 86
    sponsorship of Ferrari, 146
    takeover of Mannesmann, 54

W

Wakayama
    birthplace of Konosuke Mastushita, 60
Wal-Mart
    German employees, 7
Wayne State University, 142
Western studio system, 289
Westinghouse
    purchase by Siemens, 54

Wikstrom, Martha, 251
women in workforce, 119
world airline, 90
world markets
    coping with, 15
World Trade Center, 112
World Trade Organization (WTO), 226

Y

Yamanashi Silk Centre, 303
Yasuhiro Shoten, 254
Yea-Sacc (1026), 176
yeast culture market, 183
Yoshinobu Fujii, Professor, 118
Yoshitaro Nomura, 256
Yuzo Sakakibara, 118

Z

Zhang Yadong, 225

Other Titles on Business Studies

The 4 Rs of Asian Shopping Centre Management
by Lynda Wee Keng Neo and Tong Kok Wing
ISBN 981 210 391 0

Building Bridges, Carving Niches
by Grace Loh, Goh Chor Boon and Tan Teng Lang
(English edition)
ISBN 981 210 439 9
translated by Chew Cheng Hai and Chan Chiu Ming
(Chinese edition)
ISBN 981 210 417 8

For information on pricing and availability, please log on to
www.marshallcavendish.com/academic